Music and the Skillful Listener

❦

MUSIC, NATURE, PLACE

Denise Von Glahn and Sabine Feisst, series editors

Music
AND THE *Skillful*
Listener

AMERICAN WOMEN COMPOSE
THE NATURAL WORLD

DENISE VON GLAHN

INDIANA UNIVERSITY PRESS

Bloomington & Indianapolis

This book is a publication of

INDIANA UNIVERSITY PRESS
601 North Morton Street
Bloomington, Indiana 47404-3797 USA

iupress.indiana.edu

Telephone orders 800-842-6796
Fax orders 812-855-7931

Parts of the discussion and analysis of
Ellen Taaffe Zwilich's Symphony No. 4,
"The Gardens" first appeared in the au-
thor's book *The Sounds of Place: Music
and the American Cultural Landscape.*
© Northeastern University Published by
University Press of New England, Leba-
non, NH. Reprinted with permission.

♾ The paper used in this publication
meets the minimum requirements of
the American National Standard for
Information Sciences – Permanence of
Paper for Printed Library Materials,
ANSI Z39.48-1992.

*Manufactured in the
United States of America*

*Library of Congress
Cataloging-in-Publication Data*

Von Glahn, Denise, [date]- author.
  Music and the skillful listener : Ameri-
can women compose the natural world /
Denise Von Glahn.
     pages cm
  Includes bibliographical references and
index.
  ISBN 978-0-253-00662-2 (cloth : alka-
line paper) – ISBN 978-0-253-00793-3
(ebook) 1. Women composers – United
States. 2. Music by women composers
– History and criticism. 3. Nature in
music. I. Title.
  ML390.V66 2013
  780.92′520973 – dc23

                                    2012033296

1 2 3 4 5   18 17 16 15 14 13

For my mother

CONTENTS

ACKNOWLEDGMENTS

Among the themes weaving together the women in this study, none is more fundamental than collaboration. And so it is with the book itself. Over years and miles I have benefited from the generous collaborative spirit of dozens of people, some close friends and colleagues, and others professionals I've never met. If, as my skillful listeners conclude, we are all parts of a larger endeavor, *Music and the Skillful Listener* is most assuredly the product of an ecosystem of efforts. My thanks must go first to the composers whose music captured my imagination. Victoria Bond, Emily Doolittle, Libby Larsen, Pauline Oliveros, Joan Tower, and Ellen Zwilich invited me into their lives and helped me to understand the nuances of their relationships to "nature." They have enlarged my world. I hope that readers will find their way to the pieces that I discuss so that they too can be challenged, transported, and changed.

I'm grateful to administrators, faculty colleagues, and graduate students at the Florida State University, College of Music, for encouraging my work. No one questioned me when I proposed courses on music and place in the early 2000s, or offered a doctoral seminar titled "Ecocriticism and Musicology" in spring 2006. Everyone assumed my ideas had merit. I hope this book proves their trust to be well founded. Travel to archives was made possible by support from my area's Curtis Mayes Orpheus Fund in Musicology. I'm indebted to Douglass Seaton, Frank Gunderson, Charles Brewer, and Michael Bakan for nurturing creativity. In 2009 the university awarded me financial assistance and time away from teaching duties through a grant from the Committee on Faculty Research Support (COFRS). The grant proved essential to conducting interviews, consulting research, and writing the first three chapters. Numerous other colleagues in the College of Music offered a collaborative hand. Sarah Hess Cohen and Sara Nodine, librarians in the

Warren D. Allen Music Library, joined me in many a search for elusive materials. Marcia Porter, Alice-Ann Darrow, and Heidi Williams generously
listened, sent me to sources, played with ideas, and cheered me on. Dean Don
Gibson of the College of Music is a uniquely talented administrator; each day
he creates anew an ideal environment to foster growth. This project would not
have come to fruition without his personal support. Dean Gibson's door is
always open. His commitment to his faculty is palpable. Each of us is certain
we are his favorite. My colleagues and I will miss him when he retires as dean
at the end of the 2012–13 academic year. Leigh Edwards, my colleague in the
English Department, provided bibliographical ideas and a lunchtime sounding board. Her excitement about the potential of this project and her belief
that I was the person to do it were crucial to its happening at all.

I've been fortunate to work with exceptional students in classes, in semi-
nars, and as my assistants; they've contributed to this particular project in a
variety of ways, some of which I'm sure they are unaware. Many of them have
graduated, but even so in a number of cases our conversations continue. While
it is dangerous to name names and risk overlooking someone, I'd rather make
that mistake than to not try. With that caveat I want to thank Caitlin Brown,
Toni Casamassina, Amy Dunning, Katherine Etheridge, Andrew Gades,
Gonzalo Gallardo, Ashley Geer, Dennis Hutchison, Amy Keyser, Megan
MacDonald, Charles Mueller, Crystal Peebles, Erin Scheffer, John Spilker,
Stephanie Stallings, Dana Terres, Stephanie Thorne, Lyndsey Thornton,
Steve Thursby, Catherine Williams, and Felicia Youngblood; Brianna Rhodes
took on the Herculean task of creating the musical examples. Their questions,
challenges, curiosity, and excitement inform everything I do.

Collaborators recognize no geographic boundaries, and many of mine live
well beyond my university home. The very first images that appear in *Music
and the Skillful Listener* come from Tina Gianquitto's book *"Good Observers
of Nature": American Women and the Scientific Study of the Natural World,
1820–1885.* Her study was an inspiration for mine. Robin Rausch and Sarah
Dorsey made my work on the MacDowell Colony and on Louise Talma possible. I'm regularly emboldened by Sabine Feisst, who lives her commitment
to the environment and is a scholar's scholar. Susan Pickett responded to an
inquiry from a total stranger and agreed to share her unpublished work on
Marion Bauer with me. While I was visiting his university, Dereck Daschke
engaged with me in a thought-provoking conversation regarding the many
meanings of "translation." I'm still thinking about what we discussed. Since
we met for the first time at a music and nature symposium in 2006, Aaron

Allen has helped me nuance my ideas and sharpen my prose. He is a most skillful thinker. Kailan Rubinoff suggested that I might be interested in contacting a Canadian composer friend of hers named Emily Doolittle. None of us could have imagined that Emily would become the focus of my last chapter. Elizabeth Keathley challenged my assumptions regarding women's roles and women's places. In marathon phone conversations and brief meetings, Tammy Kernodle continues to gently steer me where I need to go. Larry Starr asks questions that no one else thinks of. In certain ways I will always be his student.

Over the decades a number of scholars have provided needed criticism, counsel, encouragement, information, good humor, and perhaps most importantly real-time models of who and what I might become. Unknowingly, they are part of this study as well. Karen Ahlquist, Mary Davis, Annegret Fauser, Sarah (Sally) Fuller, Carol Hess, Ellie Hisama, Barbara Lambert, Beth Levy, Leta Miller, Carol Oja, Kitty Preston, Deborah Schwartz-Kates, Anne Shreffler, Judith Tick, and the late Adrienne Fried Block and Catherine Parsons Smith have all guided me. They've convinced me of the necessity of role models. I look up to them all.

This project has involved the cooperation of a host of publishers, photographers, archivists, and associations. I want to acknowledge the Manfred E. Bukofzer Endowment of the American Musicological Society and thank the society's publications committee for their subvention award. I am honored. I'm grateful to the Society for American Music for the many opportunities I've been given to present my developing research and for the collegial atmosphere that accompanies any gathering of this society's members. I am grateful to key people at various music publishing houses who endured dozens of permission requests. They include Gene Caprioglio, Aida Garcia-Cole, John Guertin, Subin Lim, Christa Lyons, Edward Matthews, and David Murray. I wanted, when possible, to have visual images to accompany my discussions, and so I appreciate Becky Cohen's moving photograph of Pauline Oliveros, and Bernard Mindich's lively likeness of Joan Tower. Kathleen Adams located a photo that captured Ellen Zwilich at the Beal Botanical Garden. Quan Tre generously allowed me to use his picture of a strangler fig, and Amy McLaughlin, among the many things she made possible, saw to it that I could reproduce a picture of MacDowell Colony fellows that included Louise Talma. She also took care of permissions to include the photograph of the Regina Watson Studio, where Amy Beach worked. William Rose, head of Milne Special Collections and Archives at the University of New Hampshire, saw to it that I had full access to Beach's voluminous papers. My week working at the Milne Collections was epiphanic. Sheri DeJan, executive assistant at the Thomas Cole National Historic Site, deftly put me in contact with the private collectors who own the Harriet Cany Peale painting, *Kaaterskill Clove*, that graces the cover of the book. I'm grateful to Sheri and the generous owners, who prefer to remain anonymous, for entrusting me and the Indiana University Press design department with this beautiful work. Suzanna Tamminen at Wesleyan University Press paved the way for me to secure permission to publish Joy Harjo's "Eagle Poem." Rae Crossman provided permission to quote from his set of poems "all spring." Christopher Wagstaff of the Jess Collins Trust gave me permission to quote Robert Duncan's poem "An interlude of Rare Beauty," and Sylvia Smith allowed me to include an Oliveros recipe from *Sonic Meditations*. George Tombs granted me permission to quote from an interview he conducted with Emily Doolittle. Kenneth Cooper shared his extraordinary music making, encyclopedic knowledge, and good humor, and he gave permission to quote from his co-written limericks for Victoria Bond's piece *Peculiar Plants*. Alvin Curran was among the most gracious of collaborators. Beyond the gift of his music, I appreciate his willingness to engage in an email conversation with me and then allow me to quote from that exchange.

All the goodwill and help from those I've listed above would come to nothing if it weren't for the dedicated professionals at Indiana University Press. I'm grateful to Jane Kupersmith, who deftly cultivated this project in its beginning stages. She encouraged me to write the book that I imagined free of constraints, either from without or within. It was a joy to work with Jane. *Music and the Skillful Listener* also benefited from the careful stewardship of Sarah Wyatt Swanson. When both Sarah and Jane chose to leave the publishing world to spend time with their young families, my project was embraced by the new music, film, and humanities editor, Raina Polivka. I could not ask for a more engaged, informed, attentive, and committed editor. I'm not sure that Raina fully appreciated the ramifications of what she had inherited when she took on a project that had over ninety musical examples and images, but to her credit, she never blinked. She is the consummate professional. Daniel Pyle good-naturedly helped me through the process of delivering high-quality digital images. I appreciate his patience and kindness; it does not go unnoticed. My project manager, Darja Malcolm-Clarke, answered questions before I formulated them. My copyeditor, Angela Arcese, understands the music of language and listened to what I wrote. I'm grateful that she found those occasions that needed fine tuning. In time I'm sure I will regret the few instances I didn't take her advice. Kathy Bennett provided indexing expertise. She actually thinks about what she's indexing and shares her ideas. This is the second project we've worked on together, and I look forward to more in the future.

Family and friends are collaborators of an indescribable kind, but once again, I will try. I continue to benefit from the long-distance support of my friends Sherry Williams and Kathy Strickland. Listening to their voices makes the thousands of miles of separation bearable. My sisters, Carol and Janet, follow my activities with a kind of loving tolerance that only very close siblings possess. In moments of weakness they tell me they're proud of me. My sons, Haynes and Evan, now a full decade older than when I first acknowledged them in a book, remain unequaled sources of delight and pride for me. There's nothing like discussing the finer points of the latest book you've read with the children you first read bedtime stories to. Books have been a constant in our lives. It has been one of my greatest pleasures to watch my sons become who they are. I'm lucky to be their mother and humbled by their love.

My husband, Michael Broyles, is such an integral part of my life that I can't imagine what it would look like without him. From the beginning he believed that I could do anything. He has accompanied me to interviews, archives, concerts, and museums, listened to the music that I was studying, and endured what must seem to be endless discussions of evolving ideas. He has read and then reread various passages of the book, offered clear-headed advice, played the role of all-purpose tech-support guy, and endured the vicissitudes of what sometimes became an all-consuming project. He has encouraged and supported me with humor, and grace, and love. Everyone should have such a collaborator.

And finally, I need to acknowledge the person who was my very first collaborator. Each evening I talk with my mother, Lorraine Von Glahn. At ninety years of age and at the distance of a thousand miles, she still possesses some kind of super-sensitive auditory gift that enables her to detect when I'm coming down with a cold or have had a difficult day. And she hears all this before I'm done with "Hi, Mom." The notion of a skillful listener was not new for me: I was born to one. This book is for her.

Music and the Skillful Listener

Introduction

This is a book about nature, and women, and music. It reflects a lifetime of curiosity regarding rocks and plants and animals and my relation to them: in that regard it is a quite personal study. Its title was inspired in part by a book by Tina Gianquitto, *"Good Observers of Nature": American Women and the Scientific Study of the Natural World, 1820–1885,*[1] and a poem written in 1887 by John Vance Cheney (1848–1922), "The Skilful Listener":

> THE SKILFUL listener, he, methinks, may hear
> The grass blades clash in sunny field together,
> The roses kissing, and the lily, whether
> It joy or sorrow in the summer's ear,
> The jewel dew-bells of the mead ring clear
> When morning lightly moves them in June weather,
> The flocked hours flitting by on stealthy feather,
> The last leaves' wail at waning of the year.
> Haply, from these we catch a passing sound,
> (The best of verities, perchance, but seem)
> We overhear close Nature, on her round,
> When least she thinks it; bird and bough and stream
> Not only, but her silences profound,
> Surprised by softer footfall of our dream.
>
> JOHN VANCE CHENEY[2]

Gianquitto's study provoked me to search for the listener equivalent of her "good observer," and Cheney provided me with the phrase. While the poet's listener is a "he," the nature to which his auditor is attuned is a "she." I am interested to know what a "she" auditor might hear and think about *herself.*

Music and the Skillful Listener explores a variety of ways American composers have understood nature and expressed those understandings in their music. Finding a single word that conveys the many processes individual composers engage in when they reflect nature's presence in music is problematic, in part because the kind or degree of "inspiration" that nature provides varies.[3] Do composers "translate," or "simulate"; "transcribe," or "imitate"? Do they "reproduce," or "musicalize"? Each word presents its own problems, and the composers recognize and often reject their limitations. The term "ekphrasis," traditionally reserved for a literary discussion of a visual work of art, but more generally denoting a practice in which one artistic mode is used to describe or represent another, comes close.[4] I have become more comfortable with the likelihood that there isn't a single satisfactory word, but I remain mindful that anytime I discuss music that is about something else, at least two degrees of "translation" are occurring. In the case of this particular study, the first degree is the composer's translation of nature's sounds or inspiration into human music; the second is my translation of their music into words.[5] Readers will have to accept my claim that I have tried to represent my composers as fully and accurately as I am able. The book is neither comprehensive nor complete, but it does allow a reader to dig deeply into more than two dozen works by nine women and develop a sense of what about nature matters most to them. The findings may surprise some readers, but more likely they will confirm what many already suspect.

No composer argues outright for a privileged understanding of or closeness to nature based exclusively on her biology, although the topic of motherhood and its unique opportunity for creativity surfaces in this study. And no woman expresses the belief that her insights are *a priori* the exclusive domain of women, although many composers acknowledge that centuries of acculturation have reinforced behaviors that have become associated primarily with *the* female character: Quiet patience was her virtue. John Vance Cheney notwithstanding, through the early decades of the twentieth century, American women were taught to listen and observe rather than to speak. This very training in patience, observation, and listening has served women well in developing a heightened ecological consciousness. It is not serendipity that the title of Rachel Carson's most famous environmental tract referred to the *silence* of a spring. She had been *listening*.[6] Starting with the first composer, *listening* is a rondo theme in this book.

Focused upon a single, homogeneous demographic – educated, white, middle-class women – *Music and the Skillful Listener* runs the risk of excluding more than it includes. But the decision to limit the study to Amy Beach, Marion Bauer, Louise Talma, Pauline Oliveros, Joan Tower, Ellen Taaffe Zwilich, Victoria Bond, Libby Larsen, and Emily Doolittle was a conscious one, and driven by a quartet of concerns: Having been brought up on a diet of Ralph Waldo Emerson and Henry David Thoreau, George Perkins Marsh, and Edward Abbey, I wanted to hear what an analogous group of American women had to say about nature; I wanted to study my topic in depth, which meant fewer rather than more subjects; I wanted a strong set of commonalities among my subjects so that I could speak to the variety of interactions with nature that was possible within a group of ostensibly similar people; and I wanted all of my subjects to be inheritors of the same dominant national narrative, which eliminated the possibility of including subjects who came to the United States later in their lives. Growing up being taught that your country is uniquely endowed and destined by its natural bounty – which stretches "from sea to shining sea" – to be God's chosen land and its people God's chosen people is an inheritance impossible to assume without training during one's most impressionable years: as the song says, "you've got to be taught before it's too late; you've got to be carefully taught."[7]

As is obvious in 2011, the narrative of a nation driven by a divine mission has produced and excused ill-conceived policies regarding the very natural resources that purportedly distinguished the New World from the Old; it encouraged an assumption of human superiority over all other life forms and has resulted in the exploitation and extinction of numerous species of flora and fauna. While nature has inspired musicians, artists, poets, and writers across centuries and the globe, it was the resonance of the particular relationship of nature and national identity in the United States as it had been presented that most interested me. I believe this is essential background for appreciating these nine composers' attitudes toward nature as reflected in their music. Do women who were observing and listening rather than felling trees fit into the dominant reading of America's relationship to nature they inherited? How does Mother Earth square with the Marlboro Man? Do these composers set out to offer an alternative American reading? Does American-ness play a role at all? Given their exclusion from a narrative that often paired American identity with a conquering spirit – whether in the name of God or government, for personal gain or commercial interest – it may come as no surprise to find that while all nine women acknowledge their citizenship and are cognizant of the variety of the natural world available to them in the United States, they do not talk about nationality. They see themselves as citizens of a larger place. Their concerns are global and universal, as is their understanding of nature.

My criteria and the practical considerations of time and space have eliminated many exceptional nature-composing women from the discussion – too many to list by name – but a few of them deserve brief mention. I had originally planned to include discussions of the nature music of Chen Yi, Margaret Bonds, and Annea Lockwood in this study. Together they have produced a range of beautiful and meaningful works in a variety of genres. A personal interview with Chen Yi (b. 1953), on February 3, 2007, made me aware, however, of the depth and range of differences of her formative nature and educational experiences from the U.S. culture I was most interested in studying. The political and cultural turmoil that engulfed China in Chen Yi's youth introduced a raft of new concerns that would have required more specific contextualizing than I was willing to devote to a single composer. In addition, the history and treatment of Chinese Americans in the United States, which would have had to have been discussed, deserved more space than I could give it. Altogether these concerns caused me to rethink the idea of including women from a range of ethnic groups beyond the one I was most interested in exploring.

African American composer Margaret Bonds (1913–1972) presented a different set of challenges. While born in the United States, and hence exposed to stories of American heroes taming the wilderness and the nation's *natural* identity, as an African American woman she was further outside the conquering narrative than even her white female counterparts. Bonds was highly educated and widely respected by musicians across color lines, yet her experiences of America's nature were unique to her. She could not be asked to function as a spokesperson for her race. Her song setting of Langston Hughes's "The Negro Speaks of Rivers" deserves serious scholarly attention, but perhaps in a study that considers it as one example of the rich range of African American female experiences of nature. No such systematic study has ever been undertaken. I decided to risk exclusion rather than engage in tokenism.[8]

Annea Lockwood's (b. 1939) commitment to nature and nature-related music was difficult to resist, but her birth in New Zealand and late arrival in the United States (she moved to the country in 1973 when she was thirty-four years old after having previously moved to England in 1961) meant that she came to the country without having experienced the impact of the American nature myth for herself on location. Since this criterion was as important for inclusion in this study as having composed nature-related music at all, Lockwood was most regretfully removed from the study. I am hopeful that some other scholar will dive into her large catalogue of environmental works. They would have provided a lively counterpoint to other pieces I discuss.

And so it is with dozens of other composers whose works could easily fill multiple volumes and nuance our understanding of how nature and music and humanity interact. I trust that future studies focusing on a variety of Americans will document the reach of nature experiences as they are understood by other marginalized groups: I have chosen one, the one to which I belong. My goal is to say something meaningful about a coherent group of composers who, heretofore, have not been investigated in relation to a shared topic, a topic that is important, to varying degrees, to each of them and all of us.

For purposes of establishing a common starting point for this study, clarification of a few terms is useful. I use the word "American" to mean North American. All of the women I discuss are U.S. citizens. Although Emily Doolittle was born in Canada to American parents, she spent considerable time growing up in the United States and especially in the past fifteen years attending American universities and teaching at one. She identifies herself as a North American. Louise Talma was born in France to American parents but came to the United States as a child. Despite her complete fluency in French and her many trips to France throughout her life, she was thoroughly American.

Among the nine *women* included in this study there are heterosexual, lesbian, married, and unmarried women. In 2011 the contemporary composers range in age from thirty-nine to seventy-nine. Amy Beach, Marion Bauer, and Louise Talma died in 1944, 1955, and 1996 respectively. The nine women were born as far apart as Nova Scotia; Miami; Houston; Walla Walla, Washington; and France, and some have spent considerable amounts of time in Europe, China, South America, and in various cities on the East and West coasts of the United States. The group is well traveled. By any measure, they are highly educated and accomplished. All women compose what is broadly understood as "art" music.[9]

"Nature" is by far the most difficult word to define. Books have been written acknowledging just that problem, and they will be referred to throughout the study. Is nature something real and discrete, or is it a construction? Is nature everything living that isn't us, or are we part of nature? Does nature have intrinsic value, or is its worth determined by human measurement? Is nature the glowing landscape of a Frederick Edwin Church painting, or the destructive winds of a category-five hurricane? I will avoid the trap of creating a definition whose inclusivity denies nature meaning. Instead I will call upon Perry Miller, who when asked to define America boldly responded that "the meaning of America is simply that its meaning cannot be fixed."[10] The protean quality of the natural world makes his response even more appropriate for the term "nature."

Music and the Skillful Listener tracks a number of ideas that are important to this group of composers and that serve as unifying themes: I've already mentioned the ubiquity of composers' references to listening. The women of this study – a microcosm of women more generally, it is presumed – are also drawn to collaborative approaches to problem solving. They welcome and seek out collaborators in their creative process – sometimes other human collaborators, and sometimes nonhuman others; they also see the interrelatedness of humanity and nonhuman nature as a work of supreme collaboration. Whether, like listening, this behavioral inclination is biologically determined and imprinted on the X chromosome, or the result of cultural conditioning, is not for this study to decide, although if forced to choose, I'd cast my vote for the latter. As readers will discover, the twin ideas of *listening* and *collaboration* weave themselves through this study effortlessly but undeniably.

The book draws upon scholarship from an array of fields: American studies, nature writing, art history, environmental studies, ecocriticism, gender studies, ecofeminism, ecomusicology, and the larger world of contemporary musicological thought. The formation of the Ecocriticism Study Group (ESG) of the American Musicological Society in 2007 reflects the efforts of a number of scholars to bring into conversation fields that have much to say to each other.[11] Together these multiple disciplines provide theoretical underpinnings for my argument that expanded access to education and the natural world for white, middle-class composing women reflects larger societal changes, and is manifested in increasingly varied artistic responses, which are observable in their music. *Music and the Skillful Listener* begins with a chapter that situates "nature composing," for lack of a better term, within a larger tradition of nature writing, and specifically women's nature writing. It briefly mentions women nature painters. Music as a sounding, temporal art provides a sympathetic expressive mode for suggesting the essence of the natural world. It can get beyond words and offer a *moving* account denied more static arts. That music occurs in time also allows it to easily suggest nature's cycles. In addition, acoustic instruments are made from nature's materials; their vibrations float in the air. The very sources of acoustic music make it *of* the natural world. That it surrounds and enfolds us in space simulates our relationship within the all-embracing natural world. This contextualizing chapter is followed by nine composer studies grouped into three sections of three composers each. Each section is preceded by a brief introduction. Composers are arranged chronologically by date of birth. A brief concluding chapter offers thoughts on what we might learn from this group of skillful listeners.

1

A Context for Composers

WITHIN THE NATURE-WRITING TRADITION

Until the 1980s, noted American women composers were few in number; their activities were limited in scope. Social mores and circumscribed educational opportunities had discouraged and denied women's pursuits of professional musical careers. The situation regarding women and music composition, in particular, differed from the long tradition of notable American women writers, and more particularly for purposes of this study, American women *nature* writers whose history of public participation went back to the earliest colonial times.

Inadequate or nonexistent musical education beyond that which guaranteed a desirable level of "accomplishment" and limiting codes of behavior, which confined women's musical sphere to the home or school, meant that most aspiring American women composers prior to the twentieth century looked no further than parlor performances as sites for their original songs and piano pieces.[1] Public performances that hinted at virtuosic displays would have been construed as unseemly and in certain circles would have drawn severe criticism and even censure.[2] Like some of their literary counterpoints, women composers often kept their identities hidden with pen names, or at the very least disguised behind initials or the use of "Mrs."[3] Prior to the closing decades of the nineteenth century, most American women with musical talent confined themselves to singing "sweetly," or playing violin, organ, piano, or guitar and within a private sphere, often with a goal of attracting an appropriate mate and educating the resulting children.[4]

While women's literary and musical traditions differed in significant ways, including their duration and degree of public engagement, both developed within similar social circumstances. This chapter provides a context for the study of American women composers and their interactions with nature by considering some of the nation's earliest women nature writers and the themes that dominated their works. It documents their desire for silence, solitude, and the opportunity to pursue their work, conditions that eluded many women. As becomes clear, the subject matter and perspective of the nation's earliest women writers and composers have much in common.

In England, in 1650, the first book of poetry by an American author was published. Without her knowledge, Anne Bradstreet's brother-in-law, John Woodbridge, had taken her writings with him when he sailed across the Atlantic.[5] There they were published as *The Tenth Muse Lately Sprung Up in America . . . By a Gentlewoman in Those Parts;* the book found its way to the library of King George III. Anticipating by a good seventy years the more famous writings in natural philosophy by Puritan theologians Cotton Mather and Jonathan Edwards, Anne Bradstreet's *Tenth Muse* meditated on the deep connection that she perceived existed between nature and God. Appearing 186 years before Ralph Waldo Emerson's 1836 essay "Nature," Bradstreet depicted nature as a moral text ripe with lessons to guide one's personal behavior. Over the next two centuries, women would become increasingly responsible for and identified with the moral instruction of the nation, as that duty was assigned to them and their sphere, the home. Women would use nature's lessons to teach their families.

In 1704, Sarah Kemble Knight (Mrs. Richard Knight) traveled from Boston to New York, a distance of about 150 miles, to help a cousin.[6] She did this with no single, steady companion, but with a series of hired guides to assist her passage over uneven countryside and swollen waterways. She recorded her alternately humorous, terrifying, and rapturous experiences in a book published posthumously in 1825 as *The Journal of Madam Knight.* Within its pages, an eighteen-line paean to the moon, that "Bright Aspect" who diffused Joy through [her] soul, aroused a more secular appreciation of nature than Bradstreet had expressed. While Sarah Knight's journey without a proper escort – which according to social custom would have been a husband, brother, son, or other male relative – might suggest behavior far outside the norms of acceptability for respectable thirty-eight-year-old women at the time, her descriptions of the woods reveal what was then considered a suitable female sensibility. Mrs. Knight portrayed her unaccustomed natural surroundings as comfortable. She employed domestic imagery, which would become the standard vocabulary for women nature writers in the nineteenth century: "the pleasant delusion of a Sumptuous city, filled with famous Buildings and churches, with their spiring steeples, Balconies, Galleries and I know not what."[7] Making the natural world home-like, with its balconies and galleries, or at least familiar, was commonplace for early American women nature writers, who seldom ranged far from their domiciles or towns. By drawing analogies between the potentially dangerous climes and domestic features, Knight claimed her right to be there: she stayed within her sphere, even if only rhetorically.

As the nation expanded, however, the nineteenth century saw the publication of a number of accounts by women who ventured from their northeastern birthplaces and went west to stay. Books by Caroline Kirkland, Margaret Fuller, Susan Fenimore Cooper, and Eliza Farnham reveal additional aspects of women's experiences with nature. Kirkland's *A New Home – Who'll Follow? or Glimpses of Western Life by Mrs. Mary Clavers, an Actual Settler,* published in 1839, is the story of the New York City–born Caroline Matilda (Stansbury) Kirkland (Mary Clavers is a pseudonym) and her husband traveling by horse-drawn wagon to Michigan, which was then the edge of the frontier. Although she described a broad range of experiences, including fording treacherous bog holes, and the unusual practices associated with purchasing land and naming and constructing towns in the west, Kirkland focused on the domestic sphere, with its specific challenges to women and family life. While not primarily about nature or the spiritual or religious lessons it contained, the natural elements regularly informed and decided her actions, activities, and attitudes; like her predecessors, Kirkland wrote from a decidedly female perspective.

A more widely circulated account of a city-bred northeastern woman interacting with nature was Margaret Fuller's *Summer on the Lakes, in 1843.* Fuller's trip around the Great Lakes lasted only a few months, June 10 to September 19, 1843, so the author did not develop the emic perspective achieved by Kirkland during her eight-year residence in the frontier. But she too used the physical journey to meditate on social issues and explore more interior landscapes. The book became, in Susan Belasco Smith's words, "an expression of self-discovery."[8]

Like Sarah Kemble Knight, Fuller was often transfixed by the beauty of nature; this is nowhere more evident than in her description of the start of her journey at Niagara Falls, considered at the time to be the nation's most famous natural phenomenon and the symbol of American power and promise. While she despaired that her own reactions to the cataract were thoroughly influenced by those who had already captured it in prose and pictures, and thus denied their full originality, Fuller achieved a personal, epiphanic moment during an uncommon solitary moonlight visit to the falls. Her description reflects the easy blending of nature with spirituality characteristic of many women nature writers and more generally of the Transcendentalist group, of which she was a prominent member.

> I felt a foreboding of a mightier emotion to rise up and swallow all others, and I passed on to the terrapin bridge. Everything was changed, the misty apparition had taken off its many-colored crown which it had worn by day, and a bow of silvery white spanned its summit. The moonlight gave a poetical indefiniteness to the distant parts of the waters, and while the rapids were glancing in her beams, the river below the falls was black as night, save where the reflection of the sky gave it the appearance of a shield of blued steel. No gaping tourists loitered, eyeing with their glasses, or sketching on cards the hoary locks of the ancient river god. All tended to harmonize with the natural grandeur of the scene. I gazed long. I saw how here mutability and unchangeableness were united. I surveyed the conspiring waters rushing against the rocky ledge to overthrow it at one mad plunge, till, like topping ambition, o'erleaping themselves, they fall on t'other side, expanding into foam ere they reach the deep channel where they creep submissively away.
>
> Then arose in my breast a genuine admiration, and a humble adoration of the Being who was the architect of this and of all. Happy were the first discoverers of Niagara, those who could come unawares upon this view and upon that, whose feelings were entirely their own.[9]

Fuller revels in her personal, individual, solitary encounter with nature writ large.[10] The extreme rarity of such experiences for women, especially in relation to grand, iconic natural phenomena such as Niagara Falls, undoubtedly fueled the passion of Fuller's reaction. Women were more often members of large parties of tourists on grand tours of natural wonders who came weighted down with Claude glasses, portable easels, picnic hampers, and pets. The opportunity to interact solitarily with a site of such unique power and beauty was of incalculable importance to Fuller. The experience was hers. As readers will discover, more than one composer in this study has sought out similarly unaccompanied interactions with the natural world. With the urging and intercession of Ralph Waldo Emerson, Fuller turned her journey into her first book.

Women writers continued to acknowledge nature's moral, spiritual, and aesthetic qualities, although practical exigencies associated with the nation's western expansion encouraged additional insights and understanding. Eliza Farnham's *Life in Prairie Land* from 1846 is a third midcentury chronicle of women's experiences of the enlarging nation. Moving from her New York home, Farnham lived along the Illinois River in Tazewell County, Illinois, for nearly five years in the mid-1830s. Her account, simultaneously realistic and romantic, benefits from the sobering experiences of extended time spent in an often unforgiving landscape. Farnham, who would become one of the first and most effective advocates of equality for women, was especially aware of the challenges the West presented to her sex, and she attributed many of them to inadequate education and social constraints: "Very many ladies are so unfortunate as to have had their minds thoroughly distorted from all true and natural modes of action by an artificial and pernicious course of education, or the influence of a false social position. They cannot endure the sudden and complete transition which is forced upon them by emigration to the West."[11]

Her real-life informed pragmatism, however, did not prevent Farnham from appreciating the inherent beauty of her surroundings. While avoiding the religious overtones of Fuller's prose, Farnham captured the unique landscape of Tazewell County. The final passage from part 2, chapter 2 shows the author responding to the variety of this prairie place:

> The great road from the northern to the southern extremities of the state passes, for the most part, over large prairies. These are sometimes divided by groves two or three miles in extent, sometimes by open, sparsely timbered tracts, called barrens, and sometimes by a mere thread of timber, towering above the swelling plain, showing a dark green line at the distance of miles, the first glimpse of which often elicits a cheerful 'land ho' from travelers who are unaccustomed to these long voyages by *terra firma*. This road intersects at Peoria the Illinois river, with which it runs nearly parallel for sixty or seventy miles, at a distance varying from four to eight, ten, and fifteen miles from the stream. The wood which crowns the bluffs of the stream stretches back at frequent intervals in long lines, and fringes the plains over which the road passes. These groves are generally very beautiful. They are usually seen on the high swells of the prairies, their outlines clearly defined on the horizon, long before you reach them. Their edges are bordered with the plum, hazel,

and other fruit-bearing trees, and shrubs, which are frequented by birds, hares, squirrels, et cet. The music, life, and freshness of these woodlands, together with their utility to the husbandmen, led the early settlers to select them as the sites of their new homes. There the cabin was laid up under the spreading boughs of the outermost trees; and there the hardy frontiersman placed his family, remote from every artificial means of comfort, "alone with nature," rich, beautiful, majestic, nature in the silent prairie land.[12]

Farnham sees the woods as crowning and fringing the plains. She construes the landscape as "rich, beautiful [and] majestic" and takes aesthetic pleasure in its "music, life, and freshness." In the context of her values, Farnham's distance from artificial comforts and solitary communion with nature in "the silent prairie land" has become a desirable condition. Eight years later, Henry David Thoreau would similarly plump the benefits of a wide margin between oneself and softening comforts. The inadequately educated ladies referred to in her preface, however, would likely have thought otherwise.

Back in the Northeast, in 1850, two hundred years after Bradstreet's *Tenth Muse* and four years before Thoreau's *Walden*, Susan Fenimore Cooper wrote *Rural Hours*, "a record of our simple rural life."[13] Thoreau read her book, referred to it in his journal, and perhaps even used parts of it as models for his own record of time "alone, in the woods."[14] Like *Walden*, which would focus on Thoreau's stay at his cabin by the eponymous pond in Concord, Massachusetts, *Rural Hours* explored the natural world of Susan Cooper's hometown, the one founded by her grandfather William Cooper, the one now famous for its Baseball Hall of Fame: Cooperstown, New York.

Thoreau would ponder the tall timbers that became railroad ties; Cooper had commented upon the less easily calculable value of trees: "Independently of their market values in dollars and cents, the trees have other values . . . they have their importance in an intellectual and in a moral sense."[15] "The great trees, stretching their arms above us in a thousand forms of grace and strength . . . fill the mind with wonder and praise."[16] While Cooper doesn't quite assign value to trees simply as trees (devoid of any useful purpose to humankind), her recognition that trees have intellectual and moral value beyond their potential as material commodities suggests the resonance of her thinking with what Kate Soper and other modern environmental philosophers have identified as the argument for the "intrinsic" value of nature: value that resides in its mere being.[17] The connection between nature and religion first seen in Bradstreet, and then echoed in Fuller, persisted in Cooper with her attributions of grace, strength, and praise. She mourned for the ancient forests where now only tree stumps stood. Later in her "record," she noted the significantly declining bird populations and wondered what their disappearance augured. Cooper understood the interrelatedness of humanity and nature; she believed that the civilization of a nation could be measured by its treatment of the natural world, and that over time people would recognize the connection. Passing the afternoon in the woods on Saturday, July 28, 1848, Cooper contemplated "the noble gift to man [of] the forests":

> But time is a very essential element, absolutely indispensable, indeed, in true civilization; and in the course of years we shall, it is to be hoped, learn farther lessons of this kind. Closer observation will reveal to us the beauty and excellence of simplicity, a quality as yet too little valued or understood in this country. And when we have made this farther progress, then we shall take better care of our trees. We shall not be satisfied with setting out a dozen naked saplings before our door, because our neighbor on the left did so last year, nor cut down a whole wood, within a stone's throw of our dwelling, to pay for a Brussels carpet from the same piece as our neighbor's on the right; no, we shall not care a stiver for mere show and parade, in any shape whatever, but we shall look to the general proprieties and fitness of things, whether our neighbors to the right or the left do so or not.[18]

We can hear the pre-echoes of the Concord woodsman and his urging toward simplicity, a trope closely associated with Thoreau in *Walden* although present in Cooper years earlier.[19] By the mid-1800s, numerous common themes characterized the works of women nature writers: Nature was a moral and spiritual force; nature was an extension of the domestic sphere; and nature possessed aesthetic value.[20] Women writers lamented the rarity of solitary experiences with nature, the limitations of women's educational opportunities, and the expectations of society regarding women's roles *vis-à-vis* nature. In *Rural Hours*, we read the roots of a modern ecological sensibility: the individual, the home, and nature are part of a single domain. And such thinking carried over to encounters with the natural world by other creative women and in unexpected places.

The experiences of a small group of women painters associated with the Hudson River School, whose works have only recently been displayed and received public recognition, provide additional evidence of women's engagement with and responses to their natural surroundings in the mid-nineteenth century. In May 2010, the Thomas Cole National Historic Site in Catskill, New York, mounted a small exhibition of twenty-five artworks created by accomplished women artists whose last names were more often associated with their famous male relatives, much like Susan Fenimore Cooper. "Remember the Ladies: Women of the Hudson River School" included works by Sarah Cole, Thomas Cole's sister, and his niece Emily Cole; Harriet Cany Peale, wife of Charles Wilson Peale's son Rembrandt Peale; and Evelina (Nina) Mount, daughter of Henry Mount and niece of William Sidney Mount; among a handful of pieces by other nature-inspired painting women. Among the paintings are works by Elizabeth Gilbert Jerome. Her stepmother considered her painting activities so socially transgressive that she destroyed Elizabeth's works. It was only as an adult that Jerome could return to her art. Susie M. Barstow challenged all notions of good behavior by climbing local mountains and painting as she went. Perhaps her freedom from famous male artist relatives allowed Barstow to imagine a larger world for herself. With the exception of rare women like Barstow, the boundaries that confined the range of expression of female writers and artists had expanded little by the mid-1800s from Sarah Kemble's time a century earlier. As exhibit curator Nancy Siegel explained, her hopes for the exhibition were "to expand the discussion of Hudson River School painting beyond the celebrated male artists." The exhibit was a recovery effort that endeavored to create "a more inclusive conversation that addresse[d] the vast number of women who venture[d] in the American landscape with artistic ambition."[21] That these women's paintings are not different in their content or artistic values – and, many would argue, in their overall quality – from works by their more famous male colleagues begs the question why they have been ignored.[22]

At the end of the nineteenth century, when the first organized groups of women mountain climbers wrote essays, reports, and articles about their experiences, they seemingly legitimized their activities by casting them in prose that spoke of nature in domestic terms, even if this nature was hundreds of miles away from their homes and thousands of feet up. Working within what William Cronon identified as the "domestic sublime" sensibility, these women referred to the room-like hollows they found within the mountain valleys, the canopy-like boughs of trees, and the carpets of flowers.[23] As Susan R. Schrepfer explained in her study of turn-of-the-century female alpinists: "Having identified (and often named) a wildflower, gathered specimens and seed, and learned a plant's habits, they spoke of it as an old friend, describing 'the special haunts and the special times of blooming of these children of the hills.'" Schrepfer understood this practice as "reflect[ing] lingering expectations about appropriate female behavior."[24]

By emphasizing the familiar comfort of their surroundings, by stressing the beauty of nature rather than its inherent danger, by focusing upon the similar social structures found in bird families and human ones rather than the predatory practices of animals, and by reading nature as a corollary to and even an extension of the home, the out-of-doors was made an acceptable place for women. In identifying with nature, they made themselves a part of it. As this study will demonstrate, many women composers behaved similarly.

Tina Gianquitto's book *"Good Observers of Nature": American Women and the Scientific Study of the Natural World, 1820–1885,* explores additional expressions of women's interactions with nature in the nineteenth century. Gianquitto explains that few disciplines in science were open to women at the time, with the exception of botany and ornithology, and these only to a limited degree. Women's drawings and paintings of flowers and their careful descriptions and renderings of birds simultaneously manifested and reinforced the acceptable realm for female interaction with nature, nature that was observable close to home, nature that was associated with the domestic sphere. In the first of her four case studies, "Botany's Beautiful Arrangement," Gianquitto introduces Almira Hart Lincoln Phelps.

In 1829, educational reformer Almira Phelps published a botanical manual specifically for students at the Troy Female Seminary. *Familiar Lectures on Botany* argued for the value of botanical education for girls, in part because it got them out-of-doors, "leading to exercise in the open air," something unusual for women at the time, as Eliza Farnham would concur. But perhaps its greater value, as Gianquitto observed, was that "botanical study . . . bare[d] the designs of nature and reveal[ed] to women their close and necessary connection to the natural world."[25] Phelps's book contained a number of illustrations by Miss Thirza Lee, a drawing teacher at the seminary. Individual parts of plants are carefully identified by letters, which refer to an accompanying key (figure 1.1).

Additional figures from *Familiar Lectures* offered more detailed studies of potentially delicate subject matter, including multiple drawings of stamens and pistils. But, as Gianquitto noted, "Illustrations [were] an essential element of the textbook, . . . [so] Phelps sanitize[d] the figures by enclosing them in descriptions of the *divine* aspects of nature."[26] The supposed religious lessons available in nature provided women entrée into this realm of scientific inquiry. It was argued that such study was appropriate and necessary preparation for their roles as wives and mothers. *"Good Observers"* shows educated, progressive women working with and within the sphere delineated for them

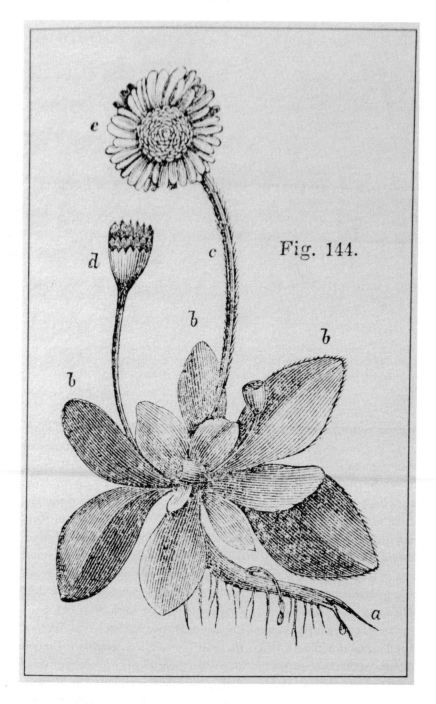

FIGURE I.I. Daisy. From Almira Hart Lincoln Phelps, *Familiar Lectures on Botany*, 183. From "*Good Observers of Nature*": *American Women and the Scientific Study of the Natural World, 1820–1885*. Courtesy of Tina Gianquitto.

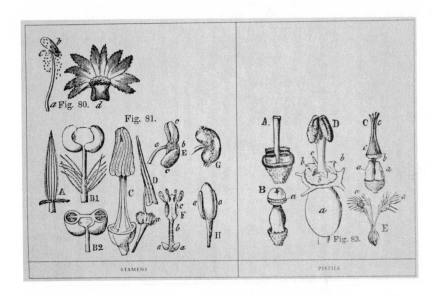

FIGURE 1.2. Stamens and pistils. From Almira Hart Lincoln Phelps, *Familiar Lectures on Botany*, 76, 78. From "*Good Observers of Nature*": *American Women and the Scientific Study of the Natural World, 1820–1885*. Courtesy of Tina Gianquitto.

by their society, even as they tried to expand it: Almira Phelps was of her time. The nine composers in this study will similarly reflect their time and place (figure 1.2).

In the late twentieth and early twenty-first centuries, women from across disciplines, scientific and humanistic, have reassessed their places within the world, natural and humanly constructed. Like Gianquitto, many of them move beyond the confines of a single discipline.[27] Pushing disciplinary boundaries will, in fact, become a hallmark of the youngest composers in this study. It is little surprise that a number of these scholars have turned their attention specifically to women's relationships with nature and questioned their inherited roles.

In 1975, Rosemary Radford Ruether published her book *New Woman, New Earth* and, without knowing the term "ecofeminism," established herself among the first contemporary scholars to systematically explore the idea of female relationships to nature and place.[28] Twenty years later, she acknowledged her primacy in the field in the preface to the second edition of her book.[29] From her vantage point as a theologian, Ruether surveyed the history of Western religious thought and concluded that contemporary class, race, and gender struggles shared similar origins and objectives; they needed to overthrow dominant ideologies that were rooted in falsely polarized thinking – rich/poor; white/black; male/female – much of which could be traced to religious beliefs and practices. While betraying potentially polarized thinking of her own by speaking broadly of "*the* male ideology,"[30] and by essentializing women's attitudes toward nature with such statements as "the commitment of women today continues to be what it has always been: a commitment to the survival of children and of the earth,"[31] Ruether ultimately moved beyond delimiting dichotomies and asked a question directed at all humankind: "How do we change the self-concept of a society from the drives toward possession, conquest, and accumulation to the values of reciprocity and acceptance of mutual limitation?"[32] The answer, she concluded, lies in thinking that is "oriented toward [the] preservation of the earth."[33] She envisioned "a society no longer bent on 'conquering' the earth," one that had more time for "the cultivation of interiority, for contemplation, for artistic work that celebrated being for its own sake."[34]

In the groundbreaking collection *The Ecocriticism Reader: Landmarks in Literary Ecology* of 1999, separate essays originally written in 1984 by Annette Kolodny and Vera Norwood considered the ways women's responses to the American place had often been ignored or, if they had been acknowledged at all, were read as inferior (too sentimental, too tender) by comparison with the prevailing discourse, which had been shaped by a language of aggression, conquest, and gratification. Norwood spoke of a common "lament": women felt unable "to escape from a variety of protectors" to experience nature in solitude.[35] Kolodny explored the ways a "single dominating metaphor: . . . the feminine landscape" had become "embedded in the [American] fantasy."[36] Themes of man's dominance over nature, and nature's *raison d'être* as a resource for human goods, convenience, and service, were reinforced in the plots of dime-store novels and pioneer myths, and in the language used to propagate them. Kolodny and Norwood each questioned whether there was/is a female environmental ethic, a way that women more often responded to nature in America that was distinct from the conquest-driven actions of heroes who were celebrated in so many stories.[37]

Lorraine Anderson's 2003 collection *Sisters of the Earth: Women's Prose and Poetry about Nature*,[38] contains writings by over a hundred American women writers, born between 1791 and 1974, that address the natural world and our relationships to it.[39] The collection's pieces oscillate between quiet meditations and thrilling revelations, hymnic paeans and calls to action.

Nature alternately provides sources of inspiration and solace, and opportunities for adventure.[40] Regardless of the variety of the perspectives, the seven sections of the collection – "Our Kinship with Her," "Her Pleasures," "Her Wildness," "Her Solace," "Her Creatures," "Her Rape," and "Healing Her" – underscore what appears to be a common deep empathy the writers feel for their mother earth. The book reveals an unexpectedly fecund literary tradition, a whole chorus of voices.

But, as Anderson observed, with few exceptions and until recently, these writers' reflections on nature went unread and unheard except by small sympathetic groups. Instead, Anderson explained, Ralph Waldo Emerson, Henry David Thoreau, John Muir, Aldo Leopold, and more recently Edward Abbey, Wallace Stegner, Leo Marx, Roderick Frazier Nash, Barry Lopez, and Lawrence Buell, have dominated and shaped the nation's conversation regarding nature in our personal lives and national culture. To be sure, writers as diverse as Emerson and Lopez do not speak with a single voice, nor do they advocate a single stance in relation to the natural world. Muir in particular spoke to and for large, diverse groups of people with differing views early on. We are all the richer for the eloquent variety of their thinking and prose. They do, however, speak from a common privileged position, first because of the types of relationships with nature that were available to and pursued more commonly by men – purportedly unmediated, solitary, direct encounters with nature on the grandest scale; and second because of the way those types of relationships had been privileged and imbued with significance.[41] They have directed and defined public discourse. While Anderson acknowledged the validity of men's experiences and men's voices, she concluded something was missing: "the world as perceived by women."[42] When it comes to writing about nature, it is no different than writing history: those who write get to decide what is most important. As Ruether expressed it in 1975: "Language is the prime reflection of the power of the ruling group to define reality in its own terms. . . . Women, more than any other group, are overwhelmed by a linguistic form that excludes them from visible existence."[43]

Anderson's collection, along with numerous recent publications, demonstrates the existence of an established tradition of women writing about nature, even if it is only now being recognized, and even if it does not reflect predominantly solitary, direct "confrontations" with nature writ large, with nature as a limitless unknown (an abyss), with nature in need of conquest. Given society's constrictions, more often Anderson's writers speak of intense emotional, physical, and often spiritual relationships with nature as revealed

on the most intimate scale. Overwhelmingly, women's nature narratives emphasize the delicate, detailed, familiar, home-like features of their surroundings, even when encountered at elevations of thousands of feet.[44] Many women
have seen themselves and their lives in nature close to home.

As a case in point, in an excerpt from the 1937 novel *Their Eyes Were
Watching God*, Zora Neale Hurston's sixteen-year-old protagonist Janie
Crawford sees her own burgeoning self in the soon-to-blossom pear tree in
her grandmother's yard. Janie is intoxicated with the sights, smells, and songs
of nature, and she aches "to be a pear tree – any tree in bloom!"[45] In Brenda
Peterson's 1990 collection *Living by Water: Essays on Life, Land, and Spirit*,
the author wrote about a transformative experience. Feeling an inexplicable
electric-like pulse course through her body as she walked along the shores of
Puget Sound, she understood: "Never again will this Earth feel the same to
me. I remember now that I live on a vibrant, breathing being that is a greater
body encompassing mine."[46] Intimate encounters permeate Anderson's collection. While the hundred-plus women don't speak with a single voice or
advocate a single stance, any more than male nature writers do, their writings reveal that women, like their male counterparts, have also given serious
thought to their relationships with the natural environment, both as individuals and as citizens of a nation closely identified with its nature.[47]

A survey of music from the late nineteenth and early twentieth centuries reveals few works by female composers that celebrate large, natural
iconographic places; such pieces would have to wait until women had access
to those wonders and the tools to craft compositions that were appropriately
grand in size. It is hard to write about what one does not know, or about that
to which one does not have unmediated access. There are, however, numerous
parlor songs and character pieces inspired by nature that is close to home, or
even outside one's window; pieces whose themes celebrate birds, flowers, and
occasionally small brooks and streams are most common. These brief, intimate pieces, so appropriate for domestic music making, spoke personally to
the predominantly female consumers of such music and are a rich source for
insights into women's and women composers' more typical interactions with
nature through the early twentieth century.

For a musicologist interested in the relationships between music and
place, the Anderson collection struck a particularly deep chord. In a previ-

ous book I had explored the ways large, iconic places had inspired fourteen American composers: of them, only one was a woman.[48] Upon completion of that project, I too questioned the want of female voices. Their near absence in my book, however, was not the result of an obviously oppressive prescriptive tradition; I had, after all, chosen my subjects. My choices, however, emerged from my criteria, which, while seemingly freely established, were influenced by dominant modes of thought: I sought out pieces that celebrated iconic American nature, and that meant large natural phenomena.[49] Accepting an American standard that valued grand nature to the near exclusion of small nature, the sublime over the beautiful, as articulated by Edmund Burke, and that had privileged dynamism and motion over placed-ness, meant that most women composers who had responded to nature with their music simply didn't speak in my book.[50] Was there an unheard chorus of women nature composers? Did American women composers who were inspired by natural environments reveal sensibilities similar to their literary or artist counterparts or to one another?

Informed to some degree or other, and consciously or not, by their natural environment, my nine composers have written music that reflects the gamut of artistic expression: it ranges from broad impressionism to razor-sharp scientific exactitude. I am interested to learn what the music says about these composers' understandings of "nature," and what their common and distinctive environmental sensibilities are in the twentieth and twenty-first centuries. With what aesthetic, philosophical, religious, or cultural values are the works imbued? Do women "nature composers" speak to and across generations and disciplines like their nature-writer or painter sisters? The study does not propose sharply etched dichotomies distinguishing between women's and men's views of nature. It does, however, argue that increased exposure to nature and educational opportunities expands women's sensibilities and provides a forum for their enactment. Music, like prose, can express deeply held beliefs regarding one's relationships to nature – beliefs that only now are being understood as intelligent, informed, insightful, and essential.

This study suggests a number of questions quite beyond its scope: Is there a fundamental difference between the ways women and men perceive nature? If such a difference exists, does it derive from experience? Is it a response to the dominant discourse? Is it encoded in genes? Does it change with hormonal levels? Fascinating questions, all of them, but perhaps more appropriately answered by those trained in cognitive psychology or neurobiology. They are not the focus of this project. *Music and the Skillful Listener* does not insist upon gender differences, per se, and does not argue that women are innately closer to nature; nor does it interrogate whether such a reading is a vestige of patriarchal oppression. It does not seek to substitute a new myth for old ones. As Ruether warned us, "the myths of spiritual femininity are as dangerous as those of denigrated female sexuality."[51]

The book endeavors to give voice to a group of American composers and explore the ways a number of them, who are female, have understood nature and brought that understanding to their music. It places them within the larger ensemble of women nature writers, artists, and ecocritics and asks how their nature-related compositions interpret common concerns, raise new ones, and offer us hope.

PART ONE

Nature as a Summer Home

AMY BEACH, MARION BAUER, LOUISE TALMA

The first three composers considered in this study – Amy Beach (1867–1944), Marion Bauer (1882–1955), and Louise Talma (1906–1996) – were born four decades and thousands of miles apart: Beach was born in Henniker, New Hampshire; Bauer in Walla Walla, Washington; and Talma in Arcachon, France – she settled in New York City when she was quite young. Beach, the oldest, was thirty-nine years Talma's senior and represents a completely different generation; however, all three women shared the common experience of multiple summers spent at the MacDowell Colony in Peterborough, New Hampshire. The artists' retreat was conceived by Marian and Edward MacDowell in 1907 and made a reality by the unstinting efforts of Marian over a period of a half century.

In the early decades of the twentieth century, the colony was a unique place for women musicians, artists, and writers to enjoy being among other professionals of their sex. In addition, at a time when uninterrupted, lengthy, solitary encounters with the natural world beyond one's local environs were still rare occurrences for the majority of women, the MacDowell, located deep in the New Hampshire woods and requiring at least a day's travel for most colonists to reach, provided a safe, quiet, bucolic escape and an opportunity to engage with nature in ways denied them in their more urban and busy lives. Unmediated access to all of nature remained an elusive experience for women in the early years of the twentieth century, as it had been for Margaret Fuller in 1843.

Beach's residencies at the colony began in 1921 and continued until 1941; she went there each year except 1939, when it was closed because of damage done by a hurricane the previous September. Marion Bauer visited Mac-Dowell twelve times between 1919 and 1944, and Louise Talma broke all records for numbers of residencies, forty-three in all, between 1943 and 1995. As the colony has grown in reputation and desirability, recurring residencies of the types enjoyed by Beach, Bauer, and Talma are no longer available; the semipermanent summer home-away-from-home, as it became for Beach and Talma, is no longer an option. But the place continues to nourish creativity even with more limited visits. The sights and sounds of the MacDowell Colony inspired specific works of all three composers as they would other artists who captured it in photographs and paintings, and writers who wove the woods into poems, plays, and stories of all kinds.

Despite the hundreds of women's music clubs that existed across the nation, which offered the closest thing to a sustained musical community for women (and provided decades of performance venues for Amy Beach), they better served amateur performers and public-spirited music initiatives than their composer members' specialized needs. The colony provided a meeting place for these composing women and many others. Supporting creative, accomplished women in a communal environment at a time when such environments were nearly nonexistent may be one of the MacDowell Colony's greatest legacies for women in the arts in the United States.

Beach met Bauer at the colony, and together they became founding members of the American Music Guild (1921) and the Society of American Women Composers (1925), an organization dedicated to nurturing and supporting women attempting to make their way in an overwhelmingly male profession.[1] Amy Beach was elected the society's first president in 1925. Bauer would also become a board member of the League of Composers, a society founded in 1923 that was dedicated to the encouragement of contemporary music. Bauer and Talma also shared the experience of having worked with Nadia Boulanger (1887–1979); the French pedagogue exerted enormous influence over many composers in the first half of the twentieth century, but especially these women, their work, and their lives. That Bauer and Talma pursued careers at major universities and secured teaching positions in New York City is likely the result of Boulanger's modeling, mentorship, and influence. Bauer became the first woman music department faculty member at New York University, where she taught from 1926 to 1951, and added in 1940 an adjunct position at the Juilliard School, where she taught until 1955. Talma earned degrees at

NYU and Columbia, attended Juilliard, and taught at the Manhattan School of Music and Hunter College of the City University of New York. Bauer's and Talma's similar institutional associations provided some degree of shared experience. Perhaps more potent than any of Talma's U.S. training, however, was the time she spent teaching with Nadia Boulanger at the American Conservatory at Fontainebleau, located outside of Paris, between 1926 and 1939. The two women formed an especially strong bond.

Although Beach never held a university position or maintained a teaching studio, and so didn't have the direct impact on students that Bauer or Talma enjoyed, it can be argued that her concertizing career and international reputation eclipsed the more focused and local work of the others and assured Beach influence over a large cadre of devoted followers. Her efforts on behalf of women's music clubs and as a devoted fund-raiser for MacDowell Clubs, which included student chapters, took her around the country; numerous articles that she wrote and that were written about her appeared in magazines and journals read by thousands.

All three women were committed to supporting and encouraging women's professional musical advancement, whether it was through performing or addressing music clubs, teaching in the classroom, writing, or personally mentoring young talent as Marion Bauer did Ruth Crawford, whom she met at the MacDowell Colony in 1929. The two forged an especially meaningful relationship, one that impacted them equally, and remained close friends, with Bauer becoming an indefatigable advocate of Crawford's music.[2] The colony was clearly an important force in identifying, encouraging, and connecting women composers in the first half of the twentieth century. The community it provided was the first of its kind.

Given the reach of Louise Talma's life into the very last years of the twentieth century and across the ocean, it may seem curious to group her with Amy Beach, who was born just two years after the close of the Civil War and enjoyed a career centered in the United States. But in the context of this study, there are compelling reasons to make them bookends of this opening section. Beyond their multiple residencies at the MacDowell Colony (with a few of them overlapping), all three wrote pieces dedicated to the founder or the place.[3] Each spoke passionately about the essential role the colony played in providing the opportunity for uninterrupted creative work. In addition, each expressed gratitude for the retreat in the form of lifelong enthusiastic advocacy, mentoring of other women fellows, and substantial monetary or material bequests to support the retreat long after they had passed away.[4] On the one hand, it is the continuous and powerful role that the colony played in these women's lives that makes them logical first subjects. But on the other hand, beyond that important shared experience, their works exhibit quite *different* relationships to nature, and this is important too. Works by the three women reflect a range of ways that nature, even very similar nature, informs music; in that regard, the first three chapters create a microcosm of the larger study. No two pieces, even when written by the same composer, manifest nature's inspiring presence similarly. The women, their relationships to nature, and their works are multifaceted.

While Beach, Bauer, and Talma encouraged one another, their efforts on behalf of women composers did not stop with their small circle. In her many articles and books, Bauer championed both her older and younger colleagues: the number and range of women she cited in *Twentieth Century Music* alone – more than two dozen – is impressive given the 1933 date of the publication. And in numerous published interviews, Beach regularly addressed the challenges faced by women who wanted to compose. Despite the efforts of other women who were composing at the time, Beach, Bauer, and Talma were the century's first, most powerful composer-champions of women musicians; they advocated for women to fulfill their creative potential.[5] Their similar understanding of the importance of educational opportunities, of the necessity of successful, encouraging female models, and of a nurturing community, all of which they experienced at the MacDowell Colony, make them a natural trio of subjects.

While none of these earliest composers will be discussed as fully as the remaining six treated in this study, for whom multiple personal interviews provided opportunities for significant questioning and cross-examination, a consideration of the different ways nature as experienced at the MacDowell Colony inspired Beach, Bauer, and Talma sets the stage for the larger project at hand. That Joan Tower, Ellen Taaffe Zwilich, and Emily Doolittle also enjoyed residencies at MacDowell – even if only onetime residencies – speaks to the continuing vitality of the retreat as a source of support and nourishment for women artists of all kinds, and perhaps to the appeal of this kind of sequestered experience of idealized nature for creative work.[6]

The focus on small nature, on flowers and birds, that dominates the prose of America's first women nature writers and even alpinists also governs the works of America's first celebrated women composers, a generation that emerged as the nineteenth century gave way to the twentieth. They too drew inspiration from nature that was closest to home, that to which they had access, that which they could experience personally. It is possible that remaining focused upon this circumscribed sphere was especially important to women at the time who, by the very act of composing, ventured into an inhospitable and overwhelmingly male-dominated domain. As Judith Tick notes, criticism could be harsh if women dared to attempt composition in the larger forms – symphonies, concerti, operas; they might be accused of "seeking after virility."[7] In 1935 the composer Mary Carr Moore (1873–1957) expressed her frustration with her lot as an American woman composer:

> But of all the difficulties I encountered, perhaps the greatest has been in the fact that I am an American and a woman. That combination, I assure you, has been the most discouraging obstacle of all! So long as a woman contents herself with writing graceful little songs about springtime and the birdies, no one resents it or thinks her presumptuous; but woe be unto her if she dares attempt the larger forms! The prejudice may die eventually, but it will be a hard and slow death.[8]

If women were going to trespass the boundaries of acceptable behavior by composing, their transgressions might be considered less egregious if they confined their attentions to the familiar and named their pieces for birds and flowers. Their actions were somewhat analogous to those of the bold women alpinists who climbed treacherous peaks and thrilled to the idea of confronting danger, but then publicly wrote about the domestic aspects of nature. It is possible, of course, that women composers happily worked within their assigned space and wrote about that which they loved. It is possible, also, that they consciously rejected the nation's seeming exclusive valuation of the breathtaking sublime and were making their own statement. Separating intentions from actions is not possible without specific commentary from the three composers addressing the question, and none is available. The tendency for later women composers to take on mountains and rivers as sources of musical subjects, however, suggests increasing frustration with any kind of restricted access.

While Eliza Farnham regretted the inadequacies of women's education as regards nature, it is likely she was unaware of the near complete exclusion of women from more specialized training in the arts and the attitudes that supported such practices, most especially in relation to musical composition.

A letter written by American composer Mabel Daniels in 1902 laid out the problem:

> You know that five years ago women were not allowed to study counter-point at the conservatory. In fact, anything more advanced than elementary harmony was debarred. The ability of the feminine intellect to comprehend the intricacies of a stretto or cope with double counterpoint in the tenth, if not openly denied, was severely questioned.[9]

Discouraged by society and circumstances, few nineteenth-century women developed the skills required to compose the most highly prized extended works, pieces such as symphonies and concerti. The question of women's fitness for composition became a topic of books, articles, and essays in the closing decades of the nineteenth century.

Among the earliest articulations of the idea of women's "innate inferiority . . . as composers" was George Upton's 1880 book *Woman in Music*.[10] Ignoring completely the question of educational opportunities, Upton saw the issue in terms of woman's intuitive, emotional being, which he surmised ill prepared her for the rigors of creative work. On the other hand, those same qualities suited her perfectly for the role of muse and inspiration for "the great compos-ers," all of whom were presumably male. Upton argued that the exactitude of the science of music, its logic and "unrelentingly mathematical" essence, rendered its creation beyond a woman's ken.[11] Upton would appear to be unaware of the likes of Almira Phelps or Miss Thirza Lee and their efforts to educate young girls about the natural world.

Women wanting to study piano, however, had different opportunities, as proficiency at the keyboard was a desirable, attractive, and useful accomplish-ment for young ladies. That it should remain an accomplishment and not a display of virtuosic skill, however, was essential to its being considered a posi-tive activity for women for much of the nineteenth century. Performing within one's home or the parlor of a friend was recreative, acceptable entertainment, not to be considered an original, creative endeavor.[12] There were exceptions, of course, and Amy Fay stands out as among the first. Born in 1844 in Bayou Goula, Louisiana, Fay helped to establish a tradition of American pianists traveling to Europe to study with master pedagogue-performers. Fay's col-lected letters detailing her six years working with Carl Tausig, Ludwig Deppe, Theodor Kullak, and Franz Liszt, which were published in 1880 as *Music-Study in Germany*, the same year as Upton's book, inspired hundreds of women and men to go abroad and get the education and imprimatur they needed.

Through her "Piano Conversations" and her increasingly activist efforts on behalf of women's issues, she became a vital voice for women's education.[13]

Studying piano was one thing, but acquiring the skills needed to compose substantial works was another. Denied access to essential conservatory classes in orchestration, score reading, and counterpoint until the closing years of the century meant that highly motivated women who aspired to compose had to undertake private or independent study, a costly and time-consuming endeavor, and this seldom happened. Women were without an institutionalized network of colleagues that could sustain them. Thus limited by the absence of educational opportunities and a supportive cohort, women focused upon composing and performing brief programmatic character pieces and songs for the parlor (works that didn't require knowledge of involved formal structures or extended developmental techniques), which became a specialty of their sex.[14] They wrote, sang, and played for one another in private homes and at meetings of women's music clubs, which emerged in the latter nineteenth century in towns and cities across the country and became among the most powerful institutions in America's musical culture.[15] Among her many efforts on behalf of women musicians, Amy Fay championed the work of music clubs.

One woman did, however, through dint of her enormous natural gifts, social and economic station, systematic personal efforts, disciplined independent study, and selective encouragement from family members overcome many obstacles to achieve recognition as a *serious* composer, at least by some.[16] The nation's earliest celebrated female composer, Amy Beach, provides an initial case study of the ways women have been inspired by and responded to nature with their music. As will be seen, in spite of her mastery of large forms, she is known today primarily for her songs and piano miniatures, an overwhelming number of which are nature pieces that focus on flowers and birds. Comparisons with two other twentieth-century women composers, Marion Bauer and Louise Talma, suggest the range of perspectives on nature that were enjoyed by these first American women nature composers and by others that followed them.

2

Amy Marcy Cheney Beach (Mrs. H. H. A. Beach)

At a time when serious American musicians traveled to Europe and more specifically to Germany for their education, as had Marian Nevins MacDowell and Amy Fay, Amy Marcy Cheney remained in the United States and under the watchful eye of her mother. Amy Cheney was born in 1867, and when she was eight years old her family moved to Boston, where she studied piano with Ernst Perabo and Carl Baermann. When she was fourteen, a single year of study with Julius Welch Hill, a Boston church organist and piano and voice teacher, provided Amy with her only formal lessons in composition. Given Hill's profession, it is not surprising that the young Miss Cheney composed four-part chorales.[1] Possessing prodigious talents including a remarkable ear, Beach quickly developed into a consummate musician without the benefit of travel or training in Europe, which Clara Cheney determined would not be an option for her daughter.[2] In 1883 at the age of sixteen she debuted in public on a "Programme for Mr. A. P. Peck's Anniversary Concert," which included multiple performers. Identified as a pupil of Carl Baermann, she played Moscheles's Concerto No. 2 in G Minor and Chopin's Rondo in E-flat, Op. 16. A review that appeared in the *Boston Gazette* was laudatory.[3] Six months later she played again on "Mr. A. P. Peck's Annual Concert."[4] Her achievements were publicly recognized. As Beach herself exclaimed, "No words can tell the pleasure I felt performing with a band of instrumentalists."[5] But a professional virtuosic career was not an option.

In 1885 an eighteen-year-old Amy Marcy Cheney married Dr. H. H. A. Beach, a prominent Boston physician and widower twenty-five years her senior. At his insistence, and in keeping with traditional upper-class behavior, the young Mrs. H. H. A. Beach withdrew from performing, except for the occasional charity recital.[6] Pleased, no doubt, that Amy conformed to societal expectations, H. H. A. encouraged his wife to turn her undeniable musical gifts to composition, and particularly to composing works in the "large forms," the types of works that he and his cohort likely valued most. Removing his musician-wife from the public eye, Dr. Beach advocated her pursuit of an activity that could be accomplished at home, in the private sphere.

One wonders, however, if Dr. Beach was unaware that women composers who attempted to write in the large forms might be perceived as overstepping their bounds and striving toward virility. Did he reject such an idea outright and hence not consider the possibility of such a criticism, or was he not convinced that Amy's activities would ever become known? Nothing in the existing literature suggests that Dr. Beach knowingly set up his wife for ridicule or failure. Quite the opposite, there is evidence that he protected her from negative reviews; his encouragement of Amy Beach's compositional talents appears to have been motivated by a genuine belief in her abilities. It is possible that at the time Amy Beach created her symphony, concerto, and mass in the 1890s, so few women composers were attempting such works that they didn't present a significant threat to the male-dominated profession. It was clear also that she wasn't seeking a professional position that might have put her in direct competition with the other musicians in the area. Certainly her immediate cohort of Boston composers, including George Whitefield Chadwick and John Knowles Paine, men she knew because of her similar social station and accomplishments in music, seemed supportive of her efforts and pleased for her success. While there was hostility toward the idea of women composing in the large forms, perhaps it had not yet galvanized beyond a few vocal critics because of its rarity.

But Dr. Beach's restrictions upon her music making were not without frustration for his young wife. In 1942, when she was seventy-five years old, Amy Beach reflected upon her husband's impact on her career: "My husband . . . would never allow me to have a teacher in composition. He felt that here lay my work. . . . Incidentally I didn't believe him, for I thought I was a pianist first and foremost. His encouragement and interest led me into composition more seriously, and yet upon one point he remained firm – I should not have a teacher lest through an outside influence my ideas be moulded into something foreign to myself."[7] A year later Beach repeated similar ideas in an interview that appeared in *Etude*: "My husband refused to allow me to study formally – which, in my earlier days, I sometimes wanted to do – in the belief that set instruction might rob my work of some of its freedom and originality. But that doesn't mean I did not work! I taught myself – and I learned through my own efforts."[8]

While the contemporary reader might bristle at Beach's use of the word "allow," which today seems more appropriate to the description of a parent's interactions with a child than a husband's interactions with his wife, more interesting in the context of this study, especially as it pertains to the issue of women's educability, is to consider H. H. A.'s attitude toward his wife's susceptibility to outside influences: in this case the influence of a composition teacher. Unspoken, but obvious, is Dr. Beach's assumption that his wife's musical competency is intuitive; a gift, not a learned skill; received, not achieved. She came by her music "naturally." And he would not have been alone in casting her musical abilities as such. The very review that praised her pianism at her debut cast her achievements in light of "her natural gifts and her innate artistic intelligence."[9] Such a reading reflected the belief that women were instinctive, intuitive creatures, ill equipped by biology or temperament to benefit from intellectually rigorous training. Rather than encourage systematic study to develop, expand, and enhance her abilities, Beach denied his wife the education she desired and cast it as a negative force, something that was potentially threatening to her most natural self. Once again, Amy Beach's musical development was restricted by the decisions of others. It is impossible to imagine a similar argument being mounted if the musician in question had been a young male. At some level, although for different reasons, Upton's thinking was enacted in the Beach household.

Amy Beach's papers are a moving testimony to the seriousness of her personal efforts to study composition: symphony scores became her texts, orchestral concerts became her classes. In 1894 she recorded her reactions to the works of Smetana, Strauss, Tchaikovsky, Dvořák, Brahms, and Max Bruch in a small (four-by-six-inch) journal that she kept; it provides additional evidence of her disciplined approach to learning composition. Beach wrote detailed descriptions of musical behavior and included numerous excerpts of musical themes, which she notated in her own hand on separate score paper and then pasted in the book. An entry on Tchaikovsky's *Pathétique* is typical of the tone of the remarks that often followed the more purely descriptive prose and the carefully notated musical excerpts: "The minor version of it at the close cannot be described. It is mournful beyond any <u>death</u>-music I have ever heard, only excepting the Siegfried funeral march. The close is heart-rending. The orchestration throughout the work is remarkable for many things. Among composers who make the orchestra speak to the hearts of the listeners, Tchaikowski stands preeminent."[10]

A "Letter from Mrs. Beach" that appeared in the April 1898 issue of *Etude* magazine shows the composer aware of her own position as a woman in a field dominated by men.

> In the best interests of those of my sex who are working in the field of musical composition, I believe that they can be advanced more rapidly and with greater certainty, not through their efforts as litterateurs, but by solid practical work that can be printed, played, or sung. In this way a record can be made of composition that should bear the test of measurement by the standards of good musicianship, and of comparison with the productions of any writer.
>
> The incontestable facts of its bearing such comparison will supply, in my opinion, the best evidence of the capacity of any composer, male or female, and will doubtless, in time, lead the public to regard writers of music in the same light as astronomers, sculptors, painters, or poets, estimating the actual value of their works without reference to their nativity, their color, or their sex.[11]

As an upper-class woman whose social circle included Boston's elite, Beach had time to perfect her craft and the resources to purchase books, materials, and concert tickets. This would not have been the case for a majority of women who might have pursued a career in composition, a fact to which Beach seems oblivious. Her large personal library of music was the subject of an extended article.[12] While her marriage restricted her options in many ways, it also bought her freedom from having to work, take care of a household, or even prepare a meal. She had no children. According to program notes provided for a "Women in Music" concert given in Baltimore in 1901, for her own "technical instruction in the art of orchestration [Beach] ... depended upon the treatises of Berlioz and Gevaert, and the constant study of scores in the presence of that best of teachers – the modern orchestra."[13] She brought leather-bound scores to symphony performances and wrote comments in the margins to call attention to particular instrument combinations and voicings that she found effective. Scores of Beethoven's Fifth, Sixth, and Ninth symphonies, which she had received as Christmas gifts, make the point. Beach recorded performances given by the Boston Symphony Orchestra between 1885 and 1900 that she attended. In addition to including dates for eight performances she heard between January 31, 1885, and October 14,

1893, the first page of the Fifth Symphony score contains numerous markings: a "Cue for horns"; places where she groups measures in twos and threes, one assumes to indicate phrasings that she heard; and numerous spectacle or eyeball-like doodles that overlook trombone and trumpet parts. Beach appears to be particularly interested in the sounds of the brass.[14] Her experiences as a student of the orchestra, even without the guidance of a teacher, undoubtedly impacted her own instrumental works of the 1890s. But these experiences would have been beyond the reach of most women who didn't enjoy her social situation and the resources of time, money, and materials that it provided.

Over the next fifteen years, Beach created works in a variety of small and large genres, and regularly made gifts of her pieces, sometimes to the surprise of her recipients.[15] Letters from Elizabeth C. Agassiz, Ferruccio Busoni, Louis Maas, Maud Powell, and Pauline Cramer all express gratitude for the receipt of an unexpected song or keyboard work. The range of correspondents provides some insight into the intellectual and musical circles Beach inhabited and her desire to reach out.

Her largest works were all written within a seven-year period and included the Grand Mass, Op. 5 (1892); the "Gaelic" Symphony in E Minor, Op. 32 (1896); and her Piano Concerto in C♯ Minor, Op. 45 (1899). Such pieces garnered the respect of her contemporaries John Knowles Paine, George Whitefield Chadwick, Arthur Foote, and Horatio Parker, the group of composers centered in and around Boston who later became known, along with Beach, as the Second New England School Composers.[16] Upon hearing the premiere of her symphony, Chadwick wrote to Beach praising her accomplishment and declaring, "I always feel a thrill of pride myself whenever I hear a fine work by any one of us, and as such you will have to be counted in, whether you will or not – one of the boys."[17] The remark simultaneously reflects upon the quality of Beach's symphonic skills and hints at the proprietary nature Chadwick felt toward the genre as one belonging to and identified with men. In Chadwick's mind, being "one of the boys" was something to be desired.

But select reviews of the piano concerto brought Amy Beach face-to-face with the potential limitations of autodidacticism. In an 1899 review of her newly completed piano concerto for the *Boston Journal*, Philip Hale expressed "pity that she has never had a thorough, severe drill in theory and orchestration." Referring to her symphony three years earlier, Hale explained, "Her symphony led one to believe that natural talent, self-study, close observation, might do much without painful labor under a pedagogue, but this piano concerto does not encourage any such belief."[18] Whether as a result of such criticism, or because she recognized her own limitations, or because she said all she had to say in these genres, Beach wrote only one of each of these large-form pieces; soon after her husband died in June 1910, she returned to her first love, playing piano. Beach continued to compose but confined herself to songs, piano pieces, and chamber works that didn't require the oversized forces of her large-form pieces.

By August 1911, Beach had engaged a concert manager, and the next month she set off on a three-year tour of Europe, where she performed many of her own piano works. When Beach returned to the United States in September 1914, she took up residence in New York City and in Centerville, Massachusetts, on Cape Cod. Contrary to our modern expectations regarding the financial security of a physician's widow, H. H. A. Beach left little money to support his much younger wife. She would be taken care of by a wide circle of devoted friends with whom she regularly stayed during the next thirty years. Beach spent months of each year on the road concertizing, addressing women's clubs, pleading the cause of music, advocating on behalf of the Mac-Dowell Colony, and composing songs and pieces especially suited for parlor performances, until ill health curtailed her travel in the 1940s. She was often the subject of published interviews and an active writer on a number of topics related to music; her articles appeared in widely circulated journals.[19] What Beach's music doesn't tell us about her specific attitudes toward nature and composition, her writings do, and with a precision and clarity that leave little room for speculation.

In the summer of 1921, Amy Beach made an initial visit to Marian Mac-Dowell's idyllic artists' colony in Peterborough, New Hampshire. But this was not her first contact with Mrs. MacDowell. A letter she had written dated February 15, 1908, just three weeks after the death of Edward Mac-Dowell, informed "Dear Mrs. MacDowell" of a "recent recital" she had given, which contained a number of MacDowell's compositions. About his pieces she wrote:

> Their reception at the hands of a most cultivated audience was deeply impressive. After the first, the silence was oppressive; not a person moved. It was a tribute that meant more than even words could have expressed, and applause would have seemed profanation. After the others, the people were heartily responsive to the different moods of the music, and at the close there was so much enthusiasm that I added the precious 'Will-o-the-Wisp.'

> I wish I could tell you of the love that I feel for these beautiful works and all the others that I play! It is quite impossible however, – as it is for one to express the overwhelming sympathy that I feel for you now.
>
> With a heartful of good wishes for your health, in which my husband joins, believe me
>
> Faithfully yours,
>
> Amy M. Beach.[20]

The colony had been conceived by Edward and Marian MacDowell as a refuge where artists from across disciplines – music, art, literature – could unwind in the sylvan setting of their Peterborough acreage, commune with nature, and draw nourishment from interactions with other inspired creative colonists. When Edward MacDowell died in 1908, Marian dedicated the rest of her life to seeing that the colony carried out his interdisciplinary vision.[21] Because separate lodgings were not available for men until 1911, an unusually large number of women artists, writers, and musicians were among the earliest colonists. As Robin Rausch describes it, "the face of the early Colony was distinctly feminine."[22] The MacDowell Colony had been in existence for fourteen years when Beach arrived; its earliest residents had included Edward's former students and Marian's artistic acquaintances. Eventually, Amy Beach and Marian MacDowell would become close friends and confidantes.[23]

As had colonists before her, Amy Beach found the protected natural surroundings of the colony deeply inspiring. She used her time there to walk in the woods, listen to the surroundings, and take in Mount Monadnock, which was visible from the back of the Regina Watson Studio, where she worked. She thrived in the solitude of nature. While Beach insisted that "for composition, I need absolute quiet,"[24] it was the *sounds* of nature that enabled her to achieve "the innermost silence" from which her own music emerged.[25] As this study will demonstrate, the need for solitude and quiet are recurring themes among many other composer subjects (figure 2.1).

Beginning with that initial visit, Beach's residencies at the colony became essential to her work. In a published interview from 1942, Beach explained, "Everything that I have written since 1921 has been sketched at the MacDowell Colony."[26] The natural setting found its way into her music. She returned regularly until illness and age kept her away. As Adrienne Fried Block, Beach's biographer, pointed out, of the eighteen piano works that Beach wrote between 1921 and 1925, all but two of them referred to nature in their titles.[27] "From Blackbird Hills," "Dancing Leaves," "The First May Flowers," "A Peter-

FIGURE 2.1. Regina Watson Memorial Studio, the MacDowell Colony, Peterborough, New Hampshire. Courtesy of the MacDowell Colony.

borough Chipmunk," and "Young Birches" are just a few of the impressionistic keyboard pieces that took root in the colony soil. A complete list of Beach's works reveals the profound effect the natural world always had on her creative oeuvre.[28] Summers at the colony didn't introduce Beach to nature; they reinforced a love of it that she had cultivated since childhood. Her compositions spoke personally to the dominantly female consumers of her music, those practitioners of the parlor tradition who played and sang her works at the turn of the century. Songs with titles such as "The Blackbird," "With Violets," "The Clover," "The Yellow Daisy," and "The Bluebell"[29] focused on the more fragile, vulnerable bits of nature with which women of her class had some experience and daily intercourse. Her works reflected the accepted boundaries of what was traditionally considered a woman's sphere.

Not content to read about nature, however, Beach needed to be in it. Like the Hudson River School painters of an earlier time, for whom direct observation had its own cachet, she preferred to sketch her compositions *en plein air*: "I like to sit out of doors, I want to be in the midst of nature when I write."[30] If poor weather prevented the composer from direct contact, she tried "to have a room with wide windows or a balcony."[31] Nature, especially as Beach experienced it during summers at the colony, was deeply nourishing to this Boston-bred pianist/composer.

Beach's first summer at MacDowell provided material she could not have imagined. As Block explains it:

> . . . one of nature's sounds was so insistent that she stopped her work to have a conversation – with 'a most voluble thrush.' A longtime collector of bird songs, she decided to record his 'lonely but appealing' music. . . . The hermit thrush became Beach's metaphor for the MacDowell Colony.[32]

We learn of Amy Beach's earliest experience with birdsong from her cousin in a "'Sketch of the life of Mrs. H. H. A. Beach – Composer and Concert Artist' by Ethel Clement, January 31, 1917. (Member of the Helktow Music Club and Coven of Mrs. Beach)." It took place when Amy was ten years old and visiting her aunt, Mrs. Franc Marcy Clement, and cousin Ethel in California.[33] According to Ethel, Amy Beach explained:

> In Berkeley, the university town, I met Edgar Rowland Sill, the poet. He was kind to me and when he heard that I was the lucky possessor of absolute pitch, he asked me to go out with him in the spring mornings, and steal from the birds! He told me that he was helping a friend in the State University, who was writing a book on California bird songs. I shall always remember that spring morning. The poet and I sat down behind a stone wall. It is a sweet memory of the kindly poet of California, of the spring flowers, of the unconscious birds. With pencil and paper, we took their melodies. We got twenty of their airs that morning.

Clement observes, "One instinctively associates with this incident the beautiful song for contralto voice dedicated to her aunt in which Mrs. Beach later set to music Prof. Sill's exquisite lyric 'The Thrush.' From that time on, Mrs. Beach has continued her observations of bird songs-immortalizing the little songsters of her summer home at Centerville, Massachusetts, – and in one of her recent and most beautiful lyrics, has incorporated the songs of the larks of southern California in her exceptionally lovely and dramatic setting of Miss Ina Coolbrish's 'Meadow-Larks.'" Clement provides still more testimony regarding the power of birdsong to inspire her cousin. Here she recounts the genesis of the song "Wind-o-the-Westland":

> The poem 'Wind-o-the-Westland' is by Dana Burnett, and came to Mrs. Beach's attention recently while she was staying in the midst of a wonderful orange grove in Riverside California. Every morning before dawn she

was awakened by the tender plaints of innumerable mourning doves, and lay listening with dreamy enjoyment to their melting tones. Subconsciously the words of Mr. Burnett's beautiful poem seemed to fit in against the background of sound, and when the composer had completed her song, she was surprised to see that she had unwittingly used the plaintive call of the mourning dove as a figure in the accompaniment.[34]

In 1911 Amy Beach had been quoted extensively in an essay titled "Bird Songs Noted in the Woods and Fields by Mrs. H. H. A. Beach for this Article" that appeared in *The Designer*, in the May 7 issue. The unnamed author included extended passages where Beach described the sounds of the chenwink (also known as the towhee bunting), the robin, the wood pewee, the song sparrow, and the thrush. Of Beach the author wrote, "she now has a large collection of bird melodies."

Years before her discovery of the MacDowell Colony, Amy Beach had consorted with birds in the thick of nature; she had taken down birdsong; she had set a poem about a thrush. When she heard a hermit thrush from the window of her MacDowell studio in 1921, it is not surprising that she responded with music by writing a pair of piano pieces. This time, however, her music would be free of the constraints of Sill's poetry and she could concentrate on the birdsong exclusively. In "A Hermit Thrush at Eve" and "A Hermit Thrush at Morn" (Op. 92, Nos. 1 and 2), Beach expressed unbridled personal delight with the avian serenader, but she also conveyed more than that. Whether by chance or design, Beach reflected the inherited nineteenth-century woman's circumscribed natural sphere; she responded to nature close to home, in this case a summer home. However, she also participated in a long tradition of philosophers, poets, and nature writers who had singled out this particular virtuosic North American songbird for special notice. In doing so, she made herself part of a national tradition of nature essayists; her essay was written in music.[35]

The hermit thrush was the symbolically charged creature that gave voice to Walt Whitman's soul in his elegiac poem "When Lilacs Last in the Dooryard Bloomed"; whom he named "the unrivall'd one" in another poem, "Starting from Paumanok"; over whom he lingered to savor the "delicious song-epilogue" in *Specimen Days*. Here was the bird that had suggested "a serene religious beatitude as no other sound in nature does" to the naturalist John Burroughs in his book *In the Catskills*. T. S. Eliot singled out the avian musician singing "in the pine trees" in *The Waste Land*, and more recently

Amy Clampitt acknowledged the power of the particular bird in her poem "A Hermit Thrush": "we drop everything to listen as a / hermit thrush distills its fragmentary, / hesitant, in the end / unbroken music." While the thrush is unassuming in appearance with its camouflaging brownish-red color and spotted breast, its song has possessed, enthralled, and elevated its hearers for well over a century in this country, and Amy Beach was among those aroused.[36]

Given the absence of any listing of books in Beach's home library, it is impossible to know whether she owned Whitman's *Leaves of Grass* or *Specimen Days*, or Burroughs's *In the Catskills*, which had been published in Boston in 1910.[37] Her use of poetry that appeared in many widely circulated magazines, along with recently published verse, suggests that she read some contemporary literature. She also set Shakespeare and poetry written by her husband, but the exact nature or breadth of her literary tastes remains unknown. Given her own connection to and dependence upon nature for artistic inspiration, and her belief in its spiritual value and meaning, however, it is hardly a leap to suggest that Beach would have seconded the poetic expressions of Whitman or Burroughs or any of a number of other well-circulated writer-naturalists.

It is clear that Beach was familiar with at least some nature poetry. She excerpted brief lines referring specifically to the hermit thrush from works by the popular American poet John Vance Cheney (1848–1922) and from the earlier English "Northamptonshire Peasant Poet" John Clare (1793–1864), which she placed at the tops of the two hermit thrush pieces.[38] As is evident from the verses she chose, John Vance Cheney and John Clare subscribed to an early nineteenth-century ideology that easily connected nature and religion. Cheney's lines at the top of "A Hermit Thrush at Eve" ascribed holiness to the bird:

> Holy, Holy! – in the hush
> Hearken to the hermit thrush;
> All the air is in prayer.[39]

Less insistent on a direct connection to the divine, but still drawing an analogy with a hymn, John Clare, like Mrs. Knight, appreciated the pure joyousness of nature. The lines Beach included at the top of "A Hermit Thrush at Morn" are brief but especially appropriate to the piece:

> I heard from morn to morn a merry thrush
> Sing hymns of rapture, while I drank the sound
> With joy.[40]

Beach's quoted lines differ slightly from those found in Clare's "The Thrush's Nest." By altering the second line from "Sing hymns to sunrise" to "Sing hymns of rapture," Beach may have consciously introduced her own response to the sound of the bird. For Beach, nature was numinous; listening to the bird's song became a thoroughly religious experience; she was transported beyond herself.[41] As Adrienne Fried Block observed: "a number of Beach's songs begin with nature images or human love and end by invoking the divine."[42] Here again, in understanding music as naturally religious, Beach participated in thinking that was common to many nineteenth-century writers and thinkers. Once again Block explains: "It was common coin of the late nineteenth century to speak of music as the divine art." She points to the influential music critic Henry Edward Krehbiel (1854–1923), who in 1899 defined "a new trinity consisting of God, nature, and music" as capturing the tone of the time.[43] In fact, Krehbiel's paradigm was infused with earlier nineteenth-century thinking.

While Beach embraced a religio-romantic nature ideology on the one hand, the pair of hermit thrush pieces shows the composer balancing two paradigms of nature. At the same time that Beach held fast to many aspects of a God-imbued nature ideology, and by so doing continued to champion one aspect of the nation's presumed exceptionalism, she also moved beyond a pre-Darwinian reading of the natural world.[44] The importance that Beach attached to her transcription of the hermit thrush song suggests different thinking, that which was privileged later in the century and especially among those scientifically inclined ornithologists and botanists who prided themselves on their accurate observation and precise description of natural phenomena. Because of Beach's valuation of her transcription and the music that resulted, the chapter will focus upon this single work.

In an interview with Una L. Allen, assistant to the head of Arthur P. Schmidt Company, publishers of many of Beach's works, Beach described her late July encounter with "a most voluble thrush."

> I took the songs down at the bird's dictation, and oh, how hard I worked! Even the most expert stenographer would have had difficulty keeping up with him! I took them exactly, even as to key (except for a few intervals too small to be transcribed) and rewrote and corrected as he sang them over and over. Then I played them back to him and he would answer.[45]

Her note at the bottom of "A Hermit Thrush at Morn," "These bird-calls are exact notations of hermit thrush songs, in the original keys but an octave lower, obtained at MacDowell Colony, Peterborough, N.H.,"[46] was not the remark of a romantic, or a nature-religion ideologue, or even of a moralist, but rather of a careful observer of nature who valued a high degree of scientific exactitude. Her remark privileged precision, rigor, and correctness; she took pride in her accomplishment. Beach brought the bird to life in a remarkably accurate rendering of its song. Comparison with examples of live hermit thrush songs or those that are available online support her claim, which is made all the more impressive when one considers that the first recordings of wild birds captured in the fields of North America were done in 1929 (example 2.1).[47]

Four measures of a seemingly generic waltz-like vamp set the stage for the entrance of the thrush. The bird's song, however, reveals the vamp to be intimately connected to what follows: both are built upon triadic structures and minor–major harmonic behavior that Beach introduced in the quiet, unassuming opening.[48] The undulating but ultimately uplifting birdsong melody, with its prominent rising fifths and fourths, informs both the right and left hands of the piano part, as does the dotted rhythm, which appears throughout the piece, sometimes in literal repetitions, but also in offset, compressed, syncopated versions and elongated, augmented forms.[49] The chirping, rising sixteenth-note pair that rounds off the bird's initial vocalization previews even faster and more delicately arpeggiated passages starting at measure 8. These flickering figures, repeated throughout, like in the bird's song, glisten in Beach's soundscape.

Even when Beach's paean turns more agitated, as it does at measure 28 and again at 79, the right-hand figuration still relates to the opening triads and the bird's arpeggiated song. In these passages the piano part appears to be modeled upon the bird's more energetic flourishes. Beginning at measure 29, the left hand engages in a modified inversion of the bird's wide-spread opening arpeggio figure (example 2.2).

Regardless of the relative agitation or serenity of particular passages, Beach's materials are all taken from the song of the thrush, which she mines thoroughly for its music.[50] Scientific exactitude aside, with its hushed, respectful, observational quality, there is something reverential about Beach's treatment of the thrush's song: this is not merely the efficient use of one's resources, nor a bravura display of compositional craft or cleverness. "A Hermit Thrush at Morn" is Beach's own "hymn of rapture": a quietly ecstatic, transparent reflection of her religiously inflected understanding of the natural world.

A Hermit Thrush at Morn

"I heard from morn to morn a merry thrush
Sing hymns of rapture, while I drank the sound
With joy."   J. CLARE

Mrs. H.H.A. BEACH
Op. 92,No2

*These bird-calls are exact notations of hermit thrush songs, in the original keys but an octave lower,
obtained at Mac Dowell Colony, Peterborough, N.H.*

EXAMPLE 2.1. *A Hermit Thrush at Morn.* By Amy Beach., mm. 1–17. Copyright © 1922
by the Arthur P. Schmidt Co. Amy Beach Papers, Milne Special Collections and
Archives Department, University of New Hampshire Library, Durham.

EXAMPLE 2.2. *A Hermit Thrush at Morn.* By Amy Beach., mm. 28–33. Copyright 1922 by the Arthur P. Schmidt Co. Amy Beach Papers. Milne Special Collections and Archives Department, University of New Hampshire Library, Durham.

While Olivier Messiaen is often celebrated for pioneering the careful use of birdsong in many compositions of the 1940s and 1950s, decades earlier and without access to recorded or taped birdsongs that could be replayed, Amy Beach transcribed and interpolated the sounds of this celebrated songster in her music.[51] Equipped only with patience, an extraordinary ear, and complete devotion to the task at hand, she listened. Just as nineteenth-century composers had responded to Niagara Falls with large and occasionally bombastic symphonies, Beach matched form to function when she wrote a character piece for piano whose dimensions and dynamic palette reflected her subject.

Once again a comparison with *plein-air* paintings seems apt. As art historian Eleanor Jones Harvey explains, "the sketches were understood to be truthful renderings of actual scenery, a benchmark of veracity for the artist's easel paintings."[52] Beach claims that her pieces are accurate and precise and, hence, authoritative artistic expressions of what she heard in nature. The veracity of Beach's renderings is not, however, the primary issue here, although her aspiration to truthfulness is clearly an important and resonant one. More essential for purposes of this study is that Beach was receptive to and respectful of what nature had to say; she took care in listening to and decoding it. She cast herself as amanuensis to the thrush and thus put herself in a position of service to nature, and her art, and the colony. Beach expressed her interconnectedness with the natural world by integrating its sounds within her own regularized, waltzlike musical frame.[53] Not quite willing to incorporate the long and irregularly spaced silences that characterize actual birds' songs, Beach made herself and nature parts of a single, more human-sounding musical whole. While she may have bent nature's song to her own purposes, and in so doing revealed larger assumptions regarding humanity's dominion over nature, in the process of creating her piece Beach showed herself a most skillful listener.

3

Marion Bauer

In *Modern Music-Makers: Contemporary American Composers*, a collection of interview-based writings published by Madeleine Goss in 1952, the author quoted Marion Bauer (1882–1955): "To Mrs. Edward MacDowell, I owe a debt of gratitude for having founded a haven where many other composers, writers, and painters have shared with me the extraordinary opportunity and privilege of doing creative work in peaceful, stimulating and beautiful surroundings."[1] While the subject of Bauer's tribute was clearly Marian Mac-Dowell, her reference to the colony as a "haven" with "peaceful, stimulating and beautiful surroundings" spoke to the impact the place had on her, as well. Like for Amy Beach, the chance to work uninterrupted in the idyllic setting was an "extraordinary opportunity" for Bauer. Her acknowledgment of the power of the *natural* place is, however, unusual, because unlike Beach, whose personal papers and compositions offer multiple references to the important role the natural world played in her music and life, Marion Bauer seems not to have felt compelled to single out "nature" on its own for comment in any other context.

Without recurring acknowledgments, however, the place was clearly inspiring to Bauer. As Goss further explained: "One year 'out of sheer joy of being at the colony' she was inspired the moment of her arrival. Not waiting to unpack her trunk, she borrowed music-paper from a fellow-colonist and at once wrote down a Prelude – last in her group of *Six Preludes for the Piano*."[2] There are no records where Bauer writes of her eagerness to capture the colony's unique sounds or soak up its inspiring scents or sights, despite the fact that a number of her works written after her initial trip refer to nature. In Bauer's music, nature functions more as a source for atmospheric musical responses than as an archive of specific sonic events. It is there but doesn't require worship, identification, approbation, or appropriation. By juxtaposing Beach and Bauer, readers can begin to appreciate the range of composer responses not only to specific environments, but also to nature more generally.

Many of Marion Bauer's earliest compositions, those from the 1910s and 1920s, were written for voice, chorus, or piano solo in a tonal idiom similar to Beach's works, and a large number of them, including some composed prior to her first residency at the MacDowell Colony in 1919, refer to nature in their titles. Among the most noteworthy is probably "Up the Ocklawaha" (op. 6), for violin and piano written for and dedicated to Maud Powell, which she composed in 1912. It was inspired by a poem the concertizing violinist sent to Bauer describing her otherworldly encounter as she toured in Florida on the eponymous "bark-stained . . . tortuous river."[3] We will come back to this work. Other nature-related pieces include "Fair Daffodils" (1914), a piece for women's chorus based upon R. Herrick's poem "To Daffodils"; and "The Lay of the Four Winds" (op. 8) written in 1915, with poetry by C. Y. Rice for male chorus.

Beginning with her first residency at the MacDowell, still more nature-related titles appeared in Bauer's works list:[4] in 1919 she set text from Oscar Wilde's poem "In the Forest" in her song "My Faun," and in 1921, the summer of Beach's first residency, Bauer composed "Night in the Woods" using words from E. R. Sill's poem "Night in Peace."[5] This is the same poet with whom Beach made her California birding trip as a child, and whose poem "The Thrush" she set in 1891. Bauer could easily have read Sill's poetry in a number of magazines – *The Atlantic Monthly* and the *Century Magazine* are just two – or she might have learned of the poet from Beach, whom she met that year.[6] Once again, Bauer left no commentary. The year 1921 also saw the publication of the vocal solo "The Epitaph of a Butterfly," which set poetry by Thomas Walsh, and the following year "A Parable (The Blade of Grass)" with words by Stephen Crane.

In selecting such poems, Bauer, like her nineteenth-century, women nature-writing forebears, focused on small, delicate, ephemeral manifestations of nature that were close to home and easily anthropomorphized. As Beach had formed a close alliance with her companion thrush, Bauer, through Herrick, empathized with the daffodils and mourned their short season: "Fair Daffodils, we weep to see / You haste away so soon." Both poet and composer understood the common fate of humanity and flora: "We have short time to stay, as you, / We have as short a Spring."[7] With Oscar Wilde, Bauer longed to "snare the shadow" and "catch . . . the strain" of the "ivory limbed and brown-eyed . . . Faun" who "skips through the copses singing" while "his shadow dances along."[8] Thomas Walsh's butterfly floated lifeless toward "Yon mirrored pool made ready for her fall / A grave as lovely as her native sky." That these sensitive lines were written by male poets underscores the point that observational (rather than conquering) attitudes toward nature were not the exclusive purview of the female sex, even if they were, overwhelmingly, the dominant one among women. That a number of these poets are household names and Bauer is not may speak more to the point that for decades, women's voices were not heard even when they explored similar subject matter as their male colleagues.

"From the New Hampshire Woods," a set of three pieces for piano solo written between 1922 and 1923, was inspired directly by Bauer's time at the colony, as will be made clear in the discussion of her music that follows.[9] By the time Bauer first visited the MacDowell Colony in 1919, she had lived in New York City and abroad in France and Germany for a total of sixteen years; she had become international in her training, outlook, and circle of acquaintances. But growing up in the Pacific Northwest, in Walla Walla, Washington, and then in Portland, Oregon, in the last years of the nineteenth century meant that Bauer would have gone to the East Coast and the New Hampshire woods with a perspective quite different from her northeastern and more urban colleagues'. And this perspective was likely most different when it came to what constituted nature – its shapes, its colors, its dimensions, and its near-limitlessness.[10] While Bauer left no extant remarks addressing the impact of her natal place on her consciousness, it is impossible to imagine that her first twenty-one years spent exclusively in that furthest northwest corner of the nation did not imprint themselves in some way.[11]

Walla Walla is located in the far southeastern part of Washington State, thirteen miles from the Oregon border; in 2008 it had a population of just under 58,000. In 1880, however, Walla Walla was a city of 3,600 people in what was then the Washington Territory; statehood was still nine years off.[12] The city and the region thrived as part of the wheat-growing Northwest Inland Empire, that landlocked expanse bookended by the Cascade Mountains on the west and the Rocky Mountains on the east.

When Marion's father, Jacques (Joe) Bauer, initially emigrated from France to the Northwest in 1854, he became an infantryman in the Ninth Infantry, which had been mustered to fight in the Indian Wars. According to Marion Bauer biographer Susan Pickett, he later joined the infantry's band,

and when the wars subsided, he opened a tobacco shop selling to "transient gold prospectors who traveled up the Columbia River, gathered supplies in Walla Walla, and then headed to mines in Idaho and Montana."[13] Playing numerous instruments and singing would remain an important part of Jacques Bauer's life that he shared with his children. If Beach had a musical mother, Bauer had a musical father, and both encouraged their daughters to different degrees. The same early tobacco shop would become a general store and provide amply for the large Bauer family.

As Walla Walla's current chamber of commerce boasts: "Walla Walla became home to the first commercial bank in the northwest, the first college in the region, and . . . the oldest, continuous symphony west of the Mississippi River.[14] Whitman College was important in Marion Bauer's life, as it would employ her mother, Julia Heyman Bauer, a French-Jewish émigré, like Jacques, and "an erudite young woman who spoke English, French, German, Italian, Spanish, and Hebrew."[15] Sometime early in the 1860s, Julia had joined family members who lived in Portland, Oregon, and through the intercession of Robert Bauer, Jacques's brother, she met the entrepreneurial shopkeeper. They married in 1864 in Portland and returned to Walla Walla, where, after having seven children, Julia taught at Whitman College from 1882 to 1888.

Together Jacques and Julia created a culturally rich home life for their family that was augmented by Walla Walla's two opera houses, the regular appearance of touring companies, military band concerts, and numerous local musical groups.[16] But even such an environment as this could not have distracted the young Marion completely from the exceptional natural beauty that surrounded her in Walla Walla. Miles of rolling fields, undulating silt dunes as far as the eye can see, the Blue Mountains to the east, and a half-dozen rivers including the Snake, Palouse, Columbia, Touchet, and Walla Walla weave through this corner of the country. The particular spaciousness of the Northwest is without equal in New York or in Paris, two places where Marion Bauer would spend considerable parts of her life once she moved east. What Marion Bauer's territorial hometown may have lacked in more cultivated refinements or conveniences it made up for in expansive natural beauty. Whether she was conscious of it or not, the place would have left some kind of mark; it may be that Bauer's receptivity to nature poetry was one manifestation of her early years. There are no signature, equivalent open-spaced textures in Bauer's music, although she was raised within the very countryside that Copland would musicalize expansively. Being born into this environment may have obscured its distinctiveness.

The importance of family encouragement in the success of the composers discussed in this study is borne out in the case of Marion Bauer. She was the youngest of the seven children born to Jacques and Julia. While her mother started teaching languages at Whitman within a month of Marion's birth and devoted much of her time to her books and work, Marion benefited from the attentions of other family members, most especially her father and eldest sister. Emilie Frances, born in 1865, had inherited her father's musical gifts, and she seriously pursued piano study at a time when such an ambitious act by a woman was not widely applauded unless she intended to become a professional, which was often considered, as has been discussed, a questionable goal. It is clear that Emilie was not going to be content with music as a mere accomplishment. She moved to San Francisco to study with Miguel Espinosa, 1879–1880, before returning to Walla Walla in 1881 to establish her own piano studio. The following year, Marion was born. More than one biographer tells of Emilie placing Marion's cradle on top of the piano while she practiced or gave lessons. As Susan Pickett observed: at seventeen years apart, the sisters enjoyed a multifaceted relationship: "mother–daughter, teacher–pupil, mentor–sister, sister–sister. . . . Later as Marion entered adulthood, their connection transcended familial affection; they shared a passion for the arts, literature, languages, journalism, and most especially music."[17] The two were inseparable companions; Emilie Frances became an indefatigable champion of her sister's musical career, often putting aside her own aspirations to support Marion.

In 1888, Emilie Frances joined her brother Cecil in Portland, where he was studying law; she again established a piano studio but also began working as a music journalist, a career that would eventually take her across the continent. When Jacques Bauer unexpectedly died in 1890, Julia Bauer left Walla Walla and took her youngest children to Portland to rejoin her family; she once again taught languages in a variety of settings, including her home and at the St. Helen's Hall Girls School, where Marion would enroll. St. Helen's Hall had been established by the Episcopal diocese in 1869 and boasted a strong music department that prided itself on its German standard of music education.[18] What musical gifts Jacques had bequeathed to Marion were reinforced and expanded under the loving tutelage of her sister and the systematic instruction at St. Helen's Hall.[19] If later in life Marion Bauer demonstrated musical giftedness, it would not be attributed to intuition or instinct alone, as had been the case with Amy Beach. From a young age Marion benefited from regular, organized, expert encouragement, training, and guidance. Her training would ultimately legitimize her claim on a professorship.

Emilie Frances eventually moved to New York to pursue her own professional interests, and Marion followed in 1903 to do the same; the two lived together until the elder sister's death in 1926. Emilie enjoyed a successful career as a music critic for the *Musical Leader*, a position that Marion assumed when Emilie passed away. In the intervening years, however, Marion's musical horizons were expanded in ways that would never have been available to her had she stayed in the still-frontier-like Pacific Northwest. Educational opportunities denied Amy Beach by a mother who refused to allow her daughter to travel to Europe for study, and by a husband who insisted that education might warp his wife's natural talents, were heaped upon Marion Bauer by the selfless Emilie Frances, and Marion took advantage of them all.[20]

Soon after her arrival in New York, Marion began harmony studies with Henry Holden Huss, an American composer and pianist who had studied with a Leipzig-trained composer in the United States and then gone to the Royal Conservatory in Munich to work with Josef Rheinberger. Marion's German training at St. Helen's Hall would have prepared her well for Huss. In 1904, Marion's first piano works, "Arabesque" and "Elegie," were published by John Church Company, and she dedicated them to her sister Emilie and Henry Huss in gratitude for their nurture and support. The next year the Bauer sisters met French pianist and composer Raoul Pugno, who was on tour in the United States. Recognizing Marion's potential and her need for a broadened world vision, Pugno invited her to visit and stay with his family the following year. Marion Bauer's French-speaking family home in Walla Walla had provided the young composer with impeccable language skills, which served her well since Pugno did not speak English. Pugno introduced Bauer to Lili and Nadia Boulanger, the latter of whom was a close friend and collaborator, and within a short time, in addition to teaching English to Pugno's daughter, Renee, Marion began teaching English to both Boulanger sisters. Bauer benefited from this association perhaps more than either Boulanger benefited from the language lessons. As Peggy Horrocks explains: "In return, she received harmony and composition lessons, earning the distinction of becoming the first American student of the legendary Nadia Boulanger."[21] This was fifteen years before Boulanger's most celebrated American student, Aaron Copland, began his studies in 1921. Prior to returning to New York in 1907, Bauer studied with the American-born composer and theorist Louis Campbell-Tipton, who had come to Paris in 1901, and the violinist-violistconductor Pierre Monteux, who would eventually leave Europe to become an American citizen. Throughout this time, Bauer composed and got her works published.[22] She immersed herself in French musical thinking, developed friendships, and established a network of professional associates that lasted her entire life. Her musical education included serious study in a least two national traditions.

Once back in the United States, Bauer taught, studied, composed, and honed her playing skills working with the highly regarded piano pedagogue Eugene Heffley. He had come to New York from Pittsburgh in 1900 at the express invitation of Edward MacDowell, who was then professor of music at Columbia University, a post he held from 1896 to 1904. Heffley was among MacDowell's greatest proponents and committed to introducing his students to the then "ultra-modern" school, which included Debussy, Rachmaninoff, Florent Schmitt, Reger, Liadow, and Poldini.[23] His own focus on tone color and the refined use of the pedal would have made the two men sympathetic spirits, as MacDowell was often described as especially sensitive to tonal gradations, which he created through a uniquely effective pedaling technique. The two men were also committed to cultivating the interrelatedness of the arts. In remarks prepared for Harriett Brower's 1915 collection of interviews with leading piano pedagogues, which incidentally included one with Raoul Pugno, Heffley explained that he "endeavor[ed] to stimulate the imagination of the pupil through reading, through knowledge of art, [and] through a comprehension of the connection of all the arts."[24] With such close aesthetic sympathies, it is not surprising that Heffley became the founder and first president of the MacDowell Club of New York in 1905.[25] Bauer studied with Heffley from 1907 until 1910 and during that time became friends with the conductor Walter Henry Rothwell.

It is almost certain that Marion Bauer's association with the MacDowell Colony can be traced directly to Eugene Heffley. It was only months after she began her studies with Heffley that MacDowell died, in January 1908, and the composer's widow, Marian, commenced her life's work promoting her husband's music and their shared vision of an artists' colony. MacDowell Clubs, which would emerge across the nation in response to her own and Heffley's efforts, among others, championed not only Edward MacDowell's music, but the retreat that had been a part of the composer's dream for a place where artists from all disciplines could share the common experience of an inspiring natural environment. Whereas Amy Beach had come to the MacDowell Colony after having cultivated a collegial relationship with Marian MacDowell and established a reputation through her work with women's music clubs, Bauer arrived at the colony as the student of the man Edward MacDowell had hand-picked as his champion. Their different paths to the colony suggest two options that were available to women who sought a more professional relationship to music in the early years of the twentieth century. Where Beach's connection to the colony was dominantly through women's musical-social clubs and networks, Bauer's connection was through her work as a serious student of music, as someone trained and endorsed by international performers and pedagogues alike, and as a person pursuing a professional career. Although born just fifteen years apart, the two women's trajectories suggest gradually enlarging horizons for female musicians. Both started with piano study, an acceptable instrument and pursuit for young women, before turning to composition. Both also demonstrated unusual degrees of musical ability that took them far beyond what was needed (or, in certain social strata, acceptable) for simple parlor entertainments. While Beach's performing career was interrupted for twenty-five years, during which time she gave herself over almost exclusively to composition and being a society matron, Bauer continued her studies of both piano and composition. Family encouragement and educational opportunities will remain the chief determinants of a woman's pursuit of a career in music.[26]

Bauer made two more trips to Europe before her first visit to the colony. In 1910–11, Bauer traveled to Berlin, where she studied counterpoint with Paul Ertel. It was during this trip that Marion detected the extent of German disparagement of American musical culture and even more especially of the idea of American women composers. She used the attribution "M. Bauer" when she published some songs there, the only time she ever denied her first name or disguised her sex. Upon her return to the United States she was immediately offered a seven-year publishing contract by Arthur P. Schmidt, and between 1912 and 1921 his company published eighteen of her songs. She briefly returned to Berlin in the summer of 1914 for additional work. Horrocks believes these studies "contributed to a more linear approach to harmonic writing, which became an important feature of her style."[27] What is perhaps most noteworthy about Bauer's training is its equal parts French and German. While studies with Ertel may have strengthened her contrapuntal skills, Bauer's time with Pugno, her work with Boulanger, and her own fascination with tone color, which was reinforced by the influence of Heffley, who in addition to being a colleague of MacDowell's was also a champion of Debussy, rounded out her thoroughly European education.[28] The contrast between Beach's experiences and Bauer's could not be more stark. Beach's mother and then husband refused Amy the opportunity to learn from master teachers, using various rationales to deny her a musical education beyond that which she could cobble together herself. Bauer's sister Emilie gave up her own musical aspirations in order to support and encourage her sister's development. She made sure Marion benefited from the best teachers available.

The unrest roiling in Europe in 1914 and the outbreak of World War I that summer terminated many American musicians' European studies and altered career plans on both sides of the Atlantic.[29] One can only speculate where Bauer might have pursued the next stages of her career had all options been available. Beach, too, returned from Europe in September of that year. Beginning in 1914, however, Bauer commenced composition lessons in New York with Walter Henry Rothwell. Although she was his first student, Bauer fondly recalled his training as among her most valuable.[30] Their lessons continued until Rothwell left in 1919 to assume a conducting position with the Los Angeles Philharmonic Orchestra. It was the summer of that same year that Marion first visited the MacDowell Colony. While Amy Beach's access to like-minded musical professionals who could have cultivated and challenged her development was circumscribed at best and suffered long periods of drought, Bauer seems never to have lacked contact with music makers and creators, teachers and champions; she was in constant stimulating company; no social circles, with their suffocating rules of conduct, constrained her. The absence of social constraints may be one of Bauer's inheritances of her birth in the Pacific Northwest. Unlike the Brahmans of Boston, or the Blue Book, Social Register members of New York, groups whose expectations for behavior exerted enormous restrictions on their elite members, Bauer would have enjoyed no such diamond-studded chains. As a professional woman, who was a musician, she belonged to no such elevated spheres. Quite the opposite.

A study of "Up the Ocklawaha" and "From the New Hampshire Woods" illuminates Bauer's employment of nature imagery in two of her earlier works and reinforces the point that nature served and serves a variety of uses for different composers in different pieces. When Arthur Foote heard "Up the Ocklawaha" for the first time, he exclaimed, "This is the best piece of descriptive music I ever heard!"[31] Foote was a member of the same loosely affiliated group of Boston composers who supported Beach's music. Maud Powell, the virtuoso dedicatee, insisted that she had "never experienced a more remarkable expression of color and picture drawing in music than this work."[32] Such praise must have been encouraging to a young woman composer just beginning to make a name for herself.

Bauer and Powell had met in New York and become friends prior to Powell's February 1912 concert tour of the South. While in Florida, the violinist endured a nightmarish overnight boat ride on "A stream of bark-stained waters, / A swift and turgid river. / A restless, twisting, tortuous river" as she wended her way to a concert venue.[33] Powell captured the scene in a sixty-six-line prose poem that she titled "Up the Ocklawaha."[34] She sent the poem to Bauer, who responded with an appropriately moody musical evocation of the exotic and forbidding place that Powell had described. Unlike Beach, who had had a personal experience with the subject of her hermit-thrush pieces, Bauer imagined the scene Powell had described and created a similarly brooding sonic picture. Her personal remove from the subject meant that Bauer wrote about a natural world that was not familiar or close by at all, but a thousand miles away. The picture of the Ocklawaha River that Powell conjured was also not a comforting one. Her "forest of doom" where "gaunt trees . . . are buried alive in the terrible swamp" was a place rife with danger. One wonders if "Up the Ocklawaha," although it celebrated Powell's courageous trek on behalf of music, was also a warning to others, and women especially, not to venture so far from home lest they risk their lives.

Although Powell's references to the "rank" and "noisome" smells of the river might not have translated easily into music, her many allusions to motion and sounds lent themselves perfectly to musical expression, and more especially to what Judith Tick characterized as "the prevailing ideal of continuous movement [which] 'implies a fluidic or dynamic state.'" This is a recurring idea in Bauer's book *Twentieth Century Music*.[35] Referring to the boat that transported her, Powell wrote, "Up the Ocklawaha / The Hiawatha plows her way." She saw "Things fantastic, gruesome, grim, / That quiver and start and quicken to life." Regarding the fantastical shapes that appeared silhouetted against "the night's abysmal black," Powell described "Swinging, swaying, a phantom throng, / Meshed in a somber death-dance, / Dancing a demon death-dance." As the night finally lifted Powell recalled, "A wild bird calls across the swamp, / A new breeze blows from the far-off gulf, / A message of dawn is in the air." The poem closes with her having survived the ordeal: "The nightmare is no more. / Peace at last / Up the Ocklawaha." Bauer's music will quiver and start, it will swing and sway, and it will end with the same sounds with which it began, but it will not suggest peacefulness.

At the top of the score Bauer provided an eight-line reduction of the violinist's poetic text. While none of Bauer's lines literally quotes Powell's poem, her gloss reveals the images that most captured her attention and informed her musical response. That said, no attempt should be made to overlay Powell's or Bauer's words on specific musical passages: "Up the Ocklawaha" is not an exercise in word painting but an example of musical atmospherics. Bauer's reduction follows:

> A boat glides silently up a swift and tortuous river.
> The bark-stained waters race madly through a mighty swamp.
> Giant cypresses stand knee-deep in noisome ooze,
> losing their birthright in the vampire clutch of the deadly Tillandsia
>   (Spanish moss).
> The trees seem shrouded in death rags.
> The mournful swish of the dying branches against the Hiawatha
> as she pushes up-stream, is the primeval forest's last
> whispered appeal to humanity for release from its awful fate.[36]

Bauer's "picture drawing in music" makes its impact through the understated but palpable tensions that exist on multiple levels in her basic compositional materials. The restlessness described in Powell's poem and retained in Bauer's reduction manifests itself in the music found in both the violin and piano parts, whether heard individually and sequentially or simultaneously. A softly rocking, repetitive chordal pattern in the piano's two-measure introduction easily parses the slow $\frac{12}{8}$ meter and evokes Bauer's *molto tranquillo* scene.[37] We can imagine a boatman stroking the water in this nod to a traditional gondolier's barcarole. But Bauer's open chords float over dissonant bass notes, and the predictable repetitive pattern breaks down before its third iteration is complete: the music portends something more unsettling than tranquil (example 3.1).

The violin enters matching the *pianissimo* dynamic of the accompaniment and drawing her first notes, D–C, from the right-hand octaves of the opening piano chords. These pitches and their descending motion will become essential motives unifying the work. While the soloist's part is initially more active and rhythmically varied than the pianist's chordal pulsations, starting at measure 11 the piano takes over the violin music, and at measure 12 the violin begins a descent that recalls the music of the right-hand piano part in measure 3. The parts mingle and blend; they are stirred together in Bauer's river music. One can hear the motion of the Ocklawaha's "dynamic state." And so it goes throughout the piece, with instrumentalists exchanging ideas; there is continuous movement. Rhythms and melodic gestures that characterize the violin music at measure 20 become the piano music at measure 31. At times the

EXAMPLE 3.1. *Up the Ocklawaha.* By Marion E. Bauer, mm. 1–4. Copyright © 1998 by
Hildegard Publishing Company. All rights administered by Theodore Presser Company.

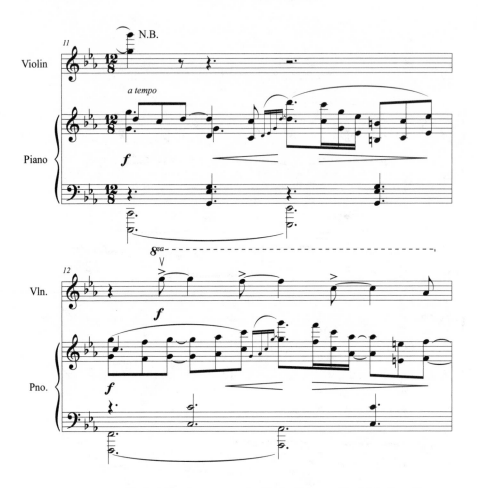

EXAMPLE 3.2. *Up the Ocklawaha* mm. 11–12 by Marion E. Bauer. Copyright © 1998 by Hildegard Publishing Company. All rights administered by Theodore Presser Company.

instrumentalists share ideas and levels of activity, and at other times they offer commentaries on each other's music. The piano's initial gentle rocking chords come back numerous times, either literally or in closely modified forms, and alternate with more tempestuous lyrical passages that occur throughout the piece. In these louder *agitato* (even *con fuoco*) lyrical passages Bauer comes closest to painting the "tortuous river" that stirs beneath the gliding boat, but the music could just as easily suggest strong winds, pelting rain, or consuming fire. It is more the idea of powerful energy being released than a literal musical manifestation of churning currents.[38] Both the gentle and the agitated musics appear in the violin part, as well; together they blend the sixty-two-measure work into a seamless stream of sound (example 3.2).

But seamlessness doesn't guarantee predictability or unity. Our conditioned expectation of four-measure phrases that answer each other and create larger meaningful structures of eight, twelve, and sixteen measures is undermined in the opening ten bars by Bauer's five-plus-five-measure statement. And while she does achieve a structural downbeat on a *forte* octave C at measure 11, it is undermined by the presence of the pitch D on beat 1. Bauer captures Powell's uneasy experience on the river in a work where consonant, restful moments are relative, undermined, or merely passing.

Although the piece begins and ends with audible octave Cs in the piano accompaniment, and there are important moments where C is structurally significant, the piece is never fully at home in its C-minor key signature. Chromatic alterations are present in every measure but one, measure 38, but even there Bauer continues her dissonant harmonies. Dissonance is a fact of the soundscape and provides the musical correlate to the "primeval forest" that Bauer envisions.[39] While "Up the Ocklawaha" is confined, more or less, within a consistent harmonic language and predictable rhythmic patterns that hold for the duration of the work, the dark undercurrent of the river permeates every moment of Bauer's moody sound picture; a listener is struck less by a sense of comforting sameness than by a feeling of unrelenting tension and impending disaster.[40] Constant chromaticism and dissonance keep the music and mood unsettled.

Ties over bar lines and overlapping entrances mean there are few neatly articulated antecedent-consequent phrases to parse the motion or define cadential moments. Like the river, the music is propelled by an unidentified force; it doesn't come to a close. The "mighty swamp" that surrounds the river means there is no defined shoreline awaiting the traveler, and this ambiguity finds a musical analogue in the final measures of the piece, where sounds eventually move beyond audibility and evaporate into the sodden atmosphere. Despite the ostensibly calm and quiet opening and close of Bauer's tone poem, a menacing energy is left hovering. If this is peace, it is at best an uneasy one.

"Up the Ocklawaha" differs in important ways from Beach's "A Hermit Thrush at Morn" and, as will be shown, from Bauer's second work considered in this study, "From the New Hampshire Woods," even though her focus on dissonance and motion will remain audible. It also differs in significant ways from the works by other composers discussed here. Chief among the differences is that Bauer did not have a personal experience with her subject.

She was not there to smell the "noisome ooze" or hear the "mournful swish of the dying branches" as they dragged against the sides of the Hiawatha. In addition, her piece is a response to someone else's reaction to a natural place, and a selective one at that. Bauer chose only the most forbidding images from Powell's more balanced observations, leaving untouched the violinist's lines referring to the call of "a wild bird" or the sound of "a new breeze" with its "message of dawn." For Bauer, it was the strangeness of this distant place that seized her senses. Bereft of any real-life experience of a similar environment upon which to draw, she conjured the Ocklawaha River from Powell's melodramatic description of an exotic, danger-laden "other" place and her own fertile imagination. For all the variety of nature available in the Pacific Northwest, there were no swampy jungles in the southeastern corner of Washington State or in the verdant hills of Portland.[41] Whether her characterization of the Ocklawaha as a deadly Tillandsia-shrouded netherworld bespoke her sense of all nature that lay beyond her experience, we don't know. If it does, and if she is representative of contemporary women composing about nature, "Up the Ocklawaha" may suggest why she and they would chose to write about nature closer to home and within their garden walls: beyond those borders might lie an "awful fate."[42]

"From the New Hampshire Woods," written one decade later, shows Bauer reveling in a wholly different relationship to nature. Rather than depend upon someone else's description to fire her imagination, this work grew from her experiences at a place with which she was intimately familiar, comfortable, and at home. The titles of each of the three pieces in the set refer to flora close by her MacDowell Colony cottage and found abundantly in the surrounding Peterborough woods: white birches, Indian pipes, and pine trees.[43] Like "Up the Ocklawaha," each piece is preceded by a poem, the second one written by Bauer herself; and each provides images that guide a listener's (or performer's) sense of what inspired the sounds. Again, looking for specific poetic-musical correspondences seems beyond the composer's intentions or what is necessary. The words function more like those that graced the tops of Beach's two hermit-thrush pieces: they provide insight into the state of mind of the composer more than they provide items for a musical scavenger hunt. This study will consider the first two pieces of the suite.

Bauer sonified the foreboding Ocklawaha with a preponderance of low, slow, dark sounds; by comparison she composed "White Birches" with softly ringing tones drawn more from the middle and higher registers. The music is graceful, lightweight, and delicate. If "Up the Ocklawaha" revealed Bauer's

EXAMPLE 3.3. *White Birches*. By Marion Bauer, mm. 1–8.
Copyright © 1922 by G. Schirmer, Inc.

general familiarity with the harmonic meanderings of the inner voices of many of Brahms's late solo piano works (and Heffley's introduction of his students to pieces by Rachmaninoff, with their impassioned minor modalities), the first work of the New Hampshire suite appears to be modeled specifically on Brahms's Intermezzo, Op. 117, No. 2 in D♭ major, the same key as Bauer's work. Brahms's piece, written as one of three intermezzi in 1892, must have appealed to Bauer, who so valued dynamic motion and harmonic ambiguity.[44] His piece moves without pause until the final chord is struck, just like "Up the Ocklawaha" and "White Birches."[45] Its harmonies rotate like a constantly changing sounding kaleidoscopic. Continuously undulating motions that characterize Brahms's D-flat Intermezzo, where hands pass materials back and forth, cross and fill in each other's lines, reach in and grab notes, become the signature gesture that frames Bauer's 1922 piece (example 3.3).

Both works also share the same general dynamic compass, beginning *piano* and ending even more quietly – Bauer *pianissimo*, and Brahms triple *piano*.[46] Whether Bauer consciously drew upon Brahms's work to fashion her own is not the issue: pointing out the similarities of the two pieces is not an indictment of her originality. What is important in the context of this study

EXAMPLE 3.4. *White Birches.* By Marion Bauer, mm. 39–42.
Copyright © 1922 by G. Schirmer, Inc.

is that Bauer drew upon sounds that had no overt relationship to nature, or at
least none that Brahms acknowledged. She didn't aspire to an onomatopoeic
creation. Rather than describe (or transcribe?) the birches in a self-conscious
pantomime of sounding arboreal gestures, whatever they might be, Bauer
evoked the delicate, shushing, flickering leaves so identified with the slender
trees. One can imagine the delicate leaves swaying to the summer breezes in a
cascading passage that emerges midway through the piece. Once again, Bauer
focused on motion, rhythmic and harmonic (example 3.4).

The white birches on the Peterborough acreage would inspire other
MacDowell fellows in the years to come, and especially painters and photographers,[47] but more importantly for Bauer, they captured the attention of

another colonist who was enjoying a residency simultaneously with her own. Pulitzer prize–winning poet and writer William Rose Benét penned the three lines that Bauer included at the top of her score:

> What is the meaning of their secret gleaming,
> What language is in their leaves, that glitter and whisper
> Where the ghostly birches glimmer under the moon?[48]

Benét didn't attempt a description of the trees, but like Bauer he commented on their effects – gleaming, glittering, and whispering – under the moon. Like the majority of the later composers considered in this study, Bauer appears not to have been after any kind of programmatic realization of her subject or carefully modeled ekphrasis-like translation. Her music is atmospheric, meant to conjure a mood, a scene, a state of being. It is unlikely that without benefit of Bauer's title to guide them, listeners would imagine white birches, but that doesn't diminish the success of her evocation.

Of the three pieces in the New Hampshire set, the one potentially able to divulge the most regarding Bauer's attitudes toward nature is the second piece, "Indian Pipes," for which she wrote not only the music, but the cryptic verses at the top of the page:

> After the rain,
> Down in the woods,
> Through last year's moss
> The ghostly Indian Pipes
> Lift up their heads . . .
> Mysterious!
> Transcendent!![49]

While the first piece of the set was dedicated to poet, composer, and ethno-musicologist John Powell, Bauer dedicated "Indian Pipes" to Mrs. Edward MacDowell. Given Bauer's fondness for Mrs. MacDowell and her gratitude for the colony, we can only speculate that this piece held some special meaning for the composer. Unfortunately, Bauer left no commentary.

The flower of the title is known by many names – ghost plant, corpse plant, and in my own experience Indian peace pipe – but in all cases, the name makes some reference to exotic or otherworldly associations.[50] And this seems reasonable if one is familiar with the pale, milky-white coloration of its single flower, which emerges from a stalk that pokes through thick humus near the bases of oak and pine trees. Protected from winds by their short stature and

dense surroundings, Indian pipes stand motionless, unperturbed sentries
guarding their host trees. Without needing sunlight to grow, the flowers
nonetheless have a quietly glowing luminescence and provide an unexpected
spot of light against the dark forest floor. There is something unassuming
about these quiet flowers found close to the ground in their self-contained
small clusters throughout the northeastern woodlands.

With no movement to musicalize, no action to emulate, "Indian Pipes"
emerges and then hovers like a suspended atmospheric moment. As with both
earlier pieces, a limited number of musical ideas provides all the materials
Bauer needs. The first is a descending, dotted-note line whose soft dynamic,
slow tempo, and unstable harmony deny a sense of home base (example 3.5).

A second idea is more obviously rhythmic, although again the unpredict-
ability of its harmonic motion reinforces its instability (example 3.6).

A third idea, loud and chordal, appears only once, but it too is related to
the descending motion of the first idea. Ironically, the *Poco marziale* passage
includes Bauer's most flexible treatment of meter in the entire piece. Harmonic instability remains a constant (example 3.7).

The chimerical qualities of the "ghostly" flower come in and out of focus
in music that resists a single key, mode, meter, tempo, or mood. Yet amid
the musical dynamism, the many stops and starts, the luxuriously elongated
silences, the unexpected accents, and the clearly enunciated triads hinting
at numerous different tonalities, the piece projects an overwhelmingly quiet
and centered mood.

It is tempting to create a backstory for Bauer's piece, one that tells of
her discovery of a mound of Indian pipes during a solitary forest ramble: it

EXAMPLE 3.6. *Indian Pipes, from the New Hampshire Woods.* By Marion Bauer, mm. 11–12. Copyright © 1923 (renewed) by G. Schirmer, Inc. (ASCAP), international copyright secured. All rights reserved. Reprinted by permission.

EXAMPLE 3.7. *Indian Pipes, from the New Hampshire Woods.* By Marion Bauer, mm. 39–48. Copyright © 1923 (renewed) by G. Schirmer, Inc. (ASCAP) international copyright secured. All rights reserved. Reprinted by permission.

is likely something of that sort occurred, but she doesn't say so. Bauer also doesn't place herself in the verses; the flowers alone are there, lifting up their (anthropomorphized) heads. Neither does she identify the woods as some numinous green cathedral. Beach's religion-infused nature is not Bauer's. She is not given to rhapsodizing over the beauties of the out-of-doors, perhaps because she was born into a rich natural environment, years earlier, and hyperbolic accounts are more often the creation of those for whom "nature" is an occasional encounter, not a daily occurrence. Do the final lines – "Mysterious! / Transcendent!!" – suggest anything regarding Bauer's attitude toward nature? Or is pinning one's hopes on such meager evidence a sure sign of an author's desperation?

The unexpected presence of glowing flowers deep within the damp, mossy New Hampshire wood must have seemed a mysterious surprise to the colonist whose inland-Washington childhood wouldn't have included encounters with the plant.[51] Additionally, one doesn't need to be Emerson or Thoreau or Susan Fenimore Cooper to appreciate the opportunities the natural world provided for transcending experiences. Bauer had cited the "extraordinary" opportunity of working at the MacDowell Colony, and here "down in the woods" was evidence of the extra-ordinary, the transcendent. As the retreat exceeded her expectations for a stimulating work environment, "Indian Pipes" exceeds our expectations for a moving musical picture whose subject is ostensibly fixed and motionless.

4

Louise Talma

In September 1946, Louise Talma wrote of her summer's experience at the MacDowell Colony: "For two months now I have had the wonderful privilege of dwelling in that enchanted little house, the Phi Beta Studio at the MacDowell Colony in Peterborough, New Hampshire. . . . It is a veritable fairy-tale house, snugly sheltered from the road by a pine grove, and, on the other side, looking out on a clearing edged by great tall sentinel pines." Talma likened "this paradise" to "entering another world." The colony provided "complete release from worldly cares, and the longed-for opportunity to concentrate without interruption on the work in hand." In her wooded studio Talma knew "I have done my best work and known the greatest peace and happiness, and I can think of no greater joy than to be the proud possessor, for a while, of the key to its hospitable door."[1] In Robin Rausch's essay "The MacDowells and Their Legacy," Rausch noted that Louise Talma had "once said that the Colony had been everything to her. 'It revolutionized my life,'" Talma explained: "The first year I came I met Lukas Foss, and year by year I've made friends and professional colleagues who have made my career as a composer possible."[2] As is clear, it was not just the natural environment that stimulated Talma, but the chance to develop professional relationships: up through the middle of the twentieth century, women had few such opportunities.[3]

Talma was born in France to two professional American musicians; her mother was her first teacher. Her parents divorced before Louise was born, and in the summer of 1914, as the initial stirrings of what would become World War I shook Europe, mother and daughter moved to New York City, where Louise received her first systematic musical training. Beach, Bauer, and Talma would all be affected by this world conflict. Louise attended the

Institute of Musical Arts between 1922 and 1930, and there she won multiple
Isaac Newton Seligman Prizes for composition; she earned a bachelor's degree
in music from NYU in 1931 and a master's degree from Columbia University in
1933. Starting in 1926, she also spent her summers in France studying piano
with Isidor Philipp at Fontainebleau. Two years later and for the next ten
years, Talma studied composition with Nadia Boulanger. In 1938 she won
the Stovall Prize, the highest student composition award, and the following year the same "Stovall Prize jury awarded Talma her second accolade as
the Conservatoire's best student composer."[4] Between 1936 and 1939, Talma
taught analysis and solfège at Fontainebleau, earning the distinction of being
the first American faculty member at the famed Conservatoire Américain.[5]
A second war would again interrupt activities in Europe, including Talma's
summer sojourns to Fontainebleau, and she wouldn't return again until the
summer of 1949.[6] At the same time, her winters were dedicated to teaching
theory and ear training, first at the Manhattan School of Music (1926–1928),
and then beginning in 1928 at Hunter College of the City University of New
York, where she was appointed to the faculty, a position she held until 1979.

As is the case for many academics, summers and semester breaks provided Talma with her only time to devote exclusively to creative work. University obligations, classes, meetings, presentations, scholarly publications,
and concerts fractured her week during the school year. Despite those responsibilities, she composed a large number of pieces across a variety of genres,
including orchestral works, chamber pieces, piano and vocal solos, sacred and
secular choral works, and a single opera, *The Alcestiad*, written to a libretto
by Thornton Wilder, another MacDowell Colony resident whom she met
there.[7] A majority of her pieces were composed in whole or part at the colony
or in other rural retreats in New Hampshire, Virginia, or New York State,
which is attested to by handwritten notations at the ends of her manuscript
pages, where she scribbled specific dates and places. Sketches for Talma's
Holy Sonnets, a collection of seven songs that set texts by John Donne, show
how summer residencies directly impacted her productivity. According to
marginalia, in the four weeks between August 11 and September 14, 1954, at
the colony, Talma composed four songs: "Annunciation," "Nativitie," "Cru-
cifying," and "Ascension," the last of which she finished back in New York.
Working with the momentum she had established in the preceding month,
in the remainder of September that year she wrote "La Corona." She did no
work on the set again until the following summer residency in 1955, when she
composed "Temple" and "Resurrection" in the two weeks between June 14

and July 1, 1955. The set becomes a testament to the necessity of unscheduled time and the power of this serene place to inspire and support creative work.

Assigning significance to a composer's marginalia can be problematic, but in the case of Louise Talma it is essential, as her response to a 1982 inquiry for information about her music makes clear:

> I am unable to comply with your request for "some words of [my] own, preferably about [my] own music or [my] view of music." I dislike talking about myself, and I have no desire to add to the rivers of verbiage that daily inundate us. Explanations, even those of composers, explain nothing. Only the work matters, and to know it one must listen to it and study the score at first hand, not via millions of words. The only other pertinent information to place it accurately in the stream of time is *date, place,* and *circumstances of composition* and its first performance.[8]

Sketches for Talma's works that are housed among her papers at the Library of Congress contain a number of surprises for the scholar who knows her music primarily through her serially derived pieces, or who identifies her as the cosmopolitan, no-nonsense teacher of Milton Babbitt. Perhaps most fascinating among the unexpected discoveries for this study are birdsong transcriptions, which sing out from dozens of pages and are associated with a variety of pieces, many of whose titles contain no hint that the natural world played any role in their creation: *Piano Sonata, Sonata for Violin and Piano,* and *Toccata* are all pieces whose sketch pages show natural sounds as an essential source. Among the dozens of boxes of papers there are instances when Talma names the particular bird species she is transcribing, although on other occasions a page of notation is simply identified as "Bird Calls."[9] Whereas Amy Beach had a long history of birdsong transcription and was expert in deciphering specific songs and calls, Talma's knowledge of ornithology seems limited to a few of the more common species: robins, thrushes, nightingales, and bobwhites. There is no evidence that she was interested in the precision or ornithological accuracy of her transcription, as was Beach; Talma wanted the songs as basic source material for her music.[10]

A more specific discovery was Talma's use of birdsong as the spur for the creation of a tone row, as will be seen in the discussion of her piece *Summer Sounds.* Here is a fruitful integration of the most "natural" of sounds, with what many consider to be the most contrived and "unnatural" of methods, serialism. Talma saw no such distinction. And this is in keeping with her integrative approach to composition, which blended tonal, atonal, and serial methods unself-consciously.[11]

A second type of revelation among her papers was related to newspaper and magazine clippings. If her birdsong transcriptions showed Louise Talma composing *from* nature, the clippings show her reading *about* nature; one of these articles may have had a direct impact upon her chamber opera *Have You Heard? Do You Know?*, which will be discussed later. The year 1975 proved auspicious for *New York Times* subscribers who were interested in nature and the environment, topics that grabbed increasing column space in the paper's pages. Talma's clippings of five articles from March through June of that year indicate not only widespread curiosity about nature, but also her concern for environmental issues. The authors writing for the *Times* in 1975 would become respected names in journalistic environmental advocacy in the last quarter of the century: David R. Brower, who had been executive director of the Sierra Club (1952–1969) and who was regarded as an aggressive and determined champion of environmental policies, was president of Friends of the Earth at the time; Walter Sullivan, whose work would inspire the Walter Sullivan Award for Excellence in Science Journalism; Charles Mohr, who had written articles and books on various aspects of nature over a period of decades; Jane E. Brody, who became the *Times'* Personal Health columnist; and Gladwin Hill, who held the position of first-ever full-time national environmental correspondent for the *Times* for a period of ten years from 1969 to 1979. Hill was there to celebrate the first Earth Day in 1970 and to warn *Times* readers in 1975 that "Ecologists Fear Peril to Nature" as the result of "man's insatiable appetite for energy."[12] Together the articles covered a range of topics, from explanations of the thinning ozone shield; to the perilous combination of fossil-fuel consumption, nuclear energy proliferation, manmade chemical compounds, and unchecked population growth; to the impact of the Department of Agriculture's aborted campaign to eradicate the fire ant; to a summary report of the four-day "Earthcare" conference, sponsored jointly by the Sierra Club and the National Audubon Society, that was held in June of that year.

Always the musician, Talma saved an article that connected nature and sound: a piece by a then young freelance writer, Edmund Morris, titled "Oases of Silence in a Desert of Din." Morris, as will be shown, struck a direct hit with Talma when he speculated what Charles Ives might have thought of various modern sonic conditions that assaulted city dwellers and when he waxed poetic about "the howl of a coyote seemingly a million miles away, hav[ing] . . . poignancy sweet as music."[13] Morris described his favorite quiet escapes and invited readers to find "their own Silent Places." Talma registered her assent regarding the issue of quiet when she underlined in red ink his phrase "silence, that pure balm of the soul."[14] These words found their way into one of her works. The article also struck a chord with many readers, if the multiple letters to the editor that the *Times* published are any indication; Talma clipped those, as well. Of course, by 1975, Louise Talma had found a number of "oases of silence" well beyond the din of the city, and the MacDowell Colony was a constant among them.

Talma's clippings reflect her alignment with a concept of nature that is in many ways significantly different from the God-infused and God-ordered one that informed Amy Beach at the beginning of the century. When John Muir founded the Sierra Club in 1892, fifteen years after Beach had accompanied Edgar Rowland Sill on his birding treks in the Berkeley Hills, Muir enjoyed a near mystical relationship with the California mountains: many of his writings reflect that otherworldly reading and his valuation, above all, of the beauty of nature, which he argued should be preserved so that others could enjoy it too. By the late twentieth century, the same club advocated for saving natural places not by making an argument for beauty primarily, although that has always been the hook used to attract many members to the group, but by employing the most sophisticated scientific findings and projections to advocate for changed relationships to the natural environment in order to ensure the mere existence of the planet.[15] Talma's late-twentieth-century view, as gleaned from the articles she saved, included an appreciation of humanity's complicity in planetary health. Talma could simultaneously crave and appreciate the wooded MacDowell Colony retreat and understand the natural environment as synonymous with the chemical-ridden air, the fragile ozone layer, and the tenacious fire ant focused upon in the articles. Her more inclusive reading of nature may help explain Talma's more matter-of-fact approach to using its sounds in her pieces. Squeaky doors as well as birdsongs were all part of her soundscape and similarly worthy musical material.[16]

Unlike Marion Bauer's set *From the New Hampshire Woods*, with its specific place title, or Amy Beach's *A Hermit Thrush at Morn*, with its footnote citing Peterborough, New Hampshire, Talma's finished works do not make references to the colony or other specific places in their titles or explanatory notes. But nature's sounds find their ways into her music in direct ways nevertheless. While Talma wrote a number of works that bear general nature-related titles – "The Bird Says 'Bob White,'" "Duck Duet," and "The Robin," to name three pieces in her larger didactic piano set *Soundshots* – for two of them she doesn't identify where she heard the sounds in the published score; her footnotes focus exclusively on the music of the bird. She wrote: "The bird's name is Bob White. These are the sounds one bob white sang. Sometime he changed his call to A-flat E-flat or A-flat D-flat or A-flat C, but most often he sang A-flat D." Her piece starts with an ascending A♭ to D; the tritone figure appears throughout the work and returns in the right hand to end the piece. What might have been, at one time, an interval to avoid is valid source material for Talma's piece, as she took it directly from the bobwhite – nature is more broad-minded than musical treatises. While the published piece does not mention the provenance of the birdsong, the sketch identifies the site of its origin as "Nelson Pond, N.H." and the precise date of its completion, "June 14, 1974"; the words "bird call" appear over the opening figure. The published piece "The Robin" is similarly devoid of information regarding its provenance. Its note reads simply: "These are the sounds one robin sang."

The note accompanying the published score of "Duck Duet," however, identifies the place specifically: "The sounds made by two ducks on the edge of Tolman Pond, Nelson, N.H."[17] The sketch also includes the date, "June 20, 1974." Why Talma includes the information she does in the published versions of her scores is not clear without commentary from the composer. It may be that Tolman Pond carried certain personal meanings that would be known to others close to the composer. In most cases, the "circumstances of composition," recorded so carefully in the sketches, become parts of the finished piece without being foregrounded. As in the more detached discussions of nature recorded in the *New York Times* articles, Talma didn't broadcast her personal connections.

A sample of Talma's sketches demonstrates the ubiquity of her detailed references to compositional circumstances. In numerous sketches from across genres and decades, Talma scribbled the sounds and identities of birds specific to local environments, whether it was Peterborough, New Hampshire; Nelson Pond; Yaddo; Wavertree (a retreat in Virginia); or the American Academy in Rome, she gathered materials from wherever she happened to be. At the bottom of a sketch for the piece that would become *Ambient Air* in 1983, Talma notated: "Song of a Nightingale in the courtyard of the American Academy in Rome, Spring 1956" (figure 4.1).[18]

Unlike Amy Beach, who faithfully transcribed her birdsong melody and gave it pride of place in pieces that boldly bore the hermit thrush's name, Talma used birdsong much as she used serial techniques in her middle and later periods. Both birdsong and tone row were starting places, "source[s]

FIGURE 4.1. Published with permission of the MacDowell Colony (© 2011 The MacDowell Colony, Inc.). Louise Talma Collection, Music Division, Library of Congress.

FIGURE 4.2. Published with permission of the MacDowell Colony (© 2011 The MacDowell Colony, Inc.). Louise Talma Collection, Music Division, Library of Congress.

of motivic material," ways of identifying and generally organizing the ideas germane to a work but not intended to be proscriptive, strict systems or templates.[19] Her birdsong-informed pieces are freely adapted responses to ambient musical ideas in the style of her freely serial works.

Talma's sketches provide rich sources for observing many other aspects of her compositional process, from the specific rhythms of her workday, to the initial sounds that sparked an idea and its development into a finished work. We can track her slow but steady progress in the consecutive dates she provides for contiguous passages of a piece.

In many cases, Talma's marginalia goes beyond simply recording the date and general place. She regularly refers to the cottage in which she lived during a residency, and occasionally to the weather. In the sketch for her *Sonata for*

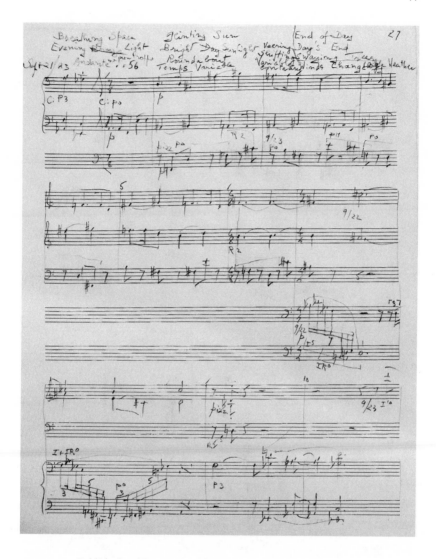

FIGURE 4.3. Published with permission of the MacDowell Colony (© 2011 The MacDowell Colony, Inc.). Louise Talma Collection, Music Division, Library of Congress.

Violin and Piano, she refers to a "big, dark, thunderstorm" that was occurring at the time (figure 4.2).

In other sketches she goes beyond references to specific weather occurrences to chronicle the more general atmospherics of a day, with their variable lighting and breezes (figure 4.3).

FIGURE 4.4. Published with permission of the MacDowell Colony (©2011 The MacDowell Colony, Inc.). Louise Talma Collection, Music Division, Library of Congress.

In another sketch she includes many of the above markers and the precise time of the day (figure 4.4).

Talma's valuation of "date, place, and circumstances of composition" is obvious from her regular notation of just these contingencies. Germane to a

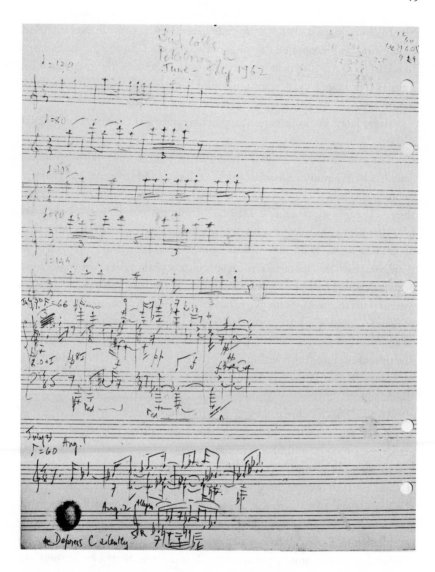

FIGURE 4.5. Published with permission of the MacDowell Colony (© 2011 The MacDowell Colony, Inc.). Louise Talma Collection, Music Division, Library of Congress.

study that focuses upon composers' refined listening skills, Talma's papers contain entire pages of sketches devoted to transcriptions of birdcalls that she heard in Peterborough, New Hampshire, in 1962, although in this instance she doesn't identify the particular species (figure 4.5).

In contrast, in a sketch of sounds heard July 4, 1969, in Nelson, New Hampshire, Talma notated the songs of two thrushes "answering" each other. In addition to the fragmentary notation of their sounds, the sketches show Talma's free adaptation of their music and her creation of an initial tone row (figure 4.6).

Pages later, we find the resulting matrix of row transformations (figure 4.7).

The two thrushes provide the essential source material for *Summer Sounds*, a twelve-minute chamber work for clarinet and string quartet that was premiered in July 1974 at the site of its initial inspiration, Nelson, New Hampshire.[20] The four movements – "Dawn," "Morning," "Noon," and "Night" – offer a rich site to observe the ways nature's sounds and cycles direct the course of Talma's work. While she is flexible in her selection and employment of basic compositional materials, she is specific about the effects she wants from her musicians. Her finely honed listening skills are observable in the detailed instructions she provides for performers. The work succeeds not only because of the care lavished on sonic subtleties, but also because of the overall sense of architecture and movement, derived from diurnal rhythms, which shape and propel the piece both within and between movements. A brief discussion of *Summer Sounds* illuminates ways nature's vocalizations and cycles inform Talma's piece.

Unlike Beach's thrush pieces, in which the bird's song became part of an established metrical structure, the music of Talma's "Dawn" moves with starts and stops resembling those of an early morning soundscape. There are few moments of sustained silence, as would characterize an actual dawn, but Talma's musical texture is transparent enough to evoke the spaces between the sounds and to conjure that quiescent interval of the day.[21] Birds softly call to each other and respond within an otherwise quiet, slowly awakening world. While "Dawn" is focused on small sounds, one senses the large, unbordered space surrounding the listener. Talma replicates the birds' rhythmic freedom with more than two dozen meter changes in a movement that lasts just three and a half minutes. Similarly abundant metrical variety characterizes all of *Summer Sounds*, as Talma captures this essential aspect of nature regardless of the time of day.[22] Talma's notational diligence when it comes to all matters pertaining to rhythm is a concession to the reality of keeping five musicians together, rather than a desire to discipline an unfettered natural world.

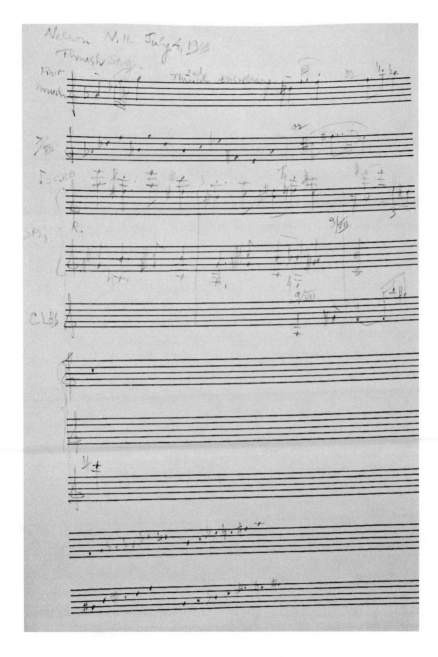

FIGURE 4.6. Published with permission of the MacDowell Colony (© 2011 The MacDowell Colony, Inc.). Louise Talma Collection, Music Division, Library of Congress.

FIGURE 4.7. Published with permission of the MacDowell Colony (©2011 The MacDowell Colony, Inc.). Louise Talma Collection, Music Division, Library of Congress.

Beyond embracing nature's temporal multifariousness, Talma also acknowledges nature's larger pitch palette. Like the birds, Talma is free of the traditional twelve tempered scale degrees. As "Dawn" opens, the first violin slowly oscillates between muted quarter tones starting on A♭; two measures later, the viola does the same. Listeners understand they have entered a different pitch domain: nature enjoys a more generous tuning system. In choosing wind and string instruments, Talma allows for more and different pitches than those isolated on a keyboard. It is distinct from Beach's piece, which was written for piano and thus confined to the twelve tempered pitches. Beach had to modify what the thrush sang in order to notate it on the five lines and four spaces of the common staff.[23] On numerous occasions throughout the four movements, Talma's use of harmonics suggests pitch realms that exist beyond human audition: an accurate understanding of the pitch spectrum of many nonhuman others, which extends both lower and higher than humans can create or detect. Talma uses all manner of extended techniques to simulate the alternately wooden, glassy, rich, thin, mellow, fluttering, sliding, pure, and hushed sounds that nature generates spontaneously. The first page of the score traces Talma's musical understanding of dawn and shows her using the prime row to introduce pitch material (example 4.1).

Talma's four-movement record of a summer day leaves an archlike sonic imprint. The first and last movements frame the set in relative quiet and stillness. With the second and third movements, the music becomes larger, faster, louder, and perhaps more human-sounding.[24] All of nature appears to be busier or at least noisier in the daylight hours. Although pitches and intervals of the original tone row unified "Dawn," and the row will continue to provide basic compositional material for the remainder of the piece, "Morning" and "Noon" possess more audible unity thanks to small, recurring rhythmic and melodic motives. Both of these movements also exhibit what appears to be more intentional, rather than serendipitous, counterpoint. Interactions sound musically driven rather than "naturally" occurring: the composer's hand is more obvious.[25] While Talma writes twenty-seven meter changes in the second movement, thus challenging any expectation of a dependable accent pattern, on multiple occasions the strings join forces in brief homo-rhythmic passages; the reinforced texture lends additional weight to that rhythmic moment, even if it too is evanescent. (Readers are directed to measures 8, 34–35, 42, and especially 49 for moments of rhythmic cohesion.) "Morning" also exhibits a softly insistent but playful momentum that is completely absent from the first movement; it is especially evident in passages where Talma

EXAMPLE 4.1 (*above and facing*). *Summer Sounds*, "Dawn," mm. 1–18. Published with permission of The MacDowell Colony (© 2011 The MacDowell Colony, Inc.). Louise Talma Collection, Music Division, Library of Congress.

instructs the lower strings to quietly play a series of staccato eighth notes *col legno battuto* (strike the string with the stick of the bow). See measures 8 and 23 of "Morning" for instances of this particular articulation (example 4.2).

"Noon" builds upon the energy of the second movement by increasing the rhythmic drive and introducing the first melodic moment in the piece. Unlike the soft openings of "Dawn" and "Morning," the third movement starts loudly

EXAMPLE 4.2. *Summer Sounds*, "Morning," mm. 1–10. Published with permission of The MacDowell Colony (© 2011 The MacDowell Colony, Inc.). Louise Talma Collection, Music Division, Library of Congress.

with a virtuosic twelve-tone plunge by clarinet followed by confirming bowed jabs from the strings.[26] Where in the previous movements the lone woodwind behaved more or less as an integrated member of the soundscape, in "Noon" the clarinet assumes a soloistic role and the strings become unquestionably the accompanying ensemble; they freely echo and respond to the clarinet's lead. Although short-lived, the single hint of melody drives the movement forward. The second page of "Noon" illustrates the new, if fleeting, relationship of parts (example 4.3). The greater rhythmic focus of "Noon," and especially those passages containing ostinati and forceful accents, conjures moments in Stravinsky's *Rite of Spring*.[27] An argument might even be made that the initial clarinet wail is Talma's answer to the bassoon solo that opened the earlier work, although Talma's is not the awakening call that Stravinsky's was. As a student of Boulanger, Talma was completely conversant with the riot-causing ballet and thoroughly admired all phases of Stravinsky's output. In "Noon" Talma didn't shy away from employing *Rite*-like techniques in her evocation of summer, even if on a much smaller scale. Beyond the opening measure, the most Stravinski-like flashbacks occur at rehearsals 8, 12, and 13. For brief periods of time, a listener is transported to the epochal pagan ritual, but then equally rhythmic series of accented offbeats suggest that Talma might also have been seeking a more syncopated, jazzlike effect. Nature's noontime concert is spirited and eclectic. The third movement, like a noontime sun, is the apex of Talma's summer day (example 4.4).

With "Night," Talma completes her musical frame: the last movement, like the first, is characterized by soft, slow (Molto lento), muted sounds. Even though the texture is thicker than in "Dawn" (a result, in part, of the cello providing a deep and quiet foundation for the other voices), there is a sense of return. The clarinet, while still distinct from the string quartet, resumes a more equal position among the instrumentalists, similar to the relationship of parts enjoyed in the first movement. Altogether, "Night" recollects the less tightly ordered (humanly ordered?) sound world of "Dawn"; Talma's music, like nature's daily cycle, has come full circle.

The composer begins "Night" by juxtaposing duple and triple divisions of beats that sound out of focus, an aural analogue to the hazy air that lingers after a warm day and that distorts the clear edges of distant markers. Slowly oscillating pitches recall the opening waverings of the first measure of the piece. Talma's nightscape is filled with barely discernible harmonics that float in the dark; like any sounds in the night, it is difficult to pinpoint their source

EXAMPLE 4.3. *Summer Sounds*, "Noon," mm. 13–18. Published with permission of The MacDowell Colony (©2011 The MacDowell Colony, Inc.). Louise Talma Collection, Music Division, Library of Congress.

or location (example 4.5). Brief chirping sounds, reminiscent of the ones that introduced the piece in "Dawn," mark Talma's "Night" and have the final word as all music fades from our hearing (example 4.6).

Talma's musicalization of summer was closely connected to specific places and what she heard there, as her sketches make clear. But her interest in those sounds had nothing to do with celebrating avian singers as heaven-sent messengers of greater truths or demonstrating her prowess as a transcriber of their songs. She made no claims for the accuracy of her transcriptions or the perfection of her secretarial skills, and she was not beholden to precise replication. Talma employed birdsong as she would any rich vein of musical material and in so doing reflected her position within an increasingly secularized American culture that included a growing number of environmentally knowledgeable citizens.

Musical works bearing some relation to nature can be found throughout Talma's oeuvre and across five decades of composition. Chamber pieces, piano solos, songs, and choral works all bear witness to the constancy of nature as a sound source or referent. And nature-related projects were clearly on her mind in the years surrounding the prolonged gestation and eventual premiere of *Summer Sounds*, an endeavor that took over five years, from July 10, 1969, to July 24, 1974. For all of her pragmatism regarding the employment of natural sounds, however, Talma consistently regarded nature and the solitude and quiet offered by her favorite rural retreats as something outside and removed from her workaday world. She shared this view of separate domains with Amy Beach. Although Talma lived until 1996 and followed current environmental debates in the newspaper, it appears that she did not consider human and nonhuman others to be fully integrated and mutually dependent parts of a whole, a perspective that would be embraced by large numbers of environmentally engaged thinkers and that gained traction and grew in the final decades of the century. Vestigial romantic notions about what nature was and where nature existed informed her thinking. As the following chapters of this book demonstrate, many other composers shared those views.

Among Talma's papers are letters written in May 1974 to Thornton Wilder, her Pulitzer Prize–winning collaborator on the 1955–1958 opera *The Alcestiad*, and in August 1974 to James D. Ireland Jr., then director of the National Endowment of the Arts, regarding a new project she titled *"Have you Heard? Do you Know?"* Her letter to Ireland dated August 11 and handwritten

EXAMPLE 4.4 (*above and facing*). *Summer Sounds*, "Noon," mm. 40–52. Published with permission of of The MacDowell Colony (©2011 The MacDowell Colony, Inc.). Louise Talma Collection, Music Division, Library of Congress.

"deep from within the woods of New Hampshire, far from any typewriter" referred to an application that she had made to the NEA for support of a project. Talma clarified that it was her understanding that her application (file # A11141–74) "was for work to be done in 1975." Rather than provide a report, which the director appears to have requested in a memorandum sent July 31, Talma offered a "synopsis of the libretto":[28]

HAVE YOU HEARD? DO YOU KNOW? for three voices and ten instruments, approximately forty-five minutes long, the object of which is to give voice to the longing felt by everyone to get away from the noise, dirt, crowds, confusion, rush, pollution, crime that presently exist everywhere to a saner way of life. I intend to do this in the comic vein with undertones of seriousness which will, I hope, convey the idea that this must be accomplished if we are to survive.[29]

The piece would ultimately require ten instrumentalists and last approximately thirty minutes.[30] Talma explained to Ireland that she had two commissions requiring completion before she could "do detailed work" on this one,

EXAMPLE 4.5. *Summer Sounds,* "Night," mm. 1–7. Published with permission
of The MacDowell Colony (©2011 The MacDowell Colony, Inc.).
Louise Talma Collection, Music Division, Library of Congress.

EXAMPLE 4.6. *Summer Sounds,* "Night," mm. 31–36. Published with permission of The MacDowell Colony (© 2011 The MacDowell Colony, Inc.). Louise Talma Collection, Music Division, Library of Congress.

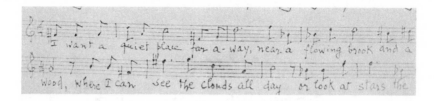

FIGURE 4.8a AND b. Published with permission of The MacDowell
Colony (© 2011 The MacDowell Colony, Inc.). Louise Talma Collection,
Music Division, Library of Congress.

thus implying that she had not focused much attention on *Have You Heard?
Do You Know?* But her letter to "Thorny" written May 7, three months earlier,
indicates that she had done significantly more than create a synopsis. After
enthusing about a recent "heavenly weekend" spent visiting mutual friends,
the Thomases, in Providence, Talma settled down to tell Wilder about her
project; the description went beyond the basic mise-en-scène. The setting is
the breakfast table of a thirtysomething couple living in Queens, New York:
Fred is off to work; an excitable neighbor, Mildred, is dispatched, but only
after she has regaled her friends with the day's most disturbing headline
stories; and "Della sinks into a chair saying: 'I'm tired, I'm tired of all this
twaddle [which Talma later replaces with the word "chatter"], all this yakety
yak.'" Della begins an aria, which Talma described as "very lyric." Starting at
the bottom of the second page of her letter, Talma neatly notated three lines
of music and the text "I want a quiet place, far away, near a flowing brook and
a wood, where I can watch the clouds go by, or look at stars the whole night
through, and hear the birds sing at dawn."[31] Following the aria's opening lines,
Talma explained to Wilder: "At the end she picks up her shopping list and
market basket and goes off" (figures 4.8a and 4.8b).

Beyond having worked out the basic storyline and important melodic
ideas in May 1974, Talma had also plotted aspects of the larger musical architecture of the divertimento, as her comments to Wilder regarding inciden-
tal music make clear. Upon Della's exit, "There is an instrumental interlude
marking the passage of time (musically this will be a first variation of the

preceding aria)." When "Fred returns from the office," he "flings his case on the table and slumps in a chair." Fred sings: "Oh, I'm tired, tired, I'm tired of all this hassle, all this rushing about." His music is, as Talma explained to Wilder, "a second variation of 'I want a quiet place far away.'" For whatever reason, Talma preferred to have Ireland believe that detailed work on the project had not yet begun, or perhaps she didn't consider what she had done to date to be significant progress.

Against the divertimento's broad depiction of harried, noisy, modern urban life – as articulated by the principal characters, Della and Fred – Talma juxtaposed an idyllic portrait of nature that expressed in remarkably similar ways what Edmund Morris would describe in his *Times* article a year later. Idealized nature provided escape. Their shared references and vocabulary and their quest for quiet make one wonder whether they were in communication during the time.[32] In her completed libretto Talma referred to "that silent place in the woods"; Morris had hoped that all travelers "have their own Silent Places." For Talma "there is a quiet place far away," while for Morris "'Far,' alas is the operative word for us inhabitants of the world's loudest city."[33] The underlined passage noted earlier, however, is imported literally into the final trio sung by Della, Fred, and Mildred. After enumerating a series of places real and imagined, ranging from the "Canaries, the Blessed Isles, the Gardens of the Hesperides, the site of the Elysian fields," and Atlantis, and quoting from Homer, the group "dreamily" sings: "All these are 'hidden clefts of peace and forgetfulness.' Places of silence, *that pure balm of the soul*. Places of refuge from the noise of the world."[34] Although Talma's musical drama was germinating prior to the appearance of Morris's story, the *Times* article reinforced her ideas, confirmed the relevance of the storyline, and gave her text. If Talma's fantasies of an Edenic retreat were predicated upon a somewhat outdated romantic reading of nature as beautiful "Other," she was in good company. She worked on the piece for five years beginning in 1975 until its completion in 1980.

If the text of Talma's complete libretto reveals widely shared attitudes toward the natural world, it also suggests the ways her residencies at the Mac-Dowell Colony and extended stays at friends' summer houses in the region provided specific imagery for her characters' fantasies. Following the opening lines of Della's aria that Talma had penned to Wilder, the disillusioned wife continued: "I want to go to that silent place in the woods where the goldenrod plumes in the sun, and the trees are aflame in the fall, and the lilac blooms in the spring, and birches stand slim and white like sentinels in the night." Fred seeks similar surroundings: "I wish I had a quiet place far away, far from the turmoil of this town, where I can hike and fish, climb a mountain, lie in the sun, plant a garden, sail a boat, or just sit and dream."[35] Talma evokes the northeastern woodlands with indigenous flora that paints and scents the seasons, the trees that stand as "sentinels," the White Mountains that are visible everywhere, and the myriad lakes and rivers that weave their way through the valleys of the worn-down peaks. It is hard not to think that Talma had the colony and its environs in mind when she wrote these lines.

It is a commonplace to assert that no single influence or event directs a person's life course, but the MacDowell Colony and a number of close-by summer haunts exerted enormous power over Louise Talma. Beyond providing sonic sources that supplied materials for numerous pieces, the colony offered a nurturing and stimulating community, an escape from the choking pace of work and life in the city, and a chance to bathe in what she heard as undisturbed quiet. Beach and Talma identified silence with their summer retreats in the woods, although both composers drew from the rich sonic environments they found there. Their association of silence with natural sounds and noise with city places raises the question of what it was they were responding to in both places. Anyone who has spent time camping knows that nature is far from quiet.[36]

In March 1986, Bruce Duffie interviewed Louise Talma by telephone.[37] Knowing of the impact the artists' retreat had had upon the eighty-year-old composer, he started his interview asking her to "Tell me about working with the MacDowell Colony!" Talma answered:

> I've been associated with it half of my life, and I owe practically my entire professional existence to it. I was a not so young, but entirely unknown and untried person applying for the first time, and they accepted me. That began this very long association which continues to this day. I have made so many of my dearest friends, not to mention professional connections which have made possible all the things that have happened since. So I have a very, very warm feeling for the MacDowell Colony and I'm going to be there again this summer.

Duffie pushed Talma to clarify why the colony was essential to her creativity.

> In New York, I am constantly interrupted either by the telephone or by the mail, which succeeds very well each day in completely disrupting whatever it was I had planned to do. And there's the noise, and there's the feeling of the neighbors whom you know you are disturbing by what you're doing. So

to be able to get away from all that, and to know that you can make all kinds of sounds, or scream 'round the place without anybody caring about it, is a wonderful feeling! I've written most of my music there.

In concluding the discussion of the colony, Duffie summarized: "So then you work best in the quiet and isolation?" Talma – like Beach, who insisted upon the necessity of a quiet, isolated place for composition, and who credited the retreat with being responsible for everything she'd written since her first visit – responded succinctly: "It's indispensable to me."[38]

A recently discovered letter that Talma drafted to Nadia Boulanger in November 1932, but never sent, sheds additional light on Talma's relationship to nature. In an attempt to explain her social awkwardness to Boulanger, Talma described her quite isolated and nearly friendless youth. Having no children her age with which to play nearby, Talma turned to nature: "The mountains, the streams, the flowers, the fruits, the animals all that rich life of the countryside was enough for me."[39] As readers will discover, looking beyond human society for companionship will be a theme that reappears in the chapters on Victoria Bond and Emily Doolittle. Talma scholar Sarah Dorsey has speculated that perhaps the composer's early experiences in nature can help explain why "MacDowell almost seemed like a homecoming for her."[40]

Lives weave themselves whole, and as it turns out, the newspaper stories Talma clipped in the 1970s and the pieces she composed with nature as their theme or source were just two indications of her lifelong attachment to "the mountains, the streams, the flowers." Although there is no evidence that she carried placards or doorbelled on behalf of environmentalist causes, Talma's deep and abiding connection to the natural world is attested to by the financial contributions she made to as many as fifteen environmental organizations later in her life. Her donations went to societies that protected her nearby Central Park through its conservancy association and the West Coast mountains and its Sierra Club. She made sure that underprivileged children in New York City had a chance to experience summer in the country with her contributions to the Fresh Air Fund. She sought to effect legal protections of the environment with financial aid to the Conservation Law Foundation and the National Resources Defense Council.[41] The number of environmental organizations that benefited from Talma's generosity suggests more than a casual response to mailbox solicitations. Among the composers discussed in this study, Louise Talma emerges as the first one to demonstrate

FIGURE 4.9. A 1954 class picture of MacDowell Fellows, including James Baldwin, Louise Talma, and Milton Avery. Louise Talma is top row, fourth from the right. Courtesy of the MacDowell Colony. Photo credit: Bernice Perry.

an environmental awareness that goes beyond an appreciation of nature; she is a behind-the-scenes activist on its behalf.

Feeling as strongly as she did about the importance of the natural world, Talma guaranteed that the MacDowell Colony, her summer home, would know and experience her gratitude. In addition to a million-dollar bequest stipulated in her will, Talma granted rights to her musical archive, the income it generated, and her Mason & Hamlin grand piano.[42] In 2011, her gift continues to support scholars and fellows[43] (figure 4.9).

PART TWO

Nature All Around Us

PAULINE OLIVEROS, JOAN TOWER, ELLEN TAAFFE ZWILICH

Composing women born in the 1930s entered a world and a national consciousness that differed significantly from their predecessors.' The nation that had acknowledged no limits to its potential now had a more realistic picture of its place in the world. For a number of years, the United States shared equally in the widely felt sense of ennui and disillusionment that attended the conclusion of World War I. Confident hopes that had been pinned to social and technological advances of the Gilded Age, and then folded into a general assumption of unending human progress in the early years of the twentieth century, were exposed as naive and then dashed. As Frederick Jackson Turner declared the end of the American frontier in 1893, and as urban centers became the new symbols of American character in the opening years of the new century, ties to the nation's rural past were strained. Niagara was replaced by skyscrapers as the new symbols of America. Manifest Destiny had served its purpose when the continent was securely united under one flag.

Hundreds of thousands of American casualties suffered in World War I, combined with the deaths of more than a half million U.S. citizens during the influenza pandemic of 1918–1919, sobered the country as it did nations around the globe whose total population, some estimate, was diminished by between 3 and 6 percent.[1] The effects of this human-medical disaster[2] were still resonating at the start of the 1920s as families regrouped and tried to put personal tragedies behind them. While the roaring twenties allowed some to temporarily forget the past, the decade closed with an international economic meltdown that was then unprecedented and remains so to this day. At the height of the Depression in 1933, just under 25 percent of the U.S. labor force was unemployed. This was the world that welcomed Pauline Oliveros (b. 1932), Joan Tower (b. 1938), and Ellen Taaffe Zwilich (b. 1939).

While women in the United States and in many nations had finally won the right to vote and seen their sphere of influence theoretically expand, it would take years for them to fully realize their newly enlarged world. Among the opportunities that emerged for women born in the 1930s was more democratic access to education, and the three women discussed in this section took advantage of it. Oliveros, Tower, and Zwilich all benefited from increased education with the best mentors in their fields and the chance to practice what they learned as professionals. They would be in their twenties and thirties when civil rights sit-ins and desegregated lunch counters and universities, second-wave feminism and its demands for equality, and environmental activism of both the peaceful and violent varieties grabbed and held on to front-page headlines. Born too early to have these social upheavals shape their formative years, Oliveros, Tower, and Zwilich would nonetheless benefit from the changed attitudes they engendered. The direction that Oliveros's music took starting in the 1970s reflects closely the combination of feminist and environmental sensibilities that were stirring, regardless of whether she considered herself an ecofeminist at the time. Her music provides an easy portal for feminist and ecomusicological studies.

The range of works created by Oliveros, Tower, and Zwilich, the recognition accorded the composers, and the influence they wielded would be unprecedented. Slightly younger women, including Sorrel Hays (b. 1941), Meredith Monk (b. 1942), Laurie Spiegel (b. 1945), and Joan La Barbara (b. 1947) have continued the trend of modeling what women composers, unencumbered by limited educations or repressive social constraints, can achieve. In 2011, as Pauline Oliveros, the oldest subject in *Music and the Skillful Listener*, approaches age eighty, each of the women considered in this section is the holder of a named professorship at an American university.

Like Beach, Bauer, and Talma before them, Oliveros, Tower, and Zwilich have evoked nature in their music in widely varied ways, sometimes attaching a leading, nature-related title to a work after the composition was complete, and at other times gathering the sounds of an environment, which then became the whole of a work. While Oliveros and Tower seem to find themselves regularly in the midst of nature and so have a constant supply of images from which to draw, Ellen Zwilich was led to her subject by a very specific commission. Their music is a testament to the continuing power of nature as an inspiring force and as a point of reference in American composers' consciousness.

5

Pauline Oliveros

For me Deep Listening is a lifetime practice.
The more I listen the more I learn to listen.
Deep Listening involves going below the surface of what is heard
and also expanding to the whole field of sound whatever one's usual focus
    might be.
This is the way to connect with the acoustic environment
and all that inhabits it.

                 — PAULINE OLIVEROS, 1993[1]

In a career spanning nearly sixty years, Pauline Oliveros (b. 1932) has been
at the forefront of multiple twentieth-and now twenty-first-century musical
movements. Starting in the late 1950s, she was among the vanguard of American composers exploring analog electronic technology and the promises it
held for musical composition; as a woman working in that field she was a rare
presence and force. In the 1960s, Oliveros expanded her composerly reach
with movement and theater pieces, collaborating with dancer/choreographers
Elizabeth Harris, Anna Halprin, and Merce Cunningham, among others,
and creating works that reached across artistic disciplines.[2] Like John Cage,
a friend and fellow explorer of new meanings of "music," "composer," and
"silence," attention to the total environment became as important to Oliveros
as attention to the sonic environment alone. At the end of the 1960s, Pauline
Oliveros began her move toward a type of sound-meditation practice that has
since become synonymous with her name.

    In a paper that she delivered at the 1978 International Studies Seminar
on Musical Creation held in Mexico City, Oliveros commented upon the fu-

ture of music, her own experiences in music, and her evolving ideas regarding focal and global modes of attention, awareness, and listening. Reflecting her pioneering work with tape music, music technology, and computer programming, she called her paper "Software for People," and in 1984 that same title became the name of her first collection of published writings.[3] In the paper Oliveros explained her gradual evolution over the 1950s and 1960s toward a practice she called "Deep Listening" and concluded her talk by inviting attendees to join in exercises that allowed them to experience the concepts she had just described. In 1994 the composer provided one of her fullest descriptions of Deep Listening: "listening in every possible way to every thing possible to hear no matter what you are doing. Such intense listening includes the sounds of daily life, of nature, of one's own thoughts as well as musical sounds."[4]

In the intervening years, *Deep Listening*® has become the trademarked name of workshops, retreats, and a three-year certified training program in which Oliveros and her team teach essential practices and skills; an ensemble, the Deep Listening Band, and the name of a CD they issued in 1989[5]; and Oliveros's Deep Listening Institute, whose mission is succinctly stated on its webpage:

> Deep Listening Institute, Ltd. fosters a unique approach to music, literature, art, and meditation, and promotes innovation among artists and audiences in creating, performing, recording, and educating with a global perspective.[6]

Oliveros has become among the most effective and beloved advocates for disciplined aural awareness in the United States and abroad. She regularly travels the globe to teach and perform. Today Oliveros is Distinguished Professor of Music at Rensselaer Polytechnic Institute (RPI) in Troy, New York, and Darius Milhaud Artist-in-Residence at Mills College in Oakland, California, positions she has earned without the highly valued doctoral degree.[7] For Pauline Oliveros, Deep Listening is a life practice; her decades-long dedication to listening – to everything, all the time – confirms her place among these skillful listeners.

As is the case with other musicians discussed in this book, starting at an early age she was deeply attuned and susceptible to her natural surroundings. In an article that appeared in *American Music* in 2007, Oliveros explained the impact of her 1930s rural Houston upbringing. She had been back in the

area to receive an award, and the ceremony was held at a studio near where
she grew up:

> Certainly my childhood in Texas opened into a 'wonderland' of natural
> sound. There were large rural areas, which I relished early on. . . . All of the
> farmland is pretty much gone now, but the studio's location is very much
> like what I knew about and experienced as a child, with a pecan orchard,
> pine woods and berry patches. In those days, what you could hear in terms
> of the natural world was just amazing: very, very dense sound that varied
> according to the time of day or night, because the lowland of Houston was
> a natural habitat filled with numerous varieties of insects and birds. The
> sounds are still present in a few places that are not paved over. But the natu-
> ral sound is diminishing and masked by technological noise. The asphalt
> and cement have covered over so much of it. The frogs, for example, have
> just about disappeared in the inner city in Houston. The seventeen-year
> cicadas cannot emerge from their underground gestation through cement
> and asphalt. The great choruses I would hear of birds and insects are not
> there anymore in force. Even so, the soundscape remains very powerful in
> my own memories.

The deep impression of those early nature sounds is present as the composer moves toward her eightieth birthday. We hear her sadness for the loss
of her early homeland soundscapes, but also the power of those "wonderland"
memories. Today she takes great pleasure in cultivating a similar awareness
of those sounds in others. As she observed, "A lot of young people go out with
recorders into natural environments . . . it's as if they are trying to recreate
that which has been lost; they get very interested in those sounds because
they *are* really beautiful."[8] Revealing her knowledge of acoustics, Oliveros
explained:

> And natural sounds are also full-range sounds, whereas a lot of electronic
> sound is not. Car radios or small speaker systems are very focused and local-
> ized sources of sound bounded by a narrow audio range. However when you
> go out into nature, sound is all around you and that immersion brings back a
> lot of something that's missing.[9]

Surveying her large and continually growing body of works, it is clear
that the sounds of nature have informed her thinking, music, and life practice in a variety of ways. And this will be an important point to keep in
mind throughout *Music and the Skillful Listener*: both within the oeuvre of
individual composers and among the works of many composers numerous,

different relationships to nature are at work. Sometimes the relationship is quite obvious, as in pieces that capture or mimic birds, insects, animals, and elemental sounds, and sometimes the relationship is more veiled. Like in the natural world itself, the diversity of nature's manifestations and the strength of nature's motivational forces vary from piece to piece. The range of nature's presence is especially large in the works of Pauline Oliveros.

Composers nurture different goals for each of their nature-related works. Where Amy Beach understood the song of the hermit thrush as a voice of God, and wrote her hermit-thrush pieces as musical offerings to the Edenic surroundings to be found at the MacDowell Colony (and eventually to fundraise on the colony's behalf), not all composers articulate specific readings or purposes for their works. While Oliveros has explained that she doesn't consciously set out to compose political music or have a programmed agenda, on multiple occasions her writings have clearly advocated on behalf of the natural environment and other topics.[10] In 1995, while in Monterrey, Mexico, Oliveros expressed her deep feelings for her surroundings in haiku-like lines she penned and titled "Wounded Mountain: to Las Mitras": "They blast you at the base! Scarred without mercy. Blighted beauty seen for miles. Houses creeping up your skirts as you bravely rest embraced by the clouds." In October of that same year, she wrote "El Fantasma al Rio: Homenaje al Rio Santa Catarina." The opening lines suggest her thinking at the time:

> They play soccer on her bed
> Led by fear the city fathers sucked her dry
> No compassion for the murdered life forms
> no desire for the pleasures she provided.[11]

Oliveros understands the mountain and river as victims of greedy builders (city fathers) who are insensitive to the beauty and pleasures they destroy. She continues the tradition of gendering the earth female, thus making her oeuvre ripe for feminist readings.[12] While such imagery can call attention to nature's (supposed) fragility and position subservient to humanity and thus encourage more responsible interactions with the environment, it can also weaken the image of woman by making her appear similarly vulnerable and powerless: in either case, it keeps nature and, by association, women, disempowered, outside, and other. But this is not how Oliveros sees nature or herself when it comes to her relationship to the natural world.

Throughout her writings, Oliveros uses a large repertoire of terms to get at the multivalent concept of nature. In *Deep Listening: A Composer's*

Sound Practice,[13] her 2005 collection of writings, she refers to "the natural environment" (xv), "surroundings" (xvii), "the outside world" (xxi), "the whole of the environment and beyond" (xxiii), "the whole of the space/time continuum" (12), "the whole field of sound" (32), "the soundscape" (49), and "country" (53), and she talks of the earth, "gripping the earth," and the "energy from the earth" (14). In an interview, Oliveros addressed the difficulty of capturing all that "nature" represents in a single term: "Well, we have the natural world, we have the world we come from, the world we're living in. We have mythic nature, we have overblown ideas of nature. . . . It's been so overworked and overblown; it's something that has to be reworked or re-understood."[14]

When asked directly, "What is nature?" Oliveros responded: "All is nature that supports life forms of all kinds."[15] Oliveros embraces a holistic worldview and thus conceives of nature differently from many earlier writers, thinkers, and composers, including Amy Beach, who understood it as something discrete and outside herself, something to which one went, something separate from humanity. Oliveros sees herself as part of a living continuum. "Nature" is present throughout Oliveros's oeuvre, inspiring some of her early works, both electronic and acoustic, and continuing to inform her most recent meditative compositions. In addition, as the chapters on Libby Larsen and Emily Doolittle will demonstrate, Oliveros's thoroughly integrative understanding of nature and humanity is not singular. Her particular perspective appears to resonate most fully with those composers in this study who are more likely to be characterized as feminists.

The text of the paper "Software for People" included a section where Oliveros shared her personal history and early involvement with music and sound. It is worth quoting at length:

> I was always interested in whatever I heard. All of music speaks to me as music, no matter how diverse, no matter what its function might be, no matter how apparently simple or complex, no matter how it affects me emotionally or intellectually, and no matter what its origin: human, animal, artificial, or extraterrestrial. No matter how much I might like or dislike something I hear, I cannot deny that it is music. Above all I believe passionately that I must respect each music in terms of its own context. For me this is one of the first steps in learning to understand and to interact appropriately with any music alien to my own culture. If nothing else, music in any of its multitudinous manifestations is a sign of life. Sound **is** intelligence.[16]

As she worked through the major points of the paper, Oliveros reflected upon the stages of her musical development and listed four sources of her musical materials: "1. All the music I have ever heard. 2. All the sounds of the natural world I have ever heard including my own inner biological sounds. 3. All the sounds of the technological world I have ever heard. 4. All the sounds from my imagination."[17] Like other composers who have spent considerable time in the West – Henry Cowell, Lou Harrison, LaMonte Young, Terry Riley, to name just a few – and whose soundscape included Asian and Native American musics as well as Western musical practices and who weren't constricted by the over-influence of European traditions, Oliveros has always had an enlarged sense of what constituted music.

Of particular interest to this study is her second point, which clarifies the notion that for Oliveros there is a natural world, and it includes humanity. The composer named specific sounds that were part of her aural upbringing:

> My childhood in a rural area of Texas sensitized me to sounds of the elements and animal life. There were those of wind and rain, cows, chickens, and wild life. I loved to hear them. There were occasional motor noises, not the constant drone that we experience in cities today. We owned a radio which we sometimes listened to at night. I loved the static and tuning whistles to be found in-between the stations. My mother and grandmother gave piano lessons. So musical sounds were also part of my early life. I learned to play the accordion and later the French horn. . . . With the advent of the LP record, I would spend hours listening to the same record at some juke box in a café. Soon we owned a record player. . . . My mother bought a wire recorder in 1948.[18]

Oliveros lived in and among a symphony of sounds with "the elements," animals, motors and machinery, radio static, traditional musical instruments, and recordings filling the airwaves. Given the sudden and intense rain and thunderstorms that plague Houston, one can imagine that the elements provided dramatic sonic moments for the young composer.

But her home was also a stimulating place for a budding musician with a finely tuned aural imagination. Beyond hearing piano lessons given by her mother and grandmother, Oliveros recalled her mother "playing for a modern dance class at the YWCA." Oliveros explained: "Modern dance, of course, was very new to people, so she was improvising music for modern dance. She would come home and play some of the things that she had improvised for the dancers. These were quirky little pieces, they were fun, and I think it was important to me that she did that and she played those things, because it was a cue, I think, from her to be able to invent new things."[19] As the following discussion demonstrates, improvisation will become a pillar of Oliveros's creative process.

Her mother's purchase of a wire recorder just after World War II must also have been thrilling for a sixteen-year-old so thoroughly engaged by the world of sounds. Although it would have been primitive by today's standards, steel wire recorders were the first reliable audio recording devices available on the mass market, and many Americans bought them. According to Oliveros's recollections, the wire recorder was a big console that stood in the living room,[20] a testament to the pride of place it enjoyed in the household. If Oliveros initially made her name in tape and electronic music, it was likely the direct result of a family environment that was more than a little interested in making, gathering, and capturing sounds. Her mother, who made music, improvised modern dance accompaniments, and purchased a wire recorder, provided Oliveros with the model, and a female one at that, that she needed to make her nontraditional musical explorations acceptable to herself. Women in her world improvised, composed, performed, taught, and listened; and that is just what Oliveros has continued to do.

In 1957, the same year she graduated from San Francisco State University, Oliveros composed a set of *Three Songs for Soprano and Piano*, two of them to the poetry of Robert Duncan ("An Interlude of Rare Beauty" and "Spider Song") and a third ("Song Number Six") to poetry by Charles Olson.[21] Given the power of the natural environment in Oliveros's childhood, it is perhaps not coincidental that she was attracted to the nature imagery of the two Duncan poems. In addition, according to Heidi von Gunden, a student of Oliveros and the composer's first biographer, Oliveros "felt a certain affinity for these writers, because they belonged to the San Francisco avant-garde and were sensitive to the musicality of poetry. Duncan, particularly, knew Anton Webern's music and liked Webern's motion and brevity."[22] "An Interlude of Rare Beauty," written with traditional piano/vocal notation, shows the composer early in her career and thus serves as a first example of Oliveros's nature-inspired pieces. Duncan's poem reads:

> The seal in the depraved wave
> glides in the green of it.
> All his true statement

made in his mere swimming.
Thus we reclaim
all senseless motion from its waves
of beauty. Naming
no more than our affection
for naming.[23]

The proximity of Seal Beach to Oliveros's San Francisco home in the 1950s must have made a poem celebrating the seals' "rare beauty" immediately resonant for the composer. The seductive sounds of the phrases "depraved wave" and "glides in the green" and the flexible rhythm of free verse, which allows certain passages to be deliberately chewed upon, captivate anyone hearing the text read aloud. But beyond the sounds, the idea that the seal's essence is contained "in his mere swimming" would likely have appealed to the young composer, who was discovering the essence of her own being and work.

Oliveros responded to the music of Duncan's suggestive imagery with her own. Flashes of sound appear and disappear like the sleek marine mammal as it "glides in the green" of the waves. The chimerical piano music darts unexpectedly from one end of the keyboard to the other: in the final half beat of the first measure, adjacent sixteenth notes move from the first G below the bass clef to the E♭ above the treble clef. Within the first five beats there are nine different pitches before any of them repeats. Like a seal that has the whole ocean for its home, Oliveros's music moves freely in harmonic and temporal space; there is no predicting where it (seal or sound) might appear next. The sixteen-measure piece enjoys nine meter changes. In addition, rests on traditional downbeats, notes tied over bar lines, and adjacent groupings of triplets and quadruplets, tremolos, accelerandos, ritards, and rallentandos guarantee a fluid space. Without seeking to translate Duncan's poetic description of a seal scudding through the waves, Oliveros conjures one doing so.

The vocal line is similarly free of any traditional moorings or a close relationship to the piano part, but Oliveros takes delight in the sounds of certain words and gives them room to resonate. The opening measures show Oliveros's musical imagery in the piano and vocal parts (example 5.1).

Bright vowels linger in the soft, slow, calm airwaves. Even the initial consonants of the word "glides," a sound combination that is not usually the recipient of *bel canto* attention, become expanded moments for sonic savoring.

EXAMPLE 5.1. "An Interlude of Rare Beauty" from *Three Songs for Soprano and Piano*.
By Pauline Oliveros, mm. 1–7. Copyright Smith Publications,
54 Lent Road, Sharon, Vermont, 05065. Reprinted by permission.

As the pianist seamlessly picks up the vocalist's final G♭ of the phrase and
races through measure 7, the seal slips through the water. With such sensitivity to Duncan's imagery, one might regret the paucity of songs in Oliveros's
works list, but the composer had her reasons. As she explained: "I was never
interested in words. I was interested in the *sounds* of words, in sound; sound
was what moved me. It felt expressive to me. I didn't have to combine words
in order to have a meaningful experience with sound. So I wasn't a song

writer." It is easy to imagine that traditional practices regarding the close association of words and music might be too prescriptive for a composer who insists, "What I don't have is a programmed agenda [for my music]."[24] Within a few years, using technology that she helped create, Oliveros found new sounds to shape.

While electronic music might not be the first genre people think of for nature-related works, *Alien Bog,* one of a series of bog pieces that Oliveros created at the Tape Music Center at Mills College in 1967, is an example of the composer's enlarged understanding of musical sound.[25] It showcases the potential of music technology, specifically the Buchla Series 100 Box, while simultaneously reflecting the impact of the natural environment.[26] Both are part of her world. In the liner notes accompanying the CD recording of *Alien Bog* Oliveros explained:

> I was deeply impressed by the sounds from the frog pond outside the studio window at Mills. I loved the accompaniment as I worked on my pieces. Though I never recorded the frogs I was of course influenced by their music. Since that time many other composers have also been influenced by the sounds from the pond.[27]

Anyone who has lived near lakes or ponds and among tree frogs, bullfrogs, and cicadas likely feels at home in Oliveros's "alien" soundscape. Her honking, burring, clicking, chirping, rapid-fire wheeping and whirring electronic symphony simulates many native environments. Over the course of the piece, however, Oliveros's bog emits sounds that also suggest a primordial nether region. Going well beyond producing sounds that simulate those of a "frog pond outside the studio window,"[28] Oliveros's manipulation of two-channel tape, patching, and delay techniques creates a whole new world. One can only imagine that Edgard Varèse would have been jealous. In moving seamlessly from what appear to be nature sounds to those that suggest something extraterrestrial, Oliveros challenges distinctions between the two spheres even when both are products of technological manipulations. A brief consideration of the work suggests the variety of Oliveros's musical responses to the natural world.

Alien Bog is a wholly electronic piece; as such, the tape is the score. It opens with a series of high-pitched, repeating, descending glissandi; a listener isn't certain whether she's hearing cicadas or synthesizers. As the falling sounds increase in frequency and then overlap, Oliveros introduces more sounds, clicks and hums, and the high tessitura of the initial cascading gestures expands to include lower, more complex sounds. The atmosphere is rich and reverberant – in that regard it sounds natural.[29] Within the first minute, the pitch A materializes in the sound mass, although its octave and timbre mean it doesn't sound like any orchestral tuning of A that listeners might expect. Is Oliveros "tuning" her alien world? At various junctures in the piece, other pitches and intervals appear; however, the structural logic of the work doesn't depend upon pitch or harmony relationships.[30]

The texture thickens, the volume increases, and in the third minute of the piece a heartbeat-like "lub-dub" pattern emerges, pulsing faintly in the background. Alien though it may be, Oliveros's bog is filled with life. Like some kind of human, super-sensitive satellite dish, Oliveros turns her head and focuses her hearing on sounds emanating from unexplored coves in her imaginary bog.

Over the course of the thirty-three-minute piece, listeners are immersed in a contrapuntal symphony of chirping (7:15), rumbling (8:40), ringing (9:09), tweeting (15:40), and bubbling (32:40) sounds that come from all directions and constantly.[31] Are we hearing memories of Oliveros's Houston lowlands? Perhaps, but this soundscape is not restricted to ersatz sonic bog emissions. There are instances when listeners hear suggestions of distant elephants trumpeting, emergency sirens, foghorns, and even the "*feeeuu*" "*feeeuu*" sounds of proto–*Star Wars* light sabers (heard for the first time at 7:54).

Intersections between nature and technology will be a major focus of the chapter on the final composer, Emily Doolittle, but its limited appearance in this study should not suggest it is the private concern of a couple of composers. In a free-wheeling conversation with Walter Zimmermann in 1975 that covered topics as eclectic as Satie, Mao Tse Tung, and Thoreau's *Journals*, John Cage spoke of that very intersection. Among its many potentials, Cage saw technology as giving "us the opportunity to record natural events, which focuses our attention back, away from theories of music to actual experience of hearing wherever we happen to be. . . . The electronics have brought our attention back to nature."[32] Cage's comments reverberate in Oliveros's observations of students going into the natural environment with recorders to capture and hear the beautiful sounds. While Oliveros didn't tape the croaking frogs and interpolate a sample into her piece, and she didn't transcribe their actual sounds like Amy Beach, neither did she attempt to fit the techno-frogs' vocalizations within existing Western tempered scales, metered time schemes, or timbral palettes. This bog needed technology to be heard.

Alien Bog challenges traditional notions of what are natural sounds and perhaps traditional notions of what is music. Is this what a bog sounds like? Are all the beeps, bleeps, blips, and low moaning sounds music? Oliveros directs our attention with her provocative title, weaves together nature-like and technologically created musics, ignores boundaries, and stirs our imagination with sound.

The 1970s saw the creation of one of Oliveros's most celebrated achievements: her set of twenty-five *Sonic Meditations*.[33] Here was a work borne of a cultural moment energized by the civil rights, second-wave feminism, and environmental movements, and equally importantly, by Pauline Oliveros's increasing attention to and understanding of sound. Oliveros had worked in the male-dominated worlds of composing and technology for over a decade and had gained the respect of her cohort, but she had always felt like an outsider.[34] Through her *Sonic Meditations* she found meaningful camaraderie, comfort, and confirmation as well as a forum to share her listening practice.

The convergence of these social movements with Oliveros's burgeoning confidence in her lesbian sexual identity and her place in the world of professional music made the collaborative, nonhierarchical, listening-focused work, originally conceived for women, among Oliveros's most personal *and* universal statements. Without her identifying *Meditations* as an ecofeminist statement, the pieces enact the tenets of ecofeminism. While providing a forum for others to test their voices (regardless of their musical skill or training), *Sonic Meditations* also created a space where Oliveros could be heard by those who would understand. She dedicated the work to a group of ten women known as the ♀ Ensemble and to Amelia Earhart. Oliveros gave Earhart's courageous spirit pride of place when she named meditation number I "Teach Yourself to Fly." The recipe for the meditation included many of the ingredients that would become essential to Oliveros's deep listening practice: circles of participants, observation of one's breathing, patience, the natural emergence of one's voice, and sensitivity to others in the group. The ♀ Ensemble gathered regularly to practice, but the results of their coming together went well beyond the refinement of aural skills. As Oliveros explained in Introduction I:

> With continuous work some of the following becomes possible with *Sonic Meditations*: Heightened states of awareness or expanded consciousness, changes in physiology and psychology from known and unknown tensions to relaxations which gradually become permanent. These changes may represent a tuning of mind and body. The group may develop positive energy which can influence others who are less experienced. Members of the Group may achieve greater awareness and sensitivity to each other. Music is a welcome by-product of this activity.[35]

The final sentence of the introduction clarified Oliveros's new vision of the composer's role as she understood it for herself. Having previously written music whose production was confined to a few expert practitioners – and, in the case of *Alien Bog*, that resulted in a "score" realizable only with the use of electronic machinery – Oliveros turned from the paradigm of the all-controlling composer to one where she shared the creative act with a group of nonspecialists. Oliveros's *Meditations* moved the focus away from the composer, the work, and the performer and toward the receiver, in this case a group of women whose primary goal was to listen to what they heard and respond. Distinctions between participants in the musical endeavor were negated and the field flattened. The deconstruction of traditional hierarchical relationships between performers and audience members is an idea that will be revisited in the chapters on Libby Larsen and Emily Doolittle.

Some might read Oliveros's metamorphosis from controlling creator to collaborative listener as a move *backward* to a more passive receiver's role, a role that modern Western culture had previously assigned to women. But Oliveros wasn't seeking to withdraw from an active role in music making. By privileging listening, Oliveros sought to restructure the music paradigm. By embracing listening, Oliveros revalued the traditional woman's domain; she simultaneously acknowledged her mother's and grandmother's work and that of numerous women in the arts who didn't appear in the history texts.

If, as Martha Mockus persuasively argues, Pauline Oliveros's music becomes a site of feminist and lesbian efforts to "challenge sexism and classism in western classical music and democratize music-making for women of all abilities,"[36] then Oliveros's listening-focused works also provide opportunities to reconsider one's place in the cosmos. At a time when the modern environmental movement was building momentum, Oliveros's redirection of energies could also be read as a reconsideration of one's relationship to the natural world. Where is our place among life forms? How do we interact with our surroundings? How do we understand and respond to the intelligence of sound that is with us at all times? Rather than advocate for passivity, Oliveros worked on behalf of engaged, attentive, disciplined listening and finding one's place within the continuum of nature. Turning away from traditional power relationships, whether as a composer or as a global citizen rejecting the idea of dominion over the earth, was a bold and courageous step.

That the environmental movement had some place in Oliveros's consciousness is borne out in Meditation VIII, "Environmental Dialogue"; it foregrounds ecological awareness. The recipe follows:

> Each person finds a place to be, either near to or distant from the others, either indoors or out-of-doors. Begin the meditation by observing your own breathing. As you become aware of sounds from the environment, gradually begin to reinforce the pitch of the sound source. Reinforce either vocally, mentally or with an instrument. If you lose touch with the source, wait quietly for another. Reinforce means to strengthen or sustain. If the pitch of the sound source is out of your range, then reinforce it mentally.[37]

Participants observe their own breathing, grow in awareness of their surroundings, and respond to the sounds of the environment by reinforcing "the pitch of the sound source." Oliveros is clear that participants are to meet an existing sound and become one with it. She eliminates the possibility of using the source as a springboard for some new sonic excursion and is careful to discourage the introduction of a sound that may overwhelm the original one. While the instructions are set, the music that results each time the meditation is "performed" is variable according to the specific time, place, and group of participants. The potential for infinite dialogues represents the limitless variety of our sounding environment and our relationships to it. "Environmental Dialogue" is all about listening to our surroundings and finding our place within the soundscape.

Sonic Meditations was conceived in the same decade that saw the emergence of ecofeminism, a movement that connected similarly disparaging attitudes and practices toward women and the environment with entrenched patriarchal cultural assumptions. The term *écologie-féminisme* or *écoféminisme* was coined by the French feminist Françoise d'Eaubonne in her 1974 book *Le féminisme ou la mort* but quickly found its way to the English-speaking world. In 1975, Rosemary Radford Ruether published her book *New Woman, New*

Earth: Sexist Ideologies and Human Liberation, and in 1991 *Ecofeminisms: Symbolic and Social Constructions between the Oppression of Women and the Domination of Nature.* In the thirty-five years since her first work appeared, hundreds of essays, articles, anthologies, and books have addressed aspects of the topic.[38] While there isn't a single ecofeminist position any more than there is a single feminist one, all versions share a basic belief that the degrading treatment of women and the environment are connected. Oliveros's collaborative-listening works were a part of this larger expanding awareness. Understanding her meditations as environmentally sensitive compositions adds another layer of meaning to these richly resonant works and one that complements feminist readings.

The environment remained a vital source of inspiration for Oliveros whether she worked exclusively with the ♀ Ensemble or with mixed groups. Other composers recognized the importance of her thinking and the premium she placed on listening when they created their own environmental projects. In the summer of 1984, composer Alvin Curran invited nine of his contemporaries to improvise works, which he then mixed and synchronized with recordings he had just made of eastern seacoast foghorns, gongs, buoy bells, bird sounds, and the voices of lighthouse keepers; among them was *Rattlesnake Mountain* by Pauline Oliveros. Curran's project, *Maritime Rites,* was presented as "ten environmental concerts for radio," which to the best of his knowledge "were broadcast by some 50 radio stations throughout the United States – leaving over the years an artistic trail like a kind of quiet myth."[39]

From a distance of twenty-six years Curran recalled: "If my memory is correct, no one of the nine artists heard the mixes which I created for them, through and around them; and with each new solo I started from absolute scratch, searching appropriate combinations of the hundreds of recordings I made in preparation for this unusual project." Although he was not certain of where he recorded each of the composers, given his practice he assumed he went to Kingston and "recorded Pauline playing that angelic music at her home." He described her music as "a structured improvisation on basic cellular gestures, melodies and forms which in those days were a common practice among many of us from Meredith Monk to Terry Riley etc. etc. etc." Clarifying the extent to which this was a collaborative project and thus emblematic of the spirit of the times, Curran explained:

What is important is that all of the performers in the *Maritime Rites* agreed to record for me for a modest (and equal) sum of money and to entrust this music completely to me to do anything I wanted with it. That in itself stands out as another iconic sign of the times, ie: giving a colleague complete freedom to utilize one's own music in any way necessary to complete a full and satisfactory fusion of the soloist's music, with my needs to make an 11 minute piece with its unique conceptual and actual compositional realization. A lot of big words to say, that these little sonic marriages between myself and selected colleagues were indeed a set of serious and trusting bonds – bonds outside the limits of normal practical law.[40]

In remarks adapted from the original program notes, Curran clarified:

The programs use specifically recorded natural sounds as musical counterpoint to the soloists, whose improvisations are freely restructured and mixed by Curran. As nature is spontaneous and unpredictable, so is the music of man. Curran simply brings the two together in a common radiophonic sound-space letting both chance and intention make the music.[41]

Curran described Oliveros "composer, and accordionist, performing her piece *Rattlesnake Mountain*":

Mixed with her solo, in a quiet rhythm that emulates breath itself, are the sounds of the whistle buoy near Robinson's Rock, a three-toned gong from the Graves near Camden, and foghorns from Rockland Harbor, all in Maine. Also heard is the voice of the only female lighthouse keeper in America, Karen McLean of the U.S. Coast Guard, Doubling Point, Maine.[42]

Born in Providence, Rhode Island, in 1938, Curran brought sonic memories of his southern New England childhood environment to his project. As he explained: "I wanted 'space' to speak for itself, and rather than narrating a story, let these monumental recorded environments speak for themselves."[43] Assessing Curran's musical achievement, David Toop concluded: "*Maritime Rites* presents the foghorn as indigenous American 'found' music par excellence and the source of one of the most enduring minimal musics around us." Toop characterized Curran's piece as "a comprehensive aural documentary of our regional and national maritime heritage."[44]

Rattlesnake Mountain is like *Alien Bog* in that there is no traditionally notated score for the sounds one hears; we have only the recording. But like *Alien Bog*, this doesn't mean the sounds lack qualities we associate with "real" music: coherence, unity, or meaning, to say nothing of timbre, texture, pitch, rhythm, harmony, or form. The bells, gongs, and foghorns are pure sound;

listening to their unique qualities when heard close up or from a distance and when combined with Oliveros's variously droning and rippling accordion music and fragments of McLean's sibilant-rich speech creates a moving, meditative musical work.

Curran interleaves Oliveros's improvised accordion solo with his sonic documentary and in so doing creates another type of environmental dialogue, but this time the conversation expands beyond a single sensitive listener and her environment. In *Rattlesnake Mountain*, lighthouse keeper Karen McLean speaks about her maritime world. She talks about the truth of sound. The piece opens with the sounds of water, bells, and distant foghorns. Starting at 0:03, McLean focuses our attention on listening:

> See, being here I control two different fog signals, but I don't have to listen to either one of them. If I really try hard, I can hear them. I have to step outside and be very quiet and still; I get this faint "ting." . . . To me it's wonderful, but to the people right next door, it might be different.[45]

Immediately foghorns, chirping birds, and cawing seagulls are heard. The pitches G and D resonate in the air. When around 0:50 Oliveros's C drone quietly begins to materialize, as if coming to us from a distance, we have heard the three pitches that will dominate the soundscape. Curran's maritime world is anchored in C major, and in the course of the piece all the pitches of that scale will sound. Over the next three and a half minutes, Oliveros's accordion music and the maritime instruments engage in a duet. Around 3:50, the cawing of a seagull is answered (perhaps reinforced) by Oliveros's own accordion call.

Starting at 4:26, McLean's voice softly reenters. Listeners pick up fragmented comments about babysitters and doctors' appointments. We hear lapping water sounds and perhaps a gentle laugh; we understand that with a husband and children, McLean is engaged in another kind of dialogue balancing her personal and professional lives. The accordion appears in a soft, scalar flourish of notes. McLean's quiet, calm delivery suggests that the myriad pieces of her life fit together naturally like the sounds of the harbor we hear enveloping her. At 5:04, McLean's voice comes to the fore for the second of her extended statements; beneath and around her are the sounds of Oliveros's accordion and foghorns.

> Well . . . when you're at sea, and in the fog, basically the only thing you have to rely on is your radar and your fog signals. [We hear a belching

foghorn sound.] If they weren't there, you're only relying on radar, which is electronic; it can fail. But when you hear that fog signal, you know, you can trust it; you can trust that's where you're supposed to be.[46]

As McLean fades into inaudibility, accordion and bell sounds become louder and the texture grows denser. During the next three minutes, we hear the soft sounds of her voice woven into the thickening soundscape. Whispery sibilants create their own watery effects. At 7:36, the piece reaches its dynamic peak. Oliveros's accordion drone sits on C, forging its own foghorn sound. Over the next minute as the drone continues, additional pitches sound, first moving upward and then moving downward: We hear C–D–F, and then C–B–A. Bells, foghorns, and accordion music seem to converse. Sounds complement and reinforce each other, much like Oliveros instructs her listeners to do in Meditation VIII, "Environmental Dialogue." The new composite soundscape breathes as one organism.

One final time, McLean's comments penetrate the soundscape. Starting at 8:48, Curran recalls McLean's comparison of radar and sounds, this time slightly varied:

> Well . . . when you're at sea and in the fog, basically the only thing you have to rely on is your radar and your fog signals. You can't put a value on those. If they're not there you're only relying maybe on your own radar, which is electronic; it can fail. But when you hear that fog signal, you know, you can trust it; you can trust bells . . . [47]

As McLean's voice fades from our hearing, we catch a few more faint words, "All the signals are different," and then she is gone. The piece disappears with ever fainter sonic traces of bells, birds, foghorns, and accordion. At 10:32, a last seagull flies through our soundscape.

McLean, like Oliveros and Curran, puts her faith in listening. She is particularly attuned to her sonic world and understands where she is by what she hears; this connects her in a profound way to Curran and Oliveros. McLean trusts the bells, as Curran trusts the maritime symphony of his childhood, and as Oliveros trusts the sounds of the Houston elements, insects, and birds. Today many of the foghorns and warning bells are gone. There are no Maine lighthouses that rely upon human keepers for their operation; all have been computerized. One wonders who is listening, and to what.

Although *Rattlesnake Mountain* challenges inherited notions of what constitutes *real* music, Curran organizes the work rather traditionally. The

FIGURE 5.1. "Pauline performing for me in her garden," Leucadia, California.
© Becky Cohen, 1980. Reprinted with the kind permission of the photographer.

pieces of *Maritime Rites* were, after all, conceived for broadcast over radio; shaping them to conform in some way to listeners' expectations would help Curran reach his audience. *Rattlesnake Mountain* has a symmetrical dynamic arch: music begins and ends quietly. The volume grows louder until minutes seven to eight of the ten-minute, forty-six-second piece, when the work reaches its apex, thus manifesting an aesthetic practice observable in many works where composers placed musical climaxes at a point analogous to the golden mean.[48] Similarly, the texture gradually thickens and then thins out over the course of the work. The consistency of the soundscape makes the unity of the work easy to apprehend.

More specifically, the work parses into three parts not unlike many works in ternary (ABA) form. In this case, each of the parts is announced by the lighthouse keeper's extended commentary. Curran guarantees that listeners focus on McLean's soliloquies by bringing her voice to the foreground and minimizing other competing sounds. But *Rattlesnake Mountain* is not a neatly packaged update of a classical readymade. The fade-out after McLean's third appearance and then the following final fade-out of nautical sounds, which moves all sounds just beyond our hearing, means the piece might be open-ended and any of the musics we've heard – avian, mechanical, or human – might reappear or still be present. Charles Ives wrote similar open endings in a number of his place-inspired works, in each case allowing for the possibility that the music continues even if it is beyond a listener's audition.[49] All three composers – Oliveros, Curran, and Ives – recognize that the soundscape is omnipresent. In all cases, listeners make sense of their pieces as they unfold. Form is perceived as it is form*ing* rather than understood in relation to some received template.[50] In this case, Curran's and Oliveros's open-ended form is an especially apt metaphor for a piece inspired by the sea, with its continuous and continuously changing tides.

The exceptional power of *Rattlesnake Mountain* that a listener perceives today was felt by Curran in 1984:

> I don't think I intervened in any major way from start to finish; once I found the appropriate fog horns (maybe I "retuned" them a little bit, maybe not), and set their cycles in motion, I clearly remember the piece composing itself into a most natural sounding tapestry, where substantial interventions on my part were clearly to be avoided . . . these tones and their looped reiterations were simply a too-perfect complement to Pauline's airy but subtle improvisational evolution. My only real structural play then was to decide the where and what of the spoken moments and how to balance them as unobtrusively as possible with the pure musics of the monophonic lines of the accordion and the cyclical tropes of the fog horns. . . . it was perhaps the easiest piece to create but certainly one of the most delicate balancing acts to create a tapestry as if with no beginning and no ending . . . without missing a stitch. The "magic" in it was evident to me and my assistant Nicola Bernardini at the end of the very first mixdown.[51]

The 1980s found Oliveros involved in a number of collaborative projects, but perhaps none more important for the course of her future work than that which she undertook in 1988 with trombone virtuoso Stuart Dempster and composer / sound designer Panaiotis (aka Peter Ward). Dempster persuaded

Oliveros to visit a 14-foot-deep, 186-foot-diameter underground cistern at Fort Warden in Port Townsend, Washington, that he had learned of ten years earlier from a composer friend, David Mahler, and to record some music there. The reverberation in this underground tank, measured at forty-five seconds, was extraordinarily long and pure and something that Dempster knew would fascinate Oliveros; this would be *deep listening* of the most literal type.

As Panaiotis explained, the cistern "once held 2 million gallons of water ... is made of reinforced concrete with more pillars per square yard than a skyscraper. The water tank, built on an army base in 1907, was probably designed to withstand heavy bombing."[52] But more than the architectural details of the space, what captivated the three musicians were the acoustic properties of the enclosure. Panaiotis spoke of the exceptional environment:

> The space is real, and unique. A large cathedral will return slap echoes, and uneven resonance characteristics. The cistern showed a very smooth frequency response and no echoes, only a smooth reverberation, the amplitude of which appears to begin at the same decibel level as the source. Consequently, it is impossible to tell where the performer stops and the reverberation takes over.[53]

One can only imagine the utter wonder felt by the Deep Listening Band, as Oliveros dubbed the three participants, as they swam in their very own sea of sounds. During the session Dempster played trombone, didjeridu, a garden hose, and a conch shell, and he whistled through his mouthpiece; Oliveros played accordion; and Panaiotis played metal pieces and pipes and whistled; all three of the musicians used their voices. The recording engineer, Al Swanson, was challenged by the lack of electricity with which to record, but more so by trying to decide "just what is the appropriate aesthetic for a two million gallon hole in the ground?"[54] Swanson had studied trombone with Stuart Dempster at the University of Washington while earning an undergraduate degree in psychology, and then undertaken graduate work in ethnomusicology as well. It turns out that his eclectic background prepared him well for the mind-bending, untraditional recording task he was asked to accomplish. As Swanson explained:

> It's funny what this does to your head. As an engineer I tried to analyze all this objectively, but I found I couldn't do it. In a kind of acoustic uncertainty principle, there was no way to simultaneously pin down both the objective audio parameters *and* the audible reality of the situation. That is, the actual act of listening influenced the cognitive result. In this situation, therefore, I, an ostensible *observer*, became a virtual *performer*.[55]

The ambiguity of Swanson's experience, the melding together of his roles as listener and performer, meshes completely with Oliveros's hopes for her practice of deep listening. Once again, one can only imagine Oliveros delighting in Swanson's realization.

Deep Listening contains four pieces, "Lear," "Suiren," "Ione," and "Nike,"[56] each using some combination of instruments and voice. While one would be hard-pressed to call an enormous subterranean concrete cistern a *natural* environment, the free-floating sounds that were captured without any kind of manipulation, added reverb, or tape-delay techniques are likely among the most natural of any heard on modern-day recordings. The one-of-a-kind setting and the musicians' interactions with it make the four pieces unique environmental dialogues where who or what is saying what or when is seldom clear.

Of the works considered in this chapter, "Lear," "Suiren," "Ione," and "Nike" are among the most difficult to describe, perhaps in part because the music resists the most basic of identifiable parameters: the discrete emergence and decay of a sound. In addition, the timbre or tone quality of the composite sound seems to be constantly growing, opening up, changing, and revealing characteristics that are not apparent in more conventional settings where listeners are likely to encounter musical instruments or voices. While the sounds move and change, they do not move toward an obvious goal as more traditional Western musics do. How does one discuss a seemingly bottomless, endless, all-encompassing, wholly reverberating environment where the utterances of instruments and voices vibrate, meld, and shape themselves into something never-before heard? Although the sounds could be charted with a spectrograph, the resulting map wouldn't come close to capturing one's experience of the sounds or their emotional impact. How is this music communicating? *Deep Listening* exposes the limitations of language; here is music that is surely supraverbal.[57]

In a paper titled "Challenging Literacies: The Significance of the Arts," music educator and researcher Susan Wright recognized that very problem and spoke of the frustrations faced by scholars grappling with "non-word-based forms of communication." Having discussed the ways infants use non-verbal communication, Wright continued:

> In a similar way, for people of all ages, the arts are not merely preverbal
> or subverbal – they are supraverbal. In other words, they involve symbolic
> modes of thinking, understanding and knowing, and express ideas in a
> unique manner. It is a commonplace to hear the arts described as 'lan-
> guages' through which we discover, express, and exchange meanings that are

otherwise unavailable (Plummeridge, 1991), thereby enabling people to say things to each other which cannot be expressed in any other way. This does, of course, present a problem. While we can enjoy and appreciate artistic experiences, it is often difficult to explain in words precisely what it is that we have come to know or understand as a result of such an experience.[58]

And yet a desire to more fully understand what is being communicated (and how) is precisely the motivation behind my attempt at some kind of description. To what are we listening? What are the aural symbols we hear? What are the ideas being expressed? How do we make sense of the experience of listening to this music?

The four pieces of the *Deep Listening* recording challenge traditional approaches to analyzing music, which emphasize the detection of formal structures that are prescribed, applied, and filled. Listeners discern patterns of continuities and contrasts as they occur within a temporal framework, which is itself articulated in a variety of ways through the combination of harmonic, melodic, and rhythmic actions. Listeners track form.[59] Theorist Judy Lochhead, however, recognizes the need to reconsider that practice.

In her 1992 article "Joan Tower's *Wings* and *Breakfast Rhythms I and II*: Some Thoughts on Form and Repetition," Lochhead argues for moving away from thinking of form as "thing-oriented" to reconsidering form as "process-oriented thought." According to Lochhead, such thinking can "account for the 'building-up' of a whole by the accumulation of parts."[60] With its focus on process, Lochhead's approach provides the needed space to appreciate what one is hearing in a piece, which is meaningful *in the process of hearing* it and is not reliant upon relationships to past or future practices. With these four works, listeners understand the idea of unity *in the process of experiencing* the pieces. Perhaps more importantly, they understand this music as about sound itself, about the overwhelmingly sensual nature of sound. Where the underlying logic of music often reveals itself in the deconstructions of its constituent parts, this music shows itself not to be *about* logic at all, but about beautiful, luscious, voluptuous sound.

A brief consideration of the first two tracks on *Deep Listening*, "Lear" and "Suiren," based on my own reactions to several listenings, hints at the workings of the pieces and what is behind their similarly calming effect. Given their focus on sound, *how* one listens to these pieces is essential to fathoming the sonic riches they contain. In a 1991 interview with Jann Pasler published in the *American Women Composers' News/Forum*, Pauline Oliveros addressed the issue of listening to recordings:

I think of recordings as documents. I want the recording to be as representative as it can possibly be. I think that perhaps in a recording like *Deep Listening* you're going to get some of that because the musicians were in fact in that state of mind when it was recorded. I mean it's there, and you can hear it. But the presentation to the listener may not be in the best circumstances. It might be backgrounded, it might be in a noisy environment, it might be coming through a two-inch speaker, it might be in a car radio when you're driving. I don't know. I don't know what those circumstances are.[61]

I listened to each of the pieces several times on different occasions while lying on the floor of a dimly lit room with my head close to and between speakers. Clearly this setting does not replicate the cistern or the experiences of the musicians as they created the music, but it was as close as I could come.

"Lear" might just as easily be called "Tuning the Cistern" or "The E-ishness of Lear," as the piece is a near-twenty-five-minute meditation on the pitch E and its overtones. I am suspended in a world of slowly rolling didjeridu, accordion, trombone, and vocal sounds. An omnipresent low E gently rumbles as other sounds join it and float in, around, and through it. While it is clear that time must be passing, I am not conscious of marking time, or of moving in a purposeful way through the music. The continuous circularity of the spinning sound makes the phrase "*long* tone," with its unavoidable image of linearity, seem inappropriate.[62] The music has momentum – the result of the liveliness of the sounds themselves and occasional increases and decreases in volume and density of texture – but it suggests no narrative; there is no sense of going "forward."[63] Even moments when the rumbling of the didjeridu or trombone becomes more growl-like (14:50), or the soft background accordion grows busier (16:40), or when two instruments combine and sound agitated (19:38), or when dissonant sounds are lingered upon (21:15) do little to disturb the overall effect of calm, fluid peacefulness. Rather than hear the piece as having moved somewhere, I perceive the entire work as a single, soothing, dilated moment in time: a rare occasion to listen to musicians listening.

"Suiren" is the second track and, at just under ten minutes, less than half the length of "Lear." However, given the relative lack of concern with time as traditionally conceived, I am not so much aware of the comparative brevity of the work as much as I am cognizant of the completely different timbral world being experienced. Except for Dempster intermittently playing a garden hose, thereby providing a drone with which other sounds interact, the three musicians "play" their voices. The focus on identifiable human sounds in "Suiren" calls attention, in retrospect, to the bit part they played in "Lear," even though they were occasionally audible.

"Suiren" sounds human where "Lear" sounded like some nonhuman other. There is a warm, personal quality to "Suiren" that seemed absent from the earlier work, as beautiful as the sounds were.[64] Panaiotis's slow whistling lightens the sonic environment, suggesting a kind of weightlessness. While the two pieces use the same basic techniques – slow, mostly quiet sounds that are given time to spin and reverberate before others are added; the presence of a low drone that supports newly entering sounds; the eventual introduction of pitches that are dissonant to the drone, which are especially audible near the ends of both pieces; and a continuous, flowing sound that resists division into traditional analytical components – the pieces set quite different moods. Is it the fact that I can discern *human* voices and *human* whistles responding to one another that makes the second piece sound more personal? Is it that likely anyone can make similar sounds with her or his own body that causes me to identify more with this work than with "Lear"? Is the audibility of Oliveros's female voice and the higher tessitura of this work something that speaks more powerfully to a woman listener?[65] Do other listeners hear these works similarly? As Oliveros explained in her interview with Jann Pasler, she isn't interested in *what* people hear, or *why* they hear what they do, but that they listen.

> I'm transmitting a cue for listening. And it's not about controlling anyone. It's an offering and it's a possibility. . . . It comes back to listening again. If you're listening, you're not wandering; when you're listening, you listen. You are listening. You become listening.[66]

Oliveros's cistern pieces continued to resonate, literally and figuratively, in her thinking throughout the 1990s and to the present day. *MirrorrorriM*, a two-minute, forty-four-second piece for piano and saxophone "or any two instruments" composed in 1994, shows her pursuing similar ideas, but this time with a more traditional-sounding result. Oliveros had told Pasler, "My ideal, and the direction I'm moving in, is mirrors. I would like not to be aware of the technology; I'd like to be aware of the music." When Pasler inquired what Oliveros meant by mirrors, the composer referred back to her Fort Warden experience:

> Mirror, I mean in the cistern, in the CD *Deep Listening*, when you play a tone, you're immediately confronted with it, you can hardly tell the difference between what you just did and what is coming back to you. I mean it's like looking in a mirror, getting the reflection instantaneously.[67]

The "score" for *MirrorrorriM* is a set of instructions to the instrumentalists, which are reproduced in *The Roots of the Moment*:

> Start with E flat 4th space
> If he goes up she goes down
> If he goes down she goes up
> Try to do this more or less simultaneously,
> without knowing what the other is going to do.
> No fair setting anything in advance.
> Spontaneity makes it work.
>
> Listen – wait awhile – anticipate or lag – play.
> If you get confused it's part of the piece.
> Play slowly at first. Increase the challenges with more or
> less notes in a phrase or gesture. One note is ok.
> Surrounded by silence of course. Play more or less notes
> faster or slower with great dynamics and articulations.
>
> When you get there
> end with E flat 3 ledger above
> and E flat 4 ledger below
>
> PAULINE OLIVEROS
> JULY 13, 1994[68]

Oliveros's instruction to "play" hints at the lightness that characterizes the conception of the work. Oliveros likes to laugh. That said, Oliveros's disciplined interest in creating music born of focused listening – music that is responsive, interdependent, interactive, collaborative, and cooperative – informs every second of this miniature.[69]

What do these six works say about Pauline Oliveros's understanding of nature? Do works created in an electronic music studio or a concrete cistern express any relationship to nature at all? Are *Alien Bog,* "Lear," and "Suiren" less nature-informed than "An Interlude of Rare Beauty," "Environmental Dialogue," or *Rattlesnake Mountain,* where the composer's attention to what are traditionally considered "natural" surroundings is more obvious? Do they tell us anything at all? I believe so. Pauline Oliveros is thoroughly embedded in her environments, wherever they are, and at the same time she enjoys complete freedom to experience her surroundings. She listens to all sounds, those from outside and those from within, the acoustic and the electronic. As she breathes in deeply, she draws life from her surroundings and just as surely breathes it back with her music and her being.

Oliveros explained: "All is nature that supports life forms of all kinds; humanity is the body of life forms called humans. . . . The relationship is symbiotic."[70] In a life practice of deep listening, Oliveros is supported by and supportive of her surroundings; she believes that listening can change conditions – moral, spiritual, social, cultural, environmental. As Oliveros breathes in the sounds of the environment, she "becomes listening";[71] boundaries become porous, dissolve, and disappear. Where Amy Beach escaped to the MacDowell Colony to find nature, Oliveros's is in a natural habitat wherever she happens to be.

6

Joan Tower

For me a piece is a completely organic process, based on itself; in other words,
the starting ideas provide the fuel for the form of the piece. The whole process
is one of listening very patiently to what that piece is trying to do, rather than
telling the piece what to do.

— JOAN TOWER[1]

Numerous published interviews, feature stories, scholarly writings, and entries
in journals, anthologies, dictionaries, and collections of various kinds – and
now Ellen K. Grolman's 2007 *Comprehensive Bio-Bibliography* – offer essential background information on Joan Tower.[2] She is among the best-known
and most well-documented composers in this study. Born to Anna Peabody
Robinson and George Warren Tower III in 1938 in Larchmont, New York,
an upper-class suburb just north of New York City that borders Long Island
Sound, as a young girl Joan Tower enjoyed "ballet lessons, belonged to Camp-
fire Girls, and studied piano."[3] In 1947, at age nine, Tower moved with her family first to La Paz, Bolivia, where she lived until 1952, then to Santiago, Chile,
where she spent two years attending an English boarding school, and then
finally to Lima, Peru, where she rejoined her family, who had moved there
in the interim. The composer would spend ages nine to seventeen in South
America, where, Grolman explains, her father "managed all the Bolivian tin
mines owned by Hochschild Mines and oversaw their daily operation."[4] Given
the singular importance of mining to the Bolivian economy, this was an extremely powerful position, which brought with it significant responsibilities
and prestige. The young Joan had enjoyed lessons with an excellent piano
teacher while living in Larchmont, and her father made sure that she con-

FIGURE 6.1. Joan Tower, © Bernard Mindich 2008. Reprinted with the
kind permission of the photographer.

tinued her studies with the best instructors available as they moved around South America. According to the composer, George Tower

> was musical and came from a very musical family. His mother was a pianist, and while he became a geologist and a mining engineer, he loved music and played the violin, banjo/mandolin, and he sang – sort of. We often did music after dinner in our house. At first I was the percussionist, because my mother played the piano. But later, as I got better, I took over the piano part, and my father and I would play. My mother sang.[5]

George Tower's appreciation of his daughter's musical talents and Joan's appreciation of her father's geological work drew the two close together.[6]

In an interview with the author in 2006, Joan Tower revealed: "I almost majored in geology; I almost went to the Colorado College of Mines. I loved [my father's] concept of geology and his love of minerals in the land, and the way formations happen and all of that."[7] Four years later, Tower expanded on the topic: "He loved his work, and exploring the land. I saw him in action."[8] One gets the sense that Joan Tower also loves her work. As Grolman explained, the Tower family "traveled frequently within the country to visit different mines . . . occasionally George would take Joan into the jungle on fishing expeditions."[9] Such treks provided Joan Tower with experiences in nature that were challenging and rare, and almost unheard-of for young "American" girls.[10] But Joan did not follow George Tower into geology. Interactions with her father and her years in South America ultimately nurtured Joan's work as a composer, providing her with sights, sounds, inspiration, and imagery that found their way into her music decades later.

After the family's return to the United States in 1955, Joan eventually attended first Bennington College in Vermont, where she earned a bachelor's degree in composition in 1961, and then Columbia University in New York City, where she completed her master's and doctoral degrees in 1967 and 1978, earning one of the first doctorates in composition awarded to a woman in the United States.[11]

Like many of the composers considered in this study, Tower has been recognized with numerous prestigious awards, including a Naumburg Award in 1973, which she won for her work with the Da Capo Chamber Players, a group she founded and administered starting in 1969 and for which she was pianist for fifteen years; a MacDowell Colony residency in 1974; a Guggenheim Fellowship in 1977; and a Grawemeyer Award in 1990 for her piece *Silver Ladders* (the first award of its kind given to a woman). In 1993 she was named a finalist for her *Concerto for Violin and Orchestra* by the Pulitzer committee, and in 1998 Tower was inducted into the American Academy of Arts and Letters, and in 2004 into the Academy of Arts and Sciences. She served as composer in residence with the St. Louis Symphony and held a similar position with the Orchestra of St. Lukes in New York City and for the Yale/Norfolk Chamber Music Festival. Joan Tower was the first composer chosen for the *Ford Made in America* commissioning program, for which she composed her orchestral piece "Made in America." The piece toured the nation and was played in all fifty states. Tower joined the faculty of Bard College in upstate New York in 1972 and is currently their Asher Edelman Endowed Professor of Music. For all the fame concomitant with such honors and awards, Joan Tower remains open to questions, thoughtful in her responses, generous with her time, continuously creative, and constantly on the move. When scholars point to the energy of her music as one of its essential characteristics, they are describing the woman, as well.

Because many of Tower's works have evocative titles, she is often asked about her compositional process and more specifically which comes first, the title or the work. Tower has a ready answer: she wants "an image with an action" and most often names her pieces during the compositional process or after a work has been composed rather than start with an extramusical idea.[12] It is important to Tower that people understand she does not start with an image, extramusical idea, or program.

If titles are any indication of a composer's frame of reference, then Tower's many pieces that allude to dance reflect her passion for the moving art: *Petroushskates* (1980), *Noon Dance* (1982), *Stepping Stones* (1993), *The Last Dance* (2000), *Chamber Dance* (2006). Carol Neuls-Bates has quoted the composer on dance:

> Dancing is so important in South American culture, and when we lived
> in La Paz, my nursemaid – who was an Inca woman – loved to go to festivals,
> and used to take me with her. I was fascinated by the colorful skirts and
> headdresses. I would be given some percussion instrument to play, like the
> maracas or the claves, and I would dance too. So that's when I developed a
> love for rhythm, which later became the basis of my music, and percussion
> and dance.[13]

The physicality of dance appealed to a young woman who was naturally athletic; it also manifested itself in a love of sports, something that had been encouraged in La Paz, and became a source of imagery for her music with titles such as *And . . . They're Off* (1997) and *Strike Zones* (2001).[14] Here too the daughter took after her father, whom she described as a "major jock." Joan played tournament tennis, taught skiing, was captain of her baseball team, and felt at home in the world of competitive sports.

While dance and athletics provide resonant analogues for her music, the number of Tower's works that allude to the natural environment far exceed any other image category. Collectively they speak to the enduring power of nature as a touchstone in Tower's life; she keeps going back to the same source. A sample of nature-related titles culled from a period of three decades suggests the centrality of natural imagery as a wellspring for her creativity: *Black Topaz* (1976), *Platinum Spirals* (1976), *Red Garnet Waltz* (1976), *Amazon* (1977), *Wings* (1981), *Sequoia* (1981), *Snow Dreams* (1983), *Island Rhythms* (1985), *Silver Ladders* (1986), *Night Fields* (1994), *Rapids* (1996), *Holding a Daisy* (1996), *Rain Waves* (1997), *Big Sky* (2000), DNA (2003), and most recently *Copperwave* (2006).[15]

When the composer was asked directly whether she felt a particular closeness, affinity, or sensitivity to nature, she cited two connections that came to mind immediately. She explained that *Black Topaz*, *Platinum Spirals*, and *Red Garnet Waltz*, "which use minerals in their titles . . . are written in memory of [my] father . . . a sort of tribute to him because I admired him and I loved him, and because he was a great influence in my life."[16] The composer reflected, "I guess that's one connection right there to nature." She then quickly offered a second association: "But there's another component working here which has to do with physics and choreography. I think very much in terms of music as being an action and a reaction. I think very much in terms of physics and the choreography of music."[17] Tower's understanding of the applications of physics to music, especially the ways energy and movement propel a piece, will become apparent later in discussions of particular works.

George Tower's love of the natural world was transmitted to his daughter in both tangible and intangible ways. Indeed, beyond inheriting her father's passion for geology, the composer inherited one of his rock collections, which includes specimens from around the world, and one of his books. As Tower explained:

> I've got a book of his called *Gems and Minerals* and it describes all the minerals and all the rocks. And every time I look for a title, I go to that book, and I see if the description of that gem or mineral is appropriate to what I am trying to say in this piece. It's always fascinating to me to look up these things and read about them.[18]

Resisting the idea that specific images or extramusical ideas *generate* pieces, Tower's descriptive remarks about certain works nonetheless provide insights into her own relationship with nature; at the same time they contain visual images for listeners who desire such guidelines.[19]

Tower's early compositions, written in the 1960s, were heavily influenced by the uptown Columbia University crowd's thinking at the time and so are serially derived, but by the mid-1970s Joan Tower felt compelled to write a different kind of music. Her decision to leave serial techniques behind was not easy given her closeness to a number of colleagues who she knew would express dismay at her seeming aesthetic retrenchment. She tacked a new course and never looked back. Her "breakaway" piece, as she calls it, was written in 1976; *Black Topaz* is a work for piano and small ensemble that includes flute, B♭ clarinet, bass clarinet, B♭ trumpet, tenor trombone, and a small arsenal of percussion instruments consisting of pairs of marimbas and vibraphones, temple blocks, and tom-toms. In *Black Topaz* the legacy of Tower's years of piano study and South American experiences with percussion emerged fully formed. The piece is the first of seven works selected to document Joan Tower's various relationships with nature.

Anyone familiar with gems will wonder about the particular color of topaz named in Tower's title; topaz, a yellowy-orange lustrous gem, exists in many shades in nature, and heating the stone adds even more color possibilities – pink and blue especially – but none of them is black. Topaz is a hard mineral, 8 on the Mohs scale, and valuable not only for its durability, but also for its brilliance and beauty.[20] But how is a rock, an inanimate aggregate of hard, consolidated, mineral matter, an appropriate image for music, a moving, changing, temporal art? What is the connection between topaz and *Black Topaz*?

According to Herbert Zim and Paul Shaffer's guide *Rocks, Gems and Minerals*, "Gems are the most prized and famous of all minerals" and are valued for their "luster, transparency, color, and hardness." Zim and Shaffer explain: "Luster depends on how light is reflected by the mineral. The transparent gems also refract or bend light and are cut to turn the light back into the observer's eye."[21] It is, at least in part, these prized interactions with light, when the gem becomes alive and engages with the observer, that connect Tower's topaz and music. Descriptions of the particulate properties and wave-like behavior of light – why it sparkles and shimmers, and how it pulses and radiates – can also describe sound and Joan Tower intuitively understood this. The program note for the score, written by Mary Lou Humphrey, explains the genesis of *Black Topaz* and its curious title.

Joan Tower's *Black Topaz* derives from a drawing she once did of color rays emanating from a black piano-like object. This single-movement work examines a similar projection of color from its focal point, the solo piano (black), to a six-member supporting instrumental ensemble. Tower selected each ensemble instrument specifically for its ability to magnify and extend the piano's timbral [color] essence.[22]

After reviewing the specific relationship of each instrument to the timbre of the piano Humphrey's note concludes:

> Even the title *Black Topaz* reflects the work's *raison d'être*: topaz is a structurally stable, yellowish mineral which can, however, transform into various hues.[23]

Tower's drawing with its rays emanating and colors projecting and magnifying "from a black, piano-like object" is a visualization of the concept behind *Black Topaz*. Here is an example of the ways the natural world provides images, rather than narrative programs, for Tower's music. As she was exposed from an early age to rocks and minerals and thinking along with her father about "the ways formations happen and all that," what might appear to others to be a lifeless mass of matter is a vital source of creative imagining for Tower. Light shined on a crystal brings it to life. Tower shines a metaphorical light on her musical materials, and we hear them shimmer.

If the piano is the focal point of *Black Topaz*, however, it takes just over a minute for the piece to come into focus. Listeners first experience a throbbing seventy seconds of sudden sounds and silences emanating from the rest of the ensemble. Tom-toms pounce, vibraphones vibrate, temple blocks pulse, and the marimba drops dissonant clusters, while a trombone, trumpet, B♭ clarinet, and flute alternately sing finely etched melodic fragments and broad sweeping lines. In this introduction, the eight instrumentalists explore various aspects of the piano's timbre and temperament as they might manifest themselves on their own instruments. Throughout the remainder of the piece, all nine instruments will interact – they'll respond to, reflect upon, and engage with each other. Regarding their various roles Humphrey specifies:

> [Tower] first chose a percussion battery to project the piano's capability for sharp articulations: the marimba and temple blocks emphasize this staccato "attack" quality. Tom-toms add depth to the sound. Brass, woodwinds and vibraphone then were chosen to augment the piano's lyrical and harmonic nature. The flute matches the piano's highest melodic registers, while the clarinet and bass clarinet can almost duplicate its middle range. A trumpet and trombone emphasize chordal strength and support.[24]

But, depending upon the situation and the ways various instruments refract musical materials, each instrument behaves in other ways, as well, and this becomes evident when the piano joins in. As two vibraphones strike unison E-flats, the piano enters for the first time with a pickup to measure 25 and takes center stage, claiming its place as the source of all that has transpired in the preceding twenty-four measures. With the sustain pedal depressed, the piano strikes its first notes *fortissimo* – B♭2 and D4; for the duration of measure 25 the pitches pulse undisturbed by any new sounds. Our focus is drawn to the widely spaced, glowing resonance (example 6.1).

By measure 26 the vibraphones' sounds have dissipated and the piano is alone, and Tower slowly reveals the pitch range of the instrument with a wedgelike gesture that expands to encompass nearly five octaves at its widest points (G1 to E♭6). This initial solo, the first of three increasingly virtuosic moments (see measures 142–153; 230–241 for the other two) discloses two aspects of the piano's essence. The spacious, transparent texture of measures 26–28, where individual notes are accented or nonlegato, allows listeners to hear the instrument's particulate components. Here are the unique crystals of sound. By keeping the piano's notes widely separated, Tower assures that we hear them as individual entities.

Measure 29, however, introduces a soft, flowing, impressionistic cascade of planed intervals and rolled chords. Although thirds dominate individual intervals and composite chords, there is no sense of key or functional harmony; the music moves "freely" through time and harmonic space.[25] Soft (*pianissimo*), *dolce* light floods the atmosphere. One can imagine the composer holding a topaz specimen, turning it slowly, and catching glimpses of its shimmering radiance. When the trombone and bass clarinet reenter at measure 31, they meet the piano's low G♯ and all three explore their lower registers. Just before the final rest of measure 35, the piano has reached the lowest note on the keyboard.

Tower's collaborative approach to composition, informed by years of being a chamber musician, is apparent in the numerous instances where timbres and pitches overlap, and instruments echo and reflect upon materials as they respond to each other. But Tower doesn't leave such connections to chance. The composer asks the piano to "balance with [the] Bs. Cl. And Tbn." as the instruments come together on unison A's. She instructs her players to "match" each other.[26] The result is a seamless flow of sound and energy that continues at various levels of intensity even through moments of silence. Tower's organic approach to form, where the logic of the piece emerges and resides in its unfolding, becomes a signature feature of her music.[27]

The piano is capable of both delicate, brilliant, and sparkling sounds and powerful, pounding, and percussive ones. As an accomplished pianist, Tower knows it can sing and keep time, be barely audible and thunderously loud, and she explores all of those possibilities. As she does, ensemble members respond and the music undergoes a process of sonic refraction. Just as light changes direction when it enters a new medium, so Tower's materials bend, extend, fracture, and reshape themselves when played by different instruments. The process of refraction produces close organic relationships free of literal repetition, which would undermine the idea of unfolding that is so essential to Tower's musical thinking. A passage beginning at measure 96, about four and a half minutes into the piece, shows Tower's application of musical refraction at work. It is just one of many instances where the composer uses this process (example 6.2).

The piano presents three transformations of a *fortissimo*, "sonorous and broad," ascending passage; each is foreshortened by a beat and exhibits minimal variations of pitch. Regardless of their differences, however, listeners relate the three iterations by their common starting note, G♯, the similar upward climb of the gestures, and the overall rhythmic design, which consists of a long-held note followed by a pair of triplet groupings. As the solo piano passage makes clear, even a single instrument is capable of reshaping materials. One's vantage point changes what we see, hear, and think. The greatest contrast, however, occurs when flute, clarinet, trumpet, trombone, and a pair of vibraphones enter at measure 100 to treat the piano's source materials in their own way. What had been a consideration of changing pitches and rhythms becomes an exploration of timbre and texture. As the timbral palette expands, it is as if the sonic wattage has increased. Once involved, the ensemble picks up a sixteenth-note pattern that the piano had introduced at measure 76 and passes it back to that instrument. What started as a deliberate exploration of pitch and timbre becomes a throbbing source of momentum that will energize much of the rest of the piece.

Black Topaz includes moments where the music radiates a gentle incandescence (measures 154–164) and other times when the music is blindingly brilliant (measures 240–241). Like the gem for which it is named, the effect of the piece depends upon how one handles the material, how it is cut and turned, how it is buffed and polished, whether it is exposed to large amounts of direct light or experienced "dans un brume" (in a fog).[28] When subjected to heat energy, the gem changes colors and so does the music. Toward the end of the piece, in a single measure the piano's chords go from triple *forte* and "full"

EXAMPLE 6.1 (*above and facing*). *Black Topaz*. By Joan Tower, mm. 24–35. Copyright © 1978 by Associated Music Publishers, Inc. (BMI). International copyright secured. All rights reserved. Reprinted by permission.

* just loud enough to make bottom pitches clearer as pitches

EXAMPLE 6.2 (*above and facing*). *Black Topaz*. By Joan Tower, mm. 96–104. Copyright © 1978 by Associated Music Publishers, Inc. (BMI). International copyright secured. All rights reserved. Reprinted by permission.

to *mezzo piano* and *dolce*, to *piano* and *diminuendo*; ultimately they evaporate into a quarter rest of silence (measure 241).

Recently, Tower explained that her piece "changes color as it goes; it moves from dissonant and hard-edged to a more colorful sound. It evolves."[29] In *Black Topaz*, the piano is the gem whose luster generates, transforms, reflects, and illuminates its surroundings. The hardness and brilliance of topaz, regardless of its color, make it a vivid image for a work whose sounds are immediately strong, bold, and assertive, shining a light on everything in its ambit, but then later shown to be capable of soft, gentle incandescence, barely a glow. For all the hesitation and self-doubt Tower experienced as she stepped away from her Columbia cohort and broke with the uptown university crowd, she took that step unequivocally. As she separated from them, she claimed her own strong voice and her family ties. Given that the largest source of the world's topaz is Brazil, the piece connects Tower to her father, the geologist, and his work in South America, as well as to the continent that was Tower's home for nine years. Sharing many qualities with the stone, Tower's piece is a unique manifestation of topaz and a touching gift from a daughter to her father.

The title of a second piece speaks directly of her South American experience and foregrounds one of its most iconographic natural phenomena. The word "choreography" comes up often in Tower's descriptions of her work; when she pairs it with the idea of "landscape," the composer provides additional insights into her creative process and the goals she harbors for her music. In an interview with Bruce Duffie in April 1987, Tower explained: "I try to choreograph a landscape of sound that reaches people in an emotional, visceral, and formal kind of way. The 'formal' being the sense of coherence of this landscape."[30] *Amazon*, written in 1977 one year after her trio of mineral pieces, and dedicated to the Da Capo Chamber Players, shows the ways real and choreographed musical landscapes come together; it also introduces Tower's interests in feminism. The composer's note prefacing the score explains:

> I grew up in South America and have long wanted to write a piece as a tribute to my experiences there. The opportunity presented itself to me when the image of a river, as a musical metaphor, became the focus of this piece. The title refers to the great Brazilian river, the Amazon, and the images and actions that a journey on such a river might provide. I was concerned with creating a kind of seamless, flowing action within which, along the way, one might sense changes of pace through the speed of the notes, sometimes resulting in a "cascade" of many notes, other times in a slowing down that almost stops the action entirely. A rippling effect can be heard in the trill sections.
>
> The other reason I chose "amazon" as a title was the fact that I was reading many books by and about women at the time, and I liked the feminist connotation of the title. I have never actually seen the Amazon river.[31]

Tower's liner notes for the recording offer a few more specific insights into the piece:

> There is generally consistent background flow that is interrupted only occasionally by "static" events or by silence, and which undergoes change

in speed and width through the spacing of notes and the type of texture being articulated. Some different kinds of associations with the river will be evident in the trill passages (ripples of water) and in the fast unison passages (which have the effect of a waterfall and water turbulence).[32]

Unlike rocks, whose apparent lifelessness seems to have precluded their being understood as a meaningful image for a temporal art by most composers, water has provided musicians with imagery and inspiration for centuries; its variable motion, depth, texture, and sounds make it an easy analogue for music.[33] With her pieces *Amazon, Rapids,* and *Rain Waves,* Tower participates in an established tradition by composing her own water music.[34]

In contrast to *Black Topaz,* but like a majority of Tower's pieces, *Amazon* starts with a few soft sounds. Like other works, the piece will develop organically from these first musical ripples and free of an imposed structural plan. *Amazon* opens slowly (quarter note = 50), with a single, long-held note on violin. The music is *pianissimo,* growing only as loud as *piano* before other instruments join in; and then each of them enters *pianissimo.* The soft, seamless sounds of Tower's barely moving music evoke the river at one of its calmer sources or tributaries. It will take time to gather the momentum needed for the Amazon to move with any sense of direction, purpose, or goal, but the composer is patient with her music and gives it time to tack its course (example 6.3).

The ensemble – violin, Bb clarinet, flute, cello, and piano – coalesces gradually; instruments enter one at a time, matching dynamic levels and sometimes even specific pitches. Although the piano doesn't appear until four minutes into the piece (at measure 55), when it does it enters playing a three-note chord whose pitches duplicate the notes most recently sounded by the violin and cello. Seamless flow is paramount.

Measures 1–54 are characterized by vacillating slow tempi, which never get faster than a quarter note = 72, and twenty-three meter changes that guarantee no single pulsing pattern can establish itself. The texture remains clear and transparent, with never more pitches sounding at a single time than can be individually discerned. Listeners focus all their attention on the minimal materials, the gentle actions, and the slight changes in sound quality that result from where and how a note is played. Tower knows the sounds she is after.[35] The dynamic compass remains similarly restrained, although there is a single occurrence of *forte* at the peak of a crescendo at measure 19. This brief surge of sound, followed as it is by a three-measure passage of paired eighths,

EXAMPLE 6.3. *Amazon.* By Joan Tower, mm. 1–7. Copyright © 1978 by
Associated Music Publishers, Inc. (BMI). International copyright secured.
All rights reserved. Reprinted by permission.

hints that the river is organizing itself. But the short-lived effort dissipates,
and the music returns to its earlier, more meandering ways.

    As if the piano must release the energy pent up from so much waiting,
within a minute of its entrance the mood of the piece changes dramatically.
The river moves from meandering to muscular, from tentative to turbulent;
the tempo increases, the dynamic level rises, and although all other instruments had dropped out between measures 55 and 75, with piano alone the
texture has become significantly thicker, the articulation more varied, and
the sounds more dissonant. When flute, clarinet, violin, and cello rejoin the

ensemble, they do so by eliding on pitches common to the piano music. They build upon the keyboard's energy, and together the entire ensemble moves *Amazon* in new directions. By measure 83, the music has decided its new course. Momentum, more than key schemes or thematic groups, becomes the integral structural force, the form-defining component of the piece[36] (see example 6.4). With few exceptions, the remaining seven minutes of *Amazon* are dominated by a stronger, louder, more continuous current of activity than by the initial meandering motions. Even when the momentum of the enlarged sound mass is briefly interrupted, as when the flute and clarinet introduce a passage of relatively soft trills that extends over a period of eight measures (measures 112–120), the energy driving the piece relaxes but is never lost. Sharp, percussive interjections from the piano, and then tremolos in the violin and cello, push the music downstream. Brief sonic whirlpools swirl the musical materials of individual instruments and the larger ensemble.[37] On a second occasion when the musical activity ostensibly slows and relaxes, thunking jabs from bass notes on the piano, which are created by the pianist stopping a vibrating string with her hand, add a level of physicality to the music that denies any sense of abating energy[38] (example 6.5).

It is not until the final minute of the piece that sounds recalling the initial surface rhythms, texture, timbre, mood, dynamic, or energy levels return. At measure 273, the cello is instructed to bow its notes in the usual manner – to play freely. The piano holds on to a single resonating middle C, which is doubled by the violin, until it disappears from our hearing two measures later; it drops out, leaving only the four instruments that started the piece twelve minutes earlier. The transparent texture is interleaved with silences as the music (and perhaps the river) slows down and returns to its *dolce sostenuto* source. One last time Tower impresses upon her players that the idea of a "seamless, flowing action" is the essence of the river and her piece. At measure 281 she instructs the violinist, "Transfer C♯ from Cello to Violin imperceptibly."[39]

The Amazon River becomes the image for Tower's musical homage to the continent she called home for nine years. In writing a tribute to the 4,200-mile waterway, one of the cleanest water sources in the world and which alone accounts for 20 percent of the world's total river flow, Tower unintentionally called attention to the plight of this life-giving natural resource. In a phone conversation, the composer explained: "The environmental movement didn't affect me in any way that I was aware of. I was looking for something more sensual, visceral, physical, and natural."[40] This professed disconnection from

EXAMPLE 6.4. *Amazon.* By Joan Tower, mm. 83–87. Copyright © 1978 by
Associated Music Publishers, Inc. (BMI). International copyright secured.
All rights reserved. Reprinted by permission.

EXAMPLE 6.5. *Amazon.* By Joan Tower, mm. 146–155. Copyright © 1978 by Associated Music Publishers, Inc. (BMI). International copyright secured. All rights reserved. Reprinted by permission.

the environmental movement distinguishes Tower from Talma and Oliveros, but then, George Tower's work in the mining industry may have made such a sensibility less likely to take root. While it was not written with environmental advocacy in mind, it is hard to hear *Amazon* today without thinking of the vulnerability of the rain forests that are home to the river or imagining ways to keep them and it alive and flowing. It is no exaggeration to say life on earth depends on the success of our efforts.

Tower chose a similarly large, one-word natural phenomenon as the image for another of her nature-referenced pieces when she wrote *Sequoia* in 1981. For this work, her first full orchestral piece, she assembled an appropriately large ensemble that included pairs of woodwind and brass, four horns, bass trombone, tuba, harp, piano (celesta), a full complement of strings, and a battery of five percussionists playing an enormous array of instruments: tom-toms, medium and large bass drums, snare drum, tenor drum, timpani, cowbells (small, medium, and large), low and high temple blocks, a large gong, xylophone, marimba, vibraphone, glockenspiel, chimes, cymbals (low, medium, and high), crotales, and medium and high triangles. The world's tallest tree evoked the composer's largest sound to date, but given Tower's more general concern with balance, there are also numerous occasions within the sixteen-minute piece for soft-spoken, soloistic passages, and time to focus on individual timbres and small details. Whereas organic seamlessness was the essence of *Amazon,* balance is the guiding principle of *Sequoia,* as the composer's note to the score makes plain:

> *Sequoia* opens with a very long "pedal point" on the note G, which expands to a four-octave G and then returns to a central G (in the trumpet part). Around this G begins a "balancing" action of harmonies that branch out on either side of the G – first above, then below – like the branching and rooting of a tree. This balancing of registers becomes more and more developed as the piece continues, and the pedal point G begins to move up and down very slowly to create a substructure of balances, a kind of counterpoint of lines.

Tower relates the idea of balance to the contrasting sounds of *Sequoia:*

> Another kind of "branching" action occurs in the contrasting of solo lines with big orchestral passages, and of soft and loud dynamics – an attempt to explore the enormous textural and dynamic range of the orchestra.

Finally she explained why, given all the large images available, she chose this tree:

The giant redwood tree, the Sequoia, seemed to me to embody these notions in at least two senses: the incredible "balancing act" achieved in the full-grown height of the tree, and the striking contrast of very small pine needles growing upon such a large structure.[41]

As Tower explained in an interview, she saw sequoias only after she had composed the piece, but she "happened to be in California" and so consciously sought them out. Upon seeing the trees her first thought, she confided, had nothing to do with their size, but rather with their sound: "they were quiet, very quiet." She "wanted to find an image in nature that had a balancing act of some kind." And she was after something big. "Growing up in South America everything was big, the mountains were really big, the rivers were really big . . . and I decided on big trees because they are such a phenomenon. They go up so high and don't fall over." But beyond the tree's impressive height, what Tower "loved" most was "these tiny pine needles that they have – no larger than a thumbnail. And my piece goes from big to little. So it was a nice metaphor or image."[42]

With *Sequoia*, Tower consciously looked for an image that embodied "the power of bigness in nature . . . the most powerful image in one word," but she admitted she was not feeling big or powerful herself at the time. "I never felt big and powerful, ever. It's sort of like a therapy: To *imagine* that you could feel big and powerful."[43]

Tower's remarks call to mind the circumscribed worlds of the majority of nineteenth-and early twentieth-century American women whose experiences of nature were more or less confined to what they could see from their homes or enjoy in their gardens. While large natural phenomena are not inherently more valuable than the smallest flower or bird, and some might argue for value in reverse proportion to size, Tower's reflection raises the question of how *access* to nature impacts not only what women have been able to experience, but also how those experiences have allowed them to *imagine* themselves. Exposure to South America's big mountains, rivers, and skies, and access to the towering heights of California's redwoods, allows everyone, men and women alike, to feel enlarged, to see themselves as part of a greater endeavor, to think big thoughts. It is impossible to calculate the effects of access denied.

As Tower's note to the score suggests, *Sequoia* is by turns muscular, bold, and powerful, with rhythms that leap and pounce and dynamic levels that rattle the brain, and then intimate, reflective, and meditative, with exquisitely expressive and tender writing for individual players. Her sensitivity to specific instrumental parts is no doubt the result of her years as a chamber musician inside a small ensemble.[44] Temporal and metrical freedom, organic unfolding, continuous momentum, a unique evolving formal structure, seamless transitions, an awareness but not a slavish adherence to traditional pitch and harmony relationships, subtle timbral effects, the balance of registers, dynamics, and the push and pull of musical energy – qualities already discussed in relation to *Black Topaz* and *Amazon* (and which will appear again in *Snow Dreams, Rain Waves,* and *Big Sky*) – are present in *Sequoia*. By 1981, Tower had found her voice, and as she had done with *Black Topaz* five years earlier, she stepped out.

Tower compared the experience of writing *Sequoia* with an earlier one she had had as a tennis player. Her remarks speak once again to the impact gendered assumptions, behaviors, and practices have on the creative process.

> I was a very good tennis player. But I was embarrassed by the fact that I could power hit; I had power strokes. It embarrassed me at first because I thought, "oh wow, I can play like a man." And that same thing applies to music. I loved drums, I love percussion, and I brought out the entire battery of my imagination. I have 64 percussion in that [piece], five players. I just went for it. Let's see, I wrote that piece in 1981, so I was 42 years old. So I was at that point when I just felt confident enough to step out, to be myself. But I was always a little embarrassed because the sound was so big. . . . I'm still embarrassed by those cowbells! . . . Three of them with brass mallets![45]

In a culture that encouraged young women to speak softly, to acquiesce, to understate their abilities, and to observe rather than to act, Tower's decision to rattle the concert hall heralded a personally courageous creative occasion. While she might be embarrassed by the cowbells now, in 1981 they were likely exactly what she needed to announce her arrival: no one can dismiss their, or her, presence.

What distinguishes *Sequoia* from Tower's earlier pieces are its overall length, enlarged sonic palette, and conceptual dimensions. In a recent conversation the composer unequivocally declared: "Sequoia changed my life; it changed my life." *Sequoia* is Tower's first work for full orchestra, and as such it is her first foray into the world of "large" instrumental forms.[46] She continued: "After I wrote that, I was launched into the orchestral world. Leonard Slatkin heard that piece, and he loved it, he just went bonkers over it, and he programmed it with three orchestras right away and took it to Europe and asked me if I'd be composer in residence at St. Louis, and wanted recording rights on it; that changed my whole life there."[47] At just over sixteen minutes, it was also her longest piece to date. An extremely sensitive listener when it comes to the qualities of individual instruments and a dancing master when it comes to handling rhythm, Tower applied those skills and acquitted herself with her debut piece in the field.[48] The music world is grateful that she "brought out the entire battery of [her] imagination."

Among a number of composers Tower acknowledges as influences upon her music, she is on record as admiring the spatial expansiveness of Edgard Varèse's musical soundscapes, and there is a similar spatial quality to *Sequoia*.[49] Given the instrumentation of *Sequoia*, one can't help but think that Tower also admired his handling of percussion instruments. With its combination of resonating gongs, pulsing drums, and a variety of pitched and nonpitched percussion, the music recalls *Ionisation*, Varèse's first all-percussion piece, written 1929–1931. But unlike Varèse, Tower gives equal time to the other instrument families and she doesn't shy away from establishing a home base with pitch; this, as she explained in her note, is an essential component of the balance of the work. A few specific observations should suffice to demonstrate the way Tower's musical "balancing act" suggests nature's own.

The principle of balance dictates both the overall structure of the piece and measure-to-measure behavior. Long passages of loud, propulsive, highly rhythmic, and often unison music meld into similarly extended passages of soft, shimmering, more freely flowing soloistic writing. Powerful, pulsing, clamorous music blends into the gentle, lyrical, expressive sounds of woodwinds and strings. Dynamic contrasts, the relative thickness or thinness of juxtaposed textures, and which instrument groups dominate a given passage all contribute to a sense of the music exploring different aspects of its own complex nature. Within the first seventy-five seconds, *Sequoia* impresses listeners with its power and with its delicacy: insisting upon both qualities assures that they understand the trees as more than skyscraping giants (examples 6.6 and 6.7).

Tower's orchestra-wide pedal points are occasions for the instruments to come together; they provide audible taproots, although they don't demarcate sections of traditional musical structures. Instead they indicate points of coalescing energy. Their verticality, so evident in the score, provides a visual image of the trees named in the title. Tower's music seems to be planted with sequoia trees. Although the viola is the first to introduce the pitch G, it comes into *fortissimo* focus at measure 11 when the entire ensemble bows, blows, and strikes the pitch. Five more iterations of G establish its importance as the axis upon which materials will be arranged and against which they will be understood.[50]

In addition to the pedal points, which appear at measures 11 (G), 78 (B), 123 (F♯), 203 (G), and 468 (G), recurring rhythmic and melodic patterns unify the work: groupings of telegraphic sixteenths and thirty-second notes and multiple series of leaping intervals, both ascending and descending, are common gestures that relate otherwise contrasting sections of music to each other. As different as they might sound, they share common roots.

Tower's concern with balance becomes apparent as soon as the *fortissimo* opening dissipates. With the clangorous sounds still resonating in a listener's memory, Tower turns her focus toward the more delicate details of the music—perhaps the sonic equivalents of the feathery foliage of the tree. At measure 25, *pianissimo* flute, clarinet, strings, and vibraphone shift a listener's attention away from the monumental and toward the minute. Soft, shimmering music provides the needed counterpoise. Although the dynamic impact of this new music cannot compete with what preceded it, the length of time Tower devotes to these less weighty or grand materials clarifies their importance to the composition and to the tree. Just as the massive sequoia cannot exist without its "tiny" leaves, so Tower's piece cannot express its essence without this musical equilibrium. The balanced relationship of large to small, loud to soft, high to low, pitched to nonpitched, and metered to free that Tower establishes in the first ninety seconds of the piece is imprinted upon the larger work.

While the use of temple blocks starting at measure 17 introduces a woody timbre that is consistent with Tower's image of the sequoia, given the order in which she arrived at the title it is clear that she did not set out to depict specific qualities of a tree or sounds that one might hear in a stand of redwoods. In fact, the composer was not originally thinking of trees or woody sounds at all, as she explained in an interview: "Originally I was thinking of tall buildings, like the Empire State Building. But I got rid of that fast because I wanted something more natural." Tower's return to nature as the more appealing frame of reference for her imagery speaks to the continuing attachment she feels for the natural world. That said, the hollow knocking sounds coming from temple blocks at measure 17 don't work against the imagery Tower ultimately decided upon; on the contrary, they help deepen a connection with the mental picture.[51]

On multiple occasions in *Sequoia*, Tower composes moments for reflection, passages of shimmering effects that evoke the wonder and awe one feels when in the presence of these arboreal giants (example 6.8). Sounds of harp, celesta, glockenspiel, and high woodwinds conjure sunlight glowing behind a fog-shrouded forest canopy.[52] Tower creates a similar effect near the end of the

EXAMPLE 6.6. *Sequoia*. By Joan Tower, mm. 1–13. Copyright © 1981 by Associated Music Publishers, Inc. (BMI). International copyright secured. All rights reserved. Reprinted by permission.

EXAMPLE 6.7 *(above and facing). Sequoia.* By Joan Tower, mm. 25–30. Copyright © 1981 by Associated Music Publishers, Inc. (BMI). International copyright secured. All rights reserved. Reprinted by permission.

EXAMPLE 6.8 (*above and facing*). *Sequoia*. By Joan Tower, mm. 175–183.
Copyright © 1981 by Associated Music Publishers, Inc. (BMI). International
copyright secured. All rights reserved. Reprinted by permission.

piece. As the solo violin takes over from the solo horn, woodwinds trill, strings
play unmeasured tremolos, and celesta, marimba, and vibraphone create a
quivering, quaking iridescent sound. There is no need to romanticize nature
or understand it as a sacred Other to feel the power of the natural world or
understand one's place in it (example 6.9).

EXAMPLE 6.9. *Sequoia.* By Joan Tower, mm. 322–326. Copyright © 1981 by Associated Music Publishers, Inc. (BMI). International copyright secured. All rights reserved. Reprinted by permission.

There is one more passage of contrasting high-energy music before Tower's balancing act is over. Rhythmic and melodic figures first heard in the opening minutes of the piece return speeded up and compressed. Loud, strong, powerfully pulsating music reminds listeners of the majesty of Tower's sound: she can write big music. But ultimately the final word goes to a solo violin singing expressively against a *pianissimo* background of violin II, vibraphone, horn, and celesta. Like the fog so common in redwood groves, the music hangs suspended and then evaporates; the trees are indeed quiet. We understand that the large, impressive sounds we heard first are just one aspect of a more complex enterprise. Whether the music is a metaphor for the towering sequoia, or vice versa, or for Tower herself remains a question that not even the composer can answer.

Tower's experiences with large sounds and large images did not keep her from continuing to explore more intimate ideas and landscapes in her nature-titled pieces. Two years after *Sequoia*, she offered insights into the imagery of *Snow Dreams*, a duet for flute and guitar that she composed in 1983:

> There are many different images of snow, its forms and its movements. Light snow flakes, pockets of swirls of snow, round drifts, long white plains of blankets of snow, light and heavy snowfalls, and so forth. Many of these images can be found in the piece if, in fact, they need to be found at all. The listener will determine that choice.[53]

Here we see the composer not wanting to lead listeners with extramusical associations but providing them nonetheless. As Sandra Hyslop explained, according to Joan Tower "the title crystallized during composition, as the unfolding moods and images suggested the wondrous variety of snow."[54]

Hyslop understands *Snow Dreams* as "a study in balancing the two *disparate* timbres and technical possibilities of the flute and guitar [where] Tower has brought them together cohesively, while celebrating their unique voices."[55] Where Hyslop hears disparate timbres, however, I hear similarities and complementarity as the guitar and flute join in a seamless exploration of snow-ish sounds. This is due not only to the virtuosity of Carol Wincenc and Sharon Isbin, the two dedicatees of the piece who have played together for years, but also to Tower's intimate understanding of the capabilities of the instruments and instrumentalists, the result of years of working closely with musicians in her Da Capo Chamber Players ensemble.

Tower was not the first to pair the flute with a plucked instrument; the combination has been a favorite across ages and continents: Mozart's *Concerto* for Flute and Harp is among the most famous of the standard repertoire; a century later, Debussy used the same two instruments to evoke the sounds of a gamelan in the "Clouds" movement from *Nocturnes*. In 1988, Ástor Piazzolla's *History of the Tango* showcased flute and guitar in a more sensuous musical coupling. In all cases, a flute and plucked string instrument form a natural pair.

Instead of hearing *Snow Dreams* as focused on working out timbral differences, I am struck by how effortlessly *Snow Dreams* emerges, especially given that my perception of its inevitability is not the result of relating what I hear to received forms or known behaviors, but rather of processing the sounds on the spot, in relation to events *as* they are occurring in the piece itself. Like in earlier pieces discussed in this chapter, Tower creates a thoroughly unified work without referencing canonized classical forms, but through a process of inspired musical unfolding, something she calls "motivated architecture."[56] One can hear the composer listening to and following the materials she sets in motion, noting the action and reacting. The music sounds effortless. Here is the composer dancing with her music, enjoying the play of actions and reactions: here is another example of where physics and nature come together.

Although it resists comparison with the formal structures of many traditional works, *Snow Dreams* does have something in common with self-contextual, dodecaphonic pieces whose germinating pitch and interval material is unique to each composition. Given Tower's decade of training in the uptown, Columbia University milieu, she is certainly conversant with serial techniques. As Jane Weiner LePage points out, prior to 1974, many of Tower's works "rel[ied] heavily on serial and other more complex structural procedures which [Tower] refers to as her early compositional 'maps' (guides to laying out her music)."[57]

As a survey of a number of pieces reveals, listening to the materials, following the musical action, and embracing formal freedom are foundational tenets of Tower's musical endeavor, but perhaps listening is most important. In an interview the composer explained the foundational role listening plays:

> I think the best composers are the ones who listen to what they do, because they are coming from what they just did instead of imposing some kind of – the hardest thing I have to do is to teach my students to listen to what they've got rather than move on, imposing their will onto something that's not particularly interesting. But they're not noticing that, because they aren't listening.[58]

Starting in the mid-1970s, Tower began listening more to herself than to the "outside information" she learned from her teachers.[59] This caused some to question her work, but unlike her serial colleagues, Tower didn't shy away from writing highly expressive, personal music; she had the confidence to "step out."[60] Since then, her work has been described as possessing "beauty of line" and sounding "full of intense, private passion."[61] While Tower shrugs off traditional formal constraints, she embraces drama and lyricism. As a chamber musician she seeks collaboration and works closely with performers on- and offstage. The practice of chamber music as conversation, with chamber musicians the conversationalists, informs all aspects of her thinking. It is perhaps not surprising, then, that Tower composes music that musicians like to play. Where much of Amy Beach's chamber music was written for the trained amateur women singers or pianists who played her works in private homes or at meetings of local music clubs, *Snow Dreams* demonstrates that Tower's chamber works are virtuosically conceived and realized in all senses of the term. A more detailed exploration of this piece provides a strategy for understanding many of Tower's works.

In a discussion of "abstract formal types," theorist Judy Lochhead identified a "process-oriented analysis" that "addresses the 'arising' of formal meanings during the temporal succession of units and events that constitute a musical whole."[62] Attending to "forming" rather than to form is a fruitful strategy for understanding *Snow Dreams*; it allows the piece the space it needs to emerge, unfold, and cohere. Key to Lochhead's understanding of Tower's formal constructions is the role played by repetition in creating a sense of continuity and unity. In repeating a musical gesture, the composer and listener relate later events to earlier ones. While repetition can assume various roles within a composition in all cases, Lochhead explains that "by replicating some features of a prior unit or event, the repetition makes more salient those features of both occurrences." She concluded that "repetition in effect 'thickens' formal process and meaning in temporally complex ways through the referential relation and the formal meanings that arise from it."[63]

Repetition, per se, doesn't occur in nature, although there are certainly cyclic patterns and rhythms that invite characterization as "referential relations." While the following discussion is not a theoretical analysis of the role of repetition in *Snow Dreams*, it suggests how one might listen to, understand, and process its recurring sounds, gestures, movements, and shapes.[64]

In her brief description of *Snow Dreams'* imagery, Tower refers to many qualities of snow – its weight, its shape, its motion, the density of a snowfall

EXAMPLE 6.10. *Snow Dreams*. By Joan Tower, mm. 1–11. Copyright © 1987 by Associated Music Publishers, Inc. (BMI). International copyright secured. All rights reserved. Reprinted by permission.

and its resulting forms – and all of these qualities have sounding corollaries in her piece. Such references reveal Tower's nature-rooted thought processes. Although the piece does not depend upon associations with snow to be meaningful, Tower's visual imagery creates an access point for listeners and a vocabulary for discussing musical events.

Snow Dreams begins with the guitar exploring a simple, rebounding (descending-ascending) gesture, G–E–G, three times: first on the bridge (*ponticello*), then in its "natural" place on the strings, and finally in a flattened version, G–E♭–G, on the fingerboard (*sulla tastiera*) (example 6.10). The three subtly different, expanding iterations of the germinating idea increasingly focus a listener's attention, much as one might pay special attention to the first tentative snowflakes of a storm. At measure 4, as the motive expands and adds a fourth note, B – and then a measure later a fifth note, D – the flute joins in. Even though it enters triple *piano* and nearly imperceptibly, on a low B, the lowest note possible on a C flute, the music is intense; a listener wonders what it portends. The flute furtively shadows the guitar, doubling the final, fleeting pitches of each measure as they whisk by. In its initial appearance, the flute's sound evokes that of a clarinet in what Kent Kennan describes as its "dark, strangely hollow" chalumeau register.[65] With the two instruments doubling each other, we hear a new timbre. The seductive, subtly morphing, expanding, contracting guitar motive, combined with the enigmatic timbre, beckons listeners.

The intense opening sounds are conveyed, however, at a very slow tempo (quarter note = 50) where notes are tied over bar lines and the rhythm is elastic – all suggestive of freedom and deliberateness.[66] In spite of Tower's many precise instructions regarding how or where to play individual notes or passages, there is no sense of the composer exerting rigid control. She sets the music in motion and it reacts. *Snow Dreams* is simultaneously intense and deliberate, exacting and relaxed, a balance of energy and rest, momentum and stillness, the composer listening and responding to the music she has created.

Although flute and guitar come from two different instrument families, they share a number of characteristics. They are both relatively soft-sounding instruments, which means they excel at conveying introspective moods. They are also similarly flexible and capable of fast and brilliant passages. In the case of the flute, the length of an extended passage is limited only by the flutist's breath control, but with the emergence of circular breathing as a standard technique for wind players, even this limitation has been significantly modified. Both instruments are often assigned similar melodic roles, although this is almost exclusively the case for the flute. As for differences, the guitar can realize contrapuntal lines; it can also play chords more easily, which is beyond many flute players' abilities, although multiphonics (playing more than a single note at a time) has become part of the standard extended technique repertoire among virtuoso wind instrument players.[67] The flute can sustain pitches longer than the plucked string of a guitar can carry. Both instruments can "massage" a note after it has been sounded, although the speed of the decay of a sound on the guitar limits the time available for such modifications. Given the manner in which sound is produced, the blown flute is capable of more *legato* than a plucked guitar, and the flute's higher tessitura and metallic timbre mean it can also penetrate a larger accompanying ensemble when needed. While in *Snow Dreams* each instrument has an opportunity to explore its distinguishing characteristics, with the guitar and flute sharing so many similar qualities, contrast and balance are achieved primarily through changing moods and the relative thickness or thinness of textures and amounts of motion, and those qualities are written into the music itself. They create the architecture of the piece more than the contrast of distinctly different instruments.

Although Tower explained, "I am not a pitch person,"[68] pitch, and perhaps more importantly the aural shapes created by pitch *relationships*, helps mold the memorable sounds that will return in different manifestations throughout the piece. On the one hand, at the most basic level, the piece begins and ends on the same pitch, E, and so to that extent, at least, pitch is a structural agent. Centering the piece on E is logical, however, given the tuning of the guitar's six strings: E–A–D–G–B–E. For those able to identify, track, and remember pitch, this is not an insignificant unifying device. On the other hand, traditional pitch and harmony relationships that one might expect to propel and bind the piece over its nine-minute duration are not present.

In *Snow Dreams*, the original guitar gesture informs everything that happens in the first minute of the piece. It reappears prominently in the flute at measure 18, only this time it is inverted, starts on a G♯, and moves up a minor third before it moves down. (The guitar first moved down by a minor third before it stretched to a major third.) Similar up-and-down motions are among the basic musical materials of the entire piece. For instance, well into the third minute of *Snow Dreams* (around measure 56), the instruments play together with the motive, but now it appears as a delicately articulated, highly metered, fast passage that starts on C and moves down to A, then A♭, then G♭, before reversing direction (example 6.11).

By this time, both instruments have also been given the opportunity to play with musical ideas in ways that showcase their strengths. Starting at measure 20, the guitar launches an extended solo of brilliant passagework. An accelerando accompanied by a crescendo intensifies momentum and exposes the range of the guitar's dynamic compass. In just over a minute, the guitar has gone from *ppp* to *fff*. If the opening of the piece suggested delicate, individual snowflakes floating undisturbed through the air, this flurry of activity conjures whirling, swirling, wind-driven snow squalls. As the guitar solo fades from its triple-*forte* peak of activity, listeners hear a gesture reminiscent of the opening motive. In three measures, Tower moves from *sffz*, to *mf*, to *mp*, to *p*.

The flute enters *ppp* and overlaps its first pitch with the final one of the

EXAMPLE 6.11. *Snow Dreams.* By Joan Tower, mm. 56–60. Copyright © 1987 by Associated Music Publishers, Inc. (BMI). International copyright secured. All rights reserved. Reprinted by permission.

guitar. They sound together briefly before the guitar drops out. At measure 37 the flute sounds a slow (quarter note= 48), "very sustained" line that evaporates into silence before starting up again and expanding. (Olivier Messiaen's *Quatuor pour la fin de temps* hovers in the air. [69]) While the music is not exactly like that which opened the piece, it is close enough to sound related. Here we experience Lochhead's "explicit reference of a later event to an earlier one,"[70] and Tower's sense of her music as driven by actions and reactions. Having experienced the pyrotechnics of the guitar's cadenza-like solo, a literal repeat of the gentle germinating materials is inappropriate. The sounds must react to what they just heard.

As the flute climbs up from the lowest parts of its range into a register more closely associated with the instrument, Tower instructs the flutist to play "smooth," something it can do exceedingly well. Within a few measures of its appearance, the flute is engaged in its own display of fast passagework, although Tower's instruction "*Quasi rubato* to end of solo (but not too fast)" predicts the gradual slowing down and close of this section of the work. The first three minutes of the piece are saturated with varied references to and recollections of the opening measures. We have tasted the many varieties of snow.

At measure 47, the tempo approaches the slow pace of the beginning (now quarter note = 54–58) and Tower again explores the sonic qualities of individual notes on the guitar. In this iteration it plays a C; then in measure 48 the same pitch an octave higher; and in measure 49, a harmonic on the same string. The quiet dynamic level, slow tempo, and transparent texture (a single guitar note in each measure) allow a listener to focus all her attention on the attack and decay of the sound. Sound quality *is* more important than pitch. By the end of the third minute of *Snow Dreams*, Tower has presented

EXAMPLE 6.12. *Snow Dreams.* By Joan Tower, mm. 144–147. Copyright © 1987 by Associated Music Publishers, Inc. (BMI). International copyright secured. All rights reserved. Reprinted by permission.

the essential materials of the piece and she turns to a new exploration of the generating ideas. Listeners have been introduced to the two instruments separately and together, and experienced varying amounts of motion and stillness; they are prepared to process what will follow in relation to what they have heard thus far.

The second section of *Snow Dreams*, eventually reached at measure 56, is characterized by highly metered and rhythmically driving treatment of a new version of the opening idea, although the variety and number of meter changes guarantees that Tower's *Dreams* are never predictable.[71] At measure 56 the tempo has doubled (eighth note=108–116) and flute and guitar join forces for seven measures of a *pianissimo, delicato* unison duet. Once again the hybrid timbre draws a listener's attention.

As the sound thickens, we are no longer watching a few free-floating flurries; we can imagine an increasingly steady snowfall. Within this section, the guitar plays its first texture-thickening chords, and when it does that, the flute breaks away to explore its own snowlike sounds. As the guitar pulses repeated notes, the music is additionally invigorated and the flute spits staccato splashes of sound. Once again, each of the instruments has its own solo that is joined to the other via a unison passage.

EXAMPLE 6.13. *Snow Dreams.* By Joan Tower, mm. 210–217. Copyright © 1987 by Associated Music Publishers, Inc. (BMI). International copyright secured. All rights reserved. Reprinted by permission.

There are ebbs and flows to the activity level of the music, as there are to any snowfall. At measure 140, for instance, (about 5:40 in the piece), as the flute embarks on its solo passage, the momentum momentarily abates as the instrumentalist is instructed to play "freely." Trilled notes and brief swirling gestures train our ears on individual actions. As if the wind has intensified, eighth-note triplets that were first heard in the flute's earlier solo now hurry past in sixteenths. When the flute gains momentum, the guitar joins in and the two instruments dance their way through a storm of changing meters, tempi, and moods. Their playful interaction underscores the natural complementarity of the instruments (example 6.12).

At the *Piu Mosso,* just about 2/3 of the way through *Dreams* (starting measure 184), musical momentum increases. A quarter note now equals 142–146, and both instruments play in the *forte* range. The guitar unleashes accented chords interrupted by repeated notes in triplet groupings, while the flute injects a new variety of down–up triplet figures first heard in its "quasi rubato" solo at measure 44. When both instruments move from triplets to groupings of four sixteenth notes, momentum increases yet again. When at measure 210 (around 7:00) flute and guitar join forces for a final whirling passage of sometimes unison and sometimes dissonant music making, listeners understand the energy pent up in Tower's seemingly gentle materials (example 6.13). With a minute left in the piece, the worst of Tower's dream-state storm appears to be dissipating, although it still has enough energy to generate short-lived bursts of activity. First the music unwinds, moving through a *Poco Meno Mosso* at measure 245 (quarter note = 100), but then it reverses its course nine measures later to *Poco Piu Mosso* (quarter note = c. 132, which increases to a half note = c. 85–90 at measure 259). The guitar strums accented six-note *rasqueado* chords as the flute spits out its own accented *fortissimo* triplet passages.[72] Here too, frequent meter changes keep predictability at bay.

Tower's *Snow Dreams* fade away as the tempo slows, the volume decreases, the texture thins out, and, like at the beginning, more silence than sound fills the air. With a last series of repeated Es, and a tremolo B from the guitar, and then trilled Bs followed by repeated Es on the flute, the music exhausts itself. The instruments join in the final measure for an extended (*lunga*), blended, triple *piano* trill/tremolo, the flute on a trilled E, and the guitar on an E–B tremolo. Listeners return to focusing on delicate individual sounds, perhaps as they might wistfully watch the last flakes of a brief storm evaporate in the air.

References to a few more pieces complete this exploration of Joan Tower's nature-titled works. Having drawn upon the imagery of minerals and monster trees, tropical rivers and wintry weather, Tower referenced avian images for her piece *Wings*, which she composed in 1991. It seems that little in the natural world escapes Tower's notice, even if none of it becomes the conscious starting point of her music. Tower wrote, "the image behind the piece is one of a large bird – perhaps a falcon – at times flying very high gliding along the thermal currents, barely moving. At other moments, the bird goes into elaborate flight patterns that loop around, diving downwards, gaining tremendous speeds." There are times when Tower's imagery seems born directly out of the sounds of *Wings* itself, most especially during high-energy passages when the music trills, swoops, twirls, and dives through the soundscape. Written for either alto saxophone or clarinet, listeners can hear the wind of the player's breath beneath the wings of the bird. In moments of calm, however, when there is less musical activity, when the music seems to slow down or even pause for a moment, a listener might be hard-pressed to conjure a falcon or any image at all without the composer's suggestion, but of course, that was not Tower's intent. In *Wings*, Tower once again explores nature's balance of action and stillness, its freedom of movement, and ultimately its ability to soar to unimaginable and, at the end of the piece, inaudible heights. Tower thinks of her music as "choreographed sound," and *Wings* is nothing if it isn't sounds dancing in the air.[73]

In 1997, nature supplied the imagery for *Rain Waves*, a one-movement, twelve-minute chamber piece for clarinet, violin, and piano.[74] Tower's interest in physics – in actions, reactions, and here more specifically in wave forms – and her familiarity with tropical environments, the result of her years in South America, are evident in her remarks:

> *Rain Waves* explores the motion of a wave form. Starting with a pointillistic rain-like pattern, the notes float upwards and downwards in increasing intensities. In the less staccato and more flowing sections, there is a sense of a wind pushing the notes into longer and wider arched patterns – perhaps like the undulating sheets of rain created in a light tropical rainfall.[75]

In a process characteristic of many of Tower's pieces considered in this chapter, *Rain Waves* begins with a few isolated pitches: in this case, piano and violin start and are quickly joined by the clarinet. Although the ascending tritone D to G♯, followed by a diving major seventh G♯ to A, doesn't establish a key or intimate a harmonic function in a traditional sense (although it could suggest a V–I gesture if the notes were aligned differently), the up–down motion creates an audible wavelike profile; it introduces the outline of an undulating motion that will distinguish the piece on both the surface and structural levels. It may also have provided the sonic starting point for the rain waves of Tower's title. Unlike other works discussed in this chapter, which begin slowly, *Rain Waves* starts very quickly (a quarter note = 120+). Any sense of speed, however, is compromised by the plentiful silence that inhabits the opening four measures. It is only as the texture thickens, articulation changes from staccato to legato, and surface rhythms increase that a listener feels the music being pushed along (example 6.14).

In *Rain Waves*, all three instruments simultaneously sound the same pitches, thus creating a hybrid timbre that blends the percussive qualities of the piano, the friction of a bow on a violin string (which comes through with the repeated figure it plays), and the breath of the clarinet. Timbre remains the primary focus for Joan Tower. At measure 7, the piano introduces an undulating passage of sixteenth notes, which is then reinforced by similarly legato violin and clarinet lines. In a move not seen in any of the works discussed heretofore, the players repeat the first fourteen measures, but now they play the passage *pianissimo*.[76] Repeating the opening music focuses a listener's attention on the particular and isolated moments of sound that chart the longer waves; it also emphasizes the different types of materials constituting the piece. As in other pieces already considered, balance remains

EXAMPLE 6.14 (*above and facing*). *Rain Waves.* By Joan Tower, mm. 1–14.
Copyright © 2000 by Associated Music Publishers, Inc. (BMI). International
copyright secured. All rights reserved. Reprinted by permission.

of paramount importance to Tower; repeating the opening measures provides an introduction that is proportionate to a piece that courses for another eleven minutes.

Rain Waves follows no traditional form, although it does make use of techniques and processes that articulate more conventionally designed musical structures: varied references to important pitches or intervals; juxtaposed passages of loud and soft, and busy and calm music; and extended ascending patterns answered by similarly long descending patterns. As in other works, Tower weaves and melds individual instruments of the ensemble using common notes and echolike effects. Passages that are introduced early in the piece return compressed, or at a new pitch level, or rhythmically altered, but still recognizable as an already-known entity.

Instances when the opening gesture returns but at different pitch levels, in new rhythmic combinations, or in variously modified or inverted combinations occur throughout the piece. Among its most conspicuous returns are at measures 199, 307, 317, and then lastly in the final measure of the piece (325), where the opening pitches, in their original up–down formation, return but are now compressed, accented, and triple *forte*. Again, as in *Snow Dreams*, Tower begins and ends her piece with the same pitch. Some might argue that the leading-tone motion from G♯ to A present in the opening and closing gestures of *Rain Waves* suggests a certain adherence to tonal function, but pitch is neither the driving force behind the piece nor the architect of the structure. *Rain Waves* is a musical exploration of motion in myriad manifestations and intensities, as a local occurrence short-lived and fleeting, and as a shape-defining element whose impact reveals itself only in the moments after the last sounds evaporate.

Big Sky, written in 2000, provides a final exploration of Joan Tower's relationship with the natural world as it manifests itself in music. A seven-minute chamber piece for violin, cello, and piano, it is among her most intimate and moving works, likely because it is directly informed by personal experience. According to the composer's note, "like many young girls . . . I had an obsession with horses." Tower's father bought her a racehorse when they lived in South America, and she "loved this horse and took very good care of it"; in her teens she enrolled in riding school and "learned to jump and hunt." The composer explained:

> *Big Sky* . . . is a piece based on a memory of riding my horse Aymara
> around in the deep valley of La Paz, Bolivia. The valley was surrounded by
> the huge and high mountains of the Andes range. As I rode I looked into a
> vast and enormous sky. It was very peaceful and extraordinarily beautiful.
> We never went over one of these mountains, but if we had, it might have felt
> like what I wrote in this piece.[77]

Big Sky includes many of Tower's signature markings – soft, slow, similar minimal materials to open and close a piece; overlapping gestures that share pitches and patterns among instruments; a form that emerges from the unique relationship of motives, both melodic and rhythmic, and their varied returns; energy that pulses through the work continuing the momentum even through moments of silence; a soundscape that privileges motion, balance, and timbre. That *Big Sky* can share so many qualities with other works and simultaneously be a distinctly meaningful musical statement speaks to

Tower's craft and creativity. *Big Sky* is singularly powerful, persuasive, and inspired.

With the opening *pianissimo, dolce sostenuto* long notes of *Big Sky* uttered first by cello, then violin, and lastly by piano, listeners are drawn into Tower's extraordinary landscape. We can imagine her as a young girl astride Aymara, holding her breath as she slowly surveys her surroundings and takes in the overwhelming beauty of the place. She sits tall in the saddle, her spine is straight, and she cranes her neck to see as far as she can.

Among Tower's achievements in *Big Sky* is the sense of spaciousness that she creates with an intimate trio of players, and she does this within the first measures of the piece using a minimum of resources. One might expect the bigness of the Andean mountain skies to be best evoked by large forces playing loudly and over a long period of time, but Tower is not so much seeking to capture the largeness of the physical environment in sound as she is intent on suggesting how "it might have felt" to be in that environment. A small chamber ensemble can get inside the internal space of feeling.

Among her limited resources are pitch materials, just four pitch classes introduced one at a time – A♭, B♭, B♮, and G – for the first ten measures of the piece. Although it is circumscribed, the pitch pool never feels enclosed or limited. Quite the opposite: the very slow tempo (quarter = c. 42), *pianissimo* dynamic level, strategic use of silence, increasing octave displacement of the pitches, and instruction to play *espressivo* encourage a listener to focus her aural gaze on the few quiet sounds; each one of them enlarges and gains in importance. Using minimal materials and momentum, Tower choreographs an expansive musical space (example 6.15).

Beginning and ending on A♭, the first ten measures create a sonic enclosure analogous to the mountains surrounding the valley. But there is an opening to the La Paz lowlands, and listeners learn of its existence over the course of the piece. With intense long lines and continual upward-reaching gestures, Tower takes listeners "over one of these mountains" and into the "vast and enormous sky" that captivated her as a youth. Instructions to the instrumentalists to play "appassionato," "intensivo," and "espressivo" hint at the composer's fervor for this mountainous expanse. Profoundly moving as Tower's experiences were, however, *Big Sky* never abandons itself to unchecked ecstasy even during extended *fortissimo* passages of rhythmically charged music.

At measure 64 and then again at measure 77, Tower composes glinting moments of sonic luminescence reminiscent of Haydn's famous C-major chord on "Licht" (light) in *The Creation* or Bartók's similar chord at the half-

EXAMPLE 6.15. *Big Sky*. By Joan Tower, mm. 1–10. Copyright © 2000 by
Associated Music Publishers, Inc. (BMI). International copyright secured.
All rights reserved. Reprinted by permission.

way point in *Bluebeard's Castle* when Judith begs Bluebeard to open the fifth
door within his castle. As his kingdom is revealed, the orchestra thunders a
C-major chord, and the stage is consumed in white light.[78] Although Tower
does not employ C major at either measure 64 or 77, the effect is similarly re-
splendent even with her much smaller ensemble.[79] Where Haydn and Bartók
used large performing forces to achieve their results, Tower accomplished
a similar celestial effect with a trio of players. Images come to mind of numerous Hudson River School paintings where artists painted shafts of light

EXAMPLE 6.16. *Big Sky*. By Joan Tower, mm. 75–79. Copyright © 2000 by Associated Music Publishers, Inc. (BMI). International copyright secured. All rights reserved. Reprinted by permission.

streaming through breaks in the clouds hovering high over mountain peaks. In the case of the Hudson River School, light emanating from the heavens was understood to be imbued with specific religious meaning: the landscape so illuminated was especially blessed by the Creator and by extension, so was the nation. While Tower does not proffer any religious or moral message behind *Big Sky*, for all of its passion the music conveys equal parts reverence and wonder (example 6.16).[80]

Like many of Tower's works meter is clearly marked and constantly changing. Freely shifting motion is an essential characteristic of this piece. In addition to myriad meters, numerous tempo changes keep the rhythm fluid. Although an eighth note never moves faster than c. 144, increased surface rhythm, culminating at measure 110, pushes the piece forward to its very slow closing passage (quarter note = 40), which begins just six measures later. Rhythm, while vital and dynamic, is not the focus of this piece; *Big Sky* is about the perception of beautiful vastness.

It may be that Tower's experiences with the natural world, starting at an early age and guided as they were through the loving mentorship of her geologist father, have so imprinted themselves on her being that she doesn't consciously think of nature as a discrete source of inspiration or as an entity outside herself at all. George Tower's work may have unknowingly complicated Tower's sympathies toward early environmental-movement activities. Nonetheless, nature and natural imagery are part of her root system, inscribed on her DNA, present at the very beginning of every creative effort and informing all aspects of her thought and expression whether she bids them or not. Perhaps like the title character in Peter Høeg's 1992 novel *Smilla's Sense of Snow*, who had a "feeling for snow," an "intuitive ice-sense," Tower has her own feeling for natural imagery, an *intuitive* nature-sense.[81] Because Tower starts with such a rich store of nature experiences and imagery, it follows that she finds sympathetic and appropriate titles in nature. If that is the case, Tower is not looking outside herself at all when she names her pieces after rocks, trees, flowers, fields, birds, water, the sky, or weather events. Her titles may simply be the final realization of a creative vision that was always present, even if it was unknown to the composer.[82]

7

Ellen Taaffe Zwilich

On first glance, Ellen Taaffe Zwilich may appear to have the weakest claim on being included in a study that focuses upon composers for whom nature is a recurring source of inspiration or reference, or whose responses to nature are well documented. Indeed, a look at her extensive works list indicates a spirit more at home in abstract musical thought than in music tied to an external idea, or bearing a specific message, or advocating a course of action. Numerous sonatas, trios, quartets, quintets, and septets; over a dozen concerti; and five symphonies, among other pieces, make it easy to assume that Zwilich would have little to contribute to a discussion of American composers and nature. A single piece, however, Symphony No. 4, "The Gardens," suggests the need for a different reading of her position in this study. Zwilich's symphony, while unique within her oeuvre, reflects the range of relations to nature that occurs among these skillful listeners and in the population more generally. That the composer doesn't foreground her environmental consciousness, or leave traces of it in the titles of her works, should not be taken as evidence that she isn't cognizant of the issues involved or doesn't care deeply about them.

Zwilich is the first to acknowledge that she does not consciously look to nature for inspiration, nor does it typically occupy a place in the forefront of her mind. Speaking directly about Symphony No. 4 "The Gardens," Zwilich explained, "I wouldn't have come to the project unless it had been suggested to me. This thing about the Symphony of the Gardens is more philosophical than naturalistic."[1] Yet in "The Gardens" Zwilich speaks quite literally to the project at hand through the voices of SATB and children's choruses. By composing a work that includes a paean to the earth and a pledge to preserve our natural inheritance, Zwilich reflects and projects widely shared attitudes regarding environmental stewardship. The work and a sixty-minute documentary film recording the genesis of its composition that was distributed by PBS in 2000, testify to the reach of efforts to increase mindfulness of the natural world and to the range of composers' responses to nature, whether consciously intended or not. Regarding a visit to the Michigan State University William James Beal Botanical Garden the composer reflected: "I knew I would find the natural beauty very moving; I didn't know that I would find the people who love the gardens and care for them very moving."[2]

Ellen Zwilich was born in Miami, Florida, in 1939 and educated at Coral Gables High School outside of Miami, which had an exceptionally broad and effective music program. She first studied violin and trumpet, her two main instruments, there and enjoyed numerous and varied opportunities to play and arrange music of all kinds. Zwilich graduated with a bachelor's degree in music from the Florida State University and then earned a doctorate in composition from the Juilliard School in New York City. She is an easterner and an urbanite, maintaining homes in both Florida and New York and dividing her time between them. In addition, she travels widely and often. A person of indefatigable energy and infectious goodwill, she recently celebrated her seventieth birthday and shows no signs of slowing down her prodigious pace.

Zwilich is often identified by a number of "firsts": first woman to earn a doctorate from Juilliard in composition (1975); first woman to be awarded a Pulitzer Prize in music (1983 – for Symphony No. 1); first person, man or woman, to occupy the Composer's Chair at Carnegie Hall (1995–1999). At the end of her tenure she was the interviewed by Ara Guzelimian, then senior director and artistic advisor of Carnegie Hall.[3] This three-hour video-taped interview provides the most thorough biographical information available on the composer beyond that which can be gotten online.[4] Zwilich sits on the boards of multiple arts institutions and foundations, has earned dozens of awards, has been the subject of two documentary films, was elected to both the American Academy of Arts and Sciences and the American Academy of Arts and Letters, received honorary doctorates from six colleges and universities, was appointed the Francis Eppes Distinguished Professor in Music at the Florida State University College of Music, and, perhaps most importantly, has had her works performed, recorded, and broadcast across the globe. While Zwilich is her own woman, she has enjoyed the support and encouragement of teachers, colleagues, and associates who have championed her and her music for decades. Her network is wide, deep, and continuous. Like Oliveros and Tower, Zwilich dared to put herself out there, and in the process she found a receptive audience. Zwilich knew she had arrived in 1990 when she discovered that she was the subject of Charles Schulz's October 13 *Peanuts* comic strip.[5]

Over a period of forty years, Ellen Zwilich has developed an identifiable musical voice that captures the eclectic millennial age. Her works are regularly praised for their expert craftsmanship, clarity of design, and timbral richness, but they are also routinely lauded for their palpable warmth, lyricism, and beauty. Although like Tower she began her compositional career writing cerebral, dissonant music, products of what she calls her "post–Second Viennese period," the sudden, soul-wrenching death in 1979 of her husband of ten years, violinist Joseph Zwilich, altered her very being, her way of seeing the world, her sense of what was important. Stunned by the loss, Zwilich didn't write for a time, but when she returned to composition her music was, by her own assessment, emotionally richer and more open and heartfelt. Her friends noticed the difference, and she did too. While capable of writing brain-twisting musical complexities, Ellen Zwilich is more likely to have her music kick up its heels and to allow her sheer joy in music making show, and she doesn't hesitate to seek after the beautiful.[6] A May 2009 review of Zwilich's Fifth Symphony led with the headline "A Composer Not Afraid to Feel." Pointing to "her music's honest emotional quality," Barrymore Laurence Scherer spoke of Zwilich's oeuvre, which "expresses a quiet, humanist skepticism in tune with the temper of our times."[7] Scherer's observation that Zwilich is at one with the times makes a study of her fourth symphony, "The Gardens," a productive undertaking, even if it is her single nature-inspired work. It reflects thinking and hopes shared by many.

Although Zwilich is thoroughly identified with the East Coast, a commission for a large-scale work brought an upper midwestern garden to her attention. When John and Dortha Withrow of Michigan State University commissioned Zwilich to write a major piece celebrating their alma mater and its famous William James Beal Botanical Garden, the place was little known to the composer except by name. She had no investment in it; it held no particular meaning for her. Given those circumstances, Zwilich automatically imagined a quasi-abstract work rooted in the general notion of organicism and growth – an apt concept for a piece intended to honor a garden, and an approach that suited her own preferences to build compositions by developing essential germinating motives.[8] It was only in the process of visiting the East

Lansing campus and becoming acquainted with the grounds and the trees and flowers and the people who tended them that Zwilich grew genuinely attached to the gardens and found herself considering something beyond abstract musical forms or instinctive processes. In walking among the acres of living things she became more mindful of the lessons they contained. Her personal experience enlarged her thinking about nature, its variety, its usefulness, and its vulnerability.

The William James Beal Botanical Garden at Michigan State University was established in 1873 and named for the American botanist, author, and teacher who founded it. It bears the distinction of being "the oldest continuously operating botanical garden of its kind in the United States."[9] Beal intended to create a teaching garden with hands-on opportunities to learn about nature. He prized careful observation above all and taught that value to his students. In her book *Gardens of the Heartland*, Laura C. Martin quotes Beal's student and later son-in-law as saying: "I learned from him the one thing I needed most of all to know. This was to look at life before I talked about it; not to look at it second-hand, by the way of books, but so far as possible to examine the thing itself, and form my own conclusions about it."[10] The necessity of firsthand experience recalls Margaret Fuller's remarks when she visited Niagara Falls and had a chance to interact with the cataract on her own. The garden as Beal envisioned it would be a site for Michigan's native plants, which he insisted should be allowed to grow wild. In 1882, he counted nearly 700 species, and by the time he died in 1924 there were 20,000 species on-site.[11] Today students, scholars, and visitors from around the world enjoy and learn firsthand from thousands of plants and trees, and from demonstration gardens and exhibits. Real fruits from Beal's garden reach beyond their Michigan home through international seed-exchange programs; and metaphorical fruits are heard 'round the world with Zwilich's symphony.

As Martin describes it, "Walking into the garden today is like walking into a living botany textbook. . . . The garden is divided into different 'chapters' so that both academic and casual students can learn quickly and easily. There are four main groups: Plant Families, Useful Plants, Forest Communities, and Landscape Plants."[12] Zwilich's four-movement symphony has an analogous chapterlike structure, even if it is not modeled directly on the groups of plant families at the gardens. Within the Forest Communities, visitors can confront threatened and endangered plants and trees. Among the Useful Plants are individual beds devoted to perfume plants, fiber plants, food plants, flavoring plants, and medicinal plants that introduce observers to the idea of nature as an essential resource for human benefit and consumption. From its inception, the Beal Garden was "an outdoor laboratory for the study and appreciation of plants by students in botany, horticulture, forestry, agriculture, biology, pharmacology, natural science, veterinary science, landscape architecture, anthropology, and art."[13] And so it is today, but it is also much more (figure 7.1).

Tucked in the northern corner of the five-acre site is the section dedicated to endangered and threatened species; it was this spot in particular that captured Zwilich's imagination. In an interview the composer confided that the visit to the gardens of threatened and endangered plants "profoundly affected me." She explained: "Here we are destroying species while contemporaneously finding pharmaceutical uses for those same plants; destroying species that potentially hold something essential and life-saving. We don't know what they might do for the world."[14] Program notes that Zwilich wrote for the premiere performance expand upon those basic ideas. Regarding the first movement Zwilich explained:

> The text of the first movement consists of the Latin names of some threatened or endangered plants in the exhibit in the W. J. Beal Botanical Garden. This garden provides a living example of our human urge to plant and nurture as well as our capacity to uproot and destroy, and I found myself thinking about it long after the day of my visit to the gardens on the campus of Michigan State. When we understand the symbiotic relationship of humans and plants, as exemplified by ancient medicinal remedies derived from the forest, and our contemporary pharmacology (I was reminded of recent headlines about Taxol being discovered in the bark of a 'worthless' tree), it would seem that our human insensitivity to the destruction of our natural heritage is repaid by a terrible foreclosure. Might not the next plant species we allow to vanish forever hold the key to curing a dread human disease? Perhaps this is why, at the musical peak of the first movement it was most natural to let the Latin word "latifolia" evolve into the word 'folia!,' recognizable as the source of our English word 'folly,' and why the end of the movement emphasizes the word 'fragilis!' (fragile).[15]

While Zwilich's comments might be read as emphasizing an anthropomorphic bias and a perspective that values nature primarily for its usefulness to humanity, for how it might best serve human beings, the composer's recognition of the "symbiotic relationship of humans and plants" reflects her broader belief in the interdependence of human and nonhuman nature, a view that has become more widely acknowledged among the general population.

FIGURE 7.1. Ellen Taaffe Zwilich at the W. J. Beal Botanical Garden and Campus Arboretum, with curator and professor of plant biology Frank Telewski. Photo, courtesy of University Relations/Michigan State University. Reprinted by permission.

The presumption of our connectedness relates Zwilich to other composers in this study. Zwilich's note underscores her deep, if not widely known, sense of our responsibility to nature. The thirty-minute symphony also reveals multiple understandings of nature: as a resource useful to humanity; as a site of mystery and spiritual revelation; and as an inheritance in need of preservation. Where other composers may have expressed this range of understanding in several different pieces, Zwilich uses individual movements of her symphony to explore her manifold readings. The composer's perception of the "tragedy of losing plants" became the impetus for the first movement, "Introduction: Litany of Endangered Plants."

Zwilich's visit to the gardens made the abstract specific, and this is nowhere more obvious than in the first movement's recitation of plant names.[16] Consulting a list of the Latin names of plants in the endangered garden, Zwilich selected nine that possessed especially sonorous and rhythmic qualities.[17] Like Oliveros, Zwilich was interested in the music of the language. Starting at measure 20, unison SATB voices begin chanting the nine: *Castanea dentate, Coreopsis palmate, Trillium nivale, Uniola latifolia, Amorpha canescens, Liatris punctata, Silphium perfoliatum, Baptisia lactea,* and *Opuntia fragilis.*

Despite having chosen the word "litany" for her opening catalogue-like chorus, Zwilich explained that she wasn't after religious associations: "Rather than suggest religion specifically, the Latin conjures something ceremonial, something more generally spiritual."[18] Zwilich is not arguing for a God-infused nature, but for a deeply respectful recognition of nature's particularity. And indeed, the recitation of names conjures a kind of sacred ritual. Four *fortissimo* strokes of the timpani that are reinforced by accented *pizzicato* figures in the strings introduce and then accompany the chorus; they simulate a cosmic clock inexorably marking the passage of time, perhaps before the endangered plants disappear completely. Although the music will be considered more thoroughly later in the chapter, it is helpful to understand how Zwilich conceives the opening of the work, as it tells much about the forces informing her piece and the way it holds together (example 7.1).

The movement begins with repeated chanting of "*Castenea dentata,*" the Latin name for the American chestnut. Although, as Zwilich acknowledges, she did not consciously seek to identify her Symphony No. 4 as an American work, she could hardly have chosen an endangered plant more closely tied to the nation's early history or at the forefront of present-day restoration projects than the chestnut. Here was a tree revered for its majestic beauty, whose over-

EXAMPLE 7.1. "Litany of Endangered Plants," mm. 19–23. Symphony No. 4 *"The Gardens."* By Ellen Taaffe Zwilich. Copyright © 2000 by Theodore Presser Company. Used with permission of Theodore Presser Company.

all size and strength made it the perfect tree for railroad ties, telegraph poles, barn beams, and house construction in the nineteenth century. Its handsome wood endeared it to furniture builders and instrument makers, who found it easy to work and welcomed its rot-resistance.[19] Its fruit appealed to humans and animals alike. The tree was found throughout the east in over 200 million acres of forests from Maine to Florida, and as far west as the Ohio Valley. The American Chestnut Foundation has estimated that "4 billion American chestnuts, 1/4 of the hardwood tree population, grew within this range."[20] By numbers alone, it was a symbolic American tree.

Zwilich's choice of *Castenea dentate* ties her not only to the early history of the nation in general, but also to America's nature-writing tradition more specifically, and this requires a digression. In *Rural Hours*, Susan Fenimore Cooper's narrative of four seasons' worth of observations of nature in up-state New York, the author mentioned the chestnut in twenty-eight different contexts, so ubiquitous, eye-catching, and important was the tree to her sense of the local environment.[21] Her entry for Wednesday, July 11 (1849), for instance, talked of the beauty of the tree: "They are one of our richest trees when in blossom, and being common about the lake, are very ornamental to the country, at this season; they look as though they wore a double crown of sunshine about their flowery heads."[22] In autumn Cooper was taken aback by the "shadeless mass of gold-color, from the highest to the lowest branch."[23] Arguing for "thinning woods and not blasting them; [and] clearing only such ground as is marked for immediate tillage," Cooper advocated "planting one or two chestnuts, or oaks, or beeches, near the gates or bars; leaving a few others scattered about every field to shade the cattle in summer."

Her entry for Wednesday, August 30 (1848), demonstrates Cooper's detailed knowledge of nature in the area around Cooperstown. While walking in the woods she noted "an old branchless trunk of the largest size, in a striking position, where it looked like a broken column." Upon closer inspection Cooper observed:

> The shaft rose, without curve or a branch, to the height of perhaps forty feet, where it had been abruptly shivered, probably in some storm. The tree was a chestnut, and the bark of a clear, unsullied gray; walking around it, we saw an opening near the ground, and to our surprise found the trunk hollow, and entirely charred within, black as a chimney, from the root to the point where it was broken off. It frequently happens that fire steals into the heart of an old tree, in this way, by some opening near the roots, and burns away the inside, leaving merely a gray outer shell. One would not ex-

pect the bark to be left in such cases, but the wood at the heart seems more
inflammable than the outer growth. What ever be the cause, such shafts are
not uncommon about our hills, gray without, charred within.[24]

Cooper speculated about what likely happened to this tree based upon
her observations of similar occurrences "about [her] hills," and years of research into the natural history of the area. Throughout the 300-plus-page
account, Cooper simultaneously exhibited aesthetic appreciation, national
pride, the disciplined observations of a scientist, the moral tone of a natural
theologian, and the conscience of a modern-day ecologist. Her multiple perspectives presaged Zwilich's 150 years later. Cooper aspired to "contribute to
the 'moral and intellectual progress' of her young nation"[25] and characterized
caring for nature as looking "beyond ourselves" and "speak[ing] of a generous
mind."[26] While Zwilich doesn't speak in terms of moral progress, her message
is quite similar. As will be seen, in the fourth movement of her symphony,
Zwilich will echo Cooper's charge to look beyond ourselves.

Not surprisingly, Cooper was not alone in her feelings for the tree. Thoreau also spoke affectionately of the chestnut in 1854 in a passage in *Walden*:
"When chestnuts were ripe I laid up half a bushel for winter. It was very
exciting at that season to roam the then boundless chestnut woods of Lincoln, – they now sleep their long sleep under the railroad." He talked of climbing the trees to shake loose their fruit, and of the "bouquet which scented
the whole neighborhood" when it was in flower.[27] History shows that neither
Thoreau nor Cooper was the first American writer to appreciate the many
qualities of the chestnut. In 1841, the tree's place in American mythology had
been secured in the opening lines of Henry Wadsworth Longfellow's poem
"The Village Blacksmith": "Under the spreading chestnut tree / The village
smithy stands." Well into the twentieth century, many a schoolchild would
be required to recite the eight-stanza poem by heart, and Zwilich was one of
them.[28]

Thoreau returned to a discussion of the American chestnut in his last
natural-history writings. Here the prescient poet warned of the "special pains"
that would be necessary to "secure and encourage" this tree and others also
threatened.[29] It was as if he anticipated the blight, first detected in New York
in 1904, which nearly wiped out the entire species. Today the tree is making a
comeback thanks to the dedicated work of scientists from the United States
and China who have succeeded in breeding a blight-resistant strain of the
American chestnut, just one example of the global efforts required to save
the environment.

Like Cooper, Thoreau's close kinship with nature can be found almost anywhere in his writings but is perhaps most succinctly stated in a journal entry dated October 23, 1855, where the Concord woodsman observed, "Old trees are our parents and our parents' parents."[30] This mid-nineteenth-century reading survived into the twentieth century and made its way into "The Gardens." The theme of humankind as nature's progeny reappears in the opening text of Zwilich's final movement, where the children's chorus resolutely promises, "We will protect our heritage." It is a small leap to suggest that protecting and nurturing plants, trees, and flowers is closely tied with the survival of humanity itself. And here is a recurring theme of the modern-day environmental movement. So ubiquitous is this trope, it became the foundational idea of Zwilich's work, without the composer consciously manipulating the idea.

A final brief digression ties mid-nineteenth-century nature writing, art, and science to Zwilich's piece. In her book *Nature and Culture: American Landscape and Painting, 1825–1875,* art historian Barbara Novak explained the basic confluence of nature, art, and science with religion in the history of the nation. "The gathering and rendering of plants – part artistic, part scientific – was a prominent part of the earliest American explorations."[31] Regarding Mark Catesby, an eighteenth-century English explorer who drew pictures of freshly gathered plants and then "apologized for his primitivism" as he "was not bred a Painter," she observed, "This interaction of the empirical eye with the categories of natural history became a major theme of the nineteenth-century artist. The early urge to label, with its emphasis on classification, persisted longer in America than abroad, as Americans held tenaciously to the 'artificial' system of Linnaeus. Since this was bound to absolute fixity of species, the American devotion to this concept and to its religious implications is easily understood."[32] As Zwilich's singers chant their binomial Latin plant names, Linnaeus's hierarchical system of classifications persists and so too do, perhaps, their quasi-religious implications.[33] Mid-nineteenth-century arguments for an evolutionary reading of nature challenged the idea of hard lines separating species, but such thinking and the well-established idea of nature as a mirror in which human beings were reflected and deified became essential to Emerson's version of Transcendentalism. Natural history was meaningful to the degree it expressed human history.

Tying one's heritage to nature was a goal for both individuals and the young nation in the nineteenth century, and science offered a way to do this. Pointing to the work of botanists, biologists, and geologists, America's vast wildernesses were presented as a pristine laboratory in which to observe the earth's ancient geological past. Here was something that Europe's civilization and culture couldn't match. Regular references in the W. J. Beal Botanical Garden literature to the site as an "outdoor laboratory" maintain this vision of nature and the nation. Rereading America's potentially frightening and primitive territories as untouched examples of God's handiwork helped America reinterpret itself to the world. What could have been a deficit became a unique and divine asset.[34]

Zwilich's symphony participates in these traditions and still others. In addition to recalling nineteenth-century art and literature about nature, the opening movement conjures a sacred work written in 1930 by Igor Stravinsky, his *Symphony of Psalms* for orchestra and chorus. The three psalms Stravinsky used made no specific references to nature, beyond the metaphorical ones in Psalm 150 to "Praise God in his *sanctuary*; praise him in his mighty *firmament*," but Zwilich's creation of a sound world similar to Stravinsky's brings the indisputable sanctity of the earlier work to bear on her own.[35] Large-scale comparisons between the pieces go beyond symphonic forces, the use of Latin, and overall mood. Both works include not only choruses, but children's choruses.[36] Pulsing rhythms undergird extremely legato vocal lines in the first movements of Symphony No. 4 and *Symphony of Psalms*. Voices enter in unison in both works and within a few measures expand to four parts. Where Stravinsky uses solo voices or parts singing in octaves to contrast with the multipart choral sound, Zwilich alternates octave chant sections with punctuating fuller chords. Both composers use fourths and fifths, intervals rich with early polyphonic sacred music connotations, and both movements build similarly to *fortissimo* closes. Whereas *Symphony of Psalms* was composed "to the glory of GOD,"[37] Zwilich's "The Gardens" was composed to "celebrate" what some might argue to be the handiwork of the Creator.[38] Without consciously intending either, in Zwilich's symphony spirituality and modern environmentalism come together in sound.

"The Gardens" starts out majestically. Celli and string basses sustain a pedal-tone A while brass and percussion deliver a sharply etched fanfare figure that is echoed in the upper strings. The heraldic double-dotted eighth-and thirty-second-note figure that opens the first movement will become a simple dotted eighth and sixteenth in the fourth movement when it articulates the word "heritage."[39] While the symphony is unified in a general programmatic way via the overarching theme of nature, Zwilich also creates artistic unity in more traditional ways by harmonic, motivic, and rhythmic behavior. She preserves musical tradition as she employs organically informed compositional techniques and argues for environmental preservation. The composer sets us up to understand that her symphony is about inheritance, musical and otherwise – what we inherit and what we bequeath – and we can trace the bequest through the music.

The bright-sounding glockenspiel, one of the bell-like instruments so important to Zwilich's timbral palette, signals the composer's ultimately positive message. But it is not a wholly optimistic work; there is much of the tragic in the opening movement, and it reflects Zwilich's realization of the precariousness of our relationship with nature. Perhaps this is the skepticism to which Scherer referred in his review of her later work. She interleaves her environmental concerns in numerous ways, but one of the more seamless is in her manipulation of the text. As the composer explained, to underscore the "folly" of our past attitudes toward nature, she redivided and re-accented the Latin word "folia" (leaves, or foliage) from *Uniola latifolia*, which in its initial appearances she had set as a two-syllable word, "fol ia" (see measures 35–46). Starting at measure 48, however, the chorus chides FOL I a, FOL I a, FOL I a, diminishing from *fortissimo* to *forte* to *piano*.[40] As anger and outrage subside to grief, Zwilich makes her point: we have erred[41] (example 7.2).

But Zwilich is not one to rant, wallow, or scold. She and her music move on. At measure 74, the opening unison chant music reappears a sixth higher, now sung as *"Baptisia lactea"* (milky wild indigo), the eighth of the nine named plants. As the movement comes to a close, the chorus cites the final plant: *Opuntia fragilis*, commonly known as the fragile or brittle prickly pear. Zwilich zeros in on that part of the name that allows her to speak her mind and to impress upon listeners the urgency of the cause. Our relationship with nature is a fragile one. Seven times the chorus reminds us, "Fragilis!" (example 7.3).

If Zwilich's music initially suggested that she was grieved to learn of the endangered state of so many plants, her music tells us she is now committed to action. Listeners feel her resolve as the orchestra joins together on a final *fortissimo* F♯-minor chord. There is no fading into the distance, no slinking away, no ambiguity. Zwilich tells percussionists: "Damp anything still ringing."[42] She has laid down the gauntlet and taken a stand.

The second movement, "Meditation on Living Fossils," is an instrumental reflection on a different exhibit at the Beal Botanical Garden. Zwilich explained:

EXAMPLE 7.2 (*above and facing*). "Litany of Endangered Plants," mm. 43–54. Symphony No. 4 *"The Gardens."* By Ellen Taaffe Zwilich. Copyright © 2000 by Theodore Presser Company. Used with permission of Theodore Presser Company.

EXAMPLE 7.3. "Litany of Endangered Plants," mm. 84–94. Symphony No. 4 *"The Gardens"*
By Ellen Taaffe Zwilich. Copyright © 2000 by Theodore Presser Company.
Used with permission of Theodore Presser Company.

> I found the "Living Fossils" exhibit in the Beal garden particularly moving
> and exciting – the magnificence of the ancient trees; the notion of rebirth;
> the living continuity with the deep past; the mystery of it all. This inspired a
> purely musical and personal meditation that became the second movement.[43]

During Zwilich's visit she saw a dawn redwood, *Metasequoia glyptostroboides*, a variety of sequoia that grows to over 200 feet. The tree had flourished during the Miocene epoch and was thought to be extinct until its rediscovery in China in the early 1940s. Since then it has been called a "living fossil." In the PBS film and in notes Zwilich wrote for the recording of Symphony No. 4, she spoke of a "deep, deep connection with the past" that she experienced in this garden.[44] The past became part of her present. To capture the seamlessness of time, Zwilich composed an expanded musical moment with sounds that seemingly emerge from nowhere and everywhere simultaneously.

Shimmering *pianissimo* tam-tam reverberations and then similarly soft celli and cantabile basses slowly rise up as if from the ground itself. We hear "the magnificence of the ancient trees" in the deep, quietly dignified music of the string basses, but only gradually attend to their presence. Over the course of eight measures they rise from low F♯ to C♯ above middle C, before sinking down two octaves and coming to rest on C. Ultimately their pitch path will prove to be structurally significant. Murmuring flutes and a clarinet flicker into our consciousness and disappear. Their music recalls a prominent melodic fragment heard initially in the "Litany." A sizzle cymbal comments and is gone. Zwilich gives us little to mark the passage of time or to locate us in a particular place; rather, the music suggests some ancient, other world, one beyond our ability to comprehend, perhaps one where the dawn redwood first grew. Consistent, however, with Zwilich's preferences for tightly structured large forms, she connects the final F♯ of the first movement with the first note of the second movement. There is no harmonic break. Throughout the "Meditation," Zwilich refers to melodic and rhythmic gestures that characterized the "Litany" and in so doing recalls her earlier clearly articulated concerns in this untexted, abstract second section.[45] As public and outspoken as the first movement was, this movement is private and introspective. Listeners get to hear Zwilich's personal meditation. Initially the movement is characterized by subdued sounds of all kinds: muted strings and brass, and woodwinds that mutter extended, low trill-like figures. Zwilich composes voices for the living fossils, but they speak from the distance of ages past and are barely audible. When horns and trumpet enter at measure 29 with a figure recalling the

EXAMPLE 7.4. "Meditation on Living Fossils," mm. 6–13. Symphony No. 4 *"The Gardens."*
By Ellen Taaffe Zwilich. Copyright © 2000 by Theodore Presser Company.
Used with permission of Theodore Presser Company.

earlier flute passage, the dynamic level rises and clear accents and repetitive
rhythms mark the passage of time. Zwilich brings the past into the present
(example 7.4).

Although F♯ returns to a place of prominence at measure 56 in the string
bass, the pitch motion first observed in the opening string bass solo forecasts
the overall harmonic motion of the entire movement: the second movement
will end on C.[46] When "Meditation" eventually fades from our hearing, soft
tam-tams and bass drum strokes return listeners to the ambiguous other-
world that opened the movement. The ending of this movement is as equivocal
as the previous movement's was decisive. Closing on C creates a structural tritone relationship with the F♯ that had opened the movement. While harmonic

ambiguity may provide an apt analogue for the problematic environmental issues Zwilich addresses in the larger symphony, the use of a tritone in this movement may speak more directly to the ambiguity of what is past and what is present.[47] When walking among "living fossils," the question can't be far from one's mind.

With the litany and meditation, Zwilich simultaneously reveals her pragmatic and contemplative understandings of nature. She appreciates both the science and the mystery of nature, and she understands the necessity of finding her place within the larger environment. The third movement is more clearly a celebration of the beauty of the natural world.

In "A Pastoral Journey," the vocalists return, and this time they muse on two ideas inspired by lines from the Bible, the book of Matthew, chapter 6, verses 28–29: "Behold the lilies of the fields. They toil not, they spin not, but Solomon in all his glory was not adorned like one of these." Zwilich explains: "Rather than a depiction of the many magnificent gardens at Michigan State University, the third movement simply offers a musical celebration of them. For me, this became a kind of spiritual journey parallel to the musical one. Freely adapted from a line in the Bible, the text serves as an integral part of the musical exploration."[48] Without previously ascribing religious meaning or significance to nature, in conversations, in filmed interviews, or in any of her works, Zwilich's experience at the gardens, nonetheless, compelled her to engage with religious texts, analogies, and themes. In the documentary film, Zwilich explained there was "something of richness, and beauty, and wonderful form" in the gardens. "I think those of us who write music are awed by the kind of form and evolution and growth you find in nature."[49] She allowed herself to be awed.

The composer is clear that she is not after a literal "depiction" of anything, and indeed, like many composers of her generation she takes pains to clarify that she didn't seek close programmatic musicalizations of places or phenomena. But capturing the celebratory mood of the brightly colored lilies is front and center in the sounds; the music alternately shivers with delight, bounces weightlessly, struts, and rings out. Zwilich revels in the beauty and richness of the Beal gardens. In "A Pastoral Journey," nature simultaneously summons religious associations with the text and excites a purely aesthetic experience with the sounds. As a composer drawn to traditional musical genres and structures, she feels a special kinship with the form, evolution, and organic growth at work in nature. Zwilich hears the music of the gardens and captures it in various effects as well: string harmonics, glissandi, instructions to the brass and later violas to play "bell-like,"[50] and directions to the singers to "hum."[51] She is precise in her intentions. At one point the composer tells the brass to play "into [their] stands,"[52] and at another she instructs instrumentalists to "keep ringing through fermata."[53] Zwilich uses an assortment of cymbals, tubular bells, and handbells played by the children to create shimmering, lingering effects. In "A Pastoral Journey," Zwilich is immersed in and swept away by nature as it is revealed in the gardens.

The "Journey" begins with the outline of a C-major arpeggio that connects it with the final C of the second movement, and also with a brass fanfare that recalls the opening mood of the first movement. Dotted rhythms that dominated the "Litany" become background commentary in the "Pastoral Journey." Glissandi that had behaved in a purely accompanimental role in the second movement are now a featured effect and reappear at prominent places throughout the third movement.[54] An entire melody first heard in the "Litany" at the introduction of the supercharged phrase *Uniola latifolia* (measure 34) is augmented and hummed by a unison chorus in "A Pastoral Journey." The third movement recollects all that Zwilich has observed in the gardens, and listeners understand that that experience has been multifaceted and perhaps even overflowing. The piece has moved far beyond her initial quasi-abstract imaginings.

"Behold the lilies of the fields" rings out in *forte* octaves sung by the four-part chorus at measure 56; their announcement heralds the newly important pitch E.[55] The remainder of the text is declaimed in similar octaves until the line "was not adorned" at measure 92, where the text compares the beauty of the lily to King Solomon. At this point Zwilich *adorns* what had been a simple declarative delivery with imitative, overlapping vocal entrances. With each iteration the composer reconsiders the eloquent, understated beauty of the lily, a common flower. When the same text reappears (at measure 219), the contrapuntal texture returns as well, but these are the only occasions that deviate from the simplest unison choral writing.

Immediately after the imitative passage describing Solomon's adornment, Zwilich moves to an *a cappella* unison on the line "like *one* of these." Without any instrumental accompaniment, the unison chorus becomes a single entity, together alone. We focus upon and hear the abundant beauty of a single common flower. Zwilich is not above employing tried-and-true techniques to communicate her text, including word painting. This device, first used during the Renaissance, pairs musical activity with the sound and meaning of the word being sung. When overused it becomes little more than a gimmick, but when applied thoughtfully it has the power to bind music and text intimately and supercharge the meaning of the sounds. Zwilich has supercharged the message. Throughout the movement, voices and instruments alternate and share a number of similar gestures, creating an effortless weave of text and music. Among the most effective instances of shared materials is a descending scalar passage that makes its first appearance accompanying the words "Solomon in all his glory" (example 7.5).

Vocalists sing the descending scale a second time as they lead out of the preceding counterpoint on the word "adorned."[56] The third time the same passage appears, voices sing, "Behold the lilies of the fields," but in this instance they are joined by trumpets.[57] At measure 198, tubular bells, sounding very much like distant church bells, ring out an augmented version of the same descending pattern. The bells repeat their passage another four times and reinforce, deliberately or not, the connection of nature and religion in these gardens.

Zwilich also commands listeners to "Behold" in both vocal and instrumental parts. Immediately after the initial vocal entrance at measure 56, handbells and brass imitate the voices with their own assertive repeated pitch "E." At measure 151, horns are instructed to play their two chords "bell-like"; as they do, we hear the echo of the vocalists' admonition to "Behold." A similar instance of instrumental ventriloquism occurs at measure 167 when tubular bells strike out two consecutive octaves. The composer speaking through her music insists that listeners look around them: "Behold!" Zwilich is obvious in her desire to integrate voices and instruments. At measure 189, the unison chorus hums a melody based upon an earlier one heard for the first time in the "Litany." While in both appearances instruments accompany the vocal melody, in the third movement the instrumentalists are directed to "blend into [the] chorus."[58] The same holds true for the next joint appearance at measure 203. Zwilich's programmatic note "the text serves as an integral part of the musical exploration"[59] is made clear before our very eyes. Using this last opportunity to impress upon listeners her desire that they heed nature, Zwilich ends her movement with trumpets, handbells, tubular bells, and strings all singing out two iterations of the chorus's initial pitch E, the one where they first commanded listeners to "Behold!" Pay attention. Look. There is no need for words; the music is the message.

"The Children's Promise," movement IV, provides still more insight into Zwilich's thinking about nature as it was awakened and shaped by her experiences at the Beal garden. As the composer explained:

EXAMPLE 7.5. "A Pastoral Journey," mm. 86–89. Symphony No. 4 *"The Gardens."*
By Ellen Taaffe Zwilich. Copyright © 2000 by Theodore Presser Company.
Used with permission of Theodore Presser Company.

The final movement was inspired by the Michigan 4-H Children's Garden, a place of powerful beauty (the replica of Monet's garden at Giverny) and delightful education (the A, B, C, garden; the Pizza Garden). I was moved by the care given to helping children understand their need to cherish and preserve the natural world they inherit. I asked Erik LaMont for a short and simple text freely interpreting a Native American lyric for the children's chorus, and used Latin names of plants in the Children's Garden for the adult chorus.[60]

LaMont's "short and simple text" is a pledge: "We will protect our heritage; nourish our plants and trees; nourish from root to bough; leave a verdant earth; gather our corn and herbs; gather from forest to plow." The final chorus ends with repetitions of the promise "We will leave a verdant earth."

Pairing the children's and adult choruses, Zwilich has the youth lead the way. They draw the adults to their concerns with the result that the adults adopt their pledge. The idea of children leading the way suggests the last line of a biblical verse taken from the book of Isaiah, chapter 11, verse 6: "The wolf shall dwell with the lamb, and the leopard shall lie down with the kid, and the calf and the lion and the fatling together, and *a little child shall lead them.*" The composer makes no reference to biblical verses, but the notion of learning from children and recognizing their wisdom is one that Zwilich would embrace, and she doesn't shy away from suggesting spiritual connections. By referring to a Native American lyric as a source for her own message, she invests the movement with the spiritual relationship to nature that is regularly ascribed to the first dwellers of the continent.[61]

After a brief fanfare figure whose dotted rhythm recalls the opening of the first movement (while simultaneously anticipating the word "heritage"), the children enter in unison singing: "We will protect our heritage. We will nourish our plants and trees." At measure 28, SATB adult voices chant a new set of Latin plant names reinforcing the connection with the first-movement litany. But as the children continue to enumerate all they promise to do, the adults appear overwhelmed by the simple intensity of their pledge and make it their own: "We will, we will leave a verdant earth" (example 7.6).

Thereafter, the adults are part owners in the children's promise. At measure 80, adult women's voices join with the children's, and at measure 106, all singers, men, women, and children join in an ecstatic "We will, we will leave a verdant earth." Their affirmation explodes into joyous music. As the children promise to enrich the earth, the divisi adult chorus enriches the musical texture. Thereafter, the recitation of Latin plant names becomes more than a

EXAMPLE 7.6 (*above, facing, and next page*). "The Children's Promise," mm. 53–67. Symphony No. 4 *"The Gardens."* By Ellen Taaffe Zwilich. Copyright © 2000 by Theodore Presser Company. Used with permission of Theodore Presser Company.

taxonomic exercise; the names are released from their exclusive scientific identities and become part of a greater endeavor: that of safeguarding the earth.
If the text addresses the moral dilemma introduced in the "Litany" of endangered plants, the music resolves harmonic tensions that motivated, connected,
and propelled the four movements forward. The initial A that anchored the
opening of the first movement returns to close the symphony. A consummate
craftsperson, Zwilich revisits melodies, rhythms, timbres, and gestures that
characterized the previous three movements. The music is formally tight and
unified, growing out of materials first introduced in the opening movement.
As the composer's thinking about nature has evolved and coalesced, so too
does the symphony. Here is the "wonderful organic form" that Zwilich sees
everywhere in the gardens; she has made it music.[62]

Ellen Zwilich's symphonic celebration of a garden and the uniqueness
of that work within her oeuvre raise a number of issues. For much of the
nineteenth century, gardens contained the sum of many middle-class women's
interactions with nature. Proximity to the home, freedom from wilderness
dangers, and aesthetic character rendered the contents of the cultivated private garden the entire curriculum of many a woman's education about the
flora and fauna of the natural world; it was also the one place where she
could be guaranteed a solitary experience with nature – molded, shaped, and
constructed as it was. Young girls, fortunate to attend a progressive school
such as the Troy Female Seminary, where the botanist Almira Hart Lincoln
Phelps taught, and which devoted considerable time to training students in a
scientific appreciation of flowers, plants, trees, or birds and other small creatures, developed a larger and more systematic understanding of the variety
of the natural environment. Although their botanical training was in many
ways equivalent to that which their male siblings received, young girls were
not encouraged to wander alone in the out-of-doors, to contemplate nature
free from shaping commentaries, or to venture beyond what was considered
a safe distance. The garden, in other words, became an outdoor domestic
space; barely an extension of the private, indoor sphere deemed the woman's
domain. Cherished for its beauty, as well as the lessons it contained, it was
still a "circumscribed firmament."[63]

It is noteworthy then that the world-traveling, internationally applauded
composer, who regularly commutes thousands of miles between her homes,
who is a creature of the cultivated, urban East, and who has succeeded, by any
measure, in a profession dominated by males, was profoundly inspired by a
garden, a place that has historically represented a much-valued but ostensibly

limited site for women. For Zwilich, the garden expanded her thinking and her world.

The particular garden that excited her was, of course, not an extension of a private, domestic sphere, but the creation of a highly regarded trained botanist who was also a faculty member at a university. It was Professor Beal's creation, with its endangered specimens and native plants, that brought her face-to-face with current environmental concerns and stirred her imagination. And this, according to philosopher Stephanie Ross, is what gardens do best.

In *What Gardens Mean*, Ross characterized a garden as "a springboard for investigating important and enduring philosophical issues." And readers will recall that Zwilich characterized her own interest as "more philosophical than naturalistic." Ross asked: "How are gardens experienced by those who view them or walk through them? How does imagination enter in? What sorts of messages can they convey? Can they have moral force?[64] Ross's study becomes a springboard for a few final considerations of Zwilich's symphony.

According to the composer, when she was commissioned to write a piece about the Michigan State University gardens, she "began thinking along the line of natural processes: the scientific side of nature." Such a response seems in character with the thoughtful, well-read, pragmatic, and ultimately accessible composer. Science, however, took a back seat to deep reflection and then celebration when Zwilich got to the campus. Her experience among the acres of flowers, plants, and trees shifted her focus away from a purely intellectual investigation toward one that embraced her visceral response. Something changed when the empathetic and imaginative musician partook of the sensorially explosive sights and smells of the Beal gardens and considered the costs of mindless human actions to the environment. Zwilich talked of "a spiritual experience writing the symphony."[65] What powers did the gardens possess to so move this seasoned, creative soul?

Ross observes: "Gardens yield prodigal pleasures. Their bounty includes not only fruits and flowers, vegetables and herbs, but also beauty, respite, and reflection."[66] The opportunity for respite and reflection seems especially significant to busy urbanites, such as Zwilich, whose daily contact with restorative, sylvan scenes is limited and whose dependence upon nature is not always apparent. As Louise Talma understood, modern routines distance most people from what is traditionally considered "nature" and encourage thinking of it as a separate entity, something outside ourselves or confined to our minds. To be in the midst of growing things, as Zwilich was, and to discover the intricate relationships between plants and humans is to understand one's collaborative presence in nature. It is no longer exclusively a mental construct or a PBS series; it is us and what we are, and music can bridge the divide and drive home the point.[67]

In the film documenting the composition of "The Gardens," Zwilich offered some final thoughts on the larger meaning of the work: "I believe a composer belongs at the center of the musical world, not on some fringe, locked up somewhere in an ivory tower writing music that no one wants to hear. We belong in the thick of things, with all that that entails. This has been a particularly profound example of something that involves music and a composer, and something very basic and wonderful about life."[68] While nature doesn't find its way into the titles of her pieces and is not an obvious source of inspiration for her music, Ellen Zwilich nonetheless created a personal response to an experience in nature that resonates with broad segments of the nation's population. Keeping nature an abstracted other allows human beings to ignore their complicity in its condition. Being in and with nature compels a confrontation with one's intimate role in the ecological enterprise. Symphony No. 4 speaks of a fully connected natural world, one where humans are part of something larger than themselves.

PART THREE

Beyond the EPA and Earth Day

VICTORIA BOND, LIBBY LARSEN, EMILY DOOLITTLE

The final group of composers includes two women born in the years closely following World War II, Victoria Bond (b. 1945) and Libby Larsen (b. 1950), and one woman born two years after the celebration of the first Earth Day, Emily Doolittle (b. 1972).[1] Tumultuous changes that swept through American society beginning in the mid-1960s divide these women into subgenerations popularly known as "baby boomers," a term used to describe people born roughly between 1945 and 1964, and Gen Xers, those born from the mid-1960s through 1981 or 1982.[2] While just twenty-seven years separate the births of Bond and Doolittle, the range and reach of economic, political, and social transformations that occurred during that time upended traditional assumptions and attitudes regarding sexual behavior, racial (in)equality, religious beliefs, gender roles, and the relationship of humans and an ever-expanding environment to a degree unmatched in recent history. The number of government agencies, acts, and initiatives that were created between the 1940s and the 1970s and dedicated to some aspect of national and/or environmental health speaks to one aspect of a paradigm shift in public thinking.

In 1950, Congress created the National Science Foundation (NSF) "to promote the progress of science; to advance the national health, prosperity, and welfare; to secure the national defense."[3] Its formation was, in part, the government's response to the barely won armaments race of World War II. And then another race, this one conducted in space, consumed part of the nation's attention for the latter part of the 1950s and 1960s as the United States found itself behind the Soviet Union in space technology. The Soviet's *Sputnik 1*, launched October 4, 1957, begat America's *Explorer 1*, which was launched on January 31, 1958. When, eleven years later, *Apollo 11* landed on the moon (July 20, 1969) and Neil Armstrong took his first bouncing steps on its surface, the United States had won that race too.

But other scientific initiatives were not as successful, despite their enthusiastic application. Suburban baby boomers were sprayed with DDT as they enjoyed their summer barbecues, compliments of mosquito-eradication programs. Children from Houston to the Hamptons danced in the fine white mist assured by their parents, who had been assured by the government, that there was nothing to fear. The long-term dangers of chemical-sprayed hot dogs and hamburgers, and the impact of DDT on biodiversity would eventually convince Washington, D.C., to find alternative methods of controlling the disease-carrying insect. DDT would be banned from general use in 1972 by the Environmental Protection Agency, which had been formed in December of 1970.[4] The EPA came into being just eight months after the first Earth Day in April 1970. The Environmental Quality Improvement Act was passed in 1970, and NOAA, the National Oceanic and Atmospheric Administration, was created that same year as well. It brought together three of the oldest agencies dedicated to the nation's physical health: the United States Coast and Geodetic Survey (founded in 1807), the Weather Bureau (founded in 1870), and the Bureau of Commercial Fisheries (founded in 1871). But not everyone waited for government reports or group protests to sound the alarm about the nation's toxic ways.

Gen Xers were born into a world informed by Rachel Carson (1907–1964). The marine biologist, author, and environmental champion became a one-woman CR (consciousness-raising) group determined to change people's thinking about their place in the world.[5] A series of books starting with *Under the Sea-World* in 1941, followed by *The Sea around Us* in 1952 and *The Edge of the Sea* in 1955, won Carson an audience of believers. When *Silent Spring* appeared in 1962, the soft-spoken call to action changed the way large numbers of Americans thought about the environment and their relation to it. With civil and social unrest roiling all around, who could not respond to: "There was once a town in the heart of America where all life seemed to live in harmony with its surroundings."[6] Although numerous attempts were made to discredit

Carson as a dilettante and an alarmist, increasing regard for her careful work brought the scientist face-to-face with Congress.[7] In 1963, she testified on behalf of the intricate and undeniable connections between human and environmental health. The Clean Air Act passed later that year.[8] *Silent Spring* had become essential reading. That it was written by a female marine biologist, the possessor of a graduate degree in zoology from Johns Hopkins University, is not inconsequential in a study that has as one of its themes the relationships between women, educational opportunities, and nature. That the book grew out of Carson noticing an ever-quieter spring underscores the essential role of careful listening: she listened, and people listened to her.

The lessons learned by listening have been embraced well beyond music and environmental-studies classrooms. In 1981, Roger Fisher and William Ury, former Harvard Law School faculty who specialized in negotiation, published what became a best-selling book on the subject, *Getting to Yes: Negotiating Agreement without Giving In*. The book is a guide for getting what one wants; however, a large section of chapter 2, "The Method," is devoted to understanding the need for listening, which the authors agree is difficult, "especially under the stress of an ongoing negotiation."[9] They observed that "often people don't seem to pay enough attention" to what is being said. While I would not argue that the Fisher and Ury text addresses all aspects of the ideal relationship humans ought to develop with the natural world (or with each other), the authors' acknowledgment that attentive listening is the starting point for any successful negotiation underscores the moral of *Silent Spring* and the instructive power of music. Whether to talk down terrorists, close a business deal, or to increase awareness of one's place in the larger environmental enterprise, the impact of skillful listening is limitless.

The years between 1972 and 1977 saw a series of actions that focused more specifically upon animal health and, pertinent to this study and Emily Doolittle's piece *Social sounds from whales at night*, legislation directed at marine mammals. The Marine Mammal Protection Act (1972), the Marine Protection Research and Sanctuaries Act (1972), the Federal Water Pollution Control Amendment (1973), the Endangered Species Act (1973), the Deepwater Ports and Waterways Safety Act (1974), and the Fish and Wildlife Coordination Act (1974) were enacted in close succession. In 1976 the Center for Whale Research was created in the San Juan Islands of Washington State to monitor orca whale populations. In 1977, a teenaged Maris Sidenstecker, who would later become a marine biologist and zoologist, founded Save the Whales. By 1985, the efforts of a number of interested groups brought about a moratorium in commercial whaling. In 2002, a network of over forty NGOS joined together to form Whalewatch, a group whose ultimate goal is to ban whaling for any purpose.

Bond, Larsen, and Doolittle all possess earned doctoral degrees and have been lauded with numerous awards. Each of them has benefited directly from the changes wrought by the social movements of the 1960s and from the pioneering work done by their predecessors, immediate and distant. They are all physically robust, enjoy extended periods of time in the out-of-doors, are broadly read, and are thoroughly engaged world travelers. At the time this book goes to press, one of them, Libby Larsen, is a mother. She is unique among the subjects of this book in that regard and aware of her position as such, as her remarks will demonstrate. Each of them has written at least one nature-related work that shows her to be at home in a natural world far beyond the garden gate. Among the trio are romanticists, feminists, and pragmatists, and sometimes each of the women is all three. None of the categories is mutually exclusive or fully descriptive of these multifaceted composers. Defying categories is a point of pride among them. One can't help but think that Amy Beach and Marion Bauer, founding members of the short-lived Society of American Women Composers, would have been ecstatic to see the strides made by their composing progeny.

The nature-related works of Victoria Bond, Libby Larsen, and Emily Doolittle are variously informed by personal experiences, family dynamics, canonical environmental tracts, poetry, sculpture, the Gaia hypothesis, a commitment to advocacy, and cutting-edge bioacoustic discoveries. The breadth of their influences suggests a connection to a larger world. Their music emerges against a backdrop of expanding popular efforts on behalf of environmental stewardship and the emergence of ecofeminism – an approach to environmentalism that recognizes a connection between the mistreatment of the earth and the mistreatment of marginalized peoples. Ecofeminists understand that the health of the earth is inextricably bound to the health of its inhabitants, and vice versa. Bond draws upon her unlimited and fearless access to the out-of-doors and an appreciation of the relativity of time, whether epochal or musical. She thinks in terms of life scales and brings that understanding to her music. Larsen embraces attitudes encouraged by second-wave feminism without donning the feminist label for herself. Her music contains both coded and explicit messages reflecting her position as a woman deeply committed to preservation of the environment. Bond, Larsen, and Doolittle have seen the acceptance of such terms as acoustic ecology and zoomusicology.[10] While these concepts inform the work of Doolittle, she doesn't employ the terms to describe her own music.

But the currentness of many of their formative ideas should not suggest that the composers are divorced from the past or that they reject constructions of the natural world advanced by their predecessors. Among the three composers readers will find continuing strong strains of romanticism and deism. In addition, the works of Igor Stravinsky continue to suggest their influence upon these most contemporary composers. While it is likely that any survey of twentieth-century music would reveal a similarly strong presence of the Russian master, his use of nature's sounds and his references to nature in the titles of multiple works make his impact on composers especially logical and apt. Little has been let go, but much has been added.

New to the attitudes toward nature discussed in this final part of the study is humor. As the following chapters will demonstrate, in these most recent assessments of what constitutes nature, composers have made room for the lighter moments that occur daily in the lives of humans and nonhuman others. There is space for laughter as well as reverence in a new construction and understanding of what constitutes nature. The last three subjects of this study substantiate the idea of diversity within and between the nature-inspired works of composing women. The variety of their music performs the variety of nature and the variety of ways of perceiving it.

8

Victoria Bond

"Of Stones and Stars"

Nature is the shrine where I worship.
It is the creator made tangible.
It nourishes me.
It inspires me.
It comforts me.
I need no other proof of the Divine.
It is there in all its glory,
in all its delicacy,
in all its intelligence.
It teaches me daily
if only I can understand its lessons.
When I listen, I can hear.
When I observe, I can see.
When I am not blinded by my own ambitions
I can learn:
the hidden patterns that wait in seeds;
the invisible paths along which birds fly;
the language of whales;
the infinite variety of shapes, sizes, colors
ingeniously tailed.
How can I observe these
without knowing a power higher than mine?
I recognize it,
celebrate it,
embrace it.
I do not know its name,
but I do know that it is.

— VICTORIA BOND, MAY 2009[1]

As Bond's poem demonstrates, the idea of numinous nature continues to be a powerful force motivating musical creation in the early years of the twenty-first century. But as this chapter will also show, it will not keep Bond from outright irreverence regarding nature's peskier agents. As has been the case with the previous composers considered in this study, nature informs Bond and her works to various degrees and in a variety of ways. We hear her environmental advocacy and stewardship in *Thinking Like a Mountain*, share her desire to take flight like a bird in *Dreams of Flying*, and laugh with the composer as she acknowledges the more humorous aspects of the natural world in *Peculiar Plants*. The three pieces considered in this chapter suggest her range of perception.

If pursuing a career in composition was considered a risky undertaking for women until quite recently, pursuing graduate work in orchestral conducting must have seemed an act of mad insubordination in the 1970s, especially to those who were still reeling from the increasing presence of women instrumentalists in their symphony ensembles. But that was the course taken by Victoria Bond, and against the odds, she succeeded.[2] Bond was the first woman to receive a doctorate in conducting from the Juilliard School of Music.[3] Immediately upon graduation in 1977, she was appointed Exxon/ Arts Endowment Conductor by André Previn and the Pittsburgh Symphony Orchestra. In 1986, Bond accepted the position as music director and principal conductor of the Roanoke Symphony in Roanoke, Virginia, and after an initial trip to China in 1993, she worked also with the Shanghai Symphony as guest conductor. Bond formed a deep attachment to that ensemble and to Chinese music. While she had studied composition with Roger Sessions at Juilliard, the need to focus her energies in a single degree program meant that composing took a back seat. Even so, throughout her years as a student and decades as a conductor, Bond continued to write her own music. In 1995, Bond decided to leave her post as music director in Roanoke, and although she continues to guest conduct, she devotes most of her time to composing. Her music provides another forum in which to observe the connections between women and nature on the one hand, and access and advocacy on the other.

Born in Los Angeles in 1945, Bond moved with her family to New York City when she was eight months old. According to the composer, her earliest and most powerful memory was of a summer vacation that she spent on a farm in upstate New York while she was a preschooler. In recalling that initial encounter with the out-of-doors, Bond reflected: "a mysterious bond . . .

connected me to a much larger world, a larger intelligence, a larger presence. I didn't take the country for granted." Bond's use of the term "the country" suggests a deeply embedded understanding of the two places – city and country – as being distinct and opposite locations. She'll use it often.[4] Regular field trips to Bear Mountain with her classmates from the Rudolf Steiner School, where she hiked among the hills and within the woods, solidified her attachment to nature, and most especially to its rocks, plants, and mosses, which today threaten to overtake her Greenwich Village and East Hampton homes. She learned to "love to climb . . . to discover[] the mountain."[5] When not on field trips, Steiner students spent recess in Central Park. Nature study was a part of the daily curriculum, and students engaged with nature wherever they could find it, even in the wholly constructed "natural" environment of Central Park. Although a city girl, Victoria Bond was completely at home "outside," where she instinctively understood that the natural world was emotionally and physically restorative to her; to this day she maintains her belief in nature's healing powers.

As with many of the composers studied thus far, Bond's family provided fertile soil for the cultivation of her interests in music and nature. Her father, a physician by profession, accompanied the young Victoria on her school field trips to the mountains, and he enjoyed walking, which included daily outings with the family dog, Tristan. Of her father's relationship to animals, Bond recalled: "He could connect with any animal; they knew that he was not patronizing them. He was always respectful, playful, but respectful to their right to be what they were and not try to make them into little people."[6] Father and daughter hiked a great deal; the composer remembers camping with her family in the Blue Ridge Mountains.

Having no siblings, the young Victoria was especially close to her pets. She played games with them and learned important lessons from them. "My animals, my animal friends really taught me what an important sense smell is. How much you can tell about something from the aromas; and of course we know how evocative it is in terms of stirring memories." While Bond described her mother as much more of an urban person who liked plants, flowers, and the nature of gardens rather than wilderness, she was also "a good sport about it" and accompanied aunts, uncles, and cousins on a camping trip to Yellowstone. Bond acknowledged, "My mother did enjoy doing that."[7]

Bond was also close to her maternal grandmother, who "grew the most beautiful roses," and from whom she "learned to love vegetables" freshly picked from the earth. "As a kid vegetables were something that came out of a can, or were frozen, and then when my grandmother planted a vegetable garden! Oh my god! Pulling a carrot out of the ground, pinching it off and eating it!" It was her grandmother who helped Victoria's parents buy their "first country house in Amityville, Long Island," where they would spend summers. Bond's grandmother provided Victoria with her own version of a young artist's retreat. "She was the one who was more of an earth person, . . . very much in touch with nature." Given the time spent with beloved family members in nature and with animals, it is not surprising that the composer described herself as "just inconsolable the first time we came back to our apartment after I had spent almost a whole summer out in the country."[8]

As a teenager Bond read *Walden:* according to the composer it changed her life. Years later, she determined to compose something related to Thoreau's text. But a friend suggested that she acquaint herself with Aldo Leopold's *Sand County Almanac* as a more contemporary take on Thoreauvian themes.[9] When she read Leopold's opening lines, "There are some who can live without wild things, and some who can not," she grasped the profound truth of the words for her own life, and that connecting to wildness was essential for her too. Putting it bluntly, she said: "Deprived of it, I would die."

Imagining a work that combined text and music was easy for Bond; her mother was a trained singer, her father had sung in the New York City Opera chorus, and she was a member of the children's chorus there. Words and music formed an effortless pairing. In composing a piece for narrator and orchestra, Bond drew upon not only Leopold's text, but also her experiences growing up in a musical household and her own deep love of mountains and the natural world. Her 1994 piece became a collaboration of sorts, a joint effort with Aldo Leopold, a musical-ecological manifesto that expressed her beliefs in the interrelatedness of all nature and the need for global action to preserve it. Her piece *Thinking Like a Mountain*, named after Leopold's famous essay in *Sand County Almanac*, publicly announced Bond's commitment to environmental stewardship. Although as recently as 2000, Karen J. Warren "argued for an updated interpretation of Leopold's land ethic that makes it . . . compatible with the . . . version of ecofeminist philosophy [she] is defending."[10] Bond is equally assertive about "not wanting to make a political statement about being a woman writing about nature." While Bond is sympathetic to many of the basic tenets of ecofeminism, she does not write from an ecofeminist's position. She writes as a human being with a global conscience.[11] By melding a Chinese folk tune with Western high-art compositional techniques, the composer gave voice to her hopes for global cooperation. Her subtle use of rhythmic, harmonic, and timbral variations of essential melodic motives expressed the intimate relationships we have with one another, even if they are not always immediately apparent.

Using the knowledge and insights she gained climbing and hiking hills and mountains, Bond composed a musical portrait of an *every-mountain* that focused upon the multiple time frames, or "life scales," present in such places.[12] When discovering a mountain, the composer explained, one encounters rocks, trees, animals, flowers, and insects, and each lives its own "life scale." For Bond, rocks represent eons, trees centuries, animals decades, and flowers and insects just days or even hours. There are moments when they coexist, but they don't necessarily appear or disappear simultaneously: each has its own time.[13] While a painter might have observed the light and shade on a mountain's face, and responded to the ways its different features emerged or vanished over the course of a day or a season, Bond listened and heard the mountain's life rhythms and understood them as "wonderfully contrapuntal."[14] She listened to the mountain.

The composer captured the mountain's rhythmic counterpoint using augmentation and diminution – conventional Western procedures that extend or shorten the original duration of notes while maintaining their essential proportions – and applied the methods to a fragment of the traditional Chinese melody, "A Hundred Birds Worshipping the Phoenix."[15] By employing a single recurring four-note melodic fragment to unify the work she offered a musical analogue to the interrelatedness of the natural environment. Drawing upon a tune that refers to birds, and more specifically to the phoenix, a mythical bird that dies and is reborn, fit well with Bond's hopes for a rebirth of environmental mindfulness.[16] By choosing a Chinese melody for her otherwise traditional Western composition, she accomplished two additional goals: she paid tribute to the Shanghai Symphony, which premiered and recorded the piece, and she also foregrounded the global character of the environmental issues at stake. Like the composers of the decade before her, Bond had experiences with nature beyond her immediate environs that enlarged her thinking. They sensitized her to the size of the struggle and the complexity of the solution: both are global.

Bond considered the rhythmically varied melodic fragments as analogues to the different life scales of the rocks, trees, animals, flowers, and insects. Transposing the melody and assigning it to contrasting instruments further reinforced the idea of nature's unity in diversity. While Bond denies any direct programmatic associations between her piece and Leopold's story, meaning that she did not pair specific words with mimetic musical gestures (a practice known as "text painting" or "word painting"), it is clear that music and story reflect each other quite closely. For instance, Bond used French horns to underline Leopold's text that refer to the hunter, thereby adopting a traditional Western association of sound and topic (hunters announce the hunt with horns), and she carefully simulated wolves howling with a series of string glissandi that sound eerily real.

The first measures of the piece introduce the fragmentary Chinese melody in numerous rhythmically varied iterations; here are musical analogues to the mountain's life scales (example 8.1). Beyond the multifarious melodic and rhythmic appearances of the tune, it also emerges at numerous pitch levels and in different timbres – violins, harp, glockenspiel, alto flute, solo violin, C flute, and later oboe, clarinet, horn, trombone, trumpet, and bassoon – thereby guaranteeing maximum variety and freshness. While the tune undergoes rhythmic, timbral, and pitch changes, it maintains its rising, optimistic contour: an ascending perfect fourth, followed by an ascending major second and minor third. Here too, however, diversity is achieved within a unified sonic landscape. In the first sixteen measures, while successive entrances of the tune fragment begin on different notes, the first note of each entrance spells out the original four-note fragment: B–E–F♯– A. The first entrance on B begins in measure 1 in violins, harp, and glockenspiel, followed by alto flute in measure 3 and solo violin in measure 4. The second entrance of the tune begins on E in measure 5 in the C flute, E–A–B–D; the third entrance begins on F♯ in measure 10 in the solo violin, F♯–B–C♯–E. Then there is a break in the pattern; perhaps Bond is concerned that we assume nature is predictable.[17] The sixth entrance completes the initial series, beginning on A and completing the pattern D–E–(G♯) in the second flute at measure 16. A seventh entrance at measure 23 reiterates the pitches of the third entrance, thus suggesting a new palindromic pattern, but it doesn't materialize. Bond achieves unity in diversity, a musical *E pluribus unum*. A soft dynamic level, soloistic writing, and a high tessitura summon nature to wake similarly to Stravinsky's opening bassoon solo in the *Rite of Spring*; nature sounds new and vulnerable.[18]

Music sets the tone and prepares a sympathetic sonic environment for Leopold's thoughts. When, close to two minutes into the piece, the narrator enters for the first time, the now familiar melodic fragment underlies the words: "There are some who can live without wild things, and some who cannot. . . . Like winds and sunsets, wild things were taken for granted until

EXAMPLE 8.1. *Thinking Like a Mountain.* By Victoria Bond, mm. 1–8. Copyright © 1994 by Subito Music Publishing, Inc. (ASCAP), New York, N.Y. All rights reserved. International copyright secured. Used by kind permission.

progress began to do away with them."[19] We hear the rising melodic fragment in a solo cello answered by violas and then string basses. Bond and Leopold have joined forces.

In the eponymous essay "Thinking Like a Mountain," Leopold shared the lessons he learned from having hunted and killed a wolf as a young man. The mountain, he realized in retrospect, understood the balance of predator and prey, and mourned the destruction of the wolf population, which kept the deer population in check. When left to multiply freely, deer denuded mountains of trees and shrubs that protected the soil against erosion. Ironically, they stripped a mountain of their own essential food source and left behind stumps and dying trees unable to hold nutrients in the soil. Leopold concluded that mountains understood the relationship of wolf to deer to mountain; mountains possessed an intelligence that humans had to learn.[20] Leopold's long view of human and animal impacts on nature, and his appreciation of the relationships between geological and human time, have a direct corollary in Bond's concern with life scales.

As the wolf is both the victim and hero of Leopold's parable, it plays a large role in Bond's composition. Beginning at 3:33, the composer introduces string glissandi that prepare the listener for the text that begins: "A deep chesty bawl echoes . . . " When the narrator enters at 4:16, keening wolves are already part of the soundscape. Text and music are intimately reflexive. Listeners hear their sound echoing, as if from "rimrock to rimrock" (example 8.2). Halfway through the near-sixteen-minute piece, Bond captures Leopold's "melee of wagging tails" in her *Cappriccioso* "Dances of Wolves."[21] The playful pack members tumble over one another in a fugal section that features the omnipresent melodic fragment as fugal subject. Bond pulls seemingly infinite possibilities out of the four-note tune, perhaps a fitting analogue to the infinite variety she finds in nature.

A minute from the end of the piece, trumpets and trombones herald a final section iterating the unifying melodic fragment (example 8.3). The triple *piano* (*ppp*) opening of the piece gathers energy over the course of the work to finish triple *forte* (*fff*). The entire ensemble comes together, varied life scales and all, to proclaim that nature's variety occurs within a greater unity, that unwise behavior can be corrected, that obstacles can be overcome, and that regeneration is possible. The kaleidoscope-like treatment of musical materials embodies Bond's belief that musical forms and procedures "grow out of observing nature," where "theme and variation [is] probably . . . among the most abundant forms. Nature's intelligence is a model for music's intelligence."[22]

Like the phoenix of her Chinese song, Bond's music overcomes its apparent fate and boldly achieves its victorious conclusion. *Thinking Like a Mountain* professes Bond's belief in the wisdom of the mountain and our need to listen to what it has to say. In this regard, Bond shares the belief with Zwilich that we must think about the consequences of our actions toward the natural world. The piece is one example of the composer's interactions with nature, and a clear statement of Bond's environmental advocacy, but it alone doesn't disclose the range of her relationships to the natural world. To get a fuller

II. A deep chesty bawl echoes from rimrock to rimrock, rolls down the mountain, and fades into the far blackness of the night. It is an outburst of wild, defiant sorrow, and of contempt for all the adversities of the world. Every living thing pays heed to that call.

EXAMPLE 8.2. *Thinking Like a Mountain*. By Victoria Bond, mm. 84–91.
Copyright © 1994 by Subito Music Publishing, Inc. (ASCAP), New York, N.Y.
All rights reserved. International copyright secured. Used by kind permission.

sense of the various ways nature informs, inspires, and entertains Victoria Bond, it is necessary to consider a few other works.

Nature was the focus of a number of pieces in the 1990s and beyond. In 1993 Bond composed *Urban Bird*, a work that simultaneously referenced nature and Charlie "Bird" Parker, and placed them both in a "deserted subway platform in New York City."[23] Martha Mooke commissioned two pieces for the electric viola in 1996, *Stalking* and *Insects*. According to the composer, *Stalking* was inspired by her "fascination with the total concentration, grace

EXAMPLE 8.3. *Thinking Like a Mountain.* By Victoria Bond, mm. 366–372.
Copyright © 1994 by Subito Music Publishing, Inc. (ASCAP), New York, N.Y.
All rights reserved. International copyright secured. Used by kind permission.

and stealth of large cats stalking their prey." *Insects* "grew out of [Bond's] interest in natural sounds and the way in which creatures communicate."[24] Time spent in China enlarged the composer's natural world. In *Three Chinese Folk Songs* of 1998, Bond set popular songs named "Digging Potatoes," "The Jasmine Flower," and The Wind Blows" for soprano, tenor, and orchestra. Each of these works testifies to the range and variety of Bond's engagement with nature. Though deserving of significant discussion, they won't be studied here.

In 1994, in addition to *Thinking Like a Mountain*, which had been co-commissioned by the Shanghai Symphony of China, Montana's Billings Symphony, the Elgin Symphony of Illinois, and Explore Park in Virginia, Bond composed a second piece, *Dreams of Flying*, a work for string quartet commissioned by the Audubon Quartet. She later arranged the piece for string orchestra.

According to the composer, the Audubon name immediately evoked images of birds, and she was inspired to write a piece that explored sensations of flying, at least as she imagined them from her human perch. As Bond explained: "The piece is actually based on my own dreams of flying, . . . these are among my favorite dreams."[25] The four movements, "Resisting Gravity," "Floating," "The Caged Bird Dreams of the Jungle," and "Flight," reveal what can only be characterized as a deep, cross-species empathy with the challenges and joys of avian flight. Nature, for Bond, is a site where the impossible (for humans) happens. One cannot help but wonder, however, whether the composer also projected a personal desire to expand her own (metaphorical) wings on the bird subjects of the chamber work. Numerous pieces by Victoria Bond have explored the themes of confinement, domination, even suffocation.[26] Birds and flight provide effective and widely understood symbols for a composer concerned with freedom.[27] The mid-1990s also saw Bond expand her personal space beyond her Manhattan home base. In 1995, Bond and her husband bought an acre of land on the eastern end of Long Island, where they built a house. She had no desire for a green carpet of lawn but wanted access to the woods, which were minimally thinned to make room for the house. Bond carved a winding path through the native trees, marked it with fallen branches, and planted moss; the mossy path became her garden. Today it is home to a rainbow of green mosses of various softnesses and patterns. Thick layers of pine needles cushion visitors' footsteps and make the garden a supremely quiet oasis. Like Beach and Talma, Bond seeks out quiet places. The "country house," as Bond refers to it, became a retreat for the composer, and the land around it became a source of inspiration for yet more nature music (figure 8.1).

FIGURE 8.1. Victoria Bond in her East Hampton, New York, garden.
Photograph by Denise Von Glahn.

In *Dreams of Flying*, the first, second, and fourth movements rise, float, and soar: avian motions become musical sounds. The third movement, "The Caged Bird Dreams of the Jungle," imagines a conscious winged creature that dreams of freedom. Bond seems comfortable attributing aspirations to nonhuman species, and perhaps avian abilities to humans, at least in her dreams.[28] But before the music enacts bird dreams, it first explores the sensation of becoming airborne.

Much like birders who must quietly await the appearance of a prized specimen, listeners must patiently attend the music to catch the first *ppp* violin entrances of "Resisting Gravity." As with *Thinking Like a Mountain*, the initial sounds of *Dreams of Flying* contain information essential to understanding the unity of the movement and ultimately the logic of the entire work. This is in keeping with Bond's practice of compositional organicism and her belief in the essential similarity between her music and nature. As the composer explained: "Nature is informed of itself. It learns from where it is, where it goes. . . . the [musical] material itself has an intelligence . . . it grows in an organic way, it learns from itself." She finds an aesthetic model in nature, much like Tower and Zwilich, whose procedural preference is an organic one.[29]

Victoria Bond's insistence that nature is literally a source of "deep inspiration" makes the opening sounds of "Resisting Gravity" especially meaningful. The soft and slow (Adagio) alternations of neighboring pitches that introduce the movement suggest gentle respirations; we hear an unknown organism breathing. As the first violin makes its gradual uphill climb from a unison G with the second violins to A, and then rocks back and forth between the two pitches before ascending to B, C, D, and E, the pitch palette expands much like lungs filling with oxygen. Over the course of fifteen measures, Bond's human–bird subject slowly overcomes gravity, and the initial, barely audible dynamic level rises with it to *mezzo forte* at measure 16. The remaining sixty measures of the first movement enact a series of similar ascending passages that take Bond, bird, and listeners up into the air. With the opening measures, she identifies essential pitch and interval material: the pitch center of the larger piece, G; and the interval of a second, which will include both rising and falling major and minor varieties (example 8.4). Ties over bar lines, series of two-beat note values within a triple rhythm, accents on second and third beats instead of on the first, and the adagio tempo (quarter note = 54) minimize a sense of expectation and metrical regularity. Thus on one level Bond removes the weightiness of strong downbeats, which could anchor her or a bird in place.[30] But she also removes the dependable sense of propulsion that results from recurring downbeats and that can generate momentum. This human flyer is going to have to work to resist gravity. When the ambiguous rhythm is combined with the slow ascent from the opening G below middle C,

EXAMPLE 8.4. *Dreams of Flying,* "Resisting Gravity." By Victoria Bond, mm. 1–16.

to the G three octaves above, which is finally achieved at the first measure of
the second movement, the music has successfully overcome gravity: the effort
has taken a full five minutes. Bond imagines the bird's and her own dreamlike
experience in sound. The bird's achievement becomes the music's achievement
and the composer's as well.

The second movement uses similar techniques to suggest "floating." Victoria Bond speaks of her music as "situational" rather than "programmatic,"
and *Dreams of Flying* is a good example of the distinction she makes. Instead
of composing a narrative work that tracks and describes the precise actions

of a subject, Bond creates a soundscape conducive to imagining actions. In spite of the composer's organic thinking, she's not so much interested in telling a story as she is in painting a scene. Ambiguous rhythms and harmonies allow the bird–human subject to drift in temporal and harmonic space. Triple piano (*ppp*) harmonics hold all aloft at the edges of our audition, and simultaneous duple and triple divisions of the $\frac{4}{4}$ meter permit unfettered movement. Instructions to the instrumentalists to play *flautando* (lightly bowing over the end of the fingerboard), which produces a flutelike tone, and *con sordino* (with mute) result in the soft, distant, weightless sound that Bond imagines as the musical analogue of floating. The movement is the briefest of all at just a minute and a half, but as it grows *attacca* (without pause) from the first movement, it builds upon the effects of the earlier sounds and gains in expressive power.

"The Caged Bird Dreams of the Jungle" is the longest of the four movements and contains music of the greatest rhythmic, melodic, dynamic, and expressive variety in the entire piece.[31] The slow unfolding of the first two movements is replaced with faster and more goal-oriented music, even though juxtaposed duple and triple meters confound predictability. In this movement, the bird reference is specific and exclusive. Passages of grouped sixteenth notes and then triplets swoop, cross, and cascade. One can hear the caged bird reveling in its imagined freedom (example 8.5).

At measure 122, Bond introduces sounds that come closest to evoking a real birdsong, although it is not;[32] she recalls the high-pitched harmonics that introduced "Floating," but they now return in a circling, repetitive "call," which is followed immediately by a modern-day *Chanson des Oiseaux*.[33] Like Clément Janequin's sixteenth-century singers, Bond's instrumentalists "make like birds." Strings chirp and call "puweee." The unifying major second first heard in "Resisting Gravity" returns as well in a repeated staccato "birdcall." The tempo nearly doubles that of the first movement.[34] With the pickup to measure 134, the circling *dolce, cantabile* tune that began the third movement now appears in the lowest strings. Is this the caged bird? Its lyricism lends itself to weaving in and around the quick, chirpier sounds of the free birds, at the same time remaining distinct from them. As "The Caged Bird Dreams of the Jungle" nears its close, however, fragments of the caged bird's song and the freed birds' calls intermingle as each tries the other's music, and for a brief three measures (228–230), the avian chorus sings excitedly as one. The dynamic level rises to triple *forte* (*fff*) at measure 230 before the birds disappear quietly. The third movement ends with a decisive pizzicato V–I cadence that prepares the way for "Flight" and a return to the pitch G, which ultimately provides a unison close to the piece.

The beginning of "Flight" shows its kinship with the first movement, "Resisting Gravity" (example 8.6). The tempo increases once again: a quarter note now equals 144, two and a half times the pace of the first movement. Bond captures the freedom of bird flight by using no fewer than thirteen different meters, which change 145 times in the 256-measure movement. A similarly inclusive array of extended string techniques reinforces the idea of liberty: pizzicatos, *flautando*, snapping strings, *sul ponticello* (playing near the bridge, which produces a thin, wispy sound), *con sordino*, glissandos, and tremolos evoke a catalogue of bird sounds. Dynamic range is both exaggerated and compressed when within a single nine-measure passage (305–313), the viola moves from fortissimo (*ff*) to triple piano (*ppp*). It seems quite clear that for Bond, flight is all about liberation, about choice. But Bond also grounds her *Dreams of Flying* and insists on the organic unity of the work by returning to the opening pitch and rocking gesture with which the piece began (example 8.7). If the bird and Bond enjoyed their liberating flight, both have also come home. Is this a musical manifestation of nature's intelligence, a correction for excess? Perhaps Bond recognizes and even welcomes *some* limitations.

Despite a similarly anthropomorphizing, organic approach to *Thinking Like a Mountain*, *Dreams of Flying* reveals a different facet of Bond's relationship with nature. If Bond's response to Aldo Leopold's essay announced her emergence as a public activist, advocate, and environmentalist, and indeed the composer has described her piece as "an ideal work for Earth Day or any concert with an environmental theme,"[35] *Dreams of Flying* is a more personal meditation on nature and reflects Bond's instinctive identification with and embrace of its symbolism for herself. Triumph over gravity becomes a shared victory. Evoking the grace of a winged creature as it floats suspended in the air allows Bond to revel in the aesthetic pleasure that nature affords her. Through tracking the dream-state bird in its jungle escapades, nature becomes a mirror in which the composer sees personal aspirations. With its alternately quiet and raucous energy, the piece embodies the vitality that Bond draws from nature. Her declaration "I draw strength directly from the ground" is everywhere evident in her being.[36]

One might assume that two such different pieces, one suggestive of an energized activist and the other of a reflective philosophe, emerged over a period of years, but they were written within months of each other: thus they reveal the richly variegated understanding of nature the composer enjoys at

EXAMPLE 8.5 (*above and facing*). *Dreams of Flying,* "The Caged Bird Dreams of the Jungle." By Victoria Bond, mm. 122–137. Copyright © 1994 by Subito Music Publishing, Inc. (ASCAP), New York, N.Y. All rights reserved. International copyright secured. Used by kind permission.

EXAMPLE 8.6. *Dreams of Flying*, "Flight." By Victoria Bond, mm. 242–248.
Copyright © 1994 by Subito Music Publishing, Inc. (ASCAP), New York, N.Y.
All rights reserved. International copyright secured. Used by kind permission.

any single time.[37] Beyond that, they are evidence of the multiple and complex
attributes associated with the term "nature." Bond's most recent nature-related
work, *Peculiar Plants* (2008), exposes yet another facet of her kinship with flora
and fauna. By foregrounding humor, something only hinted at in earlier works,
we hear the composer lightening up and enjoying what she characterizes as an

EXAMPLE 8.7. *Dreams of Flying*, "Flight." By Victoria Bond, mm. 494–498.
Copyright © 1994 by Subito Music Publishing, Inc. (ASCAP), New York, N.Y.
All rights reserved. International copyright secured. Used by kind permission.

"enlarged appreciation" and a "clearer-eyed view" of nature.[38] The composer's
program notes explain the genesis of this more recent work, a collaborative
undertaking with the virtuosic harpsichordist and musical polymath Kenneth Cooper:

> *Peculiar Plants* is a suite of character studies in the Baroque spirit. Written
> for the brilliant and inventive harpsichordist Kenneth Cooper, it is a part-
> nership of ideas, fostered through lively rehearsals, numerous e-mails and a
> meeting of the minds. The Strangler Fig was the instigator of the suite, being
> a plant I found particularly peculiar and fascinating. After showing Ken the
> initial draft, he made suggestions which prompted more ideas which then
> led to still other ideas and more music, and the garden was seeded. Since
> that initial impetus, not only music, but poetry sprouted, revealing aspects
> of each plant both humorous and instructive. . . . The garden is now in full
> bloom, peopled with plants of striking individuality.[39]

In performance, the suite consists of seven musical sketches, each preceded
by an Ogden Nash–like limerick that is read aloud. The plants spotlighted

include the strangler fig, Venus flytrap, creeping moss, blushing violet, deadly nightshade, ghost orchid, and ragweed. A consideration of a few of the pieces and their poems reveals the composer's always respectful but perhaps less high-minded attitude toward nature. Although poetry was conceived after the music, in performance the poems are read first and set the tone for each of the pieces, as the poetry of "The Strangler Fig" demonstrates:

> Among the most bizarre of flora
> Is one with a distinctive aura:
> The Strangler Fig attacks its host —
> A tree as innocent as most —
> By dropping seeds in crucial spots
> And spreading tendrils, which with knots
> And stalks and vine-like ammunition,
> Starve the tree of its nutrition.
> But as the hapless victim dies,
> A marvelous sculpture multiplies,
> Impressing on our inner mind
> How life and death are intertwined.[40]

The composer likened the larger work to "a walk in the wilderness" and marveled at the irony present in the plant world, especially the pairing of death and beauty so obvious in the strangler fig.[41] In the remnants of the fig's decimated host tree, Bond saw exquisite sculpture that reminded her of the works of the iconoclastic Spanish architect Antoni Gaudí.[42] It comes as no surprise that Bond appreciated the artistic qualities of natural forms, since at one time she briefly considered painting and sculpture as possible professions. For Bond, nature and art were reflexively imitative; boundaries between the two were not fixed. At the same time, recalling the more sober lesson of Leopold's "Thinking Like a Mountain," Bond acknowledged that "balance [in nature] is dependent upon the predator."[43] For Bond, while nature possesses intrinsic *aesthetic* qualities, it is simultaneously and perhaps ultimately *instructive*. "Of Stones and Stars," Bond's poem quoted at the top of this chapter, devotes ten of its twenty-seven lines (lines 10–20) to enumerating the ways nature teaches. The framing lines acknowledge the divine power of nature "in all its intelligence" without the andropomorphization that usually accompanies such attributions. References to a higher power are missing completely from *Peculiar Plants*. Bond engages with nature as an equal, she spars with it, and she admits being amused by its ways.

FIGURE 8.2. Strangler fig, Fraser Island. Reprinted with Permission of Photographer Quan Tre.

Bond's "Strangler Fig" catches both the delicacy and power of the predatory tree.[44] The piece begins *tranquillo*. Light, right-hand filigree fingerwork
recalls the elegant French clavecin style, an association reinforced by the
sound of the harpsichord. Intimations of the plant's deadly potential, however, are immediately audible in the highly chromatic, dissonant harmonic
palette and in a staccato accompanimental figure that resembles a ticking
clock; although the left-hand part remains in the background, the material
portends something vaguely threatening. Within seven measures, relative
tranquility gives way to trilling, punchy, agitated music (example 8.8). "Menacing" figures accelerate.[45] One can almost hear the fig's branches grasping
and wrapping themselves around their victim. At measure 66, Bond writes
"Wild!" and the harpsichordist pounces with a series of wedgelike clusters
of notes violently pounded with fists. It's as if the fig is chomping at the
harpsichord (example 8.9). Twelve measures later, dissonant clusters punch
and thrash as a rapidly cascading hybrid scale collapses "as fast as possible."[46]

Although the real-time strangling process takes years, even decades,
to be complete, Bond has portrayed the fig's attack as sudden and furious.
Compressing the action heightens the drama and drives home the moral of
this story: nature is, as Tennyson adduced, "red in tooth and claw."[47] But as
Bond admits such unrepentant destruction is essential to nature's balance,
and it requires acknowledgment even in a set of humorous pieces. Leopold's
lessons continue to resonate. After an elongated pause, which allows the preceding violent sounds to dissipate, the original mood, tempo, and *pianissimo*
dynamic level return. A "Delicato," transparent passage, reminiscent of the
beginning of the work – save for a single measure-long convulsion – restores
the opening tranquility, almost. Bond, however, won't let listeners forget
the potential of this natural killer. Thus the last measure, with its final, if
unstable, diminished sonority, clarifies that such calm is illusory. While this
strangler fig has done its work, others of its ilk are poised to create stunningly
beautiful natural sculptures out of the hollowed, contorted remains of their
hosts. And so begins Bond's deadly humorous paean to nature.

The composer fills *Peculiar Plants* with instructions to the harpsichordist to play "seductively" in "The Venus Flytrap"; "ominously" in "Creeping
Moss"; "and voluptuously," "con passione," and "timidly" in "Blushing Violet." In "Ghost Orchid" the mood should be "Misterioso," and in "Ragweed,"
Bond's portrayal of a plant that causes untold grief for allergy sufferers, the
harpsichordist is instructed to play "Jaunty and Exuberant." (No sympathy

EXAMPLE 8.8. *Peculiar Plants,* "The Strangler Fig." By Victoria Bond, mm. 1–14. Copyright © 2010 by Henmar Press, Inc. Sole Selling agent C. F. Peters Corporation. Used by kind permission. All rights reserved.

EXAMPLE 8.9. *Peculiar Plants,* "The Strangler Fig." By Victoria Bond, mm. 66–69. Copyright © 2010 by Henmar Press, Inc. Sole Selling agent C. F. Peters Corporation. Used by kind permission. All rights reserved.

from this composer or the plant.) Bond anthropomorphizes with ease; as she writes in her notes, her "garden is . . . *peopled* with plants of striking individuality."[48] And her music and poetry make no attempt to hide the human qualities she attributes to the plant world.

With its slow, dotted rhythms, "The Venus Flytrap" suggests a sultry Latin dance, a fitting aural analogue to poetry that talks of a plant that uses its "sweetly-scented bait" to seduce. The brevity of the piece matches the quickness with which the plant lures and devours its prey. The composer clearly has fun imagining personas and histories for her plants, as is evident in the poem that precedes "Blushing Violet":

> By the road a violet stood,
> A recluse in the neighborhood;
> She blushed, as she was now aghast
> To tell us of her sordid past.
>
> Angelic though she seemed to be,
> She led a life both fast and free;
> She liked to stimulate the bees
> And send them into ecstasies;
> She liked to drink and dance and feast
> Voraciously as any beast,
> And terrorize the flower beds!
> While slashing stems and splitting heads,
> She caused the very buds to weep,
> Then threw them on the compost heap.
>
> But that was then, and now a hush
> Conceals her deeds with bashful blush.[49]

By turns Bond's blushing violet suggests a "delicato," angelic character (appropriate, perhaps, for a small, simple, five-petaled flower), and then a "voluptuoso," wanton one. We hear the seduction scene (the composer writes "Seduttuoso") that leads the bees into ecstasies and witness the passion ("Con passione!") before Violet shrinks "timidly" from the flower beds she has terrorized.[50] The music is full of surprises like Bond's imagined character; the composer allows the flower the full range of contradictions Walt Whitman so poetically permitted himself and humanity.[51]

Bond sees herself and her nature pieces as part of the Austro-German music-nature tradition, and she likens her inspiring walks to those taken by Brahms: as nature nourished the nineteenth-century master, it feeds this modern American too. Among the many mosses in Bond's East Hampton garden is one grown from moss fragments gotten at Brahms's house in Baden-Baden, Germany, where he spent summers between 1865 and 1874 hiking in the area. Bond has had residences there on multiple occasions and feels great kinship with the late-nineteenth-century master. She sees daily communion with nature as bringing herself "into a larger context."[52]

But traditions beyond the German romantic one inspire Bond as well, and the final piece in the set shows the composer drawing upon an American musical style for added meaning and humor: "Ragweed" bursts on the scene riding the sounds of a rag. The American reference is especially apt given this peculiar plant's provenance in North America.[53] The jaunty syncopated duple rhythm is unmistakable even if the jangly sounds of the harpsichord momentarily defamiliarize it for us. A scattering of measures in $\frac{3}{4}$ and $\frac{6}{8}$ isn't enough to "denature" the rag for us, and save for them and a preponderance of clashing right-hand chord clusters, Scott Joplin would have happily claimed this piece as his own. Dissonance and an occasional unexpected rhythm seem appropriate, however, when one considers the widespread misery and upset of daily routine caused by the miniature flowers that top the stalks of this resilient torturer. The poem sets the tone:

Nature made the Ragweed glorious
Because its features are notorious.
Its rampant growth has proved insidious:
Apparently its taste is hideous.
Its leaves, when brewed, might cure your cold –
The Puritans tried this, we are told.
Among the ragweed's plusses and minuses:
Pure disaster for our sinuses.[54]

While Bond collaborated with Kenneth Cooper on *Peculiar Plants*, she also dedicated the work to him and freely admits it was written with his particular virtuosic and temperamental gifts in mind. "Ragweed" gives Cooper ample space to show his keyboard chops and his irrepressible sense of humor. Clocking in at less than two minutes, "Ragweed" whisks by, much like the weightless airborne pollen. In keeping with the relationship between hands in traditional rags, the left hand maintains a steady eighth-note patter. Dramatic contrasts result from dynamic adjustments – shifts from *forte* passages to *pianissimo* and *sotto voce* ones. Eight measures from the end, Bond instructs Cooper to become suddenly *fortissimo* and to "broaden" his playing. Thereafter, measure by measure, momentum builds and accents create momentary spasms; one can hear someone suppressing a sneeze. After a final accelerando and a momentary silence, Cooper is splayed on the keyboard, left elbow smashing a thirteen-note cluster and both hands grabbing an additional ten notes in the upper register. The insidious pollen has overtaken the harpsichordist, and the only release is a thunderous, if musical, "Ah-choo" (example 8.10).

There are no signs here of a reverential attitude toward a numinous nature. No attempts to suggest its transcending powers. This is mundane reality treated with a light touch. We are amused, but we are also mindful. Unexpectedly, perhaps, despite its rollicking good humor, *Peculiar Plants* offers a profound commentary. Nature continues to instruct. As allergy-medicine sales attest, ragweed mocks the idea that we control nature; the best we can do is respond and adapt. We don't need a category-five hurricane to understand that nature is simultaneously beautiful and deadly, and the distinction is not always obvious. With her darkly humorous work, Bond exposes the complexity of nature and our connections to it.

Victoria Bond finds spiritual nourishment, creative inspiration, aesthetic pleasure, a source of belly laughs, and analogies for musical forms in nature. The essential temporal quality of music makes it the ideal expressive art for nature, where dynamism is the steady state. As regards the impact of being a woman on her attitudes toward nature, Bond points to her inexperience with the alternatives; she is unwilling to attribute her particular perspective on nature to being female, but sees creativity as "ambi-sextrist," her own word.[55] Bond prefers to think less in terms of discrete or oppositional categories of male and female and more in terms of the Chinese concept of yin and yang, where complementary opposites are always at work animating a greater whole. While being thoroughly sympathetic to the reality of women's subjugation across the globe, she rejects the idea that as a woman she can speak for women.

EXAMPLE 8.10. *Peculiar Plants,* "Ragweed." By Victoria Bond, mm. 34–37.
Copyright © 2010 by Henmar Press, Inc. Sole selling agent C. F. Peters
Corporation. Used by kind permission. All rights reserved.

In response to the question "Does being a woman, and having inherited the
identification of women with nature, inform your work as a composer?" the
composer had much to say:

> The best I can do is tell the world how I see it. That's the most honest
> thing I can do. . . . I hope that the elements that people usually associate
> with masculinity, you know aggressive and driving, and all those things, I
> wouldn't want *not* to incorporate, because I feel that way very often. . . .
>
> Women have long been identified with nature and the fact that we were
> the first agriculturalists and able to use plants for food and for medicinal
> purposes in so many different cultures, I mean in Native American and
> Eskimo, . . . where women are really identified [with nature], I feel that very
> strongly.

> It's a great privilege to be able to give to other women a gift of being
> satisfied in [one's] womanhood, and not being threatened and being able to
> celebrate it. I think that's a very important gift to give women who probably
> wish that they hadn't been born women because of the way they are treated,
> and whose lives are just filled with misery and frustration.[56]

When asked whether she thought of her music "as giving those women a voice," the composer responded, "I hope so. One hopes that in the personal lies the universal. I can't speak for the world at large, but I can be [as] honest and clear in terms of letting the ideas filter through me as I possibly can."[57] We hear the hopes of many of these skillful listeners echoing in Bond's words.

In Victoria Bond, one appreciates the important roles played by family and schooling in laying the foundation for a respectful relationship with the natural world. She traces her connection to animals and plants through her father and grandmother. She fondly recalls conversations with her cousin while sitting in a tree. By hiking and gardening, she experienced nature at a pace deliberate enough to allow observation, education, and enjoyment. Her pets helped her develop a heightened sense of smell. As the natural world stimulated Victoria Bond, she concluded that "my fondest hope is that my pieces will stimulate a listener's imagination; that they will somehow unlock doors, or maybe be for the listener what the experience was for me. I'd like to be able to can my experiences in notes and let the aroma, as it were, be activated on the listener."[58]

Adjusting the balance of conducting and composing responsibilities toward the latter has allowed Bond to work with musicians in a "collegial relationship," something that was difficult to achieve when she was the conductor ("management") of orchestral musicians. Regarding the role of conductor as it is traditionally defined, Bond sees "that hierarchical position [as] antithetic to what women desire." And here Bond is willing to speak more broadly about possible differences between men and women, or at least her experiences in the context of gender differences. "I think we want to have a circle of equals; it's much more interesting when everybody contributes to something. When we're talking about feminism, I would say that is one significant difference, not that a man can't access that, but in general what I see about relationships between men and men and women and women is that there does seem to be more of a desire for equality, for that level playing field."[59]

The metaphor of a "circle of equals" describes not only Bond's aspiration for her personal and professional relationships, but also her understanding of one's place within the natural world. We can imagine Oliveros offering an enthusiastic "Huzzah!" While Bond believes that we have become "disconnected from our true parent, the earth," she understands our "moments of connectedness [as a] kind of *reconnecting*, rather than a connecting for the first time."[60] Circles and cycles, so often associated with females and with nature, will remain key images for the final two composers in this study.

9

Libby Larsen

Music exists in an infinity of sound.
I think of all music as existing in the substance of the air itself.
It is the composer's task to order and make sense of sound, in time and space,
to communicate something about being alive through music.

— LIBBY LARSEN[1]

Of the composers studied thus far, Libby Larsen is among a very few to ascribe extramusical intent to her works. In contrast to Victoria Bond, whose music making is, by her own admission, *not* driven primarily by political issues, Libby Larsen acknowledges that many of her pieces were conceived with clear agendas, although they aren't always audible to listeners. About a 1992 composition Larsen explained: "I have been political about ecology through my music. In the *Marimba Concerto: After Hampton*, in the orchestral part I embedded Morse Code for 'save the rain forest' in the percussion part." About *Missa Gaia*, composed around the same time, she asserted: "It *is* ecology, and meant to be about ecology," but as this chapter will demonstrate, the piece is about much more as well.[2]

As with all the composers in this study, Larsen's relationship to nature is extremely personal, multifaceted, and dynamic. Interactions with the natural world have been recurring themes in Larsen's music her entire composing life. Born in Wilmington, Delaware, at the exact midcentury mark, 1950, she moved as a young child to Minnesota, away from dense eastern urban culture. She would attend the University of Minnesota and earn bachelor's through doctoral degrees there. As a new graduate student in 1973, Larsen, along with other young composers including Stephen Paulus, founded the Minnesota Composers Forum, which in 1996 became the American Composers Forum. What started as a regional initiative is now a thriving national organization with a presence in every state. The activist streak present then is still at work. Larsen has remained a steadfast advocate of young American composers and new American music. From early on, her home included the outdoors. While her works list contains plenty of compositions celebrating historically female (small-nature) subjects, Larsen, like Bond, is not hesitant to take on big nature too. Ants and grasshoppers, blackbirds and swallows, winter, spring, summer, gardens, skies and sea, sun and moon, rivers, wind, snow and roses, thin air and red hills, the atmosphere as a fluid system – she has composed them all.

Hearing Larsen speak about her childhood confirms that nature was a powerful presence in the front and at the depths of her consciousness. Her definition of nature is embracing: "For me nature is life force, *life force*, global and way beyond global . . . the physical forces that allow those who are imbued with it to recognize their state of being."[3] It is immediately apparent to anyone who has been in Libby Larsen's presence that she is imbued with "life force."

Numerous experiences shaped the receptive and thoughtful youth into the supremely "natural" adult. Larsen tells of a Girl Scout reforestation project in northern Minnesota when, as a child of eleven or twelve, she spent a day planting "hundreds and hundreds of tiny pine trees" with her troop. Later that evening, bedded down in a tent she shared with a few girls, Libby and her friends thought about their project and wondered: "Are we now, or are we then?" As Larsen explained, the girls had identified completely with the trees, they had become the trees, and they pondered whether they, like the seedlings, contained their future. Were they their future at that very moment? Was there such a thing as a future, or was/is it all present? Such a discussion was likely not typical of "tent conversations," and might never have occurred without the philosophically inclined Libby Larsen, but the composer's vivid recollection reveals the depth of thought inspired by nature even at a young age.[4]

In 2009, from a distance of over forty years, Larsen revisited that experience and reconsidered the tiny pines and the energy they contained: "The energy in a young being is quite unlike mature energy. Its life force is there, it's palpable. So it may be now, but it's also then." Fully present in the teenager's observation is Larsen's adult identification with nature, and not incidentally, her understanding of time as of the moment and eternal rather than linear and moving in a single trajectory forward. In other contexts Larsen has de-

EXAMPLE 9.1. *Water Music,* from Suite in D Major. By George F. Handel.

scribed this synchronic conception of time as "vertical time." Such thinking directly impacts the works of a creative being whose expressive medium is a temporal one, and especially her pieces of a more "inward" and contemplative cast, which she distinguishes from her public "display" pieces. According to Larsen, "display" pieces are typically commissioned, "event-oriented works" that are linear and teleological. They often involve large performing forces. "Outward display is the one for which I receive public feedback in a framed kind of way, the review, the large audience." In these works Larsen is "the external verbalizer in the post-Romantic model." "Inward pieces" allow the composer "to work with great chamber musicians." These pieces are often softer, smaller works of a more personal nature even though they may also be commissioned.[5]

Sailing regularly as a young girl on Lake Harriet in Minneapolis put Larsen in direct contact with the ways of wind and water; she worked with the currents and listened to the breezes. She was in, on, and surrounded by water, and she was at home there. Like Tower, Larsen is an accomplished athlete. Years later, the lessons learned on the lake found their way into her *Symphony: Water Music* (1984), an orchestral piece whose movements are titled "Fresh Breeze," "Hot, still," "Wafting," and "Gale." The larger title, *Water Music,* pays homage to Handel's eponymous D-Major Suite, and throughout the first movement Larsen plays with the signature fanfaric motive from that earlier work (example 9.1). At measure 45, trumpets and then horns introduce Larsen's version of Handel's heraldic call (example 9.2). Over the course of the next five minutes, bassoons, trombones, strings, high woodwinds, and

EXAMPLE 9.2. *Symphony. Water Music,* "Fresh Breeze." By Libby Larsen, mm. 45–47.
Copyright © 1984 by E. C. Schirmer Music Company, a division of ECS Publishing,
Boston, Massachusetts. All rights reserved. Used with kind permission.

horns all have a go at the *Handel cum Larsen* motto; its recurrence unifies "Fresh Breeze." But Larsen's focus isn't on melody, and so she doesn't develop Handel's motive; instead she concentrates on a small number of intervallic and rhythmic gestures, and the ways the main motive sounds within and against a changing timbral palette. Her techniques recall those of Talma in *Summer Sounds*. Repeating telegraphic pulses and brief scalar passages purl. Larsen's enjoyment of glistening, shimmering sound, which she creates using vibraphone, bell tree, wind chimes, orchestral bells, and celeste, recalls Debussy's "Dialogue du vent et de la mer" (Dialogue of the wind and sea) from his orchestral suite *La Mer*, where he used cymbals, tam-tams, orchestral bells, and gongs to achieve many similar effects.[6] Larsen joins Handel and Debussy in exploring the ways wind plays on water with music that is alternately rhythmic and pulsing, and then all silvery effects. Breezes tap the surface and skip away. Larsen rigs the sails of her bouncing skiff. "Fresh Breeze" offers listeners an energizing experience: it's an outward, exuberant statement about the joys of wind and water and an example of Larsen as her public "display" self, as what she calls "the external verbalizer in the post-Romantic mode"[7] (figure 9.1).

The exhilaration of "Fresh Breeze" is balanced by the quietude of "Hot, still." Using soft dynamics and "shadowy, fleeting" woodwind figurations, Larsen paints a hazy waterscape. If the sounds were colors, this would be a movement in pastels. As much as the first movement reached out, the second movement pulls in. The absence of any continuously propelling rhythm means listeners sink deep where they are; they stop and listen to the capacious environment Larsen creates. The orchestral score looks like the sound: open, spacious, vaguely pointillistic (example 9.3).

Birdcalls and cricket chirps gently punctuate the stillness, producing a loosely contrapuntal soundscape. While the resulting sounds are completely different, the contrapuntal textures of Talma's *Summer Sounds* and Larsen's *Water Music* are similar. Despite the stillness, however, the music never stagnates; nor do listeners feel lost or without an aural path. Larsen fills "Hot, still" with evocations of nature's music: at measure 5, flutes flutter-tongue and "sound as crickets," and at measure 66, a percussionist is told "to simulate the sound of a katydid" on a sizzle cymbal. One can almost smell the heavy scent of a late August day near a lake; the air is sticky and reluctant to move. The occasional thud of timpani or bass drum suggests the sodden atmosphere.[8]

Throughout the seven-plus-minute movement, musicians play "fleeting-[ly]," "lightly," and "gently." Downbeats seem to dissipate in the natural reverberations of orchestral bells, wind chimes, celeste, and a marimba struck with

FIGURE 9.1. Libby Larsen and her sister Molly George in 1968 racing their sailboat on Lake Harriet, Minneapolis, Minnesota. With the kind permission of the composer to reprint this photograph by Dee O'Neal.

soft mallets. The composer's recurring instruction to play "warmly" makes one think that she seeks to change the temperature of the performance hall as much as guide musicians to play with tenderness. And such a reading might not be too wide of the mark: Larsen wants to heighten our awareness by creating an environment that invites becoming one with it.[9] Larsen will return to this idea with her piece *downwind of roses in Maine*, which will be discussed later.

The third and fourth movements of the symphony return Larsen and her listeners to more active water. In "Wafting," the wind moves in a brief dance on the water's surface. But gone is the courtly minuet, the traditional dance of a symphonic third movement; Larsen's dance exudes the playfulness of an energetic cha-cha; this is more Broadway than Esterháza.[10] It's hard to imagine Larsen's music being created anywhere but in the New World. Its choppy rhythms and brass and percussion stamp it American.

EXAMPLE 9.3. *Symphony. Water Music*, "Hot, still." By Libby Larsen, mm. 5–7.
Copyright © 1984 by E. C. Schirmer Music Company, a division of ECS Publishing,
Boston, Massachusetts. All rights reserved. Used with kind permission.

"Gale" musicalizes the sensation of a storm and the feelings of one who is subject to its violence. The tumultuous final movement involves the full forces of the orchestra, which produces an increasingly aggressive sound. Hard mallets replace softer ones, temple blocks and "detached and accented" piano octaves emphasize rather than diffuse beats, a wind machine "begins softly" but then "rises and falls with increasing intensity." We feel the storm surrounding us as the harp careens through a series of undulating glissandi and the dynamic level rises to triple *forte*. This is nature writ large, and Larsen is neither intimidated by it nor reluctant to take it on. She has personal experience with it; she understands, appreciates, and respects it. Despite her diminutive stature, Larsen is at home in big nature.

The relative lengths of the movements in *Water Music* provide, perhaps, some insight into Larsen and her relationship to nature in 1984. With the symphony clocking in around eighteen minutes, and the second movement lasting nearly seven and a half of them (over 40 percent), Larsen shows herself as valuing both the display nature-composer and the meditative nature-composer almost equally. During an interview in 2009, Larsen reflected upon *Water Music* and an earlier vocal work titled "Soft Pieces" that she had written while a graduate student in the 1970s: "I wonder if I've been exploring outward display and inward . . . I wonder if I've been exploring both for a long time."[11] While Larsen identifies *Symphony: Water Music* as a "display" piece, and it was commissioned by the Minnesota Orchestra and premiered by them in 1985, the second movement of the symphony also reveals Larsen's intensely personal relationship to nature. Its "inward" quality previews the direction she will turn with increasing frequency in later compositions, where she will sink into and surround herself with nature. At the same time Larsen became more reflective and inward, she became more outspoken regarding the power of music to change people's thinking and lives.

A program note she wrote for her feminist work *Missa Gaia: Mass for the Earth* clarifies the direction of her thinking in 1991–1992:

> It seems to me
> that if we perform traditional Western rituals
> with new reverence, spirit and meaning,
> then perhaps we can help effect change.
> It is, at least, one of the efforts we who make music
> can give to assist Mother Earth
> and repay her in some small way for all she has given us.
>
> LIBBY LARSEN
> PROGRAM NOTES FOR *MISSA GAIA*[12]

Larsen attended Catholic schools and was a regular churchgoer until about ninth grade, when she gave up the practice. Too many questions went unanswered and too many needs went unmet for the young Libby to remain devout. Searching for the mystical that she felt had been excised from the Roman Catholic Church with the reforms of Vatican II, on Sunday mornings a teenage Libby Larsen bicycled to a nearby lake, climbed a favorite gingko tree, and sat alone in its branches. Here she found the spirit-filled silence that she was seeking. Here she could commune with the natural world, which, she explained, "I consider dearer to me than any church edifice." Up in the tree "I could be at peace with the mystical. I could be part of the mysticism by being part of the silence in that tree. No words are necessary, and even the music was gone that's always there."[13] As is the case for many of her sister composers, nature provides Larsen with a connection to the mystical; her association of silence and trees recalls Tower's observation of the quietness of the sequoias.

The longing for silence and the opportunity to *listen* to the nurturing soundscape of nature (and perhaps to discover one's own thoughts) is as important to Larsen as it was to Beach and Talma and Bond. Larsen is outspoken on the topic; her passion is palpable. In order to compose she requires "large blocks of uninterrupted time! The ideal working situation is a quiet moment away." But she observes, "women, in general, grow up not counting on having big blocks of uninterrupted time so they can work things out."[14] Larsen notes that this situation is further complicated if a woman composer elects to have children. Her role models, Pauline Oliveros and Thea Musgrave, provided what she needed to be a composer, but not what she wanted for her personal life; to find that, she turned to her sister. For Larsen, being creative included motherhood, and she sees it, composing, and ecology as closely related and mutually informing pursuits. She is a creative world.

Given its ubiquity as a theme, one might be tempted to read a desire for solitary moments as characteristic of female nature-composers more broadly. But quiet time alone is sought by many creative people, male and female alike, and especially by composers. Hearing sounds in one's head is easier in an environment free of distracting other sounds: in that regard these women are typical of composers more generally. What appears to distinguish women composers from their male colleagues when it comes to quiet is not the particular work conditions they desire, but the too-frequent lack of *access* to those desired conditions.

Yearning for quiet time by oneself may be more keenly felt by women in a culture that has traditionally granted large blocks of dedicated, creative time to men but assumed that women could manage with the leftover bits and pieces of days spent taking care of others, or that has believed truly creative work wasn't done by women anyway. Perhaps society's endorsement of and enchantment with "the struggling artist," "the unappreciated composer," "the mad scientist," and "the tortured genius" – all of whom are assumed to be solitary, brilliant, iconoclastic males – make voicing the need for time alone less urgent for men. Male authors, artists, and composers assumed their right to solitude, and many got it. Assigning the terms "public" and "private" to men's and women's traditional spheres confused and concealed the reality of time for creative thought that was enjoyed by each of the sexes. As with access to counterpoint and orchestration classes, which came late to women who were serious about composing, regular access to conditions conducive to creative work, truly private time, was difficult to secure for many women and almost impossible if they were responsible for a household that included children. Whether familial duties, fears for personal safety, or assumptions of ineptitude were the excuse, results were the same: Women had fewer opportunities to develop their expressive skills, and they were often counseled against solitary, personal experiences in nature beyond their gardens. The consequences of the reality were and are still daunting.[15]

As of 2011, of the composers discussed in this study, Libby Larsen is the only one with a child, a distinction she finds profoundly troubling. It would appear that the majority of widely known female composers in the United States don't have children.[16] The situation is something that Larsen bemoans because she recognizes conception, childbirth, and motherhood as uniquely meaningful creative acts that are available *only* to women. In a recent interview the composer confided: "It seems odd to me to be talking about nature and women composers, and not talking about giving birth. I find it odd and very hard to talk about," perhaps precisely because she feels so very deeply about the issue. Larsen worries that women composers sacrifice the opportunity to fully "be," and she rejects the idea that compositions are like children: "[With compositions] you can put them on a shelf, you can objectify them, you can invent anything you want about them. That's probably the most dangerous thing here. The question of objectification vs. being."[17] And here Larsen reveals her thinking about nature at the most personal level. Nature is not an objective other or something outside herself. For Larsen there is no distance between nature and humanity; they are the same. As a mother she is creative nature.

Larsen rues the pressures that are insidiously present in American society to choose either a creative career or a domestic life, which causes many women to opt out of a natural experience that she believes could inform their work. Lest anyone think the sixty-year-old Larsen is out of step with current attitudes and practices, the choice she described became the focus of an acclaimed 2009 documentary film produced and directed by Academy Award–winning producer Pamela Tanner Bolls titled "Who Does She Think She Is?" The film looked at five contemporary women artists and musicians as they struggled to balance motherhood and their art. The film observes: "A woman still has to choose" and then asks the simple question: "What if she didn't?"[18] Larsen rejects this false dichotomy and wonders whether in accepting a male model of success (its behaviors, its markers, and its timelines), many women composers have given up more than they realized or intended. While recognizing that motherhood is not possible for some, or essential for every woman to achieve a meaningful life, Larsen would like the choice to have a child to be one that is made for the right reasons, reasons that acknowledge the advantages of such an experience for a creative person and for society. She would like no penalty for parenting. But inherited gender roles and codes of behavior die hard. It becomes increasingly clear why Larsen grew frustrated with her religious upbringing.

In comparison to the patriarchal church in which she'd been raised, Larsen explained that nature provided her with an ungendered place and limitless possibilities. And this was the case despite her familiarity with common terms like "mother earth." In assessing her actions Larsen concluded: "That's [one reason] I went outside: because it's not gendered."[19] There were no restrictions on her experience or imagination; she could explore her full being. In *Missa Gaia: Mass for the Earth* (1991–1992), Larsen investigated a range of issues close to her heart – religion, spirituality, regionalism, gender, and nature – and her own potential as an American woman composer.

The Gaia hypothesis, as expressed first by British environmentalist James Lovelock in the 1960s and then in concert with American biologist Lynn Margulis beginning in the 1970s, holds that the planet is a complex, unified, self-regulating system that depends upon cooperation rather than competition among its life forms for its continued evolution.[20] As science, the Gaia hypothesis recognizes the intimate interrelatedness of all nature, human and nonhuman, animate and inanimate. As religion, Gaia worship enjoys many similarities with some of the earliest known Western cultural practices in which people venerated the Great Goddess Earth, Gaia.[21] As much as can be deduced from recently discovered ancient artifacts, Goddess-worshiping cultures were nondualistic and nonhierarchical. Riane Eisler has characterized the societies as possessing "what we today call an ecological consciousness: the awareness that the Earth must be treated with reverence and respect."[22] Such a reading seems logical for a feminist, peace activist, and social historian such as Eisler, but it is not hers alone. Eisler quotes the esteemed Greek archeologist Nicolas Platon as saying of these "prehistoric" societies: "the whole of life was pervaded by an ardent faith in the goddess Nature, the source of all creation and harmony."[23] For Eisler, Gaia-informed thought didn't fade with the Paleolithic Period; she sees sisterlike Gaia figures in "Isis in Egypt, Ishtar in Canaan, Demeter in Greece, and later, as the Magna Mater of Rome and the Catholic Virgin Mary, the Mother of God."[24] Larsen's embrace of Gaia as totemic for her full-length mass, which includes a soprano solo, SATB chorus, and chamber ensemble, is a logical outgrowth of her early Roman Catholic faith overlaid with her spiritual, feminist, ecological, and bioregional sensibilities.[25] She is less concerned with Margulis's biological theories than with the spiritual metaphors Gaia provides.

When discussing the range of her frustrations with the 1960s demystification of the Roman Catholic Church, Larsen contrasted her situation to that of the devout Catholic composer Olivier Messiaen: "Messiaen, as a male, was able to give voice within the Roman Catholic Church in large, structural ways; I wouldn't be [able to]. . . . in small, modest ways [yes], but not [in] large, structural ways because of the gendering in the church."[26] As a result of having felt disenfranchised, Larsen determined that "religion is human-defined, which is the absolute ego." By comparison, Larsen's understanding of the divine resists definition, dominion, or containment. "The ultimate egotistical statement is to say you have a relationship with God. God becomes co-opted by your own ego."[27] In *Missa Gaia* Larsen makes a large personal "structural" statement that involves poets and writers from different cultures in her effort. By setting Wendell Berry, Gerard Manley Hopkins, Joy Harjo, Meister Eckhart, Maurice Kenny, and words from *The Chinook Psalter*, Larsen makes clear her belief in the immanence of the divine across gender, time, place, and culture.

If the title of the Mass were not enough to announce her nature-oriented outlook on things spiritual, in liner notes she wrote to accompany the recording of the work, Libby Larsen foregrounded her ecological agenda: "*Missa Gaia: Mass for the Earth* is a Mass for our times which adopts the form and spirit of the traditional Mass and replaces the texts with words addressing human beings' relationship to the Earth."[28] Later in the same statement, she situated herself within a particular place on the Earth and reflected on her perspective:

> *Missa Gaia* is a celebration of those of us who live on this land, a land
> which can be terribly beautiful and gentle, a land which can be harsh – but
> which is always giving and always renewing. . . . The United States of
> America is not an old country. Most of us are really still pioneers. And we
> are still learning what it is to live on this land and what it is for the land to
> let us live here. Amidst the natural abundance of our country, I live with
> the blizzards and tornadoes of the Midwest. And I see the earthquakes of
> the West Coast, the hurricanes of the South and the East coast, and the
> arid lands of the Southwest. I am reminded again and again that the Earth
> lets us live on it.[29]

The composer acknowledges her particular American perspective on nature.
She also grants the earth an intelligence akin to what Bond (and Leopold
before her) attributed to mountains. We have lots to learn from "this land."
Larsen roundly rejects an anthropocentric relationship to nature. With her
statement "the Earth lets us live on it," it is clear she believes that humankind
does not have the upper hand; on the contrary, we are like squatters. Such
remarks, which privilege a cooperative spirit between humans and nonhuman
others, suggest her sympathies with ecofeminist thinking. However, Larsen
wasn't familiar with the term "ecofeminist" when she composed *Missa Gaia*
or wrote her remarks, and she recently rejected the label for herself: "No,
I'm not going to buy it. I'm going to tell you, I may be one, but I don't want
to be called one because that's to be co-opted, which is exactly the domination model."[30] As Larsen rejected the role the Catholic Church imagined for
her, she continues to refuse labels, categories, and prescribed behaviors of all
kinds. Nonetheless, Larsen shares many values with spiritual ecofeminists,[31]
and also with bioregionalists, people who make a commitment to being in a
place and knowing the particular regional environment. Having grown up in
Minnesota and completed her schooling "in state," Larsen still lives there year-
round. When not in Minneapolis, she has a summer home near a lake not far
away. Libby Larsen knows this part of the Earth well; she is a placed person.

Missa Gaia musicalizes Larsen's connection to "this land" (the United
States of America), the Earth, and to women and men who have expressed
ecological and spiritual values similar to her own. Within the thirty-five-min-
ute work, each of the six movements allows her to focus on a particularly resonant image or issue. Larsen sets Wendell Berry's poem "Closing the Circle"
as her Introit, and she establishes the essential visual and musical symbol of
the work: circles.[32] Larsen shares her enthusiasm for this image with Oliveros
and Bond, and, as will be shown, with Doolittle as well. With an opening

melodic line whose notes trace the circle of fifths while a unison chorus sings, "Within the circles of our lives, we dance the circles of the years, the circles of the seasons," Larsen's music emphasizes cycles, connection, returning, joining together, "each by all." Farmer, conservationist, activist, Baptist Sunday school teacher, writer, and "placed" person Wendell Berry has deep roots in Kentucky, where he lives and where his family has farmed for over two centuries; he understands the cycles of nature. One senses that his words and Larsen's music are as naturally connected to each other as the authors are to their places[33] (example 9.4).

The idea of circles and connections permeates the music beyond a melody derived from the overtone series; the entire work is a musicalization of the concept of unity and wholeness.[34] Unison singing dominates the Mass: the choristers are connected by the similarity of their notes. This may be an outgrowth of Larsen's early experience singing Gregorian chant at Catholic school, a practice she thoroughly enjoyed. And Larsen uses chimes, an instrument whose reverberating sound bleeds into and blends with the surrounding music.[35] Additionally, ostinato figures (brief recurring gestures) and homogeneous rhythms – in the case of *Missa Gaia,* dominantly straightforward quarter- or eighth-note patterns with very few dotted figures – reinforce the solid congruence of the Mass.

Missa Gaia is harmonically unified and stays close to pitch centers D and A throughout. This suits Larsen's instrument of choice, the oboe, which she features in the work and uses to introduce and connect individual movements. The oboe's most characteristic range is between D4 and A5, although it can go below and above these notes. Selecting this particular double-reed woodwind instrument to carry so much of her message introduces another set of connections, but these move beyond sonic imagery. As one of a handful of instruments within the Western art music tradition historically associated with depictions of pastoral scenes and more specifically with the Siciliano – a graceful, lilting rustic dance – the oboe connects the sounds of Larsen's Earth Mass with earlier works inspired by and evocative of nature. The simple melodies, parallel thirds, and drones intrinsic to the Siciliano also characterize long passages of *Missa Gaia.*

While written in $\frac{3}{4}$, and not in the $\frac{6}{8}$ or $\frac{12}{8}$ meter typical of Sicilianos, the second movement still exhibits a lilting rhythm, simple melody, many thirds, and opening and closing pedal tones, which act like a framing drone for the piece.[36] The only mood indicator that the composer provides for the two-and-a-half-minute movement is the single word "gently"; one gets the feeling

EXAMPLE 9.4 (*above and facing*). *Missa Gaia*, "Introit." By Libby Larsen, mm. 1–7. Copyright © 1992 by ECS Publishing, Boston, Massachusetts. All rights reserved. Used with kind permission.

that the composer is rocking listeners with her music. Larsen uses the final stanza of T. S. Eliot's *Ash Wednesday*, the first lengthy poem he wrote after his conversion to Anglicanism in 1927, for her "Kyrie"[37]: "Blessed sister, holy mother, spirit of the fountains, spirit of the garden . . . " The appeal and appropriateness of Eliot's lines to Larsen's project become obvious. Having had Berry introduce the primary visual image, the circle, Eliot now introduces *Mother* Earth, Gaia. Later references in the stanza to the "spirit of the river, spirit of the sea" must have resonated deeply with a composer so at home in and on the water. As with "Hot, still" from *Symphony: Water Music*, in "Kyrie" Larsen pulls in and goes deep. Despite its presence in the public celebration that is a Mass, this movement is a quiet, meditative, personal expression of Larsen's feelings about the Earth. Its scoring for two-part, divisi, women's chorus allows the composer to identify with the singers' voices and make their supplication her own.

Like Victoria Bond, who addressed the global nature of environmental issues in her piece *Thinking Like a Mountain*, Libby Larsen recognizes the need to reach across religious and spiritual traditions for her Mass; she calls upon a variety of Christian, mystic, and Native American writers to help speak her message. "Glory be to God for dappled things" was written by the English poet, Roman Catholic convert, and Jesuit priest Gerard Manley Hopkins; it forms Larsen's "Gloria."[38] Its joyous enumeration of nature's many hidden beauties – brindled cows, stippled trout, and finches' wings – and its celebration of "all things counter, original, spare, strange" allow Larsen to fling her arms wide open and embrace nature. One wonders if in her resistance to categorization, Larsen identifies with "things counter [and] original." Her "bright" music matches the extroverted mood of traditional Glorias and the poetry of this one, most especially where Larsen's energetic sounds vivify Hopkins's upbeat message.[39]

"Credo" adapts texts by both the medieval mystic, theologian, and philosopher Meister Eckhart and the upstate New York–born contemporary Mohawk Maurice Kenny, and combines them with lines from *The Living Bible*. Where Eckhart observes, "God is in all things," and "Nature can teach us," Kenny insists, "I am nature. My chant [and] dance are nature." Larsen's affinity for Kenny's Native American perspective is clear: poet and composer *are* nature. Larsen explained: "I have quoted Native Americans because of where I live. In Minnesota the Native American tradition is very integrated, very present. I have learned a lot from the Native American tradition about my own personal relation to nature."[40] It seems logical, then, that the final two movements of *Missa Gaia* use American Indian sources for their texts.

The "Agnus Dei/Sanctus" takes lines from the *Chinook Psalter*, a Native American Christian text. The lines "How lovely are thy holy groves / God of the heaven and earth / My soul longs and faints / for the circles of thy trees. / My heart and my flesh / sing with joy to thee / O God of life"[41] are an adaptation of "Psalm 84" as found in the *King James Bible*: "How lovely is thy dwelling place / O Lord of hosts!" With its references to song and the natural world, especially trees, and to the imagery of circles, its appeal must have been obvious for Larsen. The "Credo" melds directly into the "Agnus Dei/Sanctus" using a sustained high G that closes the third movement. The oboe cascades down to A via a perfect fourth to D and then opens with a solo that uses the seven pitches of an A-major scale. Beginning at measure 6, orchestral bells reply "gently" to the oboe's call while strings play "warmly" underneath. In a joint effort with the soprano, who enters at measure 8, the ensemble moves pitch material from A major to A♭ major. In doing so, oboe, orchestral bells, and soprano present all twelve chromatic pitches and Larsen completes another conceptual circle, this one of pitch. Once again, the undulating melodic materials musicalize the larger circular theme[42] (example 9.5). Closing in measures 85 and 86 with a final solo oboe incantation, now a half step higher than that which opened the "Agnus Dei/Sanctus," the movement segues directly into "Benediction," where the continuing oboe solo immediately sinks back down a semitone (example 9.6). Echoing the exact pitches of the initial circle-of-fifths melody of the Introit, but now inverted – what had ascended now descends – the larger piece is ever changing but ever the same. Even though Larsen uses two series of pitches that together employ all twelve tones, she does not write a serialized piece. Serial techniques would likely be too prescriptive for the boundary-eschewing composer. In this regard she uses serial techniques with the same freedom demanded of them by Louise Talma. It appears, however, that Larsen uses the two series to musicalize the ideas of inclusion, accommodation, coming together, and wholeness. All twelve pitches find a home in *Missa Gaia*; each series needs the other to be complete.

Joy Harjo's "Eagle Poem," which Larsen sets in her "Benediction," may come closest to articulating in words the composer's understanding of her own relationship to nature. Once again, circles are the central symbol.

EXAMPLE 9.5. *Missa Gaia*, "Agnus Dei/Sanctus." By Libby Larsen, mm. 1–13.
Copyright © 1992 by ECS Publishing, Boston, Massachusetts.

EXAMPLE 9.6. *Missa Gaia,* "Benediction." By Libby Larsen, mm. 1–4.
Copyright © 1992 by ECS Publishing, Boston, Massachusetts.
All rights reserved. Used with kind permission.

To pray you open your whole self
To sky, to earth, to sun, to moon
To one whole voice that is you.
And know there is more
That you can't see, can't hear
Can't know except in moments
Steadily growing, and in languages
That aren't always sound but other
Circles of motion.
Like eagle that Sunday morning
Over Salt river. Circled in blue sky
In wind, swept our hearts clean
With sacred wings.
We see you, see ourselves and know
That we must take the utmost care
And kindness in all things.
Breathe in, knowing we are made of
All this, and breathe, knowing
We are truly blessed because we
Were born, and die soon, within a
True circle of motion,
Like eagle rounding out the morning
Inside us.
We pray that it will be done
In beauty.
In beauty.[43]

Images of circles and references to unified voices are manifest, once again, in large-and small-scale musical behavior: Multiple ostinato patterns energize and unify the culminating movement. Among the most important is the one introduced in measure 5; it will return in a varied form to close the

EXAMPLE 9.7. *Missa Gaia*, "Benediction." By Libby Larsen, mm. 5–7.
Copyright © 1992 by ECS Publishing, Boston, Massachusetts.
All rights reserved. Used with kind permission.

Mass (example 9.7). The pattern persists through measure 50 with just one interruption. At measures 38–40 it ceases, and the music slows down, then changes meters from $\frac{5}{8}$ to $\frac{3}{4}$; and the chorus builds an eight-part stacked chord: B♭–D–F–A–C♯–E–G♯–B. The ambiguity of the sonority, with its multiple tonal implications – is it a B♭-major 7 chord followed by a C♯-minor 7, or three major triads, B♭ major, followed by A major linked to E major, or something else? – musicalizes Larsen's wonder at the "moon." Larsen composes the mystery she finds in nature (example 9.8). The $\frac{5}{8}$ ostinato resumes at measure 41, and the once-divisi chorus now chants in unison: "To one whole voice that is you." A new $\frac{4}{4}$ ostinato that is introduced at measure 51 and continues for eight measures abruptly changes the rhythmic orientation of the movement (example 9.9). The punchy syncopated pattern is an unexpected contrast to the legato contour of the initial ostinato, however, Larsen's gear shift sets the stage for the text that follows: "And know there is more that you can't see, can't hear, can't know"—and, a listener might add, can't anticipate. The change is sudden and unexpected but perhaps forms a suitable analogue for nature's occasional impetuous behaviors.

Larsen returns to the circle-of-fifths pitch pattern that opened the movement as the chorus sings "circles of motion" in a quasi-round. The composer layers circular patterns upon circular patterns with orchestral bells striking their own circular series starting at measure 68, followed by pianos I and II at measures 73 and 74. The increased activity is invigorating. When at measures 114 and 119 Harjo commands us to "breathe," Larsen obeys, writing a *mezzo-*

EXAMPLE 9.8. *Missa Gaia,* "Benediction." By Libby Larsen, mm. 38–40.
Copyright © 1992 by ECS Publishing, Boston, Massachusetts.
All rights reserved. Used with kind permission.

EXAMPLE 9.9. *Missa Gaia,* "Benediction." By Libby Larsen, mm. 51–52.
Copyright © 1992 by ECS Publishing, Boston, Massachusetts.
All rights reserved. Used with kind permission.

di-voce a cappella choral respiration.[44] Singers and listeners are grateful for the momentary pause.

The opening rhythmic ostinato, slightly varied, returns at measure 128, followed by another form of the pattern at measure 134, and still another at 145. A final statement at measure 156 closes the piece. Larsen's musicalized circle has changed since the opening of the piece, but it is still a circle, and perhaps even a larger one. The idea of connection and relatedness, basic to the behavior of the details of the piece, and central to the texts of her authors, emerges as the defining characteristic of the entire work. This is, as Larsen asserted, a piece about ecology, and "meant to be about ecology."

Missa Gaia doesn't reference all religious traditions – no Jewish, Hindi, Buddhist, Jainist, or Islamic sources are drawn upon – and Larsen doesn't include words from some of the nation's most famous spokespersons for nature, as there's nothing from Henry David Thoreau, Susan Fenimore Cooper, John Muir, or Rachel Carson. And given the name of the work, it may strike some as surprising that there is only a single female among her contributors, Joy Harjo. But Libby Larsen isn't bullied by political correctness, and she won't submit to ideologies that demand more than she is willing to give; these are, she insists, as constraining as the patriarchal religious attitudes she rejected. The composer writes what she knows; like the midwestern place where she grew up, she is at home with her authors' thoughts about nature.

Near the end of two days of interviews, Larsen reflected upon what we'd discussed and admitted that putting ideas into words does not come naturally for her. She explained that her first language is music, her second is gesture, and only a distant third is words: "I was sort of floored last night at what I'm learning, because my language is music, and pieces just come, but to try to get a perspective on them . . . I realized that I have a twenty-year arch going that I didn't know I had going, an investigation."[45] The arch that Larsen was referring to was an arch from her early "Soft Pieces" back to quietude: "Where I'm going," the composer concluded, "is to be quiet."[46]

Larsen spoke about the practical difficulty of "setting up silence with instruments that have heavy cultural baggage." "Silence," she concluded, "is the antithesis of what Western music has co-opted about emotion."[47] But two of her recent pieces have come close to expressing the fully resonant silence Larsen values and craves: *Now I Pull Silver*, a work for amplified flute, real-time fractal imagery, manipulated spoken voice, Silvertone lap guitar, Kalimba, and brass wind chimes, which uses A. E. Stallings's poem "Arachne Gives Thanks to Athena," and *downwind of roses in Maine* a piece for flute, B♭ clarinet, and "a little hedge of mallet instruments," including marimba, vibraphone, and orchestral bells, which she asks to be played "like wind chimes in a gentle breeze, out of time."[48] Both pieces were composed in 2008.[49] *Now I Pull Silver* never rises above *pianissimo* for its three-and-a-half-minute duration, and *downwind of roses in Maine*, a piece that is almost twice as long, never rises above *mezzo forte*, and then for only a few measures. Larsen referred to *downwind of roses in Maine* as "my favorite thing I've done."[50]

Larsen conceived *downwind* in summer 2008, close by Rockport, Maine. Waiting in a motel parking lot for her group to gather and head off to the Seal Bay Festival, where she was a featured composer, Larsen didn't smell the salt-rich ocean air that was all around her but instead noted the choking odor of diesel fuel coming from the nearby throughway.[51] The composer recalled that "it was horrible." Larsen, however, was standing next to a rose hedge and willed herself "to go inside their fragrance, and not be where I was. And it was beautiful, quiet; to be inside the fragrance you *are* the fragrance, somehow."[52] And this was the genesis of the work: being the fragrance became the piece.[53]

Victoria Bond had spoken of her heightened sense of smell, which she attributed to learning from her pets. But what was the source of Libby Larsen's olfactory keenness? Did it have roots in her early upbringing in the Roman Catholic Church, with its use of incense? When the question was put to the composer, she admitted that she "hadn't thought about it before [being] asked," but then offered a possible explanation: "I would say the connection to fragrance may be more a function of growing up in a place where sub-zero temperatures create an absence of nature's aromas for enough time that the body longs to breathe them in again, so much so that a spring violet, delicate in aroma, is a fiesta to the nose in Minnesota."[54]

The piece was commissioned by the School of Visual and Performing Arts at the University of Louisiana at Monroe, and performed there for the first time in February of 2009. Larsen explained how she coached her musicians to think of their job as "conditioning the air; there are no barriers, there is no linearity."[55] Her charge to the musicians distills three themes that recur in Larsen's thinking.

The first has to do with composing music to effect change. Recognizing that music has the ability to alter the atmosphere and "condition" the environment, the composer hoped that *downwind of roses in Maine*, in its gentle, personal, and inward way, could move listeners to greater mindfulness of their place within the cosmos, a goal similar to that which she expressed for the public and overtly ecological *Missa Gaia*. Both types of pieces can inspire action, and Larsen used the opportunities they presented to sensitize listeners to ideas close to her heart. While Larsen sees herself as heading toward "quiet," and *downwind of roses in Maine* is exemplary of that movement, she also recognizes the need for public display pieces and continues to write both.[56]

The second has to do with barriers, and in this case more specifically the unnecessary obstacles that prevent people and music from being fully realized. As with her separation from the church and her rejection of labels and categories, Larsen resists tradition-bound restrictions on her music or its creation. She rejects the isolated-genius model for herself. For this composer, working collaboratively with chamber musicians excites her creativity: this is the ideal environment. And performing in venues where players and audiences are seated on the same level increases her music's ability to impact listeners. For Larsen, "it's about a full realization of self . . . this self that doesn't live within the definition of linear" or any other ill-conceived limitation.[57] As Larsen conjures and evokes the memory of fragrance through sound, *downwind of roses in Maine* celebrates multisensory stimulation, the auditory and the olfactory. It is simultaneously her most decisive and subtle statement about the dissolution of boundaries.

The third idea concerns concepts of time. Larsen's mandate regarding "no linearity" recalls the tent conversation from decades earlier when she and her friends considered the notion that present and future, now and then, are coetaneous in the tiny pines they had planted. As a mature composer, Larsen "goes deep" to fully engage an expanded, dilated moment and open herself to all that is.[58] She invites her audience to do the same. There's no room for teleological thinking, which potentially hurries people away from where they are. Taking the time to sink into the music and forget clock time becomes the essence of *downwind of roses in Maine*.

In the minutes prior to the premiere performance, Larsen addressed her audience. She explained the origins of the piece, her encounter with the rose hedge, and her hope that with the help of her music, the listeners could experience something similar, if only in their imaginations. Larsen invited them to sink deep where they were; to not seek after narratives; and to allow the music to help them "become the fragrance." A month after the performance, she recalled that the audience listened, rapt, and the railroad trains that regularly rattled through Monroe, Louisiana, and which everyone expected to do the same that evening, inexplicably ceased for the duration of the piece.[59]

Just as Larsen hadn't known the word "ecofeminism" or the movement associated with the term when she composed *Missa Gaia* in 1992, the composer was not conscious of the sense of smell having "been dubbed the sense of the postmodern" by contemporary cultural theorists when she wrote *downwind of roses in Maine* in 2009.[60] In a collection memorably titled *The Smell-Culture Reader*, Mark Graham characterized smell as "the sense that confuses categories and challenges boundaries. It is difficult to localize, hard to contain and has the character of flux and transitoriness." In a culture that has privileged sight – "the sense of differentiation par excellence" – the sense of smell offers "shifting, fluctuating and imprecise qualities of its objects, odors."[61] While the composer will only admit to "perhaps unconsciously" making a postmodern statement about the arbitrariness of sensorial boundaries, given Larsen's commitment to dissolving boundaries, it is hard to imagine a more appropriate sense to involve in the composer's musical exploration of her experience.[62] Combining the most transitory sense, smell, with the most abstract art form, music, frees Larsen from the yoke of traditional forms and expectations. Her sounds, like the remembered fragrance of roses, can waft in the air and in a listener's imaginings. Linearity dissolves as musicians and listeners douse themselves in Larsen's "gentle," "always delicate and fluid" music.[63]

Rather than use conventional time signatures, with their assumed accented and unaccented beats, Larsen organizes *downwind* with instructions for a "Pulse = 56–60," which is unchanged, and groupings of notes in bars of 2, 3, 4, or 5. Notation keeps musicians together; it does not imply meter. Any sense of momentum comes from brief rotating patterns of notes and not from larger rhythmic behaviors. The composer encourages nonlinearity with instructions to be "still" and with requests to play "out of time." The quiet dynamic range of the piece, encompassing quadruple *piano* (*pppp*) to *mezzo forte* (*mf*), is accompanied by numerous terms suggesting the nature of the soft sound Larsen wants: wafting, gossamer, hushed, murmur, rustle.[64] While pitches are precisely notated, the blending and bleeding of sounds that characterize those produced by marimba, orchestra bells, and vibraphone – and Larsen's frequent instructions to the flutist to play with a wide vibrato, or a tremolo, or to slide from pitch to pitch – combine to create a soundscape that is fragrance-like in its shifting, fluctuating "transitoriness" (example 9.10).

Like Graham's description of smells, Larsen's music is "difficult to localize, hard to contain." We recognize that sound is moving around us, but we don't know its origin or form. Sounds are carried through the air like scent or smoke, but listeners can't be certain of their conveyance. Sounds are hinted at, they hang in the air for a moment, but just as their identification seems certain, the music wafts away to nothing.

EXAMPLE 9.10. *downwind of roses in Maine*. By Libby Larsen, mm. 1–12.
Copyright © 2009 by Libby Larsen Publishing, Minneapolis, Minnesota,
U.S.A. All rights reserved. Reprinted with kind permission.

Like fragrance, whose intensification varies without apparent cause, Lars-
en's music unexpectedly rustles and murmurs; it increases momentum. And
some movement is essential if audiences are going to stay focused on a work
that lasts over seven minutes. Analogous to sustained exposure to a single
scent, which renders it imperceptible to most people, drifting unmoored in
musical space invites disengagement, and that is the opposite of Larsen's hope

EXAMPLE 9.11. *downwind of roses in Maine.* By Libby Larsen, mm. 58–61.
Copyright © 2009 by Libby Larsen Publishing, Minneapolis, Minnesota,
U.S.A. All rights reserved. Reprinted with kind permission.

for her piece. While increased momentum can't suggest a goal in this piece, it
must connect listeners to the sounds (example 9.11).

At measure 91 Larsen writes: "Serene to the end." Flute and clarinet
sustain notes and then ultimately diminuendo to a whole rest in the final measure. The marimba is instructed to "murmur" its rotating pattern. Orchestra
bells that introduced the piece make a wisp-like, *pianissimo* appearance, and
vibraphone and marimba join together in a triple *piano* (*ppp*) alternation of
notes that evaporates to "niente" (nothing) at the close of measure 96. Little

escapes Larsen's notice, and her use of the Italian term rather than its English translation "nothing" is telling. When asked why she chose this word, Larsen explained, "I suppose I could indicate 'nothing' but I feel this word suggests 'a decision to terminate sound.' Somehow 'niente' suggests slipping into the absence of sound. Strange."[65] Music, like the fragrance that inspired it, has disappeared beyond our perception, and we follow it (example 9.12).

Larsen's embrace of a nonlinear, multisensory, boundary-defying concept for *downwind* raises a number of questions regarding how to hear and understand the end of the work. Does the composer intend the music or the musicians to be "serene," the term she indicates at measure 91? Do her words "to the end" imply to the end of the piece, or beyond? As she aspired for her players and listeners to *become* the fragrance and experience what she had the summer before, it appears that Larsen also hopes they *become* serenity. Inspired by the fragrance of roses, with *downwind of roses in Maine* Larsen invites listeners to come with her, "to be quiet."

Larsen's musicalization of fragrance is unique among the pieces discussed in this book, but the work raises a number of questions that are germane to the larger study and worth brief consideration. Do roses, any more than music, speak similarly across cultures? Does *downwind of roses in Maine* have particular meaning to audiences in the West and North America, where the flower is often associated with romantic love? Would a composer in India choose jasmine or sandalwood to similar effect? Marcello Aspria, a sociologist who specializes in the study of fragrance, observes: "In the Middle East, men wear rose based fragrances, because yellow rose is the cherished flower in Islam."[66] How is that cultural practice reconciled with the more Western association of roses and the scent of rose water with females, and males with fragrances that contain citrus and musk? To whom does this music speak?

Would the piece speak equally to men and women, given research that demonstrates women's greater olfactory prowess, which includes a keener ability to identify a smell, to assess its intensity, to appreciate its complexity and subtleness, and to decode and describe it? While *downwind of roses in Maine* isn't accompanied by the actual scent of roses, would a woman's greater sensitivity to the fragrance mean that her memory of the scent was that much more intense than that of her male counterpart? Recent research suggests that this is not necessarily the case.[67]

Would the memory of the scent of roses be a welcome, enjoyable, serenity-inducing experience for listeners who associate the flower with pain or loss, two conditions that regularly attend romantic love? Beyond the chemical

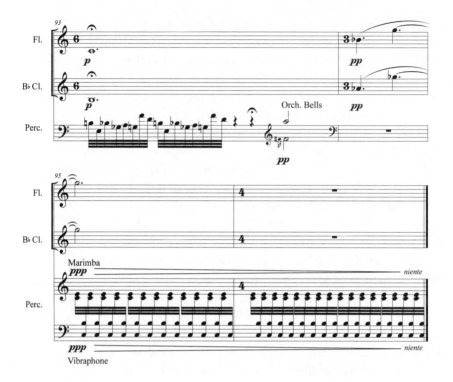

EXAMPLE 9.12 (*above and facing*). *downwind of roses in Maine*. By Libby Larsen, mm. 90–96. Copyright © 2009 by Libby Larsen Publishing, Minneapolis, Minnesota, U.S.A. All rights reserved. Reprinted with kind permission.

properties that give a fragrance its particular aroma, its effects depend to a large extent on the perceiver and the feelings, emotions, and sensations that are conjured by the smell. Does Larsen intend for her piece to be a pleasant experience for all listeners, or just a deeply felt one?

The sense of smell is complex and subjective, and describing it, like describing sound, is difficult at best. Descriptions can minimize, neutralize, or ignore essential cultural and personal differences. As Clara Origlia observes, the sense of smell involves "the body, the imagination, and memory." Our perception of the "pleasantness" of a fragrance relies upon the chemical compound, but also on our emotional responses that are tied to experiences and memories, cultural and individual.[68] While there are some universals regarding fragrance – among which is the observation that the most enduring are ones are derived from nature – responses are culture-specific, and beyond

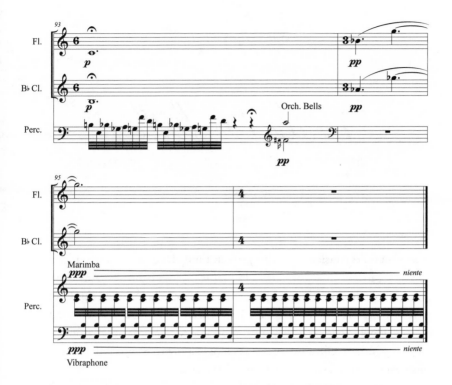

that, person-specific. When Larsen invites musicians and audience members to "become the fragrance" of roses, is she inviting them to engage in an activity that will be similarly pleasant and escapist to that which she enjoyed?

What is fragrance? What is music? Can one conjure the other for any but a handful of synesthetes? How do such ephemeral entities imprint themselves on the mind? Larsen's piece forces listeners to reconsider how music and the senses might work together and inspire or evoke each other; the composer nudges us beyond comfortable assumptions regarding discrete spheres for sounds and smells. With its roots in the scent of flowers, *downwind of roses in Maine* is yet another example, and a unique one, of the ways American women interact with nature and express that personal experience in their music.

10

Emily Doolittle

✥

Of the composers considered in this project, Emily Doolittle is the youngest by nearly a generation. Born in 1972 in Halifax, Nova Scotia, to American parents, Doolittle enjoys both Canadian and U.S. citizenship; she thinks of herself as North American. Like Pauline Oliveros and Libby Larsen most especially, Doolittle is extremely uncomfortable with categories that might confine her. Where Oliveros speaks often of valuing freedom, and has consciously tacked a professional (and personal) course that some consider to lie outside traditional boundaries, Doolittle simply *is* a free spirit. She doesn't talk about it much. There is little that is self-conscious about this young composer. As will become clear, dual citizenship is just one manifestation of Doolittle's boundary-crossing being. Where Oliveros appears almost uncomfortable with the word "nature" and uses a large repertoire of expressions to speak about the natural environment, Doolittle acknowledges the complexity of the concept it represents but embraces the term as long as she can define it. With characteristic openness, Doolittle actualizes her understanding of nature as a wholly unified entity with human beings one species among many, and she does this without romanticizing nature or taking herself too seriously. Positioning herself *within* nature means she maintains a healthy, light grasp. Doolittle and her music substantiate the ecological condition; environmental mindfulness is part of her DNA.

Given the groundswell of Green thinking in the past thirty years, it may be tempting to interpret Doolittle's outlook as typical of folks born in the decade that celebrated the first Earth Day and saw the first Greenpeace activism; and certainly there is broader awareness of environmental concerns in all sectors of society today than prior to the 1970s.[1] But to attribute her interest solely to the temper of the times would deny Doolittle the passion of her sensibility or her commitment to its practice. Not every Gen Xer shares her passions. Just as Amy Beach was a product of the late nineteenth century and its values and mores, Doolittle is a product of the late twentieth century; that said, historical circumstances alone do not explain the specific relationships each composer cultivated with the natural world. While context can make something possible, it doesn't make anything inevitable. Doolittle's particular expression of ecological awareness and her intentional advocacy on behalf of the environment place her in a unique position in the pantheon of composers considered in this study.

At least in part because of her relative youth, Emily Doolittle has benefited from significantly greater access to nature compared to many of the women considered in *Music and the Skillful Listener.* But it is not this alone that separates her from the other composers; greater access to more different opportunities of all kinds may be the single most distinguishing feature of Doolittle's late-twentieth-century formative years. She is as much the product of second-wave feminist initiatives as the concurrent environmental movement. Where Pauline Oliveros was among a small number of women breaking through barriers of all kinds in the 1950s before second-wave feminism gained momentum, Doolittle was a child of the movement and could ride its wave. She has availed herself of educational opportunities at every turn and pursued formal studies in many fields and across multiple continents. Like many of her contemporaries, she travels freely and frequently, and in contrast to the earliest women writers discussed in the introduction, she does so by herself with no escorts and no disapproving glances.

Doolittle earned a bachelor's degree in composition and theory in 1995 from Dalhousie University in Nova Scotia, where her composition teacher was Dennis Farrell and where she minored in oboe; she earned the Eerste Fase in 1998 from Koninklijk Conservatorium in the Hague, where she studied composition with Louis Andriessen and Martijn Padding; she received a master's degree in composition from Indiana University in 1999 studying composition with Don Freund; and in 2007 she completed a PhD in composition from Princeton, where she worked with a number of supportive and influential people, including Barbara White, Steve Mackey, Paul Lansky, Paul Koonce, and Peter Westergaard, and wrote a dissertation cleverly titled "Other Species' Counterpoint: An Investigation of the Relationship between Human Music and Animal Songs."[2] Her project explored the hypothesis that "some animals . . . share our ability to create and experience aesthetic sound." In her unique boundary-defying way, Doolittle continues to cultivate and enjoy close professional and personal associations with other composers, performing musicians, musicologists, artists, and scientists around the globe who interact with her as an equal. Without obligations to anyone but herself prior to her appointment as assistant professor of composition and theory at Cornish College of the Arts in Seattle in 2008, Doolittle had long periods of time alone to pursue her work. Since her appointment, she has consistently etched out time within a consuming academic position.

In her still brief career, Emily Doolittle has enjoyed residencies at multiple artist retreats, including the MacDowell Colony, the Banff Centre for the Arts in Alberta, Canada, and Ucross, a 20,000-plus-acre ranch located in the high plains and Rocky Mountain region of Wyoming, among other places.[3] According to Doolittle, her time at the Blue Mountain Center in the Adirondacks, a community for artists and activists, "was a great place for ways of thinking about combining both" art and advocacy and was important to the composer. She has taken advantage of opportunities to immerse herself in summer programs that stimulated her creativity and nurtured her activist inclinations. Doolittle participated in R. Murray Schafer's Wolf Project and spent part of the summer of 2003 at *Bread and Puppet,* a political-activist puppet theater in Vermont; she has thrived in the collaborative artistic cultures. Around the same time she took up fiddle playing and continues to pursue her love of amateur music making. Her attraction to collaborative creative opportunities echoes the preferences of Oliveros and Larsen.

But beyond Doolittle's educational experiences, perhaps nothing has impacted her thinking and her work more powerfully than her family and its culture of inclusivity. If there is a single common characteristic that can be pointed to as relating these skillful listeners, it is the importance of nurturing family environments.[4] Filled with equal numbers of potters and physicists, evolutionary biologists and artists, gardeners and hikers, Doolittle's family modeled a life where science and art were not mutually exclusive pursuits but different approaches to understanding. The potter was a math teacher; the evolutionary biologist was also an artist. And this wasn't a generational fluke. Among her grandparents there were scientists and painters alike. Just as Doolittle's dual citizenship impeded exclusive national allegiances and made possible the idea that she was the product of an entire continent, a family where the arts and the sciences were valued and pursued with equal vigor, rigor, and enthusiasm reinforced her sense that boundaries, whether between nations or academic disciplines, were arbitrary and even unreal. It doesn't require a large leap to see how such an upbringing would inform a holistic approach to the natural world and cause one to reject dichotomous thinking.

In her dissertation Doolittle acknowledged the work of biologist John T. Bonner and characterized his nondichotomous approach to nature and culture as "an inspiration."[5] She quoted Bonner:

> In principle it would appear so easy to be both [holistic and reductionist] at once, but human nature is such that it enjoys taking positions on philosophical or political dichotomies, ignoring totally the possibility that some of these dichotomies are not genuine antitheses of the either-or category, but are complementary.[6]

Doolittle concluded, "Creating an opposition between the biological and the cultural, as often occurs in comparisons between the animal and the human, is likewise unnecessary."

In a recent interview, the composer expanded upon the idea of dichotomies and complementarity:

> I think that science and art ask different questions, and deal with different things, and describe things in different ways. But there are lots of things in the world that we can look at in both a scientific way and an artistic way, and I don't think it's a matter of one way being right and the other wrong. They are just different ways of describing things or understanding things.[7]

Doolittle attributes much of her comfort in talking to scientists to years of conversations with her dad, a molecular biologist interested in molecular evolution, who had at one time considered majoring in literature or art. As Doolittle explained: "He's been doing art as an amateur all his life" and has "been in art school for about ten years. . . . He's been doing those things side by side." Most recently he's "become interested in animals . . . and has been collaborating with a photography professor at Nova Scotia College of Art and Design on some projects looking at animals and art. So now we have an unexpected convergence of some of our interests."[8]

Her first research trip to Scotland in 2007 raised Doolittle's awareness of just how valuable her family culture was to a composer wanting to learn about bioacoustics:

> The first time I spent time at Saint Andrews University was two years ago and I was just there for a couple of weeks, and it really struck me how much science is a culture, . . . a culture of how you talk about things and how you

look at things. And I realized that even though I wasn't educated in that
culture, I was at least familiar with it because of growing up around it.

In addition to her many conversations with her father, about whom Doolittle
explains, "it's primarily from talking with him that I learned about how to
talk with scientists," the composer credits the rest of her family as well with
contributing to her comfortable boundary-crossing ways:[9]

> My mother's father is a scientist and my mother was a math teacher, so she
> has some of that background as well, so . . . spending time around scientists
> made me realize how much it really is a culture and how lucky I am to be
> familiar with it, even if I haven't studied it. Other people studying animal
> songs and music don't have so much familiarity with the scientific world, and
> I think that if you don't . . . it takes a long time to get used to it.[10]

Beyond her immediate family, Doolittle's extended family played a role as well
in shaping her worldview. It was Aunt Claire who, while not a professional
musician, gave the preschooler Emily her first recorder and then composed
some simple pieces for her to play. At five Doolittle started piano, and then
Aunt Claire encouraged the eleven-year-old self-described "nerdy kid" to take
up oboe, reasoning that with a less popular instrument she'd have more opportunities to play in orchestras and ensembles, which turned out to be the
case.[11] Having no idea that the oboe was among the traditional Western art
music instruments often called upon to evoke the natural world, Emily simply
liked "playing a weird instrument . . . and making reeds."[12]

Growing up in a house whose property bumped up against the woods
meant that the natural world played a large role in Doolittle's life from the
beginning. Once again, as with many of the composers studied in this book,
early childhood exposure to nature appears to be an important commonality
among the women and a well from which they draw for their later work. The
composer recalls that she spent most of her time outdoors and, like many
young children, had animal-inspired imaginary friends: hers included a frog,
a toad, a snake, and a worm. Animals were very important to her, and birds
especially so: "I was just really fascinated by them. Not so much the song, I
just really liked the way they could imitate things . . . sounds, speech. I also
liked their general bird-ness . . . their feathers, the way they move."[13] Here
Doolittle echoes many of the sentiments expressed by Victoria Bond. As
children, both composers considered animals to be simultaneously equals and
fascinating others. Playtime laid the foundation for their adult understanding of the natural world. In 1997, close attention to a bird would inspire one

of Doolittle's first major pieces, *night black bird song*, a work to which we will return.[14]

Doolittle's own attachment to the woods and the natural world can be traced in part to her mother, who "loved spending time out of doors, and gardening and hiking." Doolittle's mother had been a Girl Scout, like Libby Larsen; she had camped and hiked in California, and she cultivated a "very wild garden" in Halifax. Doolittle lovingly credits much of her own feelings for the outdoors to her mother in a way similar to Victoria Bond's fond recollection of the taste of a carrot from her grandmother's garden igniting her senses. And as Oliveros's mother's improvising and composing made a career in music a logical choice for an impressionable Pauline, for Emily Doolittle her mother made the outdoors a natural place for a woman to be.

Connections with still other composers emerge. Like Ellen Taaffe Zwilich, who credited an exceptional public-school music program in Coral Gables, Florida, with stimulating and encouraging her love of music, Doolittle attributes much of her love of music to the Halifax school system, which had its own strong program. "Pretty much any kid could learn to play any instrument. We all went to the music department in the center of town and took lessons and orchestra and choir, and it was very accessible to people." It was in a school choir that Emily learned Murray Schafer's "Epitaph for Moonlight," a piece, as she puts it, "that every Canadian school choir sings." Schafer and his ideas and music would ultimately exert a great influence on the composer.[15] At the age of sixteen, the budding musician heard Schafer's Third String Quartet at the Scotia Festival of Music. She credits an "amazing performance" of the work with inspiring her, in large part, to become a composer.

At nineteen, Doolittle read a paragraph-length announcement in the *Globe and Mail* describing Schafer's summer music project in the Haliburton Highlands of Ontario; she wrote a lengthy letter to the composer telling him of her interests and asking for permission to participate. The next year she attended the weeklong collaborative wilderness music experience for the first of ten consecutive summers, 1992–2002.[16] With Schafer's *And Wolf Shall Inherit the Moon*, known among the participants as the *Wolf Project*, Doolittle experienced music-making that was inspired by and realized within the acoustic environment of the outdoors. Discovering that the whole world of sounds could be source material expanded her thinking.[17] Thus began a compositional career that combined Doolittle's twin interests in music and nature.

Over the course of the first four summers at Schafer's music project, Doolittle became increasingly sensitized to the ways topographical contours, waterways, and forest canopies affected sound. She was intrigued with the dryness and resonance of the outdoors, a space that was free of humanly constructed walls and the modifications created by acoustic tile. In 1996, rather than write a piece imitating any birdcall or wolf howl, of which there were many in the forest, she wrote a gentle solo work that explored how sounds linger. Reveling in pure sound, its qualities, and the way it changes over time recalls Oliveros's interest in sound and sonic environments. Doolittle composed *Aubade* for Canadian flutist-musicologist Ellen Waterman, who was a founding member of the *Wolf Project* and a fellow participant at the time; Doolittle's dawn song was used as one of a number of pieces – "folktunes or other suitable morning music" – to awaken the Wolf Project participants that summer. Excited by the musical possibilities of nature, in the same year Doolittle wrote a pair of *Weather Songs*, "Lightning" and "Snow."

Today, Doolittle's nature pieces number over a dozen and include works whose titles are obviously nature-related – *field music* (1998), *Ruby-Throated Moment* (1999), *night black bird song* (1999), *Four Pieces About Water* (2000), *music for magpies* (2003), *all spring* (2004), *Social sounds from whales at night* (2007), *Vocalise (for bees)* (2008), *Hatchlings (a set of six)* (2009), and most recently *Reeds* (2010), a collaborative work for three instrumentalists, a dancer, and a place.[18] Among the sounds featured in the thirty-six-minute *Reeds* is the song of the hermit thrush, the bird that caught the attention of Amy Beach and that continues to fascinate musicians and scientists alike today, a topic to which we will return.[19]

There are also many other compositions in her oeuvre that were inspired by natural phenomena but whose titles give no hint that that is the case. Among them are *falling still* and *Paths*. And then there are the trick pieces: *green notes*, whose title looks promisingly like an ecologically minded work, turns out to be named for the color of pen Doolittle used to notate the score; it has nothing to do with nature. But that work is more the exception than the rule. In sometimes obvious and other times more obscure ways, Doolittle's output expresses her thorough involvement, engagement, and immersion in a natural world that includes animals and elements, birds and humans, animate and inanimate beings and things (figure 10.1).

In a series of interviews and email exchanges and phone conversations conducted over a period of more than three years, the composer consistently returned to *night black bird song* as an example of one way that nature informs her music, and it was with a description of the same piece that Doolittle began her dissertation.[20] Her written account of its genesis illuminates much

FIGURE 10.1. Emily Doolittle and friends. Reprinted with kind permission of the photographer, Erika Kinetz.

of her thinking and establishes a starting point for understanding Doolittle's conception of nature:

> In the fall of 1997 I was living in Amsterdam, and one of my first nights there I awoke to hear an unfamiliar and splendid bird singing outside my window. Perhaps because I was in a new environment, I listened to the bird with greater attention and for a longer time than I usually would. I became entranced by its song. Not only the beauty of this European blackbird song (as I found out the next day that it was) intrigued me, but also my own thoughts about the ways in which this song was and was not like what one would usually consider 'music.'[21]

In our conversations Doolittle also recalled "a gentle backdrop of rain" that accompanied the blackbird's song, which made her think of the relationship between animate and inanimate nature, an issue that would later influence many of her nature pieces.[22]

Doolittle clarified how the bird's song became her own *night black bird song,* and she enumerated the many similarities between human and bird music:

> Individual motives ("syllables") of this particular bird's song were much like something we would typically hear in human music: scalar passages, major triads in a variety of inversions, simple three-or four-note diatonic patterns, little trills and ornaments.[23]

And then she noted the differences:

> The continuity of what the bird sang, however, was quite unlike what we would usually consider music: motives were repeated a seemingly arbitrary number of times in a row; motives were always repeated as is, without development; the bird jumped from one kind of motive to another with no connecting tonal, rhythmic, or melodic relation; periods of silence and sound seemed to be interspersed at random.[24]

She "ended up writing a piece of music, *night black bird song*, which explored the difference between human and blackbird ways of arranging the same collection of motives."[25] As a composer who works motivically, Doolittle likely was particularly sensitive to the way the blackbird parsed its song. But a bonus of her careful listening was the discovery of the uniqueness of each blackbird, as she explained: "While blackbirds as a species can easily be recognized, the voice of each individual blackbird can also be clearly distinguished." Of the original, inspiring blackbird, the composer bemoaned that "the beautiful night-time singer outside my window . . . was only a temporary guest, and was soon displaced by a much less inventive singer, one with only three or four dull motives which he repeated endlessly."[26] However disappointing the second singer, her long-held intuition that "each animal was an individual" was proven correct. In the composer's words, "this experience, more than any other, made me consciously aware of animals as subjective beings, each with a unique way of perceiving and relating to the world." As she "read, watched, and listened," she became "more aware of the details of various animal behaviors."[27] By tracking the distinguishing traits of individual blackbirds, Doolittle ultimately became sensitized to cross-species commonalities. In acknowledging the unequivocal individuality of blackbirds, other nonhuman animals, and human beings, Doolittle rejected the idea of a strict dichotomy between humanity and the rest of nature; it was impossible.[28]

Doolittle expanded upon the creation of the piece.

> I listened a lot . . . and I transcribed some of the motives he sang, and I made up some motives in a similar style. I wrote [the piece] first with the idea of arranging the motives as a blackbird would, and gradually making them more and more "musical." I say that in quotation marks, you know, more

and more like human music. So I was thinking that [the] piece had different motives; if a bird arranged the motives or the blackbird arranged the motives, there's often sort of repetition . . . with phrases. . . . They begin and end all sorts of strange times. Other things are . . . thrown in randomly. Whereas for us, motives are often developed, and there's some sort of harmonic connection between one motive and another. There's just more sound than silence.[29]

The pride of place given to the act of *listening* by so many of the composers, starting with Amy Beach, remains a primary value for this most modern woman. Listening, often mistaken as a passive activity, requires focused attention and practiced discipline; it is an essential behavior among these environmentally sensitive citizens. In addition to allowing her to track and transcribe the bird's song, Doolittle's skilled listening expanded her thinking about her place in the natural world. *night black bird song* became a testament to cross-species commonalities, as the following discussion demonstrates.

The first measures of the piece announce the bird's motives in their discontinuous state even as Doolittle explained, "the motives aren't direct transcriptions. They're a mix of very rough transcriptions and blackbird-inspired, made up motives."[30] A brief call by a piccolo bursts *sfp* (*subito forte-piano*) into the air and then "fades to nothing" before the sounds of a Chinese opera gong, rainstick, and bamboo wind chimes dissipate as well. Unlike Beach, who took pride in her accurate transcription of the hermit thrush, Doolittle was not so much interested in capturing the precise pitch of the bird's song as she was concerned with "where they sound good on the piccolo."[31] Except for occasional sudden appearances by the rainstick or wood blocks, the early moments of the piece reveal a world of quiet, watchful waiting. There is little to provide rhythmic or harmonic grounding. A small compass of repeated pitches suggests some kind of center, and up through measure 66 listeners feel a certain weight assigned to B♭, but the pitch doesn't materialize into a tonal home. While there are numerous episodes of heightened activity that propel the music forward, they are, as Doolittle observed, "seemingly arbitrary." The bird is content to sing where it is (example 10.1).

A transparent texture heightens the importance of individual sounds, and so it follows that Doolittle provides numerous instructions for what she is after.[32] The gong player should "hold firmly on the inclined part of the gong, just before the flat center, so that the pitch rises immediately and the sound decays quickly."[33] The rainstick remains "almost silent – just occasional drops" and then later creates an "uneven crescendo, with small variations up and down."[34] Listeners are given the opportunity to savor a variety of vocal-

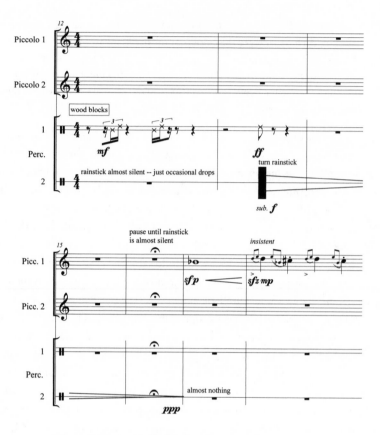

EXAMPLE 10.1 (*above and facing*). *night black bird song*. By Emily Doolittle, mm. 12–26. Copyright © 1999 by the composer. Reprinted with kind permission.

izations and background sounds. Doolittle's particular ensemble – piccolo, flute, and three percussion parts, where the flute doubles as a second piccolo on many occasions – enables maximum contrast and homogeneity at the same time. Two piccolos or a piccolo and flute allow for seamless transitions, call-and-response exchanges, and duetlike passages between equals, or at least among close relations, while a variety of unusual percussion instruments evoke the intermittently rainy background Doolittle heard that evening in her apartment. In addition to the rainstick, Chinese opera gong, wood block, and bamboo wind chimes, Doolittle uses a wave drum, temple blocks, a conga drum, marimba, bongos, and cow bells to create her soundscape. The exotic nature of the sounds and their unpredictable appearances hold our atten-

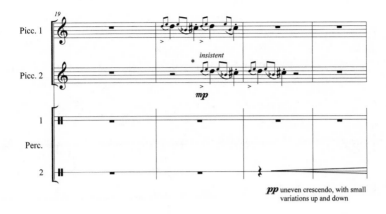

*grace notes on beat

tion and keep us aware that we are not listening to a traditionally conceived piece.

At measure 67, piccolo I leaps to a new pitch plane and a "shrill" repeated figure. Here is an example of the blackbird "jumping from one kind of motive to another." Three measures later, the call first heard at measure 27 reappears. Its "lively, sweet" song recalls the opening pitch center and provides a counterpoint to the more grating sounds of the higher-pitched newcomer. Beginning at this point, Doolittle's piece displays more humanlike musical qualities, although there are numerous instances of the composer returning to the birdsong and reminding listeners of the origins of her idea.[35] As *night black bird song* morphs from the fragmentary avian to avian-cum-human music, the texture thickens, individual motives are subject to development-like

EXAMPLE 10.2 (*above, facing, and next page*). *night black bird song.* By Emily Doolittle, mm. 71–85. Copyright © 1999 by the composer. Reprinted with kind permission.

treatments, and the percussion assumes a more conventional role by providing increased rhythmic momentum that leads to a climactic moment, itself a common feature of human music (example 10.2).

While the piece is engaging because of its obvious evocation of natural sounds, and while a listener eagerly awaits the next call, plop, or patter, the absence of transitional passages is apparent, and the amount of time given to silence in the first minutes of the piece (compared with the louder, fuller soundscape of the latter part of the piece) challenges the norms of traditional

human music.[36] We are, as Doolittle observed, accustomed to "more sound than silence," but her work encourages us to listen and reconsider that bias. She draws us into a world of animated birdsong and the inanimate sounds of the rain, the soundscape that captured her attention in Amsterdam.

Over the course of *night black bird song*, the dynamic level rises from the opening triple *piano*-to-*mezzo piano* range to a more consistently *forte*-to-*triple forte* range, and there are increased interactions between instruments. Human musicians, it appears, are much busier (or perhaps more garrulous) than avian songsters.[37] Measure 145, which occurs about five minutes into the piece, offers the last moment of complete silence until the final seconds of the work.[38] While the bird-evoking piccolo is encouraged to sound "playful" on

many occasions, at measure 142, a point where the quarter-note beat increases its tempo from 108 to 126 and the music is decidedly more "human," the piccolo is instructed to sound "playfully aggressive"; this description returns on a number of occasions thereafter. The lighter side of nature first discussed in relation to Victoria Bond's *Peculiar Plants* is present in this work as well: we hear birds at play. At measure 165, Doolittle has the piccolo play "shrill," as it did in measure 67 with the same pitch material, but moments later the indication is to play "a little nicer" at measure 167. The responding flute is alternately "insistent" and "smooth." Later on, both piccolo and flute will be "startled" and "scolding."[39] If bird and human musics are very much alike, it appears that bird and human behaviors have many correlates as well (example 10.3). While some might read Doolittle's work as suggesting that birds need human intervention to create "real" music, the composer explains that this was not her intention at all. "The piece could just as well have gone the other way around – going from 'human music' to 'bird music' – it just suited my compositional needs for this piece to have it go the way it does."[40] Rather than aiming to imply any kind of hierarchical arrangement, Doolittle was interested in exploring the possibilities inherent in the basic building blocks – "what animals might do with sounds and what humans might do with similar sounds."[41] Her approach to this work, which involves first laying out basic building blocks, recalls Louise Talma's collecting of birdsongs for their potential as source material, although Doolittle appears to develop a more personal relationship to individual birds than does Talma. It also bears some similarity to a form-building technique found in many works of the composer Charles Ives, which J. Peter Burkholder calls "cumulative form." In numerous pieces that draw upon borrowed materials – although in Ives's case these are seldom nature's sounds – the composer initially presents fragmentary melodic and rhythmic motives; heard without reference to any larger musical context, the motives appear disconnected and unrecognizable. Over the course of a piece, however, motives are expanded and connective materials are added; listeners gradually become aware of the relationship between the early disconnected fragments and the generating musical idea. Toward the end of the piece, the first full iteration of the now-recognizable borrowed theme emerges.

Although this is not directly analogous to how Doolittle conceives her piece, borrowing materials and presenting them in a fragmented form prior to their ultimate reassembly is a practice that *night black bird song* shares with many of Ives's works.[42] If in Ives's pieces we gradually discover the hidden relationships between disconnected bits and pieces of music and their generating tune, in *night black bird song* we ultimately discover the remarkable closeness between the two species' – bird and human – musics. The work corroborates Doolittle's belief in the arbitrariness of strict divisions between different species, human and other-than-human.

In the final twenty-four measures, where percussion are tacet, the tempo slows down, the dynamic level relaxes to its original *piano* range, and the piece returns to simple, transparent, nondirectional birdlike music, even though as Doolittle explains, "the motives are connected to each other harmonically,

EXAMPLE 10.3 (*above and facing*). *night black bird song.* By Emily Doolittle, mm. 165–177.
Copyright © 1999 by the composer. Reprinted with kind permission.

EXAMPLE 10.4. *night black bird song.* By Emily Doolittle, mm. 228–243.
Copyright © 1999 by the composer. Reprinted with kind permission.

they develop, etc.," which is more like human music.[43] As the piece closes, we
listen to Doolittle exploring the raw materials one last time. In addition to
the work's suggestion of compositional methods similar to Ives's cumulative
process, the opening of the piece, with its recurring, cycling, additive patterns
of bird music, once again recalls Igor Stravinsky's treatment of materials in
Rite of Spring, a piece that has been mentioned multiple times in this study
and will be cited a final time in the discussion of Doolittle's work *Reeds.*

Although she was not aware of Stravinsky's specific references to the natural world when she wrote *night black bird song*, she learned of the connections a few years later from reading François-Bernard Mâche's *Music, Myth, and Nature* and his discussion of Stravinsky and birdsong: "Mâche suggests that musical structures such as Stravinsky's, which seemed radically new to listeners at the time, are in fact no less 'natural' than the flowing melodic structures which have more traditionally been considered musical in the West – only that they are related to a different natural model. Mâche believed that this change in music model was . . . the direct result of Stravinsky having composed *Le Sacre* in Ustilug (Ukraine), by the Bug River, where many aquatic warblers . . . would have lived."[44] While meters are carefully measured in both pieces, as in the Stravinsky in *night black bird song*, it is impossible to predict accent patterns. The music quietly pops along "a little bit dance-like."[45] Ultimately, the blackbird's song winds down and disappears in the night. Doolittle explains, "I wasn't thinking about either Ives or Stravinsky at the time and didn't read Mâche until several years later, but while I was working on *night black bird song* I showed my list of blackbird and human ways of developing motives to Louis Andriessen, and he looked at the blackbird list and said 'That sounds like Stravinsky!'[46] Perhaps most importantly, like the two earlier composers, Doolittle allows musical materials to dictate formal strategies and structures (example 10.4).

Begun when she was twenty-five years old, *night black bird song* shows Doolittle possessing a devotion to sound exploration similar to Pauline Oliveros and listening skills that recall those of Amy Beach. She has a mature composer's command of her craft. But beyond demonstrating aesthetic sensitivity and technical accomplishments, *night black bird song* reveals a fully developed ecological sensibility and a commitment to nondichotomous thinking. At home in nature, Doolittle sees more similarities than differences between human and nonhuman creatures. In the following decade, nature would inform numerous works in different ways and to different degrees; however, Doolittle will remain steadfast in her belief that human beings are a part of nature, not standing outside it or above it, but one species deeply enmeshed within it.

From the distance of over a decade, the composer reflected that when writing *night black bird song* she "was really just thinking musically/observationally."[47] However, by the time she was writing her dissertation, she was interacting with people from a variety of fields, including philosophy, semiotics, ornithology, bioacoustics, cognitive ethology, and ethnomusicology. She focused on "similarities of structure, function, sound, and meaning between

certain animal and human songs." At the end of years of work on her dissertation, she concluded that her "understanding of music . . . [had] change[d]
substantially." In a conversation two years later, Doolittle also acknowledged
that her understanding of nature had undergone a change:

> I used to think of nature as wherever people aren't, and where things
> haven't been affected by humans, but more recently, I think that we're part of
> nature too, we're animals and we . . . look for food and shelter, and we have
> more technology that we use than other species but . . . I don't know where
> to draw the line . . . I guess there isn't a dividing line.[48]

It is instructive that Doolittle's project on music, and a year of "reading and
listening extensively,"[49] caused her to rethink her understanding of nature.
As she looks back on her work from a distance of a few years, Doolittle believes her approach to comparing animal songs and music has changed subtly
too. "When I was working on my dissertation, I was really thinking mostly
about how some animal songs are (like) human music, and now I think more
about how human music is animal song. Just a slight change in emphasis!
(Which maybe has to do with having spent more time with scientists.)"[50] It
makes me think that music, if listened to carefully, can change attitudes in
similar ways. Music can encourage a broader understanding of the concept
of nature.

In 2003, Doolittle completed a set of five solo pieces for viola da gamba
titled *music for magpies*. It is one of a number of works she has written since
2000 for early instruments or baroque orchestral ensembles.[51] The *magpie*
pieces were written for Karin Preslmayr, a gambist dedicated to performing
contemporary music and showing the full range of her instrument's abilities.
Preslmayr knew of Doolittle's early-instrument works and contacted her to
write something. According to the composer, she accepted Preslmayr's invitation because "quarter-tone viola da gamba sounded interesting."[52] The result
was a set that includes the "pied butcherbird," "hoopoe lark," "ringed river
snike," "pileated pocket grouse," and "green-rumped antstalker."[53] Doolittle
recalled the genesis of the five pieces:

> The way these pieces really came about [was] that I had agreed to write
> something for Karin. The deadline was approaching and I had no idea what

to do with quarter tones! I was listening to lots of bird songs, and even though they're not in quarter tones, some of them did use smaller intervals than semitones, and I thought it would be interesting to try to transcribe some of them. So I started with pied butcherbird because its song is so music-like. The result seemed like it might be interesting, so I went on with hoopoe lark. Then I felt like I was getting into a more bird-like way of thinking about music, so I thought it would be fun to make up some of my own birds![54]

Doolittle's snike, pocket grouse, and green-rumped antstalker are all imaginary creatures, but the pieces bearing their names betray her mastery of birdlike ways of thinking about music. While related to *night black bird song, music for magpies* offers a different manifestation of nature's presence in Doolittle's music. As the composer explained, "the pieces in *music for magpies* are based on bird songs . . . at least pied butcherbird and hoopoe lark I can't quite take credit for . . . [they] are like translations . . . the same way I can take credit for the music I wrote myself. I did write the other three!"[55] Despite that disclaimer, no listener would mistake Doolittle's *magpies* for the real birds, even with the much rougher and some would say more "natural" sound of the viola da gamba singing the birds' songs; these are not simple translations or transcriptions.

Beyond the expanded pitch palette, whose quarter-tone sharps and flats are carefully indicated in the score using standard symbols, the composer provides precise performance directions for all aspects of sound production.[56] She indicates metronome markings for each of the pieces, and these hold for the duration of the piece without a single instance of an accelerando or ritard, although the composer insists "the performer is certainly free to interpret."[57] In "green-rumped antstalker," the composer clarifies that a quarter note = 100 and an eighth note = 200. Such detail is helpful given the numerous instances of eighth-note triplets and dotted-eighth, thirty-second-note groupings. Even with a wholly imaginary creature, Doolittle has exact ideas about certain qualities of its sound.

The character of various birds is captured in distinctive mood indicators given at the top of each piece: The "pied butcherbird" is "flowing and lively"; the "hoopoe lark" is "expressive but restrained." the "ringed river snike" should sound "plaintive"; the "pileated pocket grouse" "lively, resonant, percussive"; and the "green-rumped antstalker" "gregarious." At turns the pied butcherbird sounds "delicate," "bold," "playful," or "emphatic." Doolittle's lighthearted attribution of human qualities to her birds recalls Bond's humorous personi-

EXAMPLE 10.5. *music for magpies,* "pied butcherbird." By Emily Doolittle,
line 1. Copyright © 2003 by the composer. Reprinted with kind permission.

fications of her *Peculiar Plants.* Regarding the first two pieces the composer
explained: "pied butcherbird is a pretty direct transcription. There are just a
few repetitions that I added. "hoopoe lark" is closely based on a recording,
but I've definitely done things to make it more 'music' like."[58] The spectrogram
and score for "pied butcherbird," the first of two pieces based upon real bird
species, show the range of Doolittle's efforts to convey the spirit of the bird's
music. She has taken Beach's detailed study of birdsong to a new level of
thoroughness and systematization (example 10.5).

Doolittle is exacting when indicating articulations. In "ringed river snike"
she explains that staccatos are "not too short, but clipped sounding." When
seeking a rough-sounding finish to a gesture in "green-rumped antstalker" she
writes, "press down on string towards end of f¼♯, so the final sound becomes a
scrape." When meters and bar lines suit the birdsong, Doolittle doesn't hesitate to use them.[59] When frequent periods of silence separate avian sounds,
Doolittle forgoes meters and depends on metronome marks and a combination of rest signs and numerals to indicate durations of sounds and silences.
The occasional "tapping on [the] wood of the gamba" constitutes the whole
of extended techniques.

Similar to her accommodating attitude toward precise pitches, Doolittle
is open-minded about the instrumental timbre of her magpies' songs. She
explained:

> You know, these pieces could really be played on anything – and have been
> played on cello, baroque flute, and modern flute. They're sort of 'translations'
> of the actual bird songs, so I think part of the interest is just in hearing how
> they'll come out on different instruments. I could imagine them being done
> on clarinet, oboe, or bassoon as well.[60]

Doolittle is interested in exploring sounds from the natural world and hearing how they "translate" to human instruments. Considered in this way, the set appears to be a continuation of Doolittle's exploration of the connections between human and avian music that first emerged in *night black bird song*. Although the birds featured in the last three pieces are imaginary, one senses that *music for magpies* is not primarily a showcase for Doolittle's imagination as much as it is an opportunity for her to think like a bird making music. The work becomes a proving ground for her listening skills, a manifestation of her intimate engagement with the natural world, and a testament to her respectful stance vis-à-vis nature.

Doolittle observes that in her piece titled *all spring*, "the relationship between my music and the birdsong is much more abstract. I feel that it is a completely composed piece."[61] *all spring* is a setting of five poems by Rae Crossman, a fellow *Wolf Project* participant and champion of collaborative artistic projects. The work was commissioned in 2004 by the Motion Ensemble by the Canada Council for the Arts and was composed and premiered that year. There have been multiple performances since then. Where Pauline Oliveros claimed to be interested only in the sounds of Robert Duncan's words in her setting of his poem "An Interlude of Rare Beauty," Doolittle draws inspiration from both the sounds and the meanings of Crossman's texts. In this way her response to text is closer to Libby Larsen's in *Missa Gaia* than to Oliveros's in "An Interlude of Rare Beauty."

Nature is a common subject for Crossman, as is performing in outdoor acoustical environments, and both composer and poet appear to share similar understandings of their place in a larger world; their works form a logical pairing. Crossman's five poems specifically name woodpeckers, geese, an anonymous bird, ruffed grouse, and goldfinches, and he is sensitive to their sounds, their movements, their fragility, the "drumming" of their wings, and their interactions with flowers. But Crossman also draws upon nature's symbolism to suggest widely understood human experiences, most specifically love: love lost, unrequited, or rediscovered. In *all spring*, Doolittle doesn't "translate" the sounds of the birds, the way she describes her process in *music for magpies*, but it is clear that even in this more abstracted construction of nature sounds, we are listening to birdlike music.[62]

Written for soprano, flute, B♭ clarinet, violin, bass (or cello), and a large variety of percussion, including wood block, sizzle cymbal, glockenspiel, bamboo wind chimes, cuíca, snare drum, small stones, kick drum, cabasa, and temple block, *all spring* demonstrates Doolittle's sensitivity to text, her preference for high tessituras, and her keen ear for timbre. Although Doolittle has no explanation for her attraction to high-pitched vocal sounds, their closer approximation to bird sounds and most of animate nature's sounds makes their choice here and in so many other pieces appropriate. The five poems – "five o'clock," "all spring," "have you ever held a bird," "ruffed grouse," and "just when" – range from three lines in "five o'clock" and "ruffled grouse," to twenty-three lines in the longest poem, "all spring."

"all spring" shows Crossman's seemingly effortless style and the poem's rich symbolism:

all spring
I have been watching
a pair of geese
in the flooded hollow

their dance of necks
among the reeds

two at first
now half a dozen

all spring
I have been listening
to them flourish

oh
I had forgotten
how loudly sometimes

life proclaims itself

my love
say it is not too late

to call you back
across the arid fields

my love
say it is not too late

to weave a nest
even from the strands of sorrow[63]

Lines 2 and 10, "I have been watching" and "I have been listening," convey Doolittle's own situation vis-à-vis nature: her senses are constantly gathering information; her steady state is attentiveness. Like Amy Beach, Pauline Oliveros, Victoria Bond, and Libby Larsen, Emily Doolittle absorbs and is absorbed by her environment. One imagines it moving through her the way she moves through it.[64] A study of this song reveals another aspect of this composer's interactions with nature.

Doolittle moves us into her springtime musical world by first playing with the sensation of the relative distance of sounds from a listener – "as if from afar" and "now closer." Her experiences at the Wolf Project in the Haliburton Forests in Canada inform her music. We are outdoors with Doolittle hearing sounds coming from all directions, some nearby and undeniable, and others barely making it to our ears and chimerical. Flute and clarinet move softly and in a tight compass of major seconds and, by measure 31, major thirds. Later they will expand their range still more. Doolittle writes precise directions for how notes should be attacked or decay, and while she provides only approximate timings for the opening bamboo wind chime, when the woodwinds enter she has specific metronome markings. The care she takes with her directions is like that of the carefully worded recipes that Oliveros writes for her *Sonic Meditations* (example 10.6).

A soprano enters with her own circumscribed melody, singing as if she is another woodwind voice, but expands her pitch palette as she explains all that she has been seeing and hearing. The singer vocalizes the composer's persona (example 10.7).

Using a bamboo wind chime throughout the song, Doolittle makes us aware of the gently moving air; a violin and a double bass playing nonvibrato, *flautando* (bowed flutelike on the fingerboard) add new voices to the natural chorus, and later a cuíca, a Brazilian friction drum that has a high-pitched squeaky timbre, joins in with instructions to "sound like a goose." Sometimes the instrument is "hit" like a drum, and other times the player "swish[es their] hand on top." The result is so convincing one wonders if the instrument was inspired by the bird (example 10.8).

When the soprano realizes she had "forgotten how loudly sometimes life proclaims itself," the ensemble crescendos to an excited *fortissimo* squawking, twittering celebration before returning to its quieter self. As if the cacophony had summoned a memory, the singer is transported outside the metaphorical natural soundscape; in a wholly unmeasured, introspective a cappella passage

EXAMPLE 10.6. *all spring*, "all spring." By Emily Doolittle, mm. 1–16.
Copyright © 2004/2006 by the composer. Reprinted with kind permission.

(save for the "occasional, quiet wind chime sound" and a cello that doubles the vocal line), she wonders whether "it is not too late to call you back across the arid fields . . . to weave a nest" (example 10.9).

The soprano floats downward from a high B♭ to an A above middle C and then springs back to the upper register of her voice. Here is Doolittle exploring the highest, birdlike reaches of the soprano voice. One wonders if perhaps the vocalist persona has been influenced by the sound of birds. The composer explained her own attraction to that tessitura: "Actually, I liked writing for high voice before I started thinking about animal songs. Not really sure why. But maybe the higher sopranos I know are more likely to be willing to sing with a pure, non-vibrato voice tone?"[65] When flute and clarinet rejoin the singer to accompany the closing words "even from strands of sorrow," the vocalist returns to earth with a final tritone G♯ to D in the same octave that began the piece, and the instruments rise above her with the hollow sounds of an open fifth.

With its Janequin-like quasi-onomatopoeic sounds and with poetry that uses nature imagery to tell of lost love, *all spring* is firmly situated in a long tradition of nature-inspired pieces even if the precise musical expression is thoroughly contemporary.[66] This is a modern springtime.

Given the attention paid to marine mammals in the decade of Doolittle's birth, it may be only logical that such an environmentally attuned composer would find herself drawn to the sound-sensitive creatures. Two decades earlier, in the 1950s, U.S. Navy scientists had learned that whales sing. While the scientists were mainly interested in the potential application of whale communication techniques to refining sonar for national security purposes, their discovery of whale song touched a nerve with people around the globe, who quickly adopted the mammals as motivation and symbol for an array of activities, environmental and aesthetic.

In deep waters, sound travels four to five times faster and much greater distances than on land, and whales have evolved to take advantage of their environment. As Zhe-Xi Luo, paleontologist at the Carnegie Museum, succinctly put it, "sound is a way of life for whales."[67] Using a large repertoire of vocalizations and acute auditory skills, including finely honed echolocation abilities, whales communicate, navigate, and position themselves in relation

EXAMPLE 10.7 *(above and facing). all spring,* "all spring."
By Emily Doolittle, mm. 18–48. Copyright © 2004/2006
by the composer. Reprinted with kind permission.

EXAMPLE 10.8 (*above and facing*). *all spring*, "all spring."
By Emily Doolittle, mm. 88–110. Copyright © 2004/2006
by the composer. Reprinted with kind permission.

EXAMPLE 10.9. *all spring,* "all spring." By Emily Doolittle, mm. 135–153.
Copyright © 2004/2006 by the composer. Reprinted with kind permission.

to prey and predators. Sound plays a role in all aspects of whale behavior. Depending upon the particular whale group, individual types can hear and produce sounds well above (ultrasonic) or below (infrasonic) the thresholds of human creation or perception. Zhe-Xi Luo notes, "with infrasonic sound, baleen whales can communicate with each other over geographic areas as large as an ocean basin." They use their version of sonar "to 'see' their environment."[68]

Inspired by recordings of whale song that were made in the 1960s, and especially by Roger Payne's "Songs of the Humpback Whales" that was released in 1970, composers saw possibilities as well.[69] Within a decade, an array of composers responded: In 1970 Alan Hovhannes composed "And God Created Great Whales" for taped whale songs and orchestra; the next year, 1971, George Crumb created "Vox Balaenae" for electric flute, electric cello, and electric piano. He asked his players to wear half masks and play under blue lighting in an attempt to capture the color of the sea and "the powerful impersonal forces of nature."[70] The composer was inspired by the singing of humpback whales that he had heard in 1969. In 1981, John Cage created "Litany for the Whale," a twenty-five-minute call-and-response work for unaccompanied vocalists who chant pitches and sounds assigned to the five letters of the word "whale." The gently curving melodic call descends a perfect fifth before it rebounds a whole tone to the final note. The five pitches provide the entirety of the pitch pool, and yet the music seems unbounded; this is due in part to the absence of meter, the particular pitches that are sung in any response, and the pauses between iterations of the call, which are separated by silences. Cage creates a virtual acoustic sea in which whalelike sounds float and echo.

Environmental groups recognized the power composed music might have to further their causes. In 1981, Greenpeace commissioned Toru Takemitsu to write "Toward the Sea" on behalf of its Save the Whales campaign. Originally composed for alto flute and guitar, it was immediately arranged for alto flute, harp, and string orchestra, and then for alto flute and harp alone in 1989. The variety of arrangements allows for greater performance possibilities. In 1982, Iannis Xenakis wrote "Pour les Baleines" for large string orchestra as his contribution to an anthology of works in support of Greenpeace. Jazz saxophonist Paul Winter created his own musical responses starting in the late 1970s with the album *Common Ground*. The performer combined his music making with the recorded sounds of whales, wolves, and birds. Today he continues his work with the music of nonhuman others. David Rothenberg, a philosopher and jazz musician, has spent decades studying and making music alongside other species. *The Book of Music and Nature: An Anthology of Sounds, Words, Thoughts*, which Rothenberg co-edited with Marta Ulvaeus, is a classic in the field of music and nature studies.[71] Human musicians and whales, it appears, form a natural pair.

In 2007, Emily Doolittle was commissioned by the Canada Council to compose *Social sounds from whales at night* for soprano Helen Pridmore. She employed advanced recording technology to provide basic musical material; it was her first work to move beyond exclusively acoustical sound. Doolittle explained: "The title comes from the jottings of the scientist who had recorded the whale sounds. I liked that phrase so I used it."[72] The social sounds emitted by whales require special hydrophones to be heard by human ears. According to Marsha Green, founder of Ocean Mammal Institute, they're produced when whales are moving slowly or resting, and a majority of them (85 percent) are communications between mother and their calves. But social sounds may also be more generally "whales within a group communicating with each other."[73]

Doolittle's *Social sounds* prescribes just two percussion instruments, which are played by the singer (bamboo chimes and an ocean drum), recorded whale songs, and a single soprano vocalist.[74] The composer is not interested in technology to create sounds per se, and so there are no newly composed pops, clicks, bleeps, screeches, or whooshes. But she welcomes the chance technology affords her to hear nature's sounds slowed down, which allows her to "pull them apart," to listen more carefully, and to hear more accurately what nonhuman nature is saying.[75] While Doolittle is increasingly curious about the possibilities of technology for her work and imagines writing other pieces using tape parts in the future, she still "tends to gravitate much more towards acoustic instruments. I think sometimes when you get too immersed in technology then you lose other things . . . I work at the piano, not an electronic keyboard. I want vibrations in the air." But she recognizes that technology changes her access to what is going on. "Technology is like a magnifying glass . . . it's more like a tool that lets me get closer to the things I'm listening to." Her remarks recall those of John Cage, who saw the great advantages technology afforded one to get closer to nature.[76] *Social sounds from whales at night* became a three-way collaboration among Doolittle, the whales, and the people who wrote the software.[77]

Doolittle explained the "music" of *Social sounds*:

There is a reversal. I could have done something where I had recordings of the whale songs and then some kind of accompaniment, but the musician is singing a transcription of what the whale sings and the whale is providing the accompaniment. For her part I just transcribed the whale part as closely as I could; so she is supposed to be sounding like the whale.[78]

The score for *Social sounds* looks similar to those of many electronic pieces. Time is measured in seconds and minutes rather than organized by meter signatures. And while Doolittle indicates that the piece is to begin and end at the tempo of a quarter note = 84, with a brief increase to a quarter note = 120 (see 4:16 to 4:37), even those seemingly absolute measurements are prefaced by the words "approximately" or "around." The composer explains "rhythmic coordination between [the] tape part and voice is only approximate, although there are a few places where it needs to line up."[79] Note values are also approximate. There should be a sense of proportion, but not of 'beat.'" This holds until 3:46, when Doolittle indicates that the alignment of tape and vocalist needs to be "as precise as possible," for a time, at least. Like Oliveros, Doolittle has a flexible sense of control. Both composers know the sounds they are after, but they also have created room for performers' choices (example 10.10).

In many places in the piece, Doolittle is similarly accommodating regarding matters of pitch, and this is likely her acknowledgement that nonhuman animals are just as free of Western music's circumscribed pitch palette as they were of traditional accent patterns.[80] At the soprano's first entrance the composer explains: "Noteheads indicate the general ballpark of the pitch to be sung: glissandi, wavers and minor alterations of pitch (within, say, a ¼ tone) may be added freely." At 3:00 Doolittle instructs the singer to "improvise using individual note leaps, and slower glissandi, as well as rests. Use mostly the notes in the box, but add others as desired. Begin by favouring individual notes and leaps, and gradually switch to favouring glissandi" (example 10.11).

The composer is more specific, however, regarding the production of the soprano's vocables: "Do not try to sing all the sections as a continuous musical thought. Rather, all the 'ah's' form one musical line, the 'eh's' another (melodically the most important), and the 'huh's' a third. 'Ah's' are always diffuse, 'eh's' always bright, and 'huh's' always pushing." As in the song "all spring," Doolittle is sensitive to spatial effects, and so the "background ocean sounds gradually become audible" and she instructs the singer to "begin as if far away, gradually coming closer until 2:49."[81]

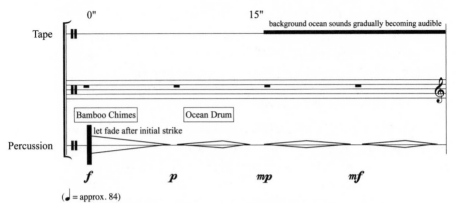

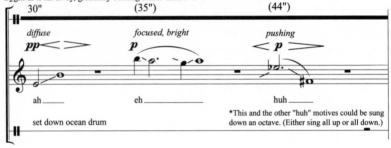

EXAMPLE 10.10. *Social sounds from whales at night.* By Emily Doolittle, page 1.
Copyright © 2007 by the composer. Reprinted with kind permission.

Doolittle unveils her delight in the musical collaboration at 3:46 when the soprano and whale sing a duet that includes "out of tune" notes. She encourages the singer to "relish the little clashes between your version and the whale's!" Her playfulness in *Social sounds* recalls Bond's *Peculiar Plants* and Oliveros's *MirrorrorriM*. While each of these musicians takes her work seriously, none is above having fun with her art and composing with a light touch (example 10.12).

Although Doolittle rejects the idea that she was making a statement about the artificiality of boundaries in *Social sounds from whales at night,*

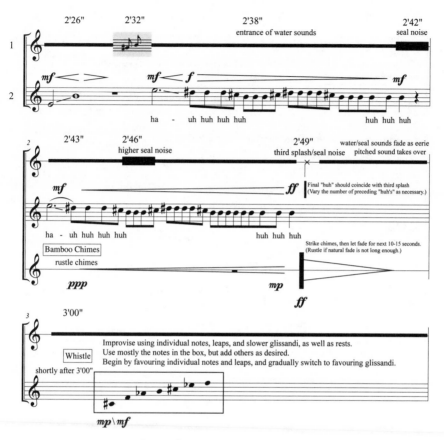

EXAMPLE 10.11. *Social sounds from whales at night.* By Emily Doolittle, page 3 (2:26–3:14). Copyright © 2007 by the composer. Reprinted with kind permission.

and clarifies that she prefers to make *suggestions* rather than statements, she acknowledges that "the piece became an exploration of breaking down boundaries" between what is human and what is nature.[82] Doolittle wrote a part for soprano that is so thoroughly modeled upon and interwoven with the recorded whale sounds, it is often impossible to distinguish between the human and nonhuman singer, and listeners discover that they are not meant to. While nature inspires Doolittle's works in varying degrees, and the composer doesn't intentionally foreground a specific agenda in all her pieces, *Social sounds* musicalizes a recurring theme for the composer: "There is not a dividing line between nature and humans."[83]

EXAMPLE 10.12. *Social sounds from whales at night.* By Emily Doolittle, page 4 (3:15–4:15). Copyright © 2007 by the composer. Reprinted with kind permission.

In the past few years, Doolittle has devoted considerable energy to researching the science of acoustic communication; she has spent time with scientists who study animal vocalization (and culture) and learned from what they know and how they perceive things. At present she is writing a collaborative paper on the hermit thrush with scientists at St. Andrews. Her embrace of technology may initially seem unusual in a person who aligns herself so thoroughly with the natural world, but, as John Cage understood, electronics that capture sounds beyond normal human hearing ranges, and computer programs that separate minute sonic occurrences into discrete bands that can be replayed, analyzed, and individually identified, allow a more intimate relationship with nonhuman subjects; she can understand them better. Here is an instance of science and art coming together and Doolittle reveling in their commingling. Her extended family, equal parts scientists and artists, continues to exert its influence.

Despite the different animal subjects, *Social sounds* is similar to *night black bird song*; both works weave together human and nonhuman musics. Like many compositions by Pauline Oliveros, both pieces complicate the idea of what is music. In addition, both pieces resist easy definition or description, and this is fine – in fact, it is freeing. Like Larsen, Doolittle is more comfortable in a world of ambiguity, complexity, and open-ended possibilities than in a world of sharp-edged, categorical, confining truths. By composing a piece with and about whales, the largest mammals on the planet, Doolittle expressed her comfort outside the circumscribed boundaries of women's early nature experiences, which for centuries took place primarily with home still in view. As her bird-inspired pieces demonstrate, she also willingly engages with nature contained in that more traditional sphere. In seamlessly weaving the whale's and vocalist's sounds and pulling the human's music from the whale's music, Doolittle composes her belief in the arbitrariness and perhaps insensibility of boundaries delineating what is human and what is animal. *Social sounds from whales at night* is Emily Doolittle expressing her belief in the connectedness of all species. Ultimately it is an example of her unique effort to bring music and activism together. She becomes part of a forty-plus-years tradition of composers to do so.

July 2010 saw the premiere of a new nature-related work by this prolific composer, and one that takes her back to the garden. As Doolittle explained in the program note, *Reeds* is a site-specific creation inspired by the soundscape of Oxen Pond in the Memorial University of Newfoundland (MUN)

Botanical Garden in St. John's, the capital city of the province, and written for the Newfoundland Sound Symposium.[84] It is the result of combined efforts by Doolittle, composer; Camille Renarhd, choreographer/dancer; and three instrumentalists of the Umbrella Ensemble – Catherine Lee, oboe; Louise Campbell, clarinet; and Alex Eastley, bassoon. But when Doolittle characterized *Reeds* as "so deeply interdisciplinary and so collaborative," it is because with this work she took the idea of collaboration to a new level. In *Reeds*, the specific features and sounds of the botanical garden were not merely sources of inspiration, but actual partners in the initial concept and its realization.[85] In point of fact, the MUN Botanical Garden was chosen by the composer, dancer, and instrumentalists specifically because of the presence of a pond, the varied avian population that made the botanical garden home year round, and the rich aural environment that water and birds created.

The intimate relationships of place and music and dance are best appreciated when one can *see* and hear the work on-site or witness the event as it has been video-recorded: only then does the full extent of its collaborative reach become apparent. Beyond the efforts of the composer, dancer, instrumentalists, and place, as the ambling audience walks down paths of crushed stone that lead to each of the designated listening sites, it too contributes to the musical landscape. Crunching footsteps signal the presence of humans as part of the natural world: auditors on a soundwalk, they are also composers.[86] Path walkers hear "bird" songs and calls long before they see the musicians playing Doolittle's transcribed avian sounds. In the service of making some of the recorded bird music audible to humans, Doolittle has slowed down and lowered by a few octaves some of the songs.[87] As Doolittle explains: "None of the music in *Reeds* is freely composed: all of it, even the parts that sound surprisingly melodic, are more or less direct transcriptions of the birdsongs or other Oxen Pond sounds."[88] Farther down the path, walkers watch and hear Renarhd enact her "Water Dance," a gentle homage to the sounds and movements of the pond and a quartet of water birds: the American bittern, common loon, spotted sandpiper, and greater yellowlegs. The lapping and slapping of waters and dancer call one's attention to still more voices in Doolittle's garden ensemble.

Doolittle divides the piece into thirteen sections, beginning and ending with "Summer Music," the most "cacophonous chorus of summer songbirds resident in Newfoundland."[89] Each of the composed sections draws from the sounds of a particular bird or two that are found in Newfoundland, except for some in section X, "Spring Peepers," which Doolittle explains are "not native to Newfoundland, but introduced."[90] Three interludes of "silence" punctuate Doolittle's thiry-six-minute soundscape, and she is emphatic that these are parts of the piece: "Just as birds and other animals come and go throughout the year and there are periods of lots of activity and periods of quiet, the piece also has periods where there is lots of music, and periods that are silent. The silent parts are parts of the piece. I would ask that you not talk at all during these parts. Just listen to the other sounds."[91]

As the final work in a book that has often seen composers employing circle imagery to get at cyclical ideas, it is happily reinforcing that the composer points out the cyclic concept of this piece:

> *Reeds* . . . follows a year's worth of birdsongs and other sounds that can be heard here. Many of these birdsongs are hard for people to hear in detail because they are so quiet, high, or fast. Yearly cycles of sound, on the other hand, may be too slow for people to experience on a day-to-day basis. By slowing down and amplifying certain aspects of each birdsong, Doolittle 'translated' them into instrumental songs which are more readily understandable by human listeners. At the same time, the yearly cycle of sounds is compressed into a time-scale that allows the listener to have a sense of the seasonal comings and goings of each species. In the creation of the dance, Renarhd draws on both the sounds and the terrain of Oxen Pond to find motions that make visible the subtle movements and energies of this place. The cumulative effect of *Reeds* is one of a shifting magnifying glass as different aspects of Oxen Pond are illuminated.[92]

She also returns to birdsong transcriptions. Although Doolittle has engaged with sounds made by the largest mammals on the planet and brought them into her music, her ear is still tuned to the vocalizations of the smallest creatures as well; she revels in their music. It is serendipitous, and more than any author has a right to expect, that the very first bird to which Doolittle devotes an entire section in *Reeds* is the hermit thrush.[93] Cycles abound.

In addition to returning to birds, *Reeds* returns to a garden. Like Ellen Zwilich, whose plans for her Symphony No. 4 were changed by the experience she underwent while visiting the Michigan State gardens, Doolittle understood that the wild and indigenous flora and fauna at the MUN Botanical Garden created a unique opportunity for engagement with the natural world. The place became the first and most important collaborator. As Doolittle explained: "a different ensemble and a different place would have resulted in a different piece."[94] Through her music and through the video-recording of the premiere performance, July 10, 2010, Doolittle's engagement with the sounds of the Memorial University of Newfoundland Botanical Garden becomes our own. Like Doolittle, we are simultaneously auditors, participants, and composers, in and of the natural world.

Conclusions

The nine composers considered in this book enjoy a variety of relationships to the natural world. Many have pointed out that within their own oeuvre, nature informs works in different ways and to different degrees; for them, no type of interaction is privileged, no single piece tells all, although specific pieces may be representative. While Amy Beach wrote a number of works whose titles refer to nature, "A Hermit Thrush at Morn" captures her most forthright statement regarding her efforts to capture nature in music. Nowhere else does Beach detail the history of a composition so completely or announce the success of her endeavor so boldly. Her pieces named for flowers are of an impressionistic type found frequently among the parlor music genre. While they are of a higher quality than many written for domestic players, these "nature pieces" are only vaguely evocative of their subjects and wouldn't be identifiable as having a relationship to a daisy or a bluebell, were it not for their titles. Other composers' works provide examples of this kind of nature-inspired music. When instructive, I have tried to suggest the fullness of a composer's interactions with the environment by examining multiple pieces. Ellen Taaffe Zwilich is an exception to this practice because of the uniqueness of her single nature-related work. The clear message contained in Symphony No. 4, "The Gardens," however, suggested to me the ways environmental issues touch a range of people beyond the most obvious sympathizers to the cause. We might not expect Zwilich to write such a rousing call to action: that she did is noteworthy.

Over a period of ten years working on this project and thinking about the relationships of music to nature, of nature to music, and of American women to music to nature, a number of themes have emerged and insisted upon themselves with something approaching consistency. Among the most emphatic of these recurring ideas is the multifariousness of composers' relationships to "nature," which reflects in part upon the ambiguity of the term. One learns that there is no monolithic concept of nature shared by these women, as there is no monolithic concept of nature shared by any group, and there is no single response to it either. There is no archetype of women's nature music. Even within the oeuvre of an individual composer, the variety of relationships and understandings of the exceedingly complex and yet commonly used term "nature" is everywhere on display. None of the composers with whom I spoke was willing to concede that a single piece embodied the entire range of her understanding of "nature," even Ellen Zwilich. The nine composers' many-faceted relationships *with* nature reflect their various understandings *of* nature and can be heard, at least in part, in the wide range of their music.

Among the composers are those who understand nature as a shrine; a vaguely programmatic extramusical referent; a source of raw materials; the embodiment of the divine; a site of aesthetic perfection; an infinite well of artistic inspiration; and a handy term for the mundane. There are also those who see "nature" as an all-encompassing humanly constructed idea for that which is outside of "us," and those who argue that there is no distinction between nature and us. They express their understandings in music that is instrumental, vocal, choral, electronic, ambient, evocative of fragrance, incorporating dance, intended for professionals, and best realized by amateurs. It is notated within traditional-looking scores, drawn with graphics, and described by the most unorthodox of recipes. It is simultaneously and by turns precise and improvisatory. It is enacted in concert halls and cisterns and botanical gardens and waterways. It is music for listening and music for participating. And this bounty of understandings emerges from a group of composers who have much in common: all are women; all are white; all are American citizens by birth. Despite differences of natal place, religious belief, sexual orientation, and aesthetic preference, they share a core cultural bond by virtue of having inherited a national narrative that casts "nature" in a principal role, even if that inherited role used a script different from the one they might have written.

Given the common national inheritance enjoyed by these women, it is significant that a strong feeling of Americanness seems to play no role in their music. It is not that they don't recognize or acknowledge their American (U.S.) citizenship, but it doesn't appear to be an essential identifier either for themselves or for their work. It is impossible to know to what degree this is a result of today's pervasive global thinking, or whether disenfranchisement from the original national narrative made it easy to ignore. Composers do refer to indigenous birds and vegetation, U.S. waterways, locations found within the nation's borders, and American musical styles including Broadway musicals and ragtime. They respond to seminal environmental tracts written by American authors, and they speak of their childhoods in specific towns and cities each with its own qualities and character that are unique to that place. But they also recognize the arbitrary quality of national boundaries when it comes to environmental concerns. Birds and whales seem not to worry about political boundaries and border crossings, and it is not a chief concern of these listeners. Emily Doolittle has written pieces that were conceived in Canada, various places throughout Europe, and the United States. Victoria Bond's caged bird dreams of flying, with no thought given to national jurisdictions of airspace. Perhaps these composers imagine their national identity is obvious; perhaps they take it as a given. They simply don't talk about it. One quality they all exhibit, which speaks volumes about their national inheritance, is an assumption that they can express themselves as they like.

Education, both formal and informal, is a theme that weaves itself through the study. When one understands the power that educational opportunities exerted upon these composers, it is easy to appreciate the historical focus of the American Association of University Women to make access to education its top priority.[1] With the exception of Amy Beach, each composer enjoyed specialized, advanced training from professionals in her field, and Beach did her best to make up for what was denied her by engaging in rigorous self-education. Of the nine composers considered, five of them have earned doctorates in music. Three others have college and graduate degrees; only Amy Beach is without any institutional credential.[2] But degrees and diplomas hardly tell the full story. By standard measures of success in the field – including publication, performance, professional employment, and public perception – all were and are high achievers. While the nine composers were born into a range of economic circumstances, they were all children of what is broadly considered the "middle to upper-middle" class. Then as now, that designation can be assigned using criteria other than material wealth: educational accomplishment remains among the most conspicuous designators of class besides money, and education can be found within and outside formal institutions of learning.

The impact of one's family is another theme that cycles through the study, and so it should come as no surprise that education and musical training were highly valued by the composers' families. Despite Mrs. Cheney's restrictive notions of how best to nurture her young daughter's musical abilities, there is no question that she valued them. While Dr. H. H. A. Beach confined his wife's public performances to infrequent charity events, he encouraged her efforts to compose. There was encouragement, even if it was not always the type that Amy Beach most desired. Bauer and Talma benefited from the extraordinary support and sacrifice of a large number of family members, friends, and teachers. It is no exaggeration to state that without her sister, Marion Bauer would not have become the successful composer, writer, or teacher she did. In the case of Pauline Oliveros, sounds of her mother practicing filled their home with improvised music. The composer credits her mother and grandmother with modeling the open-minded and playful musician she would value and become. Tower learned from the best teachers that could be found in her hometown of Larchmont, New York, and then in Bolivia, Chile, and Peru as her family followed her father's career. George Tower exposed his young daughter to experiences in the out-of-doors that were off-limits to other girls growing up in the 1940s, and she benefited from regular evening musicales with her family where each played an instrument or sang. She developed a love of dance from her nanny. In addition to a rich and varied home and family environment, Emily Doolittle benefited from a superior school music program, as did Zwilich years earlier, and Bond blossomed in the open air of the Rudolf Steiner School curriculum, a summer home in the country, and a family environment that nurtured the unlimited growth of all of Bond's abilities and interests. Larsen cites her mother and Girl Scouts and access to the lakes and lands surrounding her Minnesota home with providing a nurturing environment. At the University of Minnesota her "family" became her fellow graduate students, who combined their energies to form the Minnesota Composers Forum, which grew to become the American Composers Forum.

Professional organizations and associations provided additional communities that acted like families for these composers, and many of them, as the Larsen example demonstrates, were self-created. While the MacDowell

Colony was in place starting in 1907 as a home away from home that nurtured young artists from across disciplines, including six women in this study, Beach's and Bauer's charter memberships in the Society of American Women Composers, and Joan Tower's co-founding of the Da Capo Chamber Players, stand as testaments to the importance of professional organizations that provide opportunities for personal growth and all-important networking where none might have existed before.

A number of the women talked about early and extremely meaningful experiences with nature: Beach, Talma, Oliveros, Tower, Bond, Larsen, and Doolittle especially recalled vivid encounters with the out-of-doors, although the range of their encounters varies significantly between the earliest and the latest of the composers. From a young age they were at home in the woods, on mountains, and on open waters. Their childhood interactions with animals (birds, frogs, dogs, cats, and horses) and their youthful introduction to the idea of the reciprocal relationships of humans and the earth (Bond's discovery of the taste of a carrot yanked from the soil, and Larsen's reflection upon having planted tiny pine trees) sowed the seeds of a profound environmental awareness and connectivity that would express itself decades later in their music. Like access to education, access to the widest variety of nature's bounty has been fundamental to their understanding of what nature is and how they stand within and among it.

By far the most resilient and resonant theme of the study, however, is the idea of collaboration: joining with others to realize a common goal. Whether discussing practical preferences for how they worked best, or assessing their position in relation to nature, the overwhelming majority of the composers regarded themselves as and sought to be collaborators in a larger endeavor. While still insisting upon the need for quiet, focused, solitary time, and individual encounters with nature, they valued their collaborative relationships. Collaboration stands as a principal mode of behavior informing everything else.

Basic to the idea of collaboration is a rejection of dichotomous thinking and the power relationships that accompany it. They reject this for themselves and for others. The composers of this study refused to be confined by established disciplinary boundaries, and they repudiated categories for themselves or their work, sometimes quite vehemently. Categories, they insisted, only limit imagination, participation, perception, and solutions. Collaboration levels the field and empowers all players. Amateurs and professionals are welcome as equals; whales and birds are as legitimate sound sources as traditional folk tunes or carefully crafted musical motives by highly trained (human) composer specialists. The circle becomes the ideal image for this company of equals – among humans, including men and women, and between humans and nonhuman others. It would appear that after years of not being heard, these composers want to be careful not to repeat the mistake of silencing others.

Listening, carefully and deeply and always, is the most obvious manifestation of this collaborative compact. Pauline Oliveros understands this when she refers to her listening practice as a discipline. Collaborative relationships require listening more than talking, being a student more often than being the teacher, growing into an environment rather than insisting upon reshaping it. That so many of the composers valued listening and sought quiet places far away to do their work seems not so much a desire on their part to remove themselves from the world but, on the contrary, a deep wish to reconnect with and listen to that part of the world that regularly gets drowned out. What these composers have taught us is that listening requires the ability to hear what is being said, and that is not always possible amid the din of an overpowering, omnipresent, humanly orchestrated soundtrack.

Their lessons in listening have applications beyond increased awareness of the natural environment. In an encomium on the back cover of *Getting to Yes*, Fisher and Ury's guidebook for successful negotiation, John Kenneth Galbraith recommended: "it is equally relevant for the individual who would like to keep his friends, property, and income and the statesman who would like to keep the peace."[3] Despite Galbraith's bothersome assumption that it is men who have property or are the negotiators of peace (*pace* Madeleine Albright and Hillary Clinton), the point is clear and gender neutral: negotiating, which the authors make clear involves respectful listening, is in the best interests of everyone. How to convince a nation of talkers, texters, and tweeters that the best communication might involve unplugging for a few hours each day and listening, listening deeply, will not be easy to pull off. It might be impossible. But that there is a growing need for time to connect with ourselves and the world, unmediated, is clear and widely understood.

Music, an expressive mode involving sound, provides the raw materials to teach listening. And music that has at its source some connection to nature can teach us how to listen and tune to the world beyond the practice room and recital hall. Taking off our headphones might actually allow us to hear better. Who knows, it might even model how to keep the peace.

And when the noise dies down, we discover another concert taking place: by turns soothing and gentle and raucous and disturbing, and we are a part of it too. We can't help but pay attention, reconsider assumptions regarding the diversity of life around us, and acknowledge our place in an enterprise that is larger than ourselves.

NOTES

INTRODUCTION

1. Tina Gianquitto, *"Good Observers of Nature": American Women and the Scientific Study of the Natural World, 1820–1885* (Athens: University of Georgia Press, 2007). Quite beyond the title, Gianquitto's book provided a model of what I wanted my own study to achieve.

2. John Vance Cheney, "The Skilful Listener," in Edmund Clarence Stedman, ed., *An American Anthology, 1787–1900* (http://www.bartleby.com/248/1008.html, accessed July 18, 2007). The spelling and capitalization are as they appear in the Stedman collection.

3. "Inspiration" is a similarly problematic word. I use it here to mean something that stimulates the mind or emotions either consciously or subconsciously.

4. See Siglind Bruhn, *Musical Ekphrasis: Composers Responding to Poetry and Painting* (Hillsdale, N.Y.: Pendragon Press, 2000), for an extended treatment of this idea.

5. I am grateful to Dereck Daschke, associate professor of religion and philosophy at Truman State University, for a stimulating and free-ranging conversation regarding the idea of "translation" and what it involves, suggests, and promises.

6. Rachel Carson, *Silent Spring* (Boston: Houghton Mifflin, 1962).

7. The lines come from the song "You've Got to Be Carefully Taught," from the Broadway musical *South Pacific* by Rogers and Hammerstein.

8. I am grateful for many hours of conversation with Marcia Porter, associate professor of voice at Florida State University, for helping me nuance my understanding of Bond's position as an African American composer of art music and the range of interactions with the natural world experienced by people of color in the United States.

9. This is a difficult term and one whose use I do not wholly endorse. In the context of this study, it distinguishes the works of these composers from popular or folk musics. That said, many works by Pauline Oliveros and Emily Doolittle, in particular, challenge traditional notions of what characterizes "art" music. More contemporary understandings of the terms "art," "popular," and "folk" look to their systems of support and transmission rather than any inherent musical qualities to understand their differing roles in culture. See the author's entry "Art Music" in *AmeriGrove*.

10. Perry Miller, quoted by Kenneth B. Murdock in his introduction to Miller's posthumous collection *Nature's Nation* (Cambridge, Mass.: Belknap Press of Harvard University Press, 1967), xv.

11. See http://www.ams-esg.org for information on this group and links to its many resources, including a bibliography of works relevant to ecomusicology in general and to this study in particular. I am grateful to Aaron Allen, who has chaired the ESG from its inception, for shepherding the group and providing leadership and opportunities to discuss ideas among its members. *Music and the Skillful Listener* has benefitted from the generous spirit and critical thinking of the ESG. For an overview of the state of ecomusicology, readers are encouraged to consult the *Journal of the Society for American Music* (*JAMS*) 64, no. 2 (2011): 391–424, for a colloquy by five scholars, including this author, on the topic "Ecomusicology: Ecocriticism and Musicology."

1. A CONTEXT FOR COMPOSERS

1. That serious literary women were more acceptable than similarly talented musical women speaks to the private and public spheres where each practiced her art. While writing and reading could take place quietly within the home, musical performance required one to commandeer the airwaves: through performance, a composer's voice would be heard.

2. See Candace Bailey's book *Music and the Southern Belle: From Accomplished Lady to Confederate Composer* (Carbondale: Southern Illinois University Press, 2010) for a region-specific study of the relationships among educational practices, social codes, and women's musical achievements. Many of Bailey's observations also reflect practices far north of the Mason-Dixon Line.

3. See "Women in American Music, 1800–1918" by Adrienne Fried Block, assisted by Nancy Stewart, in Karin Pendle, ed., *Women and Music: A History* (Bloomington: Indiana University Press, 2001), 210–218, for paragraph-length discussions of a handful of American women composers of the nineteenth century.

4. Ibid., 193–204, for an overview of women who were active in opera, in theater, and on the concert stage, as well as those who participated in the larger American musical culture through their work in music clubs. Women have historically been welcome as harpists in professional orchestras. See Bailey, chapter 6, "The Singer," for a discussion of acceptable singing styles (pages 119–136).

5. Anne Bradstreet, c. 1612–1672.

6. Sarah Kemble Knight, 1666–1727.

7. Michael Branch, ed., *Reading the Roots: American Nature Writing before Walden* (Athens: University of Georgia Press, 2004), 97.

8. Margaret Fuller, *Summer on the Lakes, in 1843*, with an introduction by Susan Belasco Smith (Urbana: University of Illinois Press, 1991), ix.

9. Ibid., 8–9.

10. As will be discussed in the following chapter, eighty years later, composer Amy Beach would also speak of her need for silence and solitude in nature. The themes of silence and solitude recur in this study.

11. Eliza W. Farnham, *Life in Prairie Land* (New York: Harper, 1846), v. Downloaded from Google Books.

12. Ibid., 267–268.

13. Susan Fenimore Cooper, *Rural Hours*, edited by Rochelle Johnson and Daniel Patterson (Athens: University of Georgia Press, 1998), ix.

14. See Henry D. Thoreau, *Walden*, edited by J. Lyndon Shanley (Princeton, N.J.: Princeton University Press, 1989), 3. For Thoreau's knowledge of *Rural Hours*, see Michael P. Branch, "Five Generations of Literary Coopers: Intergenerational Valuations of the American Frontier," in Rochelle Johnson and Daniel Patterson, eds., *Susan Fenimore Cooper: New Essays*

on *Rural Hours and Other Works* (Athens: University of Georgia Press, 2001), 61–71. Branch argues for possible instances of Thoreau imitating Cooper in his discussions of loons and wild berries, the depth of the pond, and the breaking up of ice.

15. Cooper, *Rural Hours*, 133. These remarks were entered in Cooper's journal July 28, 1848.

16. Ibid., 126.

17. See Kate Soper, *What Is Nature? Culture, Politics and the Non-Human* (Malden, Mass.: Blackwell, 1995), especially the introductory chapter, for a discussion of the complex meanings of the word "nature" throughout history and for different ways of construing nature's meanings.

18. Cooper, *Rural Hours*, 133, 134.

19. In his chapter "Economy," Thoreau observes: "In short, I am convinced, both by faith and experience, that to maintain one's self on this earth is not a hardship but a pastime, if we will live simply and wisely." In his chapter "Where I Lived, and What I Lived For," Thoreau repeats, "Simplicity, simplicity, simplicity!" and a few lines later, "Simplify, simplify." See Henry D. Thoreau, *Walden*, edited by J. Lyndon Shanley (Princeton, N.J.: Princeton University Press, 1989), 70 and 91.

20. I don't argue that these themes appeared exclusively in women's writing, only that they appeared regularly in women's nature writing.

21. See the section headed "Remember the Ladies: Women of the Hudson River School," Thomas Cole National Historic Site, http://www.thomascole.org/past-events (accessed September 19, 2011). The exhibit showed from May 1 to October 31, 2010.

22. See Judith H. Dobrzynski, "Time to Rewrite the Hudson River School Chapter of Art History" (http://www.artsjournal.com/realcleararts/2010/07/

hudson_river_women.html, accessed September 13, 2011).

23. William Cronon, "The Trouble with Wilderness," in William Cronon, ed., *Uncommon Ground: Rethinking the Human Place in Nature* (New York: Norton, 1996), 75.

24. Susan R. Schrepfer, *Nature's Altars: Mountains, Gender, and American Environmentalism* (Lawrence: University Press of Kansas, 2005), 84. Schrepfer quotes from "Haunts" from Mary T. S. Schaffer, "Botanical Notes," *Canadian Alpine Journal* (1911): 131–135, among other journal articles written by women alpinists of the turn of the century.

25. Tina Gianquitto, *"Good Observers of Nature": American Women and the Scientific Study of the Natural World, 1820–1885* (Athens: University of Georgia Press, 2007), 21. Gianquitto quotes Phelps, 14.

26. Ibid., 44, italics mine. Caption to figures 80, 81, and 83 from Phelps's *Familiar Lectures*, 76, 78.

27. Tina Gianquitto earned a PhD in American literature at Columbia University in 2002 and is currently assistant professor of liberal arts and international studies at the Colorado School of Mines. Her work moves effortlessly between literature and science in general, and more specifically between women writers and their perception of nature. Besides *"Good Observers,"* Gianquitto has published on Charles Darwin and on popular science writing in the nineteenth century. She is the recipient of ACLS and NEH fellowships.

28. Rosemary Radford Ruether, *New Woman, New Earth: Sexist Ideologies and Human Liberation* (Boston: Beacon Press, 1995). Originally published in 1975 by the Seabury Press.

29. Ibid., xvii.

30. Ibid., 195. Italics are my own.

31. Ibid., xxiii.

32. Ibid., 204–205. Susan Fenimore Cooper's concern that Americans had moved away from simplicity echoes in Ruether's prose.

33. Ibid., 205.

34. Ibid., 211.

35. Vera L. Norwood, "Heroines of Nature: Four Women Respond to the American Landscape," in Cheryll Glotfelty and Harold Fromm, eds., *The Ecocriticism Reader: Landmarks in Literary Ecology* (Athens: University of Georgia Press, 1999), 327. In *Nature's Altars*, Susan R. Schrepfer considers the importance of "manless climbs" to the many women's climbing groups that hiked in the Sierras. The theme of solitude continues to resonate.

36. Annette Kolodny, "Unearthing Herstory: An Introduction," *The Ecocriticism Reader*, 173. As Susan R. Schrepfer demonstrates, the feminine metaphor was regularly co-opted by women to support their efforts on behalf of nature.

37. Michael P. Branch's collection *Reading the Roots: American Nature Writing before* Walden (Athens: University of Georgia Press, 2004) identifies numerous male nature writers of the seventeenth and eighteenth centuries, including Jasper Danckaerts, Cotton Mather, and William Bartram, who early on exhibited a more sensitive (i.e., female?) attitude toward nature prior to the utilitarian ethos that came to dominate in the mid-nineteenth century. Danckaerts's description of a summer sunset in 1679, viewed while on a sea voyage, is remarkable for its aesthetic detail and perspective (see Branch, 78–84). Mather, a leader among Puritan intellectuals, was among the first, with his work *The Christian Philosopher: A Collection of the Best Discoveries in Nature, with Religious Improvements* (1721), to advocate that "the natural world should be studied as evidence of the Creator" (Branch, 111).

And Bartram invested all living creatures with spiritual value (Branch, 184). Susan R. Schrepfer's study demonstrates that even the heartiest and most fearless of women alpine climbers at the turn of the century did *not* use a rhetoric of attack and conquest. Their narratives consistently described the comfort and hominess of the mountains.

38. Lorraine Anderson, ed., *Sisters of the Earth: Women's Prose and Poetry about Nature*, 2nd ed. (New York: Vintage Books, 2003). The book was first published with slightly different contents in 1991.

39. Lydia Huntley Sigourney lived from 1791 to 1865. She is represented in the collection by her poem "Fallen Forests," written in 1845. A poem titled "A Different Sympathy," by Maria Melendez (b. 1974), is the work of the youngest writer included in the collection.

40. Anderson, *Sisters of the Earth*, xxi.

41. Readers should consult Susan R. Schrepfer's *Nature's Altars* for an extraordinarily well-documented study of men's and women's participation in alpine sports and the rhetoric that has accompanied the descriptions of their experiences. As Schrepfer makes clear, men's accounts rarely acknowledged the presence of porters or guides, although they were certainly there and in many cases actually arrived at the peak of the mountains before the gentleman credited with that achievement.

42. Anderson, *Sisters of the Earth*, xxii.

43. Ruether, *New Woman, New Earth*, xxiii.

44. It is possible that women climbers engaged in a different description of nature in more private communications among fellow alpinists. There they would be free to drop domestic imagery and acknowledge the challenges they faced and the physical accomplishments they had achieved.

45. Zora Neale Hurston, excerpt from *Their Eyes Were Watching God*, in Anderson, *Sisters of the Earth*, 13.

46. Brenda Peterson, excerpt from *Living by Water: Essays on Life, Land, and Spirit*, in Anderson, *Sisters of the Earth*, 17.

47. As discussed above, Susan Fenimore Cooper's *Rural Hours* from 1850 is among the earliest broadly distributed books that claims the special importance of nature in the United States. Cooper followed it with numerous articles, essays, and introductions that secured her claim as the first widely published American woman nature writer. The title of Perry Miller's posthumously published book *Nature's Nation* made the connection between America and its natural environment most profoundly and pithily.

48. Denise Von Glahn, *The Sounds of Place: Music and the American Cultural Landscape* (Boston: Northeastern University Press, 2003).The composers included Anthony Philip Heinrich, William Henry Fry, George Frederick Bristow, Charles Ives, Aaron Copland, Edgard Varèse, William Grant Still, Duke Ellington, Roy Harris, Ferde Grofé, Robert Starer, Dana Paul Perna, Steve Reich, and Ellen Taaffe Zwilich.

49. In order to qualify, the work had to be predominantly of the high-art instrumental or concert tradition; its title had to make a clear reference to a place; the composer had to intentionally commemorate a place (as closely as that could be determined); and it had to be written by a native or naturalized U.S. citizen. In addition, I sought pieces whose composers had real connections to and experiences with the places they named.

50. Edmund Burke, *On the Sublime and Beautiful*, vol. 24, part 2, *The Harvard Classics* (New York: P. F. Collier, 1909–14), from Bartleby.com, 2001 (www.bartleby.com/24/2, accessed June 9, 2008). In his essay "The Sublime and Beautiful Compared," Burke explains: "On closing this general view of beauty, it naturally occurs, that we should compare it with the sublime; and in this comparison there appears a remarkable contrast. For sublime objects are vast in their dimensions, beautiful ones comparatively small: beauty should be smooth and polished; the great, rugged and negligent; beauty should shun the right line, yet deviate from it insensibly; the great in many cases loves the right line, and when it deviates it often makes a strong deviation: beauty should not be obscure; the great ought to be dark and gloomy: beauty should be light and delicate; the great ought to be solid, and even massive. They are indeed ideas of a very different nature, one being founded on pain, the other on pleasure; and however they may vary afterwards from the direct nature of their causes, yet these causes keep up an eternal distinction between them, a distinction never to be forgotten by any whose business it is to affect the passions."

51. Ruether, *New Woman, New Earth*, 25.

PART I. NATURE AS A SUMMER HOME

1. In her biography *Amy Beach, Passionate Victorian: The Life and Work of an American Composer, 1867–1944* (New York: Oxford University Press), Adrienne Fried Block provides a full account of Beach's participation in this group. See page 246 in particular, where Block also discusses Bauer's role in the society. For a list of founding members, see page 366n23. The group disbanded in 1932, although as Block points out, "in its few years of existence, [it had] kept the music of its members in the public ear and, via reviews, the public eye" (246).

2. Ellie M. Hisama's book *Gendering Musical Modernism: The Music of Ruth*

*Crawford, Marion Bauer, and Miriam
Gideon,* provides a sensitive and insightful
discussion of the multifaceted and pro-
ductive relationship of these two women.
See especially chapter 5, "Gender, Sexual-
ity, and Performance in Marion Bauer's
Toccata," pages 99–121. See also Judith
Tick's biography *Ruth Crawford Seeger:
A Composer's Search for American Music*
(New York: Oxford University Press),
97–99, especially, for an assessment of
Bauer and Crawford's interactions at the
MacDowell Colony.

3. Together the three women enjoyed
seventy-five residencies at the MacDowell
Colony.

4. Adrienne Fried Block explains
Beach's "substantial gift . . . to the Mac-
Dowell Colony," which included "royalties from publishers and performance fees
from ASCAP and other agencies [which]
were regularly paid into the Amy Beach
Fund of the Edward MacDowell Association, a bequest that yielded thousands of
dollars per year for the colony in the first
decade or so after Beach's death." Block
continues: "During the years in which her
music was neglected by almost everyone
but church musicians, the amounts de-
clined considerably and subsequently the
fund was folded into the general assets
of the MacDowell Colony. Very recently,
however, a startling change has occurred.
While royalties have diminished mark-
edly as more and more of her works are
in the public domain, performance and
recording fees have greatly increased, and
thus between 1992 and 1995 the colony's
income from Beach's music tripled."
Block summarized: "Amy Beach would
have been delighted – staunch supporter
that she was – to know that fifty years
after her death her music is again earning
thousands of dollars yearly for the colony." Block, *Amy Beach,* 297. Luann Dragone notes that upon Louise Talma's death
in 1996, she left one million dollars to

the colony (http://www.omnidisc.com/
Talma/Biography.html#INTERVIEW
(accessed May 20, 2011).

5. Florence Price (1887–1953); Elinor
Remick Warren (1900–1991); Miriam
Gideon (1906–1996), a student of Marion
Bauer; and Margaret Bonds (1913–1972)
were all actively composing at the same
time, but none of them focused their
energies in similarly systematic ways on
nurturing other women composers. The
reasons for this are likely many, including
choice to do otherwise, and for Price and
Bonds (two African American women)
the denial of access to many of the institutions and social circles that would have
allowed them to exert their influence very
broadly.

6. The multiple extended residencies
of Beach, Bauer, and Talma, which meant
the colony functioned as a regular summer home and source of inspiration, community, and nurturance for these women,
separates the first three composers from
the other MacDowell fellows studied in
Music and the Skillful Listener.

7. From Rupert Hughes, *Contemporary American Composers* (Boston: L. C.
Page, 1900), 438, as quoted by Judith Tick
in her essay "Charles Ives and Gender
Ideology," in *Musicology and Difference:
Gender and Sexuality in Music Scholarship*
(Berkeley: University of California Press,
1993), 92. The phrase originally appeared
in Hughes's discussion of the composer
Margaret Ruthven Lang in his chapter
"The Women Composers." In summariz-
ing her work Hughes explained, "It is devoid of meretriciousness and of any sus-
picion of seeking after virility." Hughes
valued "the general quality of [Margaret
Ruthven Lang's work] above that of any
other woman composer," including Mrs.
H. H. A. Beach. Besides those two more
famous women composers, Hughes
names twelve others he believes are worthy of mention (see 439–441). Marcia

Citron's seminal work *Gender and the Musical Canon* (Cambridge, UK: Cambridge University Press, 1993) remains among the most systematic and informative studies regarding the obstacles to creativity and professionalism faced by women daring to compose. See chapters 2 and 3 especially. Its value to my thinking and this study cannot be exaggerated.

8. Mary Carr Moore, "Is American Citizenship a Handicap to a Composer?" *Musician* 40 (September 1935): 5, 8 (an interview with Juliet Laine), quoted in Catherine Parsons Smith and Cynthia S. Richardson, *Mary Carr Moore, American Composer* (Ann Arbor: University of Michigan Press, 1987), 173.

9. See Carol Neuls-Bates, *Women in Music: An Anthology of Source Readings from the Middle Ages to the Present* (Boston: Northeastern University Press, 1996), 220–221.

10. See ibid., 206, for Neuls-Bates's characterization of Upton's remarks.

11. Ibid., 206–210. Neuls-Bates provides an excerpt from George Upton's *Woman in Music* (Boston: J. R. Osgood, 1880), 21–28.

12. Women were not encouraged to develop virtuosic skills, however, as that would have been unseemly. On a practical level, they would have few respectable opportunities to perform publicly. See Candace Bailey's book *Music and the Southern Belle: From Accomplished Lady to Confederate Composer* (Carbondale: Southern Illinois University Press, 2010) for a consideration of the particularly restrictive code of behavior regarding musical accomplishment that young southern women endured in the antebellum and Civil War years.

13. Among other early accomplished performers, Maud Powell (1867–1920) was the first American violinist, male or female, to enjoy international acclaim. Additionally, her recordings for Victor

Red Seal helped establish violin repertoire for a generation of students and performers. She has only recently begun to receive scholarly recognition for her remarkable achievements. For the newest addition to Powell scholarship see Catherine Williams, *"The Solution Lies with the American Woman": Maud Powell as an Advocate for Violinists, Women, and American Music*, master's thesis, Florida State University, 2012.

14. This is not to say men didn't compose smaller works as well and perhaps even prefer those dimensions: Schubert, Schumann, Mendelssohn, and Chopin come immediately to mind. In the United States, Edward MacDowell (1860–1908) was a celebrated composer of both large and small works. His collections of programmatic pieces for solo piano, most especially *Woodland Sketches* (1896), *Sea Pieces* (1898), and *New England Idyls* (1902), were favorites among parlor pianists. His two piano concerti were especially popular among concertizing virtuosi. But even MacDowell came under criticism for his tendency toward sentimentalism. Paul Rosenfeld wrote that MacDowell "minces and simpers, maidenly, and ruffled"; see Rosenfeld, *An Hour with American Music* (Philadelphia: J. B. Lippincott, 1929), 46, as quoted in Tick, *Ruth Crawford Seeger*, 95. Rosenfeld's gendered language was typical at the time.

15. According to an article published in 1919, there were "more than 600 active [music] clubs, with a combined membership of approximately 200,000." See "Women as 'Keepers of Culture': Music Clubs, Community Concert Series, and Symphony Orchestras," by Linda Whitesitt, in Ralph P. Locke and Cyrilla Barr, eds., *Cultivating Music in America: Women Patrons and Activists since 1860* (Berkeley: University of California Press, 1997), 66–67. Whitesitt summarizes an

article by Theodore H. Bauer, "Women's Clubs a Dominant Factor in Music," *Musical Monitor* 8, no. 9 (June 1919): 431. See also Michael Broyles, "Art Music from 1860 to 1920," in David Nicholls, ed., *The Cambridge History of American Music* (Cambridge, UK: Cambridge University Press, 1998), 227–232, for a discussion of the power of women's music clubs.

16. "Serious" in this context implies a composer of large orchestral music: symphonies and concerti. George Whitefield Chadwick assumed that he paid Beach a compliment when, upon hearing a performance of her "Gaelic Symphony" with the Boston Symphony Orchestra in 1896, he pronounced that she was "one of the boys," a reference to the group of composers with whom he associated, now known as the Second New England School. Chadwick made his comment in a letter he wrote to Beach dated October 31, 1896. See Amy Beach, *Quartet for Strings (in One Movement)*, Op. 89, vol. 3 of *Music of the United States of America*, ed. Adrienne Fried Block (Madison: A-R Editions, 1994), xiv. Walter Damrosch took a different view of Beach's accomplishments. See Adrienne Fried Block, *Amy Beach*, 201 and 356n24, for a different assessment of her work, and the potential of women composers more generally.

2. AMY MARCY CHENEY BEACH (MRS. H. H. A. BEACH)

1. See Adrienne Fried Block's biography *Amy Beach, Passionate Victorian: The Life and Work of an American Composer, 1867–1944* (New York: Oxford University Press, 1998), 36, for the most complete study of the composer, her music, and her milieu.

2. It is impossible to know the many considerations that went into Clara Cheney's decision to deny her remarkably gifted daughter the opportunity to study abroad, but expenses associated with

such a venture; pressures on the family, which would likely be separated for years during the time of training; and a sincere belief that Amy's talents would blossom fully on their own cannot be discounted. That Clara Cheney also identified herself as a musician and may have harbored some jealousy of her daughter's gifts might also have played into the decision to stay stateside.

3. See Block, *Amy Beach*, 322n64. The review appeared in "Musical Notes," *Boston Gazette*, October 25, 1883 (S1.3). For a copy of the program, see Mrs. H. H. A. Beach (1867–1944) Papers, 1835–1956, at the University of New Hampshire, Milne Special Collections, box 16, folder 1, Concert/performances, programs arranged by year.

4. A. P. Peck was manager of the Boston Music Hall until his death in 1885.

5. See Block, *Amy Beach*, 30, as quoted from Olin Downes, "Mrs. H. H. A. Beach of Boston, Now Noted as Composer," unidentified clipping. 1907.

6. See Mrs. H. H. A. Beach Papers, box 16, folders 4, 5, 8, and 13, for programs from benefit concerts in which she participated.

7. Mrs. H. H. A. Beach, "How Music Is Made," *Keyboard* (Winter 1942): 11, 38.

8. "The How of Creative Composition: A Conference with Mrs. H. H. A. Beach," secured expressly for *The Etude* by Benjamin Brooks" (March 1943): 151, 208; Mrs. H. H. A. Beach Papers, the University of New Hampshire, Special Collections MC 51, box 4, folio 4.

9. See Block, *Amy Beach*, 30.

10. See Mrs. H. H. A. Beach Papers, box 4/f.1, Music reviews, v. II (of the compositions of others), October 1894. The remark quoted is found on page 57. The underline is Beach's. For those who have noted close similarities between works by Beach and Brahms, this gushing praise

of Tchaikovsky's music may come as a surprise.

11. See Mrs. H. H. A. Beach Papers, box 11, part 1: Copies of Scrapbooks. This article appears on page 39 of the copied pages that make up the scrapbook.

12. See Mrs. H. H. A. Beach Papers, box 11, part 1, Copies of Scrapbooks, "Visit to the Home of Mrs. H. H. Beach, Which Is Paradise for the Lover of Music." No page number.

13. See Mrs. H. H. A. Beach Papers, box 16, folder 13, Concert/performances programs arranged by year. Women in Music: Grand Vocal and Instrumental Concert given for the benefit of "The United Women of Maryland: showing the Wonderful Progress in the Creative Power of Woman in Music during the last decade of the Closed Century." Music Hall, Baltimore, MD. Thursday Evening, March 14, 1901. Unnumbered page. The treatises were Hector Berlioz (1844): *Grand traité d'instrumentation et d'orchestration modernes* (Treatise on Instrumentation), and François-Auguste Gevaert (1863): *Traité general d'instrumentation*, which, according to Rupert Hughes, Beach translated for herself. See Rupert Hughes, *Contemporary American Composers* (Boston: L. C. Page, 1900), 438.

14. See Mrs. H. H. A. Beach Papers, box 10, folder 4, for Beach's Beethoven symphony scores.

15. See Mrs. H. H. A. Beach Papers, "Letters to Beach," box 1, folder 1.

16. The First New England Composers, although never referred to by that title, would have been those men associated with the early singing-school movement: William Billings and Oliver Holden were among the most famous Yankee tunesmiths associated with the movement.

17. See Mrs. H. H. A. Beach Papers, Autograph Album, no. 68. Also quoted in Block, *Amy Beach*, 103.

18. Philip Hale, "Symphony Night," in the *Boston Journal*, n.d. (S2, 51). The degree to which Hale's comments are honest reflections of his thinking must be weighed against the fact that Hale was married to Irene Baumgras, an American-born, European-trained pianist and composer, who received little attention for her creative work. It is possible that jealousy or at least misplaced gallantry played a part in his criticism of Beach.

19. A sampling of articles written by Beach suggests the breadth of her interests: "To the Girl Who Wants to Compose" appeared in *Etude* 35 (November 1918): 695; "The Twenty-Fifth Anniversary of a Vision" was published in the Music Teachers National Association (M.T.N.A.) *Proceedings* (1932). Beach spoke heartfully about the role of the MacDowell Colony in American musical culture. A few years later, the article "A Plea for Mercy" was addressed to the same constituency and published in the M.T.N.A. *Proceedings*, 1935. It considered the impact the new, more percussion repertoire had on pianists' "sensitive hands." M.T.N.A. *Proceedings* (1935): 163. A more philosophical article, "How Music Is Made," appeared in the winter issue of *Keyboard* in 1942.

20. Box 1, Marian MacDowell Papers, Manuscript Division, Library of Congress, Washington, D.C. It is perhaps noteworthy that Amy Beach signed her letter as she did. After her marriage to H. H. A. Beach, she adopted his name and, more often than not, was known as Mrs. H. H. A. Beach. Just two years later, Amy Beach would be a widow like Marian MacDowell. The recital to which Beach referred took place while H. H. A. was alive and almost certainly was a private performance or charity event given among friends.

21. The MacDowell Colony thrives today and is recognized as the first

continuously operating artists' colony in the United States.

22. "The MacDowells and Their Legacy," by Robin Rausch in *A Place for the Arts: The MacDowell Colony, 1907–2007*, edited by Carter Weisman (Hanover, N.H.: The MacDowell Colony, 2007), 64. Its early identification as a place that supported women artists continues uninterrupted to the present day.

23. The importance of the MacDowell Colony to Amy Beach is testified to in Adrienne Fried Block's biography of the composer, *Amy Beach, Passionate Victorian*, where the author devotes an entire chapter to its impact. See chapter 19, "At the MacDowell Colony: 'Solitude in Silence.'"

24. H. F. P., "Believes Women Composers Will Rise to Greater Heights in World Democracy," *Musical America* 25 (April 21, 1917): 3. Quoted in Block, *Amy Beach*, 213.

25. Amy Beach, "The Twenty-Fifth Anniversary of a Vision," in *Proceedings of the Music Teachers National Association, 1932*, 27th Series (Oberlin, Ohio: Music Teachers National Association, 1933), 46. See Block, *Amy Beach*, 361n.4.

26. See "How Music Is Made," 11.

27. Block, *Amy Beach*, 225.

28. For a complete list of Beach's works, see Block, *Amy Beach*, 300–309.

29. "With Violets" comes from the set *Four Songs*, published in 1885; "The Blackbird" comes from the set *Three Songs*, published in 1889; and "The Clover," The Yellow Daisy," and "The Bluebell" are from a set of choral works, *Three Flower Songs*, published in 1896. See Block, *Amy Beach*, 303, 304.

30. Block, *Amy Beach*,154.

31. Ibid., 154.

32. Ibid., 221. See Una L. Allen, "The Composer's Corner: Wherein Contemporary Writers of Teaching Material Express Views Regarding Certain of Their Own

Compositions. No. 10: Mrs. H. H. A. Beach," *Musician* 35 (July 1930): 21. As Block explains, "Una Allen was the assistant to Henry Austin, head of Arthur P. Schmidt Co. from 1916 to 1958," 361n.1

33. Mrs. Franc Clement is Amy Beach's aunt on her mother's side.

34. See Mrs. H. H. A. Beach Papers, box 4, folder 9, from the handwritten manuscript by Ethel Clement. A copy of Beach's song "The Thrush," published by Arthur P. Schmidt in 1891, is also among her papers, box 9, folder 14, pages 40–45.

35. In the essay "School of Giorgione," Walter Pater spoke of the power of different arts: Each art, he explained, "brings with it a special phase or quality of beauty, untranslatable into the forms of any other." Each "has its own special mode of reaching the imagination." Walter Pater, *The Renaissance* (New York: The Modern Library, 1919), 107.

36. Additional writers, including Thoreau, spoke at length about the wood thrush, a close relative of the hermit thrush. See Thoreau's journal entry for April 30, 1852, for his poetic responses to the song he believed expressed "the immortal beauty and wildness of the woods." See Francis H. Allen, ed., *The Journals of Henry D. Thoreau: In Fourteen Volumes Bound as Two*, vols. 1–7 (1837–October 1855), 396. In the original journal, the line quoted is found on page 486. Currently, theorist/composer Emily Doolittle (PhD Princeton, 2007) is writing a paper that analyzes the hermit thrush song from a combined musical/acoustical perspective. Her dissertation researched the relationships between human music and bird and other animal music. Emily Doolittle is discussed in the final chapter of this book. In 2009 the American composer John Luther Adams included references to the hermit thrush in his percussion work *Inuksuit*. Previously, he evoked the hermit thrush

in his works *songbirdsongs* (1974–1980), *Night Peace* (1976), and *A Northern Suite* (1979–1981).

37. Attempts to locate books from Beach's library or even a listing of books she owned have been futile. The only reference to Amy Beach's "library" is in an article that appeared in the *Chicago Times-Herald*, November 28, 1897, and it talks exclusively about her music library. The author, A. M. B. [Mrs. Brisbane], notes: "Her musical library contains one of the greatest collections in the country. Orchestral scores, complete of Wagner, and the old masters: the beautiful French edition of 'Alcestes,' bound in white vellum, of which there are but few in existence: an engraving of Brahms, autographed, sent from Ischel, the famous German watering place where the great composer spent much time: Rosenthal's gift of a small lamp for sealing wax, once used by Mozart, are there with original manuscripts given by well-known composers from every part of the world." See Mrs. H. H. A. Beach Papers, box 11, part 1, Copies of Scrapbooks, "Visit to the Home of Mrs. H. H. Beach, Which Is Paradise for the Lover of Music." No page number.

38. Only the excerpt from Cheney's poem is reproduced in the published edition of the pieces. Clare's poem "The Thrush's Nest," is available at www.poemhunter.com/poem/the-thrush-s-nest/ (accessed July 12, 2007). Excerpts from both poems, however, are present on copies of the scores found in the Mrs. H. H. A. Beach Papers.

39. See "A Hermit Thrush at Eve" (Hildegard Publishing, 1997).

40. See "A Hermit Thrush at Morn" (Arthur P. Schmidt, 1922). The University of New Hampshire, Milne Special Collections, Mrs. H. H. A. Beach Papers, MC 51, box 8, folder 17.

41. Among the first modern uses of the term "numinous" was that of German theologian Rudolf Otto (1869–1937), who invoked the word to suggest the presence of the divine or holy. A numinous experience of nature would be one that ascribed mystery, spirituality, and divinity to the natural world. See Rudolf Otto, *The Idea of the Holy*, trans. John W. Harvey (Oxford: Oxford University Press, 1923; 2nd ed., 1950).

42. Block, *Amy Beach*, 154.

43. Ibid., 152. She cites Henry Edward Krehbiel, *Music and Manners in the Classical Period*, 3rd ed. (New York: Charles Scribner's, 1899), 237. See 348n22.

44. The United States, it was argued, was exceptional because of the variety and size of the continent's natural endowments. If God resided in nature, then surely God resided in America to a degree unmatched in the Old World. The doctrine of Manifest Destiny tied together God, nature, and the nation.

45. Una L. Allen, "The Composer's Corner: Wherein Contemporary Writers of Teaching Material Express Views Regarding Certain of Their Own Compositions. No. 10: Mrs. H. H. A. Beach's *Musician* 35 (July 1930): 21. Quoted in Block, *Amy Beach*, 221. While some might discount Beach's claim that the bird answered her back, recent scholarship has demonstrated that many birds and animals do precisely that.

46. See "A Hermit Thrush at Morn" (Hildegard Publishing Company, 1997). Beach includes the same remark in "A Hermit Thrush at Eve" to refer to the birdsong that appears starting in measure 23. I have chosen to speak about the second of the set of pieces "A Hermit Thrush at Morn" because the birdsong is clearly laid out at the beginning of the work and informs all aspects of the piece.

47. In May 1929, in Stewart Park, Ithaca, New York, Arthur Allen "recorded the songs of a rose-breasted grosbeak, house wren, and song sparrow, the first

recording of wild birds in North America." See Don Stap, *Birdsong: A Natural History* (New York: Oxford University Press, 2005), 29.

48. The D-minor and C-major triads of measures 1 and 3, beats 2 and 3, are now sung melodically by the bird in measures 5 and 6. The pattern of a minor harmony followed by a major one is typical of many Irish fiddle tunes, which Beach would, no doubt, have known. Whether the thrush knew them is another question! That the thrush's song and Irish tunes shared this harmonic quality may have subconsciously been another reason the bird's music appealed to her so.

49. See the right-hand part of measure 16 for a rhythmically adjusted and syncopated version of the dotted rhythm, and the left-hand part of measure 36 for an augmented version of the basic dotted rhythm. Both of these gestures will appear numerous times in the 121-measure piece.

50. See measures 28–56 and 79–107 for the more agitated passages. Interspersed and ending the piece are Tempo I passages (measures 57–78 and 108–121) that return the music to the quiet "*poco a poco piu tranquillo*" mood that began the piece.

51. Among Olivier Messiaen's birdsong-inspired pieces are *La merle noir* (1951), *Reveil des oiseaux* (1953), *Oiseaux exotiques* (1956), *Catalogue d'oiseaux* (1958), and *La fauvette des jardins* (1972). In other pieces, birdsong is interpolated liberally throughout the work.

52. Eleanor Jones Harvey, *The Painted Sketch: American Impressions from Nature, 1830–1880* (Dallas Museum of Art in association with Harry N. Abrams, 1998), 19, 21.

53. The choice of a waltz may reflect the dance that was most popular during the closing decades of the nineteenth century, a time when Beach would have

been young and impressionable, although Mrs. H. H. A. Beach's "quasi valse" is most certainly not for dancing.

3. MARION BAUER

1. Madeleine Goss, "Marion Bauer," in *Modern Music-Makers: Contemporary American Composers* (New York: E. P. Dutton, 1952), 135. Goss does not cite the source of Bauer's words, although her foreword explains that "only those [composers] with whom the present writer has been able to talk personally" have been included; the one exception is Charles Ives, whose wife, Harmony, "supplied the necessary information." See unnumbered page 7 of front matter.

2. Ibid., 135.

3. See "Up the Ocklawaha" by Marion Bauer (Hildegard Publishing Company, 1998) for the full text of Powell's poem, and Bauer's reduction, which she placed at the top of the first page of the score.

4. Bauer summered at the colony in 1919, 1920, 1921, 1925, 1927, 1928, 1929, 1931, 1937, 1941, 1942, and 1944. See Nancy Louise Stewart, "The Solo Piano Music of Marion Bauer," PhD dissertation, University of Cincinnati, 1990, 23.

5. See Peggy A. Horrocks, "The Solo Vocal Repertoire of Marion Bauer with Selected Stylistic Analyses," PhD dissertation, University of Nebraska, 1994, 71–73, for a discussion of this song.

6. It is the only poem by E. R. Sill that Bauer set, although she frequently set only a single poem by an individual poet.

7. "To Daffodils" by R. Herrick as found in Francis T. Palgrave, ed., *The Golden Treasury*, 1875. See http://www.bartleby.com/106/110.html (accessed January 5, 2011).

8. Peggy A. Horrocks discusses the symbolist qualities of Wilde's poem and what she understands as complementary

impressionist characteristics of Bauer's piece in her dissertation "The Solo Vocal Repertoire of Marion Bauer," 71–74. The discussion of "My Faun" provides a brief description of basic musical characteristics, including the germinating arabesque-like motive, the alternating key centers, and textural changes. Horrocks also treats "The Epitaph of a Butterfly" and "Night in the Woods" in the dissertation. See pages 80–90.

9. Bauer frequently grouped sets of solo piano music in collections of three or six pieces, although each could be played separately if the performer wished.

10. In *Senses of Place* (Santa Fe, N.M.: School of American Research Press, 1996), 9, Steven Feld and Keith Basso summarize philosopher Edward S. Casey's thoughts on the inescapable resonance of place in a single sentence: "place is the most fundamental form of embodied experience – the site of a powerful fusion of self, space, and time."

11. I am extremely grateful to Susan Pickett of Whitman College for sharing the draft of a chapter she has written of an unpublished biography on Marion Bauer that details Bauer's early years in the "Wild West." Additionally, Dr. Pickett answered email questions and generally made findings from her considerable archival work available to me. I draw from her scholarly efforts in describing the dynamics of the accomplished Bauer family. Additional biographical information comes from a number of sources, including J. Michele Edwards's entry "Bauer, Marion Eugenie" in *Grove Music Online*; Madeleine Goss's entry "Marion Bauer" in *Modern Music-Makers: Contemporary American Composers* (New York: E. P. Dutton, 1952), 129–140; Melissa de Graaf's article on Bauer in the Jewish Music Web Center site "Contributions of Jewish Women to Music and Women to Jewish Music,"

http://www.jmwc.org/pdf/MarionBauer.pdf (accessed December 30, 2010); Ellie M. Hisama's 2001 book *Gendering Musical Modernism: The Music of Ruth Crawford, Marion Bauer, and Miriam Gideon* (Cambridge, UK: Cambridge University Press); and Peggy A. Horrocks's dissertation "The Solo Vocal Repertoire of Marion Bauer with Selected Stylistic Analyses."

12. See the 1880 census report for Walla Walla, Washington, which lists the population as 3,588. Ten years later it was 4,709, and in 1900 it had reached 10,049.

13. Susan Pickett, unpublished manuscript, *Marion Bauer*, chapter 1, "Wild West," 2.

14. http://www.wallawalla.org/attractions.cfm (accessed December 29, 2010). In 1883, the city of Olympia, Washington, which is now the state's capital, became home to the first women's club on the West Coast.

15. Whitman Seminary was founded in 1859 and became Whitman College in 1882. Today it enjoys a reputation as a highly selective liberal arts college.

16. American author Willa Cather (1873–1947), from Red Cloud, Nebraska, wrote passionately about the impact various touring companies had upon her as a child. See "Willa Cather Mourns Old Opera House," as quoted in Judith Tick's *Music in the USA: A Documentary Companion* (New York: Oxford University Press, 2008), 293–296. Cather and Bauer were near contemporaries: Bauer was born in 1882 and lived until 1955.

17. Pickett, *Marion Bauer*, 18.

18. Thanks in part to Amy Fay's book *Music-Study in Germany*, which was published with the help of her sister Melusina in 1880, German music instruction became the gold standard.

19. St. Helen's Hall morphed over the years and is today known as the Oregon

Episcopal School. It is the oldest Episcopal-affiliated school west of the Rocky Mountains.

20. Clara Cheney was not by any means unique in denying her daughter educational opportunities. Adella Prentiss Hughes (1869–1950), the American pianist and impresario best known for her work founding the Cleveland Symphony Orchestra, speaks of her mother twice denying her chances to continue her intellectual work, although the young Miss Prentiss did graduate from Vassar College. Mrs. Prentiss refused Adella the opportunity to teach, or to pursue a PhD degree, instead insisting that the two go on a grand tour. It seems that Mrs. Prentiss feared Adella would become a "bluestocking," the pejorative term attached to women who were intellectually focused. While in Europe, Adella and her mother attended numerous concerts and the young pianist got a chance to accompany a variety of musicians. See Adella Prentiss Hughes, *Music Is My Life* (Cleveland, Ohio: The World Publishing Company, 1947), 31.

21. Horrocks, "The Solo Vocal Repertoire of Marion Bauer," 7.

22. In 1884 and 1885, Emilie Frances had published her own original piano compositions but appears to have given up those ambitions to channel her energies into her sister's work. See Pickett, "Wild West," 11.

23. See "Piano Lessons with Master Teachers: No. 26. Eugene Heffley: Modern Tendencies in Piano Music." http://www.piano-lessons-master-teachers.com/piano-mastery/26.php (accessed January 8, 2011).

24. See Harriette Brower, *Piano Mastery: Talks with Master Pianists and Teachers and an Account of a von Bulow Class, Hints on Interpretation by Two American Teachers (Dr. William Mason and William H. Sherwood) and a Summary by the* Author. *With Sixteen Portraits* (New York: Frederick A. Stokes, 1915). http://www.gutenberg.org/files/15604/15604-h/15604-h.htm#XXVI_EUGENE_HEFFLEY. Also http:www.piano-lessons-master-teachers.com/piano-mastery/26.php (accessed January 8, 2011).

25. Ibid.

26. While males also benefit from family support and educational access, it has not been unusual for men to defy family wishes and expectations to pursue musical careers. Until recently, such independent choices and "rebellious" behavior were more difficult for a woman to exercise.

27. Horrocks, "The Solo Vocal Repertoire of Marion Bauer," 9. The author offers no specific evidence for her assertion, although it is likely that a year's worth of German counterpoint lessons would reinforce any student's appreciation of the linear dimension of musical composition. See also Ellie M. Hisama, *Gendering Musical Modernism: The Music of Ruth Crawford, Marion Bauer, and Miriam Gideon* (Cambridge, UK: Cambridge University Press, 2001), 5, 99–121.

28. This is not to say that counterpoint can't be studied in France or tone color studied in Germany, but only that Bauer studied counterpoint in Germany and had her own interests in timbre and tone color reinforced by her work with Pugno and Boulanger in France.

29. The Russian American pianist-composer Leo Ornstein, who had made a big splash in Europe with a series of concerts in winter 1914, had planned to return later that year after a few months at home. The events in Sarajevo put an end to his European concertizing, and he made the rest of his career in the United States as a composer, concert pianist, and teacher.

30. Stewart, "The Solo Piano Music of Marion Bauer," 16.

31. Madeleine Goss, "Marion Bauer," 133. When this occurred is not clear. Foote was a member of the group of composers informally known by contemporary scholars as the Second New England School or Boston Six. In addition to Foote, its members included George Whitefield Chadwick, John Knowles Paine, Horatio Parker, Amy Beach, and Edward MacDowell. Beach's inclusion in this list of academic composers is recognition of her musical style and professional achievements more than of her daily interactions with these men. They were bright enough to recognize her superior achievements, even if she could not participate in their daily circle. Chadwick was a particular supporter of her music.

32. "Maud Powell Finishing Tenth Season," *Musical Leader* (1913), 29, as quoted by Leslie Petteys, ed., in "Up the Ocklawaha" by Marion Bauer (King of Prussia, Pa.: Hildegard Publishing Company, distributed by Theodore Presser Company, 1998). Unnumbered front matter. Emilie Bauer likely wrote this piece of prose.

33. Ibid. These lines are taken directly from Powell's prose poem. Leslie Petteys suggests that the concert was the one in Ocala, Florida, February 16, 1912.

34. Powell's poem was published in the article "Here Is a Poem by Maud Powell," which appeared in the *San Francisco Examiner* on December 22, 1912, page 1, a week after her premiere of Bauer's piece.

35. Judith Tick, liner notes to Albany Records, Troy 297, 1998, referring to Bauer's ideas as stated in *Twentieth Century Music: How It Developed, How to Listen to It*. Originally published by Putnam, New York, 1933 (New York: Da Capo Press, 1978). In this study's chapter on Libby Larsen, readers will encounter the composer seeking to

musicalize the fragrance of roses in her piece "downwind of roses in Maine," but Bauer did not attempt any such thing. Bauer dedicated her book "To the memory of Eugene Heffley (1862–1925), valiant pioneer in the cause of Twentieth Century Music whose wise guidance and teachings have made this book possible." In her acknowledgments, Bauer thanks "Mrs. Edward MacDowell for a fortnight spent at the MacDowell Colony in June ... without which *Twentieth Century Music* would not now be completed." See page vii. The colony was responsible for not only musical compositions, but for scholarly texts about music.

36. Marion Bauer, "Up the Ocklawaha" (Hildegard Publishing Company, 1998), page 2.

37. Ibid. Bauer indicates the opening of the piece is to be played "Larghetto, molto tranquillo."

38. See measures 13–18, 31–36, and 45–52 for especially tumultuous musical passages.

39. Bauer devotes considerable space throughout her book to discussion of dissonance, defining it, tracking it in various composers' works, and providing multiple examples of dissonant appoggiaturas, chords, progressions, and counterpoint and its use in melody and harmony. See multiple entries in the index under "Dissonance." See page 328.

40. There are only two occasions when Bauer deviates from the $\frac{12}{8}$ time signature, at measures 30 and 36. In each case the single $\frac{6}{8}$ measure provides additional time and space to introduce a new structural section of the piece. Regardless of its incessant chromaticism, Bauer never alters the three-flat key signature.

41. There is the Olympic National Forest in the far northwestern corner of Washington State, but that is a significantly different environment, even

if water is omnipresent in both it and in Bauer's river-centered piece.

42. One is made to think of the Puritan minister Increase Mather and his admonition to his followers not to venture "beyond the hedge." Outside lay the wilderness, a dark, savage place dangerous to both body and soul. Over time, American wilderness would be reimagined and construed as a place of untouched natural beauty and purity.

43. Beach, Bauer, and Talma each memorialized the colony's birches in one of their works. These trees suffered most dramatically in the hurricane of 1938 and never returned to their pre-hurricane numbers or presence.

44. Bauer acknowledged her familiarity with Brahms's Intermezzo Op. 117, No. 1, specifically and his enriched harmonic and rhythmic materials in *Twentieth Century Music*. See pages 53–54. Rachmaninoff's *Moments Musicaux* (op.16), written in 1896, sound like another possible source of inspiration for "Up the Ocklawaha," especially No. 3, with its similarly dread-filled mood; this one set in B minor. I am grateful to Michael Broyles for first suggesting to me the vaguely Russian sound of Bauer's piece, an idea I eagerly embraced based upon my experience of having played works by both composers. Rachmaninoff is among the list of "moderns" that Heffley taught his students.

45. Bauer's "White Birches" has a single fermata at measure 38. See Marion Bauer, "From the New Hampshire Woods: A Suite of Three Pieces for Pianoforte," Op. 12 (New York: G. Schirmer, 1922). "Up the Ocklawaha" has a single instance of rest for both instruments at measure 56. Otherwise, there is always some amount of sound decaying or resonating.

46. Each of the works also has a single moment where the dynamic level climbs to *forte*. Brahms's work closes *ritard molto* and Bauer's *rallentando*, *morendo*.

47. In 1925, Jessie Tarbox Beals photographed "Birches at the Sprague Smith Studio," and in 1937, Elizabeth White painted "Birches and Pines," perhaps using Beals's photograph as a model.

48. Ibid., fn. 43. See page 3 for Benét's three lines. Benét met his second wife, Elinor Wylie, at the colony, where she was also a fellow in 1922 and 1923. They married in October 1923. I have not been able to ascertain if Bauer solicited the lines from Benét because she had already written the piece, or at least imagined the piece, or whether he wrote the lines first and thus inspired the musical work, in which case the text functioned much like Maud Powell's poem "Up the Ocklawaha."

49. Marion Bauer, "Indian Pipes" (New York: G. Schirmer, 1923), 3.

50. I recall coming upon these rare forest flowers when I was a child summering at a family cabin deep in the woods of what was then a rural part of Huntington, Long Island. My cousin James, who had a knack for finding them, insisted that they marked the grave of an Indian, which he then volunteered to dig up, much to my utter panic. He assured me that I shouldn't be afraid since these were peace-loving Indians, hence the name of the flower. His feigned efforts at comforting me had no effect, which was, of course, his intent all along. The woods contained equal parts fascination and fright for me.

51. Indian pipes are also native to the Pacific Northwest's coastal forests, but they would have been hundreds of miles and two mountain ranges away from the Bauers' home in Walla Walla, Washington. There is no evidence in any surviving accounts that the Bauer family ever visited the coast.

4. LOUISE TALMA

1. Quoted by Sarah Dorsey, in "Louise Talma (1906–1996) and the MacDowell Colony: A Saving Grace," paper presented at the Feminist Theory and Musicology Conference (FTMIO) in Greensboro, North Carolina, May 28, 2009.

2. Robin Rausch, "The MacDowells and Their Legacy," in *A Place for the Arts: The MacDowell Colony, 1907–2007* (Hanover, N.H.: University Press of New England, 2006) 50–136. See page 105 especially.

3. I am deeply grateful to Sarah Dorsey, music librarian at the University of North Carolina, Greensboro, and Talma scholar/biographer, for sharing the organizational work she accomplished on the Louise Talma papers housed at the Library of Congress. Ms. Dorsey responded to every question that I put to her and itemized a list of papers she thought would be most useful to my project. I am also grateful to Robin Rausch, senior music specialist at the Library of Congress, for locating the materials Ms. Dorsey suggested I consult. It is no exaggeration to say that without the assistance of these two women, I could not have written this chapter. They provided a network for me to test ideas and accomplish my work.

4. See Kendra Preston Leonard, *The Conservatoire Américain: A History* (Lanham, Md.: The Scarecrow Press, 2007), 33–34. Leonard's book contains many insights into Talma's relationship to Boulanger and the larger enterprise of the American Conservatory at Fontainebleau. See Leonard's appendix G for lists of the many awards Talma won, including those for her piano work.

5. Ibid., 202.

6. Talma returned to Fontainebleau on numerous occasions over the next five decades, studying there in 1949, 1951,

1961, 1968, 1971, 1972, and 1976, and teaching solfège, analysis, and harmony there in 1978, 1981, and 1982. See www.omni disc.com/Talma/Biography.html# INTERVIEW (accessed May 20, 2011).

7. Talma's "Composition List" as posted on the Louise Talma Society website includes seventy-four complete works, many of which are multipart and multimovement. Fewer than twenty of these are currently available from publishers. Last accessed May 23, 2011.

8. The quote appears in the program for "The French Connection: Louises in Paris," presented by Catherine Keen and Sarah Dorsey, which celebrated the composers Louise Farrenc and Louise Talma. The event was part of Women's History Month at the University of North Carolina at Greensboro, March 17, 2007. Italics are mine. Talma's response was to an inquiry by Thor Wood, dated February 8, 1982.

9. The Louise Talma Collection at the Library of Congress includes scores, letters, programs, clippings, and photographs. I am grateful to the MacDowell Colony for permission to quote from music and music sketches in this collection.

10. In an effort to model herself as thoroughly as possible upon her mentor Nadia Boulanger, who was a devout Catholic, Louise Talma converted to Catholicism, as would others of Boulanger's students. Her teacher became her godmother. I have not located any evidence that Talma's use of birdsong in her music was associated in any way with her religious beliefs, contrary to Olivier Messiaen, another devout Catholic, for whom birdsong and religion were closely allied. See Léonie Rosenstiel, *Nadia Boulanger: A Life in Music* (W. W. Norton, 1982), 271 for a brief discussion of Boulanger's role in Talma's conversion.

11. Whether serial arrangements of pitches are any more unnatural than

tonal ones is a question whose answer lies within specific temporal, geographical, and cultural contexts. The "naturalness" of a system is a reflection of its acceptance over a long period of time by a large number of people.

12. See David Brower, "The Third-Planet Operators Manual," *New York Times Magazine* (March 16, 1975), 53–54; Walter Sullivan, "Vanishing Shield?" *New York Times*, April 13, 1975, 212; Charles Mohr, "Tampering with Nature Perils Health, U.N. Environment Unit's Report Warns," *New York Times*, April 20, 1975, 3; and Jane E. Brody, "Agriculture Department to Abandon Campaign against the Fire Ant," *New York Times*, April 20, 1975, 46; and Gladwin Hill, "Ecologists Fear Peril to Nature," *New York Times*, 8 June 1975, 15.

13. Edmund Morris, "Oases of Silence in a Desert of Din," *New York Times*, section 10, Travel and Resorts, Sunday, May 25, 1975, pages 13–14. Edmund Morris would write additional articles later in 1975 for the *New York Times* with similar themes related to sonic overload, and then many articles on a variety of topics over the next decades. He is known today for his brilliant, if occasionally controversial, biographies of Theodore Roosevelt, Ronald Reagan, and Beethoven.

14. Ibid., 13.

15. Muir's mystical relationship to nature comes through in many of his writings. The following quote suggests that condition as well as his gendered understanding of who had access to nature: "The mountains are fountains of men as well as of rivers, of glaciers, of fertile soil. The great poets, philosophers, prophets, able men whose thoughts and deeds have moved the world, have come down from the mountains – mountain dwellers who have grown strong there with the forest trees in Nature's workshops." From Linnie Marsh Wolfe, ed., *John of the Mountains: The Unpublished Journals of John Muir* (Madison: University of Wisconsin Press, 1938, republished 1979), http://www.sierraclub.org/john_muir_exhibit/ (accessed May 27, 2011).

16. Talma notated both a "bird call" and a "backdoor squeak" in a sketch made "June 20" at the Yaddo artists colony "Tower Studio." This sketch has no year, although one directly below it is dated March 6, 1953. Talma's sketch shows how she treated both sound sources similarly. The birdcall sketch goes directly into the backdoor-squeak sketch. Each is identified with a bracket over the specific pitches. Together they create a single, elongated melodic line. See Louise Talma Papers at the Library of Congress.

17. See Louise Talma, *Soundshots* (Bryn Mawr, Pa.: Hildegard Publishing, 2000), 7, 9, 16. This set was "Printed by permission of The MacDowell Colony, Inc., 1999."

18. There is currently no published score for this work.

19. See Joseph N. Straus, *Twelve-Tone Music in America* (Cambridge: Cambridge University Press, 2009), 104 for his discussion of Talma's *Seven Episodes* from 1987.

20. This piece, originally published in 1976 by Carl Fischer, Inc., is now in the catalogue of Theodore Presser Company but currently out of print and unavailable. Personal email with Jackie Nicklas Bach, May 24, 2011. At the end of a holograph of the score Talma records: "July 10, 1969 Nelson, N.H.; Jan. 10, 1973 Wavertree, Va.; [and] Feb. 10, 1973 New York, N.Y." The piece came together over four years and three states. See Louise Talma Papers, Library of Congress.

21. Emily Doolittle, the final composer discussed in this study, will come closest to writing a bird's silences into music with her piece *night black bird song*. Doolittle discusses the quantitative

differences between sound and silence in the music of humans and birds.

22. Victoria Bond addresses the issue of nature's different "time scales" in remarks about her piece *Thinking Like a Mountain*.

23. In the final chapter of this book, readers will learn that Emily Doolittle also moved pitches around in her piece *Reeds* to make them fit traditional notation.

24. See chapter on Emily Doolittle for additional comments on this idea.

25. This is, of course, not the case, as Talma "composed" all aspects of this piece. The effect, nonetheless, remains.

26. The "row" that introduces "Noon" relates to the primary row in its opening perfect fourth, although here it is descending rather than ascending. The rest of the series appears to be freely adapted to suit Talma's musical needs for a sustained dramatic descent, something impossible in any transformation of the original row. Fourths appear three times in the prime row: between the initial ascending pitches A♭ and D♭; between the fifth and sixth descending pitches G and D; and between the final two ascending pitches E and A. Pairs of strings that respond in measure 2 also emphasize fourths: A and E; G♯ and C♯.

27. The *Rite* will be mentioned many times in this study as a possible source of inspiration for these composers, although it will not be discussed in depth within *Music and the Skillful Listener*. Its impact on twentieth-century musical thinking is undeniable, whether the topic is nature or compositional techniques.

28. Talma was awarded a fellowship grant from the National Endowment for the Arts of $3,750. See http://www.omnidisc.com/Talma/Biography.html for a listing of all of her awards. Accessed June 5, 2011. The date given in this source for the NEA award is 1975, although the

1974 correspondence suggests it might have been given in 1974 or even earlier. Attempts so far to corroborate the 1975 date have yielded no results.

29. Louise Talma letter to Mr. James D. Ireland Jr., Office of Music Programs, National Endowment for the Arts, Washington, D.C., 20506, August 11, 1974. It may be of passing interest that Talma wrote this letter from the home of Nora Kubie, to whom she had dedicated "Dawn" of *Summer Sounds*. See Louise Talma Collection, Music Division, Library of Congress, box 4, folder 2.

30. See the composer's holograph score. I appreciate the use of a perusal copy of the score from Carl Fischer Music, Theodore Presser Company, 588 Gulph Road, King of Prussia, Pennsylvania, 19406.

31. See Louise Talma Collection, Music Division, Library of Congress, box 3 and holograph score (see pages 109, 142). What Talma writes as lyrics in 1974 remain the final text in 1980, with the exception of her substitutions of the word "chatter" for "twaddle," the word "and" for "or" in the phrase "or look at stars" in Della's aria, and the word "around" for "about" in Fred's aria. The majority of the music remains as Talma wrote it to Wilder, with small modifications to the melody in the final lines she sketched.

32. I've discovered no evidence to suggest that Morris and Talma knew each other or communicated, although it is possible, since both author and composer were living in the city at the time.

33. A typed copy of the complete libretto is among the Louise Talma Collection at the Library of Congress, box 4, folder 2.

34. See composer's holograph score. Talma instructs her trio to sing "dreamily." See page 203. Although there is no mention in Talma's papers of Raymond

Williams's 1973 book *The Country and the City* (New York: Oxford University Press, 1973), its study of the ways the concepts of "the country" and "the city" have been constructed in British literature would have resonated with both Talma and Morris. Williams points to the centuries-long associations of "peace, innocence, and simple virtue" with the country and "noise, worldliness, and ambition" with the city and their deep entrenchment within British culture regardless of their truthfulness. Although Williams sees the thoroughness of the distinctions as being especially powerful in English literature, and even refers to a kind of English exceptionalism, any American conversant with these constructs would see their relevance on this side of the pond. That the book was reviewed in the *New York Times Book Review* and the *New Yorker* means both composer and writer would have had easy access to Williams's ideas. See the first chapter, "Country and City," for an introduction to Williams's thesis.

35. Ibid., 4.

36. For a foundational study of perceptions and attributions traditionally associated with rural and urban environments, see Raymond Williams, *The Country and the City*. The question of the mere existence of "silence" was foregrounded most infamously by John Cage in 1952 with his piece 4′33″, which revealed the constant presence of sound in any environment. R. Murray Schafer addressed the issue of silence multiple times in his 1977 book *The Soundscape: Our Sonic Environment and the Tuning of the World* (Rochester, Vt.: Destiny Books, 1994) and gave special attention to sounds of forests that changed depending upon the types of trees they contained. The concept of silence continues to occupy acousticians, musicians, and ecomusicologists.

37. Bruce Duffie is a radio broadcaster and producer who won an ASCAP Deems Taylor Award in 1991 for his work at WNIB in Chicago. He was honored for his commitment to introducing the works of twentieth-century American composers. His interview with Talma was one of a series of interviews he conducted over the years.

38. http://www.bruceduffie.com/talma/html (accessed June 3, 2011).

39. I am grateful to Sarah Dorsey for locating, translating, and sharing this letter with me.

40. Personal email from Sarah Dorsey, July 11, 2011.

41. Other organizations include the Wilderness Society, World Wildlife Federation, Nature Conservancy, Defenders of Wildlife, Save the Redwoods, Cousteau Society, National Parks and Conservation Association, Audubon Society, and National Wildlife Federation. Personal email from Sarah Dorsey, July 14, 2011.

42. See "Planned Giving Opportunities at the MacDowell Colony," a trifold mailing from the MacDowell Colony that included a quote from a letter that Talma wrote to William Schuman, September 25, 1983, regarding what the colony characterizes as "The Art of Giving."

43. The rights to Talma's music are held by the MacDowell Colony. I have benefited directly from their granting me permission to include excerpts from her music and musical sketches in this chapter.

PART 2. NATURE ALL AROUND US

1. Jeffery Taubenberger and David M. Morens, (2006), "1918 Influenza: The Mother of All Pandemics," *Emerging Infectious Diseases* (http://dx.doi.org/10.3201/eid1209.05-0979, accessed June 19, 2011).

2. C. W. Potter, "A History of Influenza," *Journal of Applied Microbiology*

91, no. 4 (October 2006): 572–579 (doi:10.1046/j.1365–2672.2001.01492.x. PMID 11576290, accessed June 19, 2011).

5. PAULINE OLIVEROS

1. Pauline Oliveros, "Deep Listening Training at Banff," in *The Roots of the Moment* (New York: Drogue Press, 1998), 114–115.

2. For Oliveros's own summary of her choreographic works, see *The Roots of the Moment*, "Choreography through Meditation 1/1/81," 88–95.

3. Pauline Oliveros, *Software for People: Collected Writings, 1963–1980* (Baltimore, Md.: Smith Publications, 1984).

4. This definition of "deep listening" comes from Oliveros's article "Acoustic and Virtual Space as a Dynamic Element in Music," written for the *Leonardo Journal* (August 21, 1994) and reproduced in her book *The Roots of the Moment* 3.

5. On the 1989 recording, members of the Deep Listening Band included Stuart Dempster playing trombone and didjeridu, Pauline Oliveros playing the accordion, and Panaiotis (aka Peter Ward) providing vocal and whistling sounds, as well as sounds from metal pieces and pipes in the piece "Nike." He was a member of the band from 1987 to 1993 and assisted Oliveros in the development of the Expanded Instrument System (EIS). Later David Gamper joined the band playing piano. See liner notes to "Deep Listening," New Albion Records, NA 022 CD DDD.

6. http://www.deeplistening.org/site/ (accessed May 17, 2010).

7. On numerous occasions in her writings, Oliveros has called attention to the fact that the only university credential she possesses is a bachelor of arts degree in composition (from San Francisco State University). She points out that her first university appointment occurred in a narrow window of time when graduate degrees were not mandatory. Of course, her initial appointment at the University of California at San Diego was more the result of her significant experience as a composer and founding work with the Tape Music Center in San Francisco and her studies with Robert Erickson, who was forming the music department, and might very well have occurred without additional degrees at any time. In the obsessively credential-conscious climate that characterizes academia today, such appointments still take place regularly for extraordinarily gifted or accomplished people in the creative arts. Oliveros's multiple prestigious appointments today attest to the academy's recognition of artistic achievement over diplomas and degrees, at least some of the time.

8. "My 'American Music': Soundscape, Politics, Technology, Community," *American Music* (winter 2007): 390–391. Oliveros explained that she received "the Resounding Vision Award from *Nameless Sound* (a spinoff organization from the Deep Listening Institute, Ltd.)." All italics are in the original text. Oliveros's observation underscores the contradiction inherent in the thinking of those who escape to nature to find a silent place. The natural world is a constant concert.

9. Ibid., 391.

10. In a Skype video interview, the composer explained that people read her music in various ways. Speaking directly of Martha Mockus's recent book *Sounding Out: Pauline Oliveros and Lesbian Musicality* (New York: Routledge, 2007), Oliveros observed: "she reads my music, and she reads it as feminist and as lesbian, so I mean that's her reading of it; it's not what I put into it. It was not something I was consciously dealing with. So I don't set out to do a political piece." Oliveros didn't endorse or dispute Mockus's conclusions; rather, she clarified that her intentions for her pieces were focused on

sound. "Where I'm invested is in sound and what I'm doing, and that's where my faith is; it's in sound." I am grateful to Ms. Oliveros for the time she spent talking with me on two occasions about her music and listening. Personal interview with the composer, February 16, 2005, Eugene, Oregon, and Skype video interview May 28, 2010.

11. Pauline Oliveros, *The Roots of the Moment*, "Wounded Mountain: to Las Mitras," 86; "El Fantasma al Rio: Homenaje al Rio Santa Catarina," 110–111.

12. Gendering the earth female is a complex proposition, as the works of numerous ecofeminist scholars have demonstrated. See collections and monographs by Lorraine Anderson, Greta Gaard, Carolyn Merchant, Maria Mies, Rosemary Radford Ruether, Vandana Shiva, Kate Soper, and Karen Warren, among others.

13. Pauline Oliveros, *Deep Listening: A Composer's Sound Practice* (Lincoln, Neb.: iUniverse, 2005).

14. Skype video interview with the composer, May 28, 2010.

15. Email correspondence with the composer, May 13, 2010. Libby Larsen's understanding of nature is quite similar, as will be shown in the chapter devoted to her work.

16. Oliveros, *Software for People*, 179. Bolding is original to Oliveros's text. Oliveros's equation of sound and intelligence recalls Edgard Varèse's gloss of Hoene-Wronski's definition of music, which he summarized in his lecture "Spatial Music," given at Sarah Lawrence College in 1959: "Music as spatial – as bodies of intelligent sounds moving freely in space, a concept I gradually developed and made my own." See *Contemporary Composers on Contemporary Music*, edited by Elliott Schwartz and Barney Childs (New York: Da Capo Press, 1978), 204. I do not know whether Oliveros was familiar

with Wronski's or Varèse's thinking or definition.

17. Oliveros, *Software for People*, 180–181.

18. Ibid., 181.

19. Skype video interview with the composer, May 28, 2010.

20. Ibid.

21. *Three Songs* is published by Smith Publications, copyright 1976.

22. Heidi von Gunden, *The Music of Pauline Oliveros* (Metuchen, N.J.: The Scarecrow Press, 1983), 11. Von Gunden offers additional insights into "An Interlude of Rare Beauty" in pages 10–15 of her book.

23. "An Interlude of Rare Beauty" by Robert Duncan, from *Writing Writing* (Albuquerque, N.M.: Sumbooks, 1964). Reprinted by kind permission of Christopher Wagstaff, co-trustee of the Jess Collins Trust.

24. Skype video interview with the composer, May 28, 2010. The italics indicate the composer's emphasis as she spoke. On the surface this remark may appear to challenge the value the composer places on words in her carefully shaped writings and instructions ("recipes") for later pieces, but in reality there is no contradiction. Oliveros's music must be free from any constraints beyond those *she* sets for it. While she is comfortable establishing the guidelines for a work, she resists controlling the manifestation of the instructions. John Cage provided similar kinds of precise directions that allowed for a range of sonic realizations.

25. The Tape Center has been known by a number of names. Originally it was the San Francisco Tape Music Center, then the Mills Tape Music Center, and now it is part of the Center for Contemporary Music at Mills College.

26. Emily Doolittle will argue for additional advantages technology presents.

27. Pauline Oliveros, CD liner notes to "Alien Bog," Pogus Productions, New York, 1997 P21012–2.

28. Readers are reminded that Oliveros never declared it was her intention to imitate or simulate these sounds.

29. The flatness of electronic sounds that Oliveros referred to in her 2007 remarks are made to sound more "natural" through the use of a variety of reverberation and tape-delay techniques.

30. For instance, starting at 5:35 an ascending major third E to G♯ sounds for the first time and is then repeated frequently throughout the work. Given the importance of these two pitches in the key of A (E as the dominant, and G♯ as the leading tone), one might be tempted to point to the traditional harmonic architecture of the work. But in no sense does a listener expect the music to unfold in a particular way because of these pitches or their common-practice relationships. This is still the case as the music fades from our consciousness and the final pitch we hear is another A.

31. The descriptive adjectives and timings are my own and were assigned to the sounds after many listenings to the CD *Pauline Oliveros: Alien Bog, Beautiful Soop*, Pogus Productions, 1997, P21012–2. There are many other types of sounds that are not listed here. The timings indicate the moment I first detected a particular type of sound. Similar sounds appear frequently and in combination as a result of playback techniques.

32. John Cage quoted in Walter Zimmermann, *Desert Plants: Conversations with 23 American Musicians* (Vancouver, British Columbia, Canada: A.R.C. Publications, 1976), 49–64. The particular quoted passage is found on pages 56–57.

33. Meditations I–XI were composed in 1971, and XII–XXV were composed in 1973. They were published as a single set in 1974 by Smith Publications.

34. Skype video interview with the composer, May 28, 2010. She expressed similar sentiments in conversations with Martha Mockus, which are reproduced in Mockus's book *Sounding Out: Pauline Oliveros and Lesbian Musicality* (New York: Routledge, 2008). See pages 4–8 especially.

35. Pauline Oliveros, *Sonic Meditations* (Baltimore, Md.: Smith Publications, 1974), Introduction I, unnumbered page.

36. Mockus, *Sounding Out*, 2.

37. Pauline Oliveros, *Sonic Meditations* (Baltimore, Md.: Smith Publications, 1974). Oliveros's valuation of the communal creation of music and her belief that it should be accessible to everyone regardless of specialized training shows the influence of the Fluxus movement, whose basic tenets she would have known of through John Cage, among others. *Sonic Meditations*. Copyright Smith Publications, 54 Lent Road, Sharon, Vermont 05065.

38. Readers are encouraged to Google "Ecofeminism Bibliography" (http://www.ecofem.org/biblio/) to establish a baseline for appreciating the thousands of pages of scholarship dedicated to this field. Accessed June 5, 2010. See especially Rosemary Radford Ruether, *New Woman, New Earth: Sexist Ideologies and Human Liberation* (Boston, Mass.: Beacon Press, 1995), originally published in 1975 by the Seabury Press, and *Ecofeminisms: Symbolic and Social Constructions between the Oppression of Women and the Domination of Nature* (Charlotte: University of North Carolina Press, 1991).

39. Alvin Curran, *Maritime Rites*, New World Records, 2004, CD 80625–2, 15.

40. All quoted comments come from email correspondence with Mr. Curran, July 1, 2010, and are reprinted with his kind permission.

41. Ibid., 9. Other composers on the recording include Leo Smith, Steve Lacy, Clark Coolidge, Joseph Celli, Jon Gibson, Malcolm Goldstein, George Lewis, John Cage, and Alvin Curran himself. It is noteworthy in the context of *Music and the Skillful Listener,* but thoroughly to be expected, that Pauline Oliveros was the only woman participant in the project.

42. Ibid., 11.

43. Alvin Curran, quoted in David Toop's liner notes, 8.

44. Ibid., David Toop, 10. In a July 1, 2010, email, Curran expanded upon Loop's reading: "Certainly my *Maritime Rites* had obvious peripheral connotations in its geographic and cultural origins, but it remains for me a work which goes beyond any narrative, archival or didactic intentions and remains . . . a weave of pure sound that just happens to be inspired by the music of the sea. Hence it is environmental in every sense of the word, where the 'natural' simply becomes all of us and it, without anyone having to sermonize."

45. *Rattlesnake Mountain,* mixed and synchronized with remarks by lighthouse keeper Karen McLean in Alvin Curran's work *Maritime Rites.* This is the author's transcription of McLean's remarks as heard on the CD.

46. Ibid., 5:04–5:37.

47. Ibid., 8:48–9:21.

48. The "golden mean," "golden ratio," or "golden section" occurs soon after the 2/3 mark of a piece.

49. Consider *Central Park in the Dark* and *The Unanswered Question: A Cosmic Landscape* as two examples where Ives rejects the convention of musical closure. Numerous songs and pieces leave traditional harmonic progressions unfinished.

50. See Judy Lochhead's article "Joan Tower's *Wings* and *Breakfast Rhythms I and II*: Some Thoughts on Form and Repetition" for a discussion of formal musical meaning as the result of processes and temporal successions. *Perspectives of New Music* 30, no. 1 (winter 1992), 132–156.

51. Email correspondence with the composer, July 1, 2010. Curran's aesthetic and technical achievements are all the more remarkable when one realizes they were accomplished "on magnetic tape, . . . a technology most recently confined to history's cemetery." He explained: "This is important insofar as the concept of adding tracks in contrapuntal layers – while available on eight-track recorders as I was then using – is now the stuff of everyday music composition on everyone's laptop worldwide – above all the editing – done by manual cutting and splicing – was more like neurosurgery than our flawless digital tricks of today." Email correspondence with the composer, July 2, 2010.

52. Information about the cistern and the experience of playing within its walls comes from remarks written by Oliveros, Dempster, and Panaiotis collectively titled "Statements on the Experience" for their CD *Deep Listening,* New Albion Records, 1989. NA 022 CD.

53. Ibid., Panaiotis.

54. Ibid. Information was provided by Al Swanson in the CD notes.

55. Ibid., Swanson.

56. As the CD liner notes point out, "Lear" was used in the act 5, /scene 3 production of *Lear* mounted by Mabou Mines, directed by Lee Brewer. According to Chinese legend, "Suiren" was the discoverer of fire. For an image of Suiren, see Hampden C. DuBose's 1886 book *The Dragon, Image, and Demon, or, The Three Religions of China,* available online as a digital replica through the University of Toronto Libraries.

57. For a provocative treatment of the challenges nontraditional musics pose to traditional modes of music analysis and description readers are encouraged to consult *Beyond Structural Listening?*

Postmodern Modes of Hearing, edited by Andrew Dell'Antonio (Berkeley: University of California Press, 2004).

58. Susan Wright, "Challenging Literacies: The Significance of the Arts," a paper reprinted on the Australian Association for Research in Education (AARE) website, http://www.aare.edu.au/00pap/wri00006.htm (accessed June 9, 2010). See also C. Plummeridge, *Music Education in Theory and Practice* (London: Falmer, 1991).

59. Musical "form" is a concept that has attracted much scholarly attention. Alan Theisen, in his dissertation "A Multifaceted Approach to Analyzing Form in Elliott Carter's *Boston Concerto*," the Florida State University, 2010, quotes a private conversation with composer Milton Babbitt, who described form as "perceived differentiation" (p. 7n23). Theisen himself suggests that musical form is "differentiation perceived through time."

60. Lochhead, "Joan Tower's *Wings*," 134–135.

61. *Jann Pasler, "An Interview with Pauline Oliveros," AWC News/Forum* (Spring/Summer 1991): 12.

62. "Long tone" is a term often assigned to similar pieces. Among the most famous is La Monte Young's 1961 work "Composition #7," which consists of the interval of a perfect fifth, B–F♯, and the instruction "Hold for a very long time."

63. The journals I kept for various listenings are filled with circular, swirling, looping graphics drawn with a heavier or lighter hand according to the loudness or softness of the sounds I was hearing.

64. The degree to which the sounds of "Lear" were inspired by Shakespeare's character might go a long way to explaining the lack of warmth I heard in the earlier piece. It is possible, though, that my knowledge of the king and his treatment of his three daughters might have set the stage for me to hear the piece in a way that didn't allow for warm thoughts.

65. The question of an audible preference for higher sounds is one I raised with composer Emily Doolittle. Her response is discussed in the chapter devoted to Doolittle's work.

66. Pasler, "An Interview with Pauline Oliveros," 11, 12. Oliveros's phrase "you become listening" will echo in Libby Larsen's instruction to her musicians to "become the fragrance" when they played the piece *downwind of roses in Maine*, which is discussed in the chapter devoted to Libby Larsen.

67. Ibid., 13.

68. The instructions, including capitalizations, spacing, and punctuation, are reproduced as accurately as possible given the unique format of the book *The Roots of the Moment*. See pages 30–42.

69. See Pasler interview (14) for Oliveros's use of the words "interdependence," "interaction," "collaborating," and "cooperating." One version of *MirrorrorriM* is recorded by saxophonist John Sampen and pianist Marilyn Shrude on the album *Visions in Metaphor*, Albany Records, 2001, B00005NF2U. Sampen and Shrude took Oliveros's advice to heart and appear to be having a great time chasing each other's sounds. I am grateful to Dr. Crystal Peebles, formerly a graduate theory student at the Florida State University, for initially calling my attention to this work and sharing her analysis with me.

70. Personal email correspondence with the composer, May 13, 2010.

71. Pasler interview, 11.

6. JOAN TOWER

1. Joan Tower quoted in Carol Neuls-Bates, *Women in Music: An Anthology of Source Readings from the Middle Ages to the Present* (Boston: Northeastern University Press, 1996), 354, with revisions according to a telephone conversation with the composer, September 3, 2010.

2. See Ellen K. Grolman, *Joan Tower: The Comprehensive Bio-Bibliography* (Lanham, Md.: Scarecrow Press, 2007).

3. Ibid., 4.

4. Ibid. I am grateful to conversations with Dr. Stephen Scott, anthropologist at Barnard College, for his help understanding mid-twentieth-century Bolivian culture, the importance of nature to the nation's sense of itself, and the milieu in which Tower and his family circulated at the time.

5. Telephone interview with the composer, September 3, 2010.

6. Having a parent who is sensitive to and educated in both the arts and sciences ties Joan Tower to Emily Doolittle, the last composer studied in *Music and the Skillful Listener.*

7. Telephone interview with the composer, August 15, 2006.

8. Telephone interview with the composer, September 3, 2010.

9. Grolman, *Joan Tower*, 5.

10. "American" in this case refers to citizens of the United States.

11. All of the composers in the following chapters of this study have earned doctorates. Tower is ambivalent about the worth of her doctoral degree as regards her development as a composer. She has spoken of the decade she spent earning it as a detour in her composer's life. Then again, the doctorate provided her with the credential that Oliveros is aware she doesn't have herself. If anyone questioned Tower's suitability for her teaching position, the doctorate would suggest, at the least, her minimal qualification for the job.

12. Nancy E. Leckie, "An Analysis of Joan Tower's *Wings* for Solo Clarinet." DMA dissertation, Arizona State University, 1992, 24.

13. Carol Neuls-Bates, ed., *Women in Music*, rev. ed. (Boston: Northeastern University Press, 1966), 344.

14. According to Grolman, the school Joan Tower attended in La Paz "had a well-developed physical education program, and [the composer] remembers with fondness working on the parallel bars, the gymnastics horse, and the high jump." See Grolman, *Joan Tower*, 5.

15. As notes to the score clarify, the title *Silver Ladders* is reflective of the "many contrasting qualities" of the metal, including but going beyond its color. See Sandra Hyslop (in collaboration with the composer), program note to Joan Tower's *Silver Ladders*, New York: Associated Music Publishers (BMI), 1987, unnumbered page preceding the score.

16. Telephone interview with the composer, August 15, 2006.

17. Ibid.

18. Ibid.

19. Such remarks may be especially useful when the sounds or behaviors of the music fall outside an audience's experiences or expectations.

20. A basic description of the stone can be found in Herbert S. Zim and Paul R. Shaffer, *Rocks, Gems and Minerals: A Guide to Familiar Minerals, Gems, Ores and Rocks* (New York: St. Martin's Press, 2001), 85. Friedrich Mohs developed a scale of 1–10 to identify the relative softness to hardness of minerals. (Talc is the softest, at 1, and diamond the hardest, rated 10.)

21. Zim and Shaffer, *Rocks, Gems and Minerals*, 83.

22. Mary Lou Humphrey, program note to *Black Topaz* (New York: Associated Music Publishers (BMI), 1976), unnumbered page preceding score. I am grateful to Megan MacDonald, graduate musicology student at the Florida State University, for suggesting that Tower's careful choice of instruments may be analogous to the care a gemologist takes in cutting a stone for maximal effect. The composer and gem cutter both seek to maximize the impact of the source material.

23. Ibid.

24. Ibid.

25. See score, Joan Tower, *Black Topaz*, page 3, for Tower's instruction regarding how to play this particular measure.

26. See measure 242, where the tom-toms are instructed to "match [the] piano" with a similar dynamic level and articulation.

27. This topic will be considered at greater length in the discussion of her piece *Snow Dreams*.

28. See piano part measure 157, where the composer uses this phrase.

29. Telephone interview with the composer, September 3, 2010.

30. "Joan Tower: The Composer in Conversation with Bruce Duffie," originally published in *New Music Connoisseur* (Spring 2001), revised in February 2006. See http://my.voyager.net/~duffie/tower .html (accessed June 28, 2006).

31. Joan Tower, *Amazon* (New York: Associated Music Publishers, 1978), unnumbered page preceding score.

32. Remarks on Tower's pieces come from her notes to the CD *Joan Tower*, New World Records-CRI, NWCR 582, pp. 2–3.

33. See the author's discussion of Charles Ives's piece "The Housatonic at Stockbridge" in *The Sounds of Place: Music and the American Cultural Landscape* (Boston: Northeastern University Press, 2003), 64–90 for a fuller exploration of the ways water has manifested itself in American literature and musical composition.

34. Starting in the 1960s, Annea Lockwood began what she called her "River Archive." In the intervening years she has created multiple sound maps of waterways, including what many consider her signature piece "A Sound Map of the Hudson River." The 70-minute recording, released in the same year as Pauline Oliveros's *Deep Listening* CD, is an elegant mixture of the ever-changing water sounds that Lockwood heard as she tracked the river from the upper Adirondack Mountains to where it meets the Atlantic Ocean near Staten Island. Her 2005 mega-opus "A Sound Map of the Danube" takes listeners on a 167-minute tour of the near-1,800-mile-long river. Sounds collected at fifty-nine sites are enhanced by remarks from thirteen individuals living along or dependent upon the river. In recording the multinational river, which passes through ten countries, and allowing its sounds to determine the course of her work, Lockwood enacts her respectful stance toward the natural world. Nature, like the Danube, is not the property of any single nation. Lockwood's project reflects her own international perspective. In 2009, Eve Beglarian, an experimentalist composer, launched a two-year Mississippi River project. Recording sounds as she kayaked down the river from Minnesota to Louisiana and then back up has provided Beglarian with source materials for her compositions. Aware of the river journeys of many others who preceded her, Beglarian anticipated that her experiences would be different from earlier chroniclers' simply by dint of her being female.

35. Tower has the cello play "sul tasto" (on the fingerboard) on many occasions in the opening measures. At other times she will ask an instrumentalist to play "dark" or "brighter." See measures 83 and 86. Later Tower instructs the pianist to play "*mp* (but clear)," see measure 142; and then "*f* (resonant)," see measure 162.

36. See Susan Feder, liner notes to the CD *Joan Tower: Silver Ladders, Island Prelude, Music for Cello and Orchestra, and Sequoia*, Electra/Nonesuch Records, 79245–2, page 4, for Joan Tower's remarks relating energy and musical structure. Although the composer does

not mention being inspired by Bedřich Smetana's piece "The Moldau," there are parallels between that work and Tower's *Amazon* in the ways they both evoke the momentum of a river.

37. See measures 136–138 for an example of this effect.

38. There is one instance where the stopped note is written in the treble clef. This is in measures 162–163, when first a stopped *forte* E♭ is played, followed by an ordinarily struck *fortissimo* E♭. The cello and clarinet pick up this pitch while the piano allows its E♭ to continue resonating.

39. Joan Tower, *Amazon*, 34, footnote. I am grateful to Megan MacDonald for observing that the successful "imperceptible" transfer of C♯ from the cello to violin would require great listening abilities from the performers. This would make the players skillful listeners.

40. Telephone interview with the composer, September 3, 2010.

41. Joan Tower, *Sequoia* (New York: Associated Music Publishers [BMI], 1981), unnumbered page preceding the score.

42. Tower's full remark is, "My first impression was that they were quiet, very quiet; and my piece is not quiet at all!!! It's a clamoring piece." Telephone interview with the composer, August 15, 2006.

43. Ibid. Italics added by the author.

44. Tower wrote the violin and horn parts in *Sequoia* specifically for Jean and Paul Ingram, the concert mistress and horn player in the American Composers Orchestra, and dedicated the work to them both. See Joan Tower, *Sequoia*, unnumbered page preceding the score.

45. Telephone interview with the composer, August 15, 2006.

46. The composition of a symphony was considered a rite of passage for nineteenth-century composers, and this standard was still in effect through the early years of the twentieth century. While Tower's sixteen-minute, single-movement work does not qualify as a symphony in the traditional sense, its use of compositional techniques regularly employed in symphonic writing, most especially sections of counterpoint, qualifies the piece as symphonic in its conception. With its programmatic title, it might more easily be thought of as a symphonic poem.

47. Telephone interview with the composer, September 3, 2010.

48. In point of fact, *Sequoia* was choreographed and performed by the Royal Winnipeg Ballet.

49. Two other composers of special importance to Tower are Olivier Messiaen and George Crumb. Tower also regularly cites Beethoven's understanding of musical architecture as the model she strives to emulate, as well as Stravinsky, whose *Rite of Spring* informs much of the rhythmic and timbral writing in *Sequoia*. Here is another potential instance of the last-named composer influencing the aesthetic preferences of American composers. See discussion of *Rite*-like sounds in Talma's *Summer Sounds*.

50. When the composer was asked whether the pitch had any particular significance, she pointed to it being an open string, but that was the extent of the rationale for selecting it. Telephone interview with the composer, August 15, 2006.

51. Had the piece been named *Empire State Building*, it is unlikely that I would attach any meaning to the wooden timbre of temple blocks. Such a realization underscores the important role titles play in guiding a listener's thinking. Telephone interview with the composer, August 15, 2006.

52. Fog is a regular and essential condition for the health of redwoods. Redwood forests in California receive approximately 30 to 40 percent of their moisture from coastal fog. Change in climate patterns could result in relative drought in

these areas. http://en.wikipedia.org/wiki/
Fog#cite_note-15 (accessed July 20, 2010).

53. Quoted by Sandra Hyslop in liner
notes to the CD *Black Topaz – Joan Tower*.
New World 80470-2.

54. Ibid.

55. Ibid. Italics are mine.

56. Tower explained: "Beethoven was
really my mentor in what I call motivated
architecture. And that's the thing I work
hardest on . . ." Telephone interview with
the composer, August 15, 2006.

57. Jane Weiner LePage, *Women Composers, Conductors, and Musicians of the
Twentieth Century: Selected Biographies*,
vol. 3 (Metuchen, N.J.: Scarecrow Press,
1988), 270.

58. Telephone interview with the
composer, August 15, 2006.

59. Ibid., LePage quoting Tower,
*Women Composers, Conductors, and Musi-
cians*, 267.

60. In a telephone interview with
the composer, August 15, 2006, Tower
recalled that her good friend Charles
Wuorinen "absolutely hated *Black Topaz*
when he conducted it. I felt very alone. I
was here in this uptown crowd called the
university. Ahhh . . . I remember that distinctly. That was the very first piece where
I just stepped out, and thought I can do
what I want to do and what I like to do
and I'm sorry if you don't like it; it's too
bad." The composer's insistence upon the
purity of her music's origins, its lack of
connection to any inspiring, extramusical
source, may be a vestige of the modernist,
absolutist values she absorbed from her
university colleagues. Then again, she
might be similarly insistent without their
influence. I am grateful to Aaron Allen
for a conversation on this point.

61. From reviews quoted in LePage,
*Women Composers, Conductors, and Musi-
cians*, 268–269.

62. Judy Lochhead, "Joan Tower's
'Wings' and 'Breakfast Rhythms I and II':

Some Thoughts on Form and Repetition,"
Perspectives of New Music 30, no. 1 (1992):
133, 135. I am indebted to Judy Lochhead's
article for helping shape, reinforce, and
articulate my own personal perceptions of
how I hear Joan Tower's music.

63. Lochhead, "Joan Tower's 'Wings,'"
136.

64. All references to timings or measure numbers refer to the CD recording
Black Topaz – Joan Tower, New World
Records, 80470-2, and the score by Joan
Tower, *Snow Dreams*, published by Associate Music Publishers, New York, 1986,
1987. Tower provides neither timings nor
measure numbers for her score. I have
added the latter and treat the extended
unbarred "measures" associated with
the guitar and flute solos each as a single
measure. The timings are approximate.

65. According to Kent Kennan, "The
bottom octave or so of the clarinet is
called the *chalumeau* register. It has a
dark, strangely hollow quality." See Kent
Wheeler Kennan, *The Technique of Orchestration*, 2nd ed. (Englewood Cliffs,
N.J.: Prentice-Hall, 1979), 85.

66. At measure 8, Tower indicates
"(poco piu mosso)." She explains: "tempo
indications in parentheses are only suggestions to the player." See Joan Tower,
Snow Dreams (New York: Associated
Music Publishers, 1986), 3.

67. Multiphonics in wind music are
one among twentieth-century extended
techniques, first explicitly called for in the
Sequenza for solo flute by Luciano Berio
and *Proporzioni* for solo flute by Franco
Evangelisti. See Nancy Toff, *The Flute
Book: A Complete Guide for Students and
Performers* (New York: Oxford University Press, 1996), page 276, for discussion
of this "avant-garde" device.

68. Telephone interview with the
composer, August 15, 2006.

69. Tower names this piece and
George Crumb's *Vox Balaenae* as among

the twentieth-century pieces to exert the greatest influence on her musical thinking and growth. Telephone interview with the composer, August 15, 2006.

70. Lochhead, "Joan Tower's 'Wings,'" 135.

71. The extemporaneous quality of the music mimics the unpredictable quality of many dreams.

72. *Rasqueado* is a technique for playing guitar using the backs of the fingers one after the other to create a strummed effect.

73. Christine Ammer, *Unsung: A History of Women in American Music*, 2nd rev. and expanded ed. (Portland, Ore.: Amadeus Press, 2001), 219. Originally published by Greenwood Press, Westport, Connecticut, 1980.

74. The approximate timing is based upon the 2002 Crystal Records recording of *Rain Waves* by The Verdehr Trio. CD943. The precise timing given for the piece is 11:36. Commissioned by Michigan State University for the Verdehr Trio, *Rain Waves* spotlights the virtuosic abilities of that ensemble.

75. Joan Tower, *Rain Waves*, New York: Associated Music Publishers (BMI), 1997. Composer's note on unnumbered page preceding the score.

76. It is not clear to this listener that the change in dynamics is all that apparent on the Crystal Records recording. With so little sound to process it is difficult to assign a dynamic level to the opening music, which raises the question what purpose the repeat serves. Literally repeating long passages of music seems to fly in the face of the notion of organically conceived compositions. Perhaps in the case of *Rain Waves* Tower determined that other ideas, most especially balancing different kinds of materials and calling attention to the germinating wavelike gesture, trumped the seeming contradiction of a literal repeat.

77. Joan Tower, *Big Sky*, Associated Music Publishers (BMI), New York, N.Y., 2000, 2006, unnumbered page preceding the first page of the score. Tower's choice of the name Aymara for her horse is not insignificant. According to Dr. Stephen Scott, to name a horse Aymara at that time was a romantic gesture on the part of the composer. The word is the name of a people and language indigenous to Bolivia.

78. See Béla Bartók, *Bluebeard's Castle: Opera in one Act*, English Version by Christopher Hassall (New York: Boosey and Hawkes, 1963), 99–100. Stage directions: "With a sudden movement Judith runs to the Fifth Door and flings it open. A lofty verandah is revealed, and far vistas are descried beyond. The light pours out in a glittering cascade."

79. The chord at measure 64 is a hybrid C♯ major/minor chord over an F♮ pedal tone; that at measure 77 is an F-major 7 chord. C is present at important structural moments in *Big Sky* – closing measure 32 just prior to the beginning of a new section in the following measure and serving a similar closing function at measure 115 just before the return to the opening gesture that will end the piece – but in no sense does Tower use C or any key with traditional functional purposes in mind.

80. Tower's ability to create sonic luminescence was first noted in the discussion of *Black Topaz*. In that piece Tower composed moments where music appeared to behave in ways suggestive of light reflecting off of and bouncing away from the crystals of the mineral named in the title.

81. Peter Høeg, *Smilla's Sense of Snow* (New York: Dell, 1992). Translated by Tiina Nunnally and copyrighted 1993 by Farrar, Straus and Giroux. Quoted descriptive phrases come from "Miss Smilla's Feeling for Snow," http://

en.wikipedia.org/wiki/Miss_Smilla's_ Feeling_for_Snow (accessed July 8, 2010).

82. I do not possess a degree in psychology, nor do I claim any expertise in the inner workings of the mind, but I am aware that the creative process is a complex one, the result of experience, exposure, and subconscious needs and desires. As we often find what we're looking for, if we're lucky we also create what we feel compelled to explore and understand. Creating helps us make sense of the world. I am grateful for a conversation well over a decade ago with the late Stuart Feder, musicologist and medical doctor of psychiatry, who advised me to "write the book you have to write." He understood the source of creativity was within and that we create what we know or need to know.

7. ELLEN TAAFFE ZWILICH

1. Zwilich does acknowledge that water is very important to her and she "love[s] being able to look at it. It has something to do with my work, but I've never written a piece about it. It wouldn't occur to me." Personal interview with the composer, October 20, 2004.

2. "The Gardens: Birth of a Symphony," by Ellen Taaffe Zwilich. The film shows Zwilich at the gardens – working with musicians from the Michigan State University orchestra who recorded the work – and the final performance of the symphony. The project was underwritten by the Michigan Council for Arts and Cultural Affairs. A vhs tape of the documentary film is available online.

3. Today Guzelimian is provost and dean of the Juilliard School.

4. Copies of the video-taped interview and a transcript made by the author of this study are housed at the Library of Congress, at the Carnegie Hall archives, and at Allen Music Library at the Florida State University.

5. Created just twenty-one years ago, the strip calls attention to the still-newsworthy achievement of women who are composers: Marcie and Peppermint Patty are at a concert when Marcie discovers that the next piece on the program is by Ellen Zwilich, who "just happens to be a woman." Peppermint Patty enthusiastically cheers, "Good going, Ellen." Zwilich wrote to thank Schulz, and they eventually met, which resulted in her composing a suite of pieces named *Peanuts Gallery*; it became the subject of a second documentary film.

6. Zwilich shares with Tower the experience of having been trained at a time that saw lots of attention paid to serial composition. Both women demonstrated their abilities to write using those techniques but rejected them for styles that more honestly reflected their own voices.

7. Barrymore Laurence Scherer, "Ellen Taaffe Zwilich: A Composer Not Afraid to Feel," *The Wall Street Journal*, May 5, 2009.

8. Zwilich and Tower also share a preference for working organically from small units of musical materials and coaxing them along, although Zwilich is more at home in classical forms and structures than is Tower.

9. W. J. Beal Botanical Garden, visitor's brochure. East Lansing, Mich.: University Publications, unnumbered page.

10. Laura C. Martin, *Gardens of the Heartland* (New York: Abbeville Press, 1996), 61. Martin does not name the son-in-law, and to date I have not been able to identify the author of this quote.

11. See http://anthropology.msu.edu/ saints_rest_gallery/explore/fp_beal -botanical.html (accessed December 31, 2009).

12. Martin, *Gardens of the Heartland*, 65.

13. Visitors' brochure, unnumbered page.

14. Personal interview with the composer, October 25, 2001. According to Network Science, "over 120 pharmaceutical products currently in use are plant-derived, and some 75% of these were discovered by examining the use of these plants in traditional medicine." http://www.netsci.org/Science/Special/feature11.html (accessed December 31, 2009).

15. Ellen Taaffe Zwilich's notes for the CD recording of Symphony No. 4 – "The Gardens," KOCH International Classics 3–7487–2 HI, 2000.

16. The text to John Luther Adams's piece *Earth and the Great Weather* (1990–1993) consists of eight litanies, which the composer explains are "composed of the names of place, plants, weather and the seasons of the Arctic. . . . In the last two litanies, Latin is included (the scientific binomials for plants and animals), primarily for its contrasting color and rhythmic texture." See liner notes by John Luther Adams, *Earth and the Great Weather*, New World Records, 1994. Zwilich did not know of this piece prior to composing Symphony No. 4, nor did anyone refer her to it after her piece had been recorded. It is only recently that John Luther Adams's work has reached large audiences, which might account for Zwilich's ignorance of his piece.

17. Elaine M. Chittenden. "Endangered and Threatened Plants in Michigan," W. J. Beal Botanical Garden, Michigan State University, 1996.

18. Personal interview with the composer, October 25, 2001.

19. I am grateful to Aaron Allen, who fills his hours away from ecomusicological studies with woodworking projects, for this piece of information.

20. See http://www.acf.org/mission_history.php (accessed January 2, 2010).

21. Susan Fenimore Cooper, *Rural Hours*, edited by Rochelle Johnson and Daniel Patterson (Athens: University of Georgia Press, 1998). *Rural Hours* is the distillation of written observations taken from a period of over "twenty months or so." See page x.

22. Ibid., 105. For specifics regarding the precise year of daily entries, see "Editorial Principles," xxiii.

23. Ibid., 211.

24. Ibid., 168–169.

25. Ibid., xviii.

26. Ibid., 134.

27. Henry D. Thoreau, *Walden*, edited by J. Lyndon Shanley (Princeton, N.J.: Princeton University Press, 1989), 238–239. Originally published in Boston by Ticknor and Fields in 1854 as *Walden: or, a Life in the Woods*. The original title page of the 1854 publication included an ink sketch of a small cabin in the woods drawn by Sophia Elizabeth Thoreau, Henry David's sister. The sketch shows her to be a careful observer and a talented artist, not unlike Thirza Lee at Almira Phelps's seminary.

28. When I pointed out to Ellen Zwilich the importance of the chestnut tree in American history, she immediately recalled having to memorize Longfellow's line and mused whether "*Castanea dentate*" might also have appealed to her because of that early experience reciting the poem. If so, the appeal was subconscious.

29. Henry David Thoreau, *Faith in a Seed: The Dispersion of Seeds and Other Late Natural History Writings* (Washington, D.C.: Island Press, 1993), 131. This book is a collection of excerpts from Thoreau's late natural-history writings and the full text of "The Dispersion of Seeds" edited by Bradley P. Dean. The 1993 publication was the first appearance of the complete manuscript of "The Dispersion of Seeds."

30. Henry David Thoreau, *Selected Journals of Henry David Thoreau*, edited by Carl Bode (New York: Signet, 1967), 220–221. Quoted in Barbara Novak,

Nature and Culture: American Landscape and Painting 1825–1875, rev. ed. (New York: Oxford University Press, 1995), 113.

31. Novak, *Nature and Culture*, rev. ed.104.

32. Ibid.

33. Although the binomial system of identification was popularized by Linnaeus, it had been invented almost two centuries earlier by a pair of Swiss-French botanist brothers, Gaspard (Caspar) and Johann (Jean) Bauhin.

34. In a paper read by Joyce Appleby before the American Historical Association, January 9, 1997, the distinguished historian discussed America's nineteenth-century history. She observed that "most American history was compensatory, giving to the people an account that justified the country's egregious differences," and she concluded that "American history turned the nation's deficits into assets." This paper later appeared in *The American Historical Review* 103, no. 1 (Feb. 1998). See page 13 for specific remarks.

35. There are significant differences in instrumentation of the two works. Among the most conspicuous is the absence of clarinets, violins, and violas in Stravinsky's score, and the absence of pianos in Zwilich's.

36. Stravinsky preferred children's voices to take the top two parts of the SATB chorus, whereas Zwilich composed separate vocal parts of each of the adult and children's choruses.

37. The capital letters are Stravinsky's and appear opposite the first page of music. See Igor Stravinsky, *Symphony of Psalms for Mixed Chorus and Orchestra* (London: Boosey and Hawkes, 1948). *Symphony of Psalms* is another Stravinsky work that has potentially influenced this group of composers. His impact was felt throughout the twentieth century.

38. Zwilich explained that she hadn't thought of the Michigan State University gardens as an exhibit until she saw them. After viewing them, in her own words she "wanted to celebrate the gardens." Personal interview with the composer, October 25, 2001.

39. At the first appearance of the word "heritage" (movement IV, measure 7), Zwilich explains: "Let the word make a natural-sounding rhythm; the [dotted-eighth, sixteenth] doesn't need to be precise" (score, page 66). Regardless of the amount of precision, the connection of the natural rhythm of the word "heritage" with the opening fanfaric figure is immediately audible.

40. Ibid.

41. See measures 34 through 54 of the score. Ellen Taaffe Zwilich, Symphony No. 4 ("The Gardens") for Orchestra, with Mixed Chorus and Children's Chorus. Bryn Mawr, Pa.: Theodore Presser, 2000.

42. Score, movement I, measure 98, page 17.

43. See liner notes by Ellen Taaffe Zwilich for the CD recording of Symphony No. 4 – "The Gardens." Koch International Classics 3–7487–2 HI, 2000.

44. See liner notes by Ellen Taaffe Zwilich.

45. The dotted rhythm that introduced movement I reappears for the first time in the second movement at measure 25 and is a common feature of the "Meditation on Living Fossils" from that point on.

46. From the opening of the symphony to the close of the second movement, Zwilich begins her traverse through the A-minor triad that will outline the largest harmonic motion of the work.

47. Libby Larsen will ask a similar question when she wonders what is now and what is then.

48. See liner notes by the composer.

49. See the documentary film *The Gardens: Making of a Symphony* for Zwilich's remarks.

50. See measures 58, 122, and 151 of the score.

51. See starting measure 105 of the score.

52. See measures 219–222 of the score.

53. See measures 242–243 of the score.

54. See measures 105–112; 175–188 of the score.

55. At this point Zwilich has completed her traverse of the A-minor triad. She will work her way back to A by the close of the piece.

56. See measure 97.

57. See measure 117.

58. This melody recalls that of the "Dies Irae," a sequence from the Medieval Requiem Mass (the Mass for the Dead). Throughout Western music history it has been borrowed by composers, including Berlioz, Liszt, Saint-Saëns, and Rachmaninoff, for various symbolic purposes. Whether Zwilich consciously intended to model her melody on this famous earlier one is not central to this discussion. The suggestion of the ancient melody brings with it its initial context, and the weight of its subsequent uses. It may be that the greater prominence of bells in the third movement, and their associations with churches and religion, underscores the similarities of Zwilich's melody and the "Dies Irae" at this point in the symphony.

59. See liner notes by the composer.

60. Ibid. Erik LaMont is the composer's husband.

61. The truthfulness or accuracy of romanticized reading of Native Americans' relationships to the earth is not the issue here. Neither is the question of appropriation central to the discussion at hand, important as it is. By referencing Native Americans, Zwilich participates in and benefits from that association. The simplicity of the text evokes the "purity" attributed to Native American

interactions with nature. Intentionally or not, Zwilich's interpolation of a lyric based upon a Native American source connects her to ecofeminism. See Karen J. Warren, *Ecofeminist Philosophy: A Western Perspective on What It Is and Why It Matters* (Lanham, Md.: Rowman and Littlefield, 2000), and especially pages 86–87 for a discussion of the pervasiveness of Native American thought in ecofeminist practices.

62. Personal interview with the composer, October 25, 2001.

63. See Tina Gianquitto, *"Good Observers of Nature": American Women and the Scientific Study of the Natural World, 1820–1885* (Athens: The University of Georgia Press, 2007), where the author quotes Catherine Maria Sedgwick, 19.

64. Stephanie Ross, *What Gardens Mean* (Chicago: University of Chicago Press, 1998), xi–xii.

65. Personal interview with the composer, October 25, 2001.

66. Ross, *What Gardens Mean*, xi. Talma's Divertimento *Have you Heard? Do you Know?* shows the composer through her characters seeking respite. The MacDowell Colony provided a place where that could be achieved.

67. In 2009 Ken Burns released a six-part paean, "The National Parks: America's Best Idea," that was broadcast nationally on PBS TV stations. Interweaving its breathtaking, panoramic vistas is a perspective that nature is outside ourselves. While films like this may awaken or strengthen environmental consciousness among some viewers, they may also encourage the continuation of romanticized views of what constitutes the natural world and its separation from humanity. Perhaps more useful to changing behaviors and attitudes are films like Davis Guggenheim's and Al Gore's 2006 film *An Inconvenient Truth*.

68. Composer's remarks in the documentary film *The Gardens: Birth of a Symphony*.

PART 3. BEYOND THE EPA AND EARTH DAY

1. Once again, other composers could have been considered. Maggi Payne, of Mills College, has written pieces for acoustic and electronic instruments whose titles reflect the broad impact of the natural world on her thinking and creative expression. Their breadth of references recollects the diverse array of images in Joan Tower's titles. Andrea Polli is a digital-media artist living in New Mexico who collaborates with scientists especially focused on weather and climate change. Her determination to bring science and art into conversation suggests similar efforts of Emily Doolittle. Frances White describes her music as "inspired by her love of nature." According to the composer, "her electronic works frequently include natural sound recorded around where she lives, in central New Jersey." Her use of electronic equipment recalls Pauline Oliveros's earlier work in that broad genre. See http://www.rosewhitemusic.com (accessed September 28, 2011).

2. The term "Generation X" originated with Canadian writer Douglas Coupland in his novel *Generation X: Tales for an Accelerated Culture* (New York: St. Martin's Griffin, 1991).

3. See http://www.nsf.gov/about/ for the foundation's most thorough online presence (accessed September 28, 2011).

4. For a list of the laws and regulations supported by EPA efforts, see www.epa.gov/lawsregs.

5. Consciousness-raising (CR) groups began in the 1960s in New York City and Chicago with small numbers of second-wave feminists who were determined to sensitize larger numbers of women to the various ways they were repressed by society. CR groups spread throughout the 1970s and across the nation. They were essential to the success of second-wave feminism.

6. See Rachel Carson, *Silent Spring* (Boston: Houghton Mifflin, 2002), opening line page 1.

7. Current efforts to dismiss scientists who are outspoken about the effects of global warming are only a continuation of a type of thinking that denies the role human beings play within a larger ecological system that is mutually dependent upon the health of all, animate and inanimate.

8. Significant amendments to this act were passed in 1977 and 1990.

9. Roger Fisher and William Ury, *Getting to Yes: Negotiating Agreement without Giving In* (New York: Penguin Books, 1983), 33–34. By 1991, the book had sold over two million copies and been published in eighteen languages.

10. Acoustic ecology, also known as ecoacoustics or soundscape studies, considers the relationships among sound, environment, and human interactions. Their beginnings occurred in the 1960s and are associated with R. Murray Schafer (b. 1933) and a group of students at Simon Fraser University. Dario Martinelli (b. 1974) uses the term zoomusicology, first coined in 1983, to describe "the aesthetic use of sounds among animals." Martinelli defined the term in his 2002 book *How Musical Is a Whale? Towards a Theory of Zoomusicology* and further elucidated the concept in his 2009 book *Of Birds, Whales and Other Musicians* Scranton, Pa.: University of Scranton Press, 2009, page 2.

8. VICTORIA BOND

1. After meeting with the composer on multiple occasions over a period of years to discuss her nature-related music,

I asked Victoria Bond, "What is nature to you?" She responded with this prose poem. It is reprinted with her permission.

2. To be sure, there were female orchestral conductors earlier in the century – Caroline B. Nichols (b.1864–d.?), Ethel Leginska (1886–1970), Antonia Brico (1902–1989) – but none of them pursued a doctoral degree in conducting or would have been accepted into such a program had it existed. It is also noteworthy that each of these conductors worked with female orchestras.

3. Zwilich and Bond knew each other from their overlapping years at Juilliard, and each walked away with the distinction of being "a first." They continue to stay in touch.

4. Personal interview with the composer, July 6, 2006 at her Manhattan home. I appreciate Aaron Allen's noting the similarities of Bond's language to that of Raymond Williams's in his book *The Country and the City*. When asked about her terminology, the composer explained that she was unfamiliar with Williams's book; however, she clarified that "the country" is a distinct location for her, whereas "nature," a word that some might have expected her to use in this context, is all-inclusive. Personal email correspondence with the composer, October 8, 2011.

5. Ibid.

6. Personal interview with the composer, June 20, 2009, at her East Hampton home.

7. Ibid.

8. Ibid.

9. Aldo Leopold, *A Sand County Almanac and Sketches Here and There* (New York: Oxford University Press, 1949).

10. See Karen J. Warren, *Ecofeminist Philosophy: A Western Perspective on What It Is and Why It Matters* (Maryland: Rowman and Littlefield, 2000), 147. See pages 168 and beyond for six ways Warren

believes ecofeminist thinking can update and expand Aldo Leopold's land ethic.

11. Personal interview with the composer, January 16, 2009.

12. Bond's notion of "life scales" is a variation of the scientific concept of "geologic time scales," which addresses the ages and eras of the earth's history.

13. One can hear Ecclesiastes 3:1–8 in Bond's thinking: "For everything there is a season, and a time for every matter under heaven," *The Holy Bible*, rev. standard version.

14. Paul Cézanne's *Mont Sainte-Victoire* paintings may provide a visual analogue of Bond's musical treatment.

15. The title of this tune varies. The composer has referred to it as "A Thousand Birds Worshipping the Phoenix," but other sources list it as "A Hundred Birds Paying Tribute to the Phoenix."

16. I encountered the term "environmental mindfulness" for the first time in John Elder's book *Pilgrimage to Vallombrosa: From Vermont to Italy in the Footsteps of George Perkins Marsh* (Charlottesville: University of Virginia Press, 2006), 8. While Elder used it to refer to his own journey toward increased sensitivity to the earth, it also describes the aspirations of Bond and many of this study's composers. Although none of the composers is a practicing Buddhist, mindfulness is a basic tenet of Buddhist meditation practices and teachings.

17. The fourth entrance begins on C♯ in measure 10 in the C flute, C♯–F♯–G♯–B; and the fifth entrance begins on G♯ in the same instrument in measure 14, G♯–C♯–D♯–F♯. The starting notes of these two entrances continue a circle-of-fifths pattern that connects them to the third entrance, which began on F♯. Bond demonstrates that there is a logic to her choice of pitches even in these pattern-breaking tune iterations, although it is not the initial logic we

tracked in the first three entrances of the fragment.

18. This is the third time Stravinsky has been suggested as a possible influence on composers in this study. See chapters on Louise Talma and Ellen Taaffe Zwilich for earlier occurrences.

19. Leopold, *Sand County Almanac*, 7.

20. In a personal interview with the composer, January 16, 2009, Bond referred to another result of the proliferation of deer: the surge in cases of Lyme disease, which is carried by deer ticks.

21. The film *Dances with Wolves*, starring Kevin Kostner, came out in 1990 and was perhaps a reference for the sectional title of Bond's 1994 piece.

22. Personal interview with the composer, June 20, 2009.

23. "Victoria Bond: Catalog of Works," 4. *Urban Bird* was commissioned by the Women's Philharmonic. http://www.victoriabond.com/catalog.html (accessed June 12, 2006).

24. Ibid., 11.

25. Email correspondence with the composer, June 5, 2009.

26. The composer's own commentaries on her pieces provide first-person evidence of this rondo theme. Bond describes *C A G E D for String Orchestra* (1974) as "portray[ing] the frustration of any living creature confined against its will, pacing, staring out helplessly, raging." In commentary for her 1994 opera *Travels*, Bond tells the story of Gull, "an adolescent on the verge of manhood. Suffocated by the confines of home, he begins a quest for identity, love, mystery." In her 1993 ballet *Rage*, Bond describes the pas de deux as "an impassioned cry against violence. It portrays a couple imprisoned in a vicious cycle of domination and abuse." See the *Catalog of Works*.

27. Bond's projection of a bird's dream of escape, which could be accomplished only by flying, introduces the additionally laden symbol of flying dreams. While such dreams may reflect ambition and a craving after success, flying dreams are typically associated with the exhilaration the dreamer feels in being liberated from a situation. According to Patricia L. Garfield, PhD, in *The Universal Dream Key: The 12 Most Common Dream Themes around the World* (New York: HarperCollins, 2001), "Flying Dreams extend that notion of choice to a wider sphere. Not only may you determine the route to take to a desirable spot, but now you may also choose the dimension." See pages 148–149. According to Bond, "I actually do experience resisting gravity, floating etc. The sensations are quite real in the dreams. That is where I drew these feelings." Quoted from email correspondence with the composer, June 5, 2009.

28. In a personal interview, Bond discussed dreams in which animals speak to her. She appeared to take their language abilities for granted.

29. Personal interview with the composer, January 16, 2009, Deering Estate at Cutler, Miami, Florida. In a follow-up interview that took place June 20, 2009, at her East Hampton home, the composer expressed a similar sentiment: "The seed has the plan in it for the whole tree or plant. There's an inevitability to things that grow in nature." While the model of nature's organicism fits neatly with Bond's compositional practice, where she works from a few brief musical gestures that ultimately expand and unify a larger work, it is not the only model of how nature works. Native American and Asian cultures, among others, offer alternative readings, as do others in positions of diminished power. I am grateful to Aaron Allen for calling my attention to the potential for monothematicism in Bond's music to be read as suggesting an exclusive embrace of the dominant and privileged attitude of traditional mainstream

American environmentalism. There are, as Allen suggests, a "diversity of perspectives and possibilities." Email correspondence with the author, May 29, 2009. Bond would agree with Allen's sensitive caution.

30. Ibid. Bond pointed out that "birds seem to have no difficulty resisting gravity!" My own observations of many aquatic birds, however, convince me she's not thinking of wood storks or even pelicans, who seem to struggle to become airborne.

31. Movement I is just over 4:00 minutes; movement II: 1:32; movement III: 4:40; and movement IV: 3:50.

32. Bond has clarified that the pitches were chosen for purely practical reasons: "The notes are all good notes for harmonics on the violin, which is why I chose them. Also, the melody is actually related to the Brazilian melody which I used as the canon in the next section and which is first stated by the cello at letter M. It's played pizz by the cello after letter N and then by the violin and cello in canon at letter Q, then by the 2nd violin at R with the viola playing the canon in pizz." Email correspondence with the composer, March 2, 2009.

33. In c. 1555, French composer Clément Janequin (1485–1558), who was known for his sophisticated onomatopoeic settings, composed a four-part chanson imitating bird sounds, which he titled "Chanson des Oiseaux." It has remained in the repertoire of early music vocal ensembles to this day. With the third movement of *Dreams of Flying*, Victoria Bond created another four-part work imitating birdsong, this one for instrumentalists.

34. At measure 126, a quarter note = 100, which is only the second metronome mark given in the entire piece, even though by this time we are in the third movement.

35. See Catalogue of Works, 4.

36. Personal interview with the composer, January 16, 2009, Deering Estate at Cutler, Miami, Florida.

37. *Dreams of Flying* premiered July 24, 1994, at the Maverick Festival in Woodstock, New York. *Thinking Like a Mountain* premiered three months later, in October 1994 in Roanoke, Virginia.

38. The lighthearted back-and-forth of the jungle birds in the third movement of *Dreams of Flying* had something of a humorous quality to it, especially in the "puweeep-ing" string glissandos. And the composer pointed to an even earlier piece, "Molly Manybloom" (1990), as containing moments of humor. Bond explained that she is more appreciative of the importance of predators to maintain the balance of nature. In a flash of self-effacing levity, the composer referred to herself as a "reformed vegetarian." "Enlarged appreciation" and "clearer-eyed view" are phrases Victoria Bond used to characterize her more pragmatic assessment of nature. Personal interview with the composer, January 16, 2009, Deering Estate at Cutler, Miami, Florida.

39. Victoria Bond, Program Notes, January 7, 2009. Collaboration, so valued by Joan Tower and other composers in this study, is a welcome condition for Victoria Bond who, as a conductor, knows the necessity of working together with others.

40. From *Peculiar Plants* (2006–2008), by Victoria Bond. Lyrics by Victoria Bond and Kenneth Cooper. Revised July 1, 2008. Poetry reprinted with the permission of Victoria Bond and Kenneth Cooper.

41. What precisely the composer means by "wilderness" is not the issue here. Like the word "nature," people across a wide spectrum use it freely to mean any number of things. The more orthodox use of the term would likely insist upon an area of uncultivated land uninhabited by human beings. (Compare

Webster's Unabridged Dictionary.) The absence of human beings or their easy navigation through such places would thus preclude the opportunity for a genteel "walk."

42. Antoni Gaudí (1852–1926) was known for his original and eccentric architecture often involving bright colors and large, thick forms that appeared to be melting, or alternately earth tones with filigree-like delicacy. Beyond the immediate appeal of his works, the oft-referenced "magical" quality of his creations may have drawn Bond to make this particular association.

43. All quoted passages related to the discussion of *Peculiar Plants* come from a personal interview conducted at the Deering Estate at Cutler, Miami, Florida, January 16, 2009.

44. The strangler fig can grow to between fifty and sixty feet tall, with a two- to four-foot trunk diameter. Its leaves are elliptical in shape and between two and five inches in length.

45. At measure 48 the composer instructs the harpsichordist, "Meno mosso, menacing."

46. See measures 80–86.

47. The lines come from Alfred Lord Tennyson's 1849 poem "In Memoriam A. H. H." and can be found in Canto 56.

48. Italics are mine. All plants named in *Peculiar Plants* are given human attributes, including the abilities to strategize, manipulate, emote, and frolic as appropriate.

49. *Peculiar Plants* (2006–2008), by Victoria Bond. Poetry reprinted with the permission of Victoria Bond and Kenneth Cooper.

50. See measures 1, 14, 32, 43, and 47 for these specific indications.

51. "Do I contradict myself? Very well then I contradict myself, I am large, I contain multitudes." Walt Whitman, "Song of Myself."

52. Personal interview with the composer, January 16, 2009, Deering Estate at Cutler, Miami, Florida.

53. Ragweed is originally a North American plant, but trade spread it to Europe, and now the plant can be found almost everywhere on the globe.

54. Poetry reprinted with the permission of Victoria Bond and Kenneth Cooper.

55. Pauline Oliveros was similarly unwilling to speculate why she thinks as she does, having had no experience being other than who she is.

56. Personal interview with the composer, June 20, 2009, East Hampton, New York.

57. Ibid.

58. Ibid. In a later chapter, Libby Larsen will also bring together music and the sense of smell.

59. Ibid.

60. Ibid.

9. LIBBY LARSEN

1. Taken from the back cover of *downwind of roses in Maine*. Minnesota: Libby Larsen Publishing, 2009. www .libbylarsen.com.

2. Personal interview with the composer, March 29, 2009.

3. Personal interview with the composer, March 28, 2009. Italics represent where the composer emphasized the phrase in her speech.

4. "Tent conversations" is the phrase Larsen used. The idea that seeds contain their present and future has much in common with Victoria Bond's reading of nature as containing its own potential.

5. Personal interview with the composer, March 28, 2009.

6. Debussy opens "Dialogue du vent et de la mer" with a chromatic, four-note ascending passage in the lowest strings, which is suggested in Larsen's own four-note gestures in "Fresh Breeze." Beyond

the number of notes and their general direction, however, there is little to suggest direct modeling of one on the other. It may be that the action of wind lapping water evokes such a sonic gesture. Debussy has been quoted as saying that he was destined to be a sailor but fate led him in another direction. One wonders if the same could be said of Larsen, although social mores would likely have had a greater role in denying her that vocation than fate. Until recently, women weren't sailors.

7. "Fresh breeze" exhibits large-scale harmonic structure and linearity but less inevitably than more traditionally harmonic pieces do. The first movement begins and ends on C with a dominant preparation on G in the lowest instruments prior to the final return. At no point in the piece, however, does a listener feel inevitably drawn toward a particular harmonic home. The closest one gets to experiencing harmonic expectation is when it is thwarted at measure 125, and then again when the same gesture repeats at measure 148. In both instances tubas ascend through an E-major scale, but the seventh-degree refuses to resolve to the tonic. Instead it curls backward to descend through a flatted seventh and finish on C. The movement achieves traditional harmonic unity, but it is not the driving spirit behind the work.

8. Had the drumming been more regular, it might suggest the heartbeat of the earth.

9. Seeking to change more than the aural environment is not unique to "Hot, still." When coaching a new work, *downwind of roses in Maine*, Larsen encouraged the musicians to "become the fragrance." Personal interview with the composer, March 28, 2009.

10. See especially the brass in measures 124–126, where the instruments join together in a *forte* "cha-cha-cha." Larsen

heard many Broadway musicals on the hi-fi in her family home; the genre was a favorite of her mother's.

11. Personal interview with the composer, March 29, 2009. Works lists include "Soft Pieces," but as of 2009 it is not published.

12. Libby Larsen, *Missa Gaia*. Boston: ECS Publishing, 1992. Full score, i.

13. Taken from email correspondence with the composer, November 25, 2008, and a personal interview with the composer, March 28, 2009. The "music . . . that's always there" refers to the music that Larsen is always hearing in her head.

14. Cynthia Green, "Interview with Composer Libby Larsen," *International League of Women Composers Journal* (June 1992): 24–27.

15. The author recognizes that many people both within and outside Western high-art culture work collaboratively to create art, and that the high value placed upon solitary, quiet time is not universally shared. That many subjects discussed in this book volunteered and focused on this issue, however, underscores its importance within the context of this study.

16. The number of women composers who have children and have achieved a degree of name recognition beyond a local or regional sphere is growing but still small. The same could be said of women in a number of professions, including academia. It is impossible to tease out all the reasons this is the case, but the absence of a supportive social structure, including adequate daycare and health policies, is a contributing factor. There are numerous additional arguments for not bearing children, to be sure, some of which are vaguely environmental at their roots, including a concern that limited resources are unable to sustain an increasing population. This argument, first articulated in the eighteenth century by Thomas Robert Malthus, continues

to have its adherents today. It is often referred to as the Malthusian theory of population.

17. Personal interview with the composer, March 28, 2009.

18. Pamela Tanner Bolls, "Who Does She Think She Is?" 2009, Mystic Artists Film Productions Documentary. See www.Whodoesshethinksheis.net. Accessed most recently June 29, 2011.

19. Personal interview with the composer, March 28, 2009.

20. See James Lovelock, *Gaia: A New Look at Life on Earth.* Oxford, UK: Oxford University Press, 2000, for an update of his original 1960s ideas.

21. See Riane Eisler's essay "The Gaia Tradition and the Partnership Future: An Ecofeminist Manifesto" in the 1990 book *Reweaving the World: The Emergence of Ecofeminism.* edited by Irene Diamond and Gloria Feman Orenstein. In Greek mythology, "Gaia" is the goddess of the earth.

22. Ibid., 23.

23. Eisler (24) quoting from Nicolas Platon's *Crete* (Geneva: Nagel Publishers, 1966), 148, 143.

24. Ibid. 24.

25. Judith Plant explains bioregionalism: "Bioregionalism, with its emphasis on distinct regional cultures and identities strongly attached to their natural environments, may well be the kind of framework within which the philosophy of ecofeminism could realize its full potential as part of a practical social movement." See "Searching for Common Ground: Ecofeminism and Bioregionalism," in Diamond and Orenstein, *Reweaving the World,* 155–161.

26. Personal interview with the composer, March 29, 2009, Greensboro, North Carolina.

27. Ibid.

28. Libby Larsen, *Mass for the Earth: Missa Gaia,* Koch International Classics, 1995, 3–7279–2.

29. Ibid., unnumbered page.

30. Personal interview with the composer, March 28, 2009.

31. According to Karen J. Warren in *Ecofeminist Philosophy: A Western Perspective on What It Is and Why It Matters,* "spiritual ecofeminists agree that earth-based, feminist spiritualities and symbols (such as Gaia and Goddess) are essential to ecofeminism." See page 31+.

32. Victoria Bond had used the metaphor of "a circle of equals" to describe the ideal creative environment.

33. Larsen, like Bond, Oliveros, and Doolittle, collaborates often and freely with women and men, whoever shares her values and message.

34. The circle of fifths represents the modification of the "overtone series," an acoustical phenomenon wherein a succession of pitches is present in a predictable order within any single (fundamental) pitch.

35. Resonating instruments including bells and chimes are also favorites of Ellen Taaffe Zwilich and the percussion-loving Joan Tower. See "The Gardens: Birth of a Symphony" for Zwilich's comments on her fascination with reverberating sounds. Larsen's chimes might also suggest church bells she heard in her youth.

36. The A drone connects the Kyrie to the closing A-major chord of the preceding Introit and acts as V to the following Gloria, which begins with a D pedal.

37. The 1992 satb/piano score for *Missa Gaia* quotes a poem by M. K. Dean, "Mother, Sister; Blessed, Honored," for the Kyrie rather than the T. S. Eliot stanza from *Ash Wednesday.* The 1995 Koch recording, however, uses Eliot's lines in the performance and includes them in the cd liner notes. Larsen explained: "I set the T.S. Eliot poem. When it came time to publish the piece, the Eliot estate would not grant permission." Email correspondence with the composer, July 22, 2009.

38. In 1949, Louise Talma also set a version of Hopkins's poem and published it as one of her *Seven Songs for Voice and Piano*. See *Seven Songs* (New York: Carl Fischer, facs. ed., 1986), 211.

39. Larsen instructs the musicians to play and sing "brightly." See Libby Larsen, *Missa Gaia: Mass for the Earth* (ECS Publishing, 1999), 18.

40. Personal interview with the composer, March 29, 2009. See Lawrence Buell's *The Environmental Imagination* (Cambridge, Mass.: The Belknap Press of Harvard University Press, 1995), 16–20, for one take on why Anglo- and Native American environmental thought may interrelate more easily that of other subcultures.

41. Libby Larsen, *Missa Gaia: Mass for the Earth* (ECS Publishing, 1999), vii. The *Chinook Psalter* text stays close to that of "Psalm 84" as it is translated in the *King James Bible*: "How lovely is thy dwelling place, / O Lord of hosts! / My soul longs, yea, faints / for the courts of the Lord; / my heart and flesh sing for joy to the / living God."

42. Larsen regularly used the word "musicalize" to convey the notion of an idea becoming music. In my 1995 dissertation titled "Reconciliations: Time, Space, and the American Place in the Music of Charles Ives," I coined the term "sonification" to express a similar idea (PhD dissertation, University of Washington, 1995, page 13). In this context I prefer Larsen's term, which clarifies that a nonmusical idea or event has become "music" and not merely "sound."

43. "Eagle Poem" by Joy Harjo, from *In Mad Love and War* (Wesleyan University Press, 1990). © 1990 by Joy Harjo and reprinted by permission of Wesleyan University Press.

44. *Mezzo di voce* describes a process whereby long notes gradually swell from a soft dynamic to a louder dynamic and

then back again. To execute *mezzo di voce* well requires extremely fine command of one's instrument or voice.

45. Personal interview with the composer, March 29, 2009.

46. Ibid. The ramifications of such a trajectory are significant for a composer.

47. Ibid.

48. Libby Larsen, *downwind of roses in Maine*, 2009. See measure 1 for instructions to the percussionist. Larsen spells the title with lowercase letters.

49. Personal interview with composer, March 28, 2009. "A little hedge of mallet instruments" is the composer's phrase.

50. Ibid.

51. Larsen was a composer-in-residence at the Seal Bay Festival of American Chamber Music, June 2–14, 2008 where her string quartet received its world premiere.

52. Ibid. Italics represent Larsen's emphasis on the word in the interview.

53. This total identification with nature recalls the Girl Scout who became the pine trees decades earlier. Larsen's association of "beautiful, quiet" with the roses recalls Tower's observation of the sequoia trees: "They were quiet, very quiet." See chapter 5, Joan Tower.

54. Personal email from the composer, July 22, 2009.

55. Libby Larsen was composer in residence, February 16–19, 2009. The work was premiered by ULM faculty members. Personal interview with the composer, March 29, 2009.

56. Among the most public of music genres is opera. Larsen's newest opera, *Picnic*, premiered in March 2009, just a month after *downwind of roses in Maine*.

57. Personal interview with the composer, March 28, 2009.

58. Ibid. Larsen used the phrase "going deep" in a conversation about motherhood and creativity and the balancing act they require. The composer wondered: "How

do you hold the deep construct in your head amidst constant interruptions?" And then answered her own question: "We become virtuosos at going deep quickly."

59. An amateur tape of this performance confirms the composer's recollection: there are no train sounds.

60. See Constance Classen, David Howes, and Anthony Synnott, *Aroma* (London: Routledge, 1994), 203–205. The sense of sight is typically understood to be the preferred sense since the Enlightenment, and most especially among modernists. David Michael. Levin, ed., *Modernity and the Hegemony of Vision* (Berkeley: University of California Press, 1993).

61. See Mark Graham, "Queer Smells: Fragrances of Late Capitalism or Scents of Subversion?" in Jim Drobnick, ed., *The Smell-Culture Reader*, (Oxford, UK: Berg Publishers, 2006), 305, 315. For a more general study of the history of the senses, see Mark M. Smith, *Sensing the Past: Seeing, Hearing, Smelling, Tasting, and Touching in History* (Berkeley: University of California Press, 2007).

62. Personal email from the composer, July 22, 2009.

63. Libby Larsen, *downwind of roses in Maine*, 2009. At the top of the score the composer instructs musicians: "Always delicate and fluid; no stressed inflection." The percussionist playing orchestra bells is told to play "like wind chimes in a gentle breeze, out of time." Libby Larsen Publishing, 1.

64. The peak volume, *mezzo forte*, is reached at measures 53 through 57 and revisited only once more at measure 64.

65. Personal email from the composer, July 22, 2009.

66. Marcello Aspria, "Perfume and Gender Identity," *Scented Pages*. Accessed online July 16, 2009.

67. See Richard L. Doty's and David G. Laing's essay "Psychophysical

Measurement of Human Olfactory Function, Including Odorant Mixture Assessment" for an insightful discussion of the ways language and fragrance memory are related. Relevant to Larsen's piece is Doty and Laing's observation: "Despite attempts to minimize labeling of the inspection odor with a familiar word or item on the part of a subject, such labeling undoubtedly occurs, and, thus, what is being measured across intervals is the memory of the label, not the memory of the odor. In other words, once an individual recognizes an odor as that of an orange, all that has to be remembered over time is the concept 'orange,' not the specific smell of the orange." *The Handbook of Olfaction and Gustation*, edited by Richard L. Doty, 2003, 213.

68. See Clara Origlia, "Sensory Semiotics: Culture-sensitive, holistic research approaches to explore sensory complexity." Paper presented at the ESOMAR Fragrance Research Conference, Lausanne (Switzerland), March 2003, and published online by The World Association of Research Professionals. See page 4.

10. EMILY DOOLITTLE

1. The first Earth Day was celebrated April 22, 1970; it is regularly credited with formally announcing the modern environmental movement. The first Greenpeace protest occurred the following year, in 1971, when a small group of activists from Vancouver, B.C., attempted to prevent the detonation of a nuclear bomb off the coast of an Alaskan island that was home to rare wildlife. While they didn't prevent the explosion, their work ultimately resulted in having Amchitka declared a bird sanctuary. In both cases, it was youthful protestors who initiated the events.

2. See Emily Lenore Doolittle, "Other Species' Counterpoint: An Investigation of the Relationship between Human

Music and Animal Songs," PhD dissertation, Princeton University, 2007. For an
introduction to Doolittle's writings about
animals and Western music, see Emily
Doolittle, 2008, "Crickets in the Concert
Hall: A History of Animals in Western
Music." TRANS-*Transcultural Music Review* 12. See http://www.sibetrans.com/
trans/a94/crickets-in-the-concert-hall
-a-history-of-animals-in-western-music
(accessed October 28, 2011).

3. All told, six of the nine composers discussed in this book have enjoyed
residencies at MacDowell. It continues to
support women and men in the arts. According to the composer, her experience
at Ucross, most specifically, reinforced
her sense of being one among many
species.

4. "Family," for most subjects of this
book, means all those people, biologically
related or not, who provide close encouragement and support for them and their
work.

5. See Emily Lenore Doolittle, *Other
Species' Counterpoint: An Investigation of
the Relationship between Human Music
and Animal Songs*, PhD dissertation,
Princeton University, 2007, page 13. She
references John T. Bonner's *The Evolution
of Culture in Animals* (Princeton, N.J.:
Princeton University Press, 1983).

6. Bonner, *Evolution of Culture*, 8.

7. Personal interview with the composer, June 10, 2009.

8. Personal interview, June 10, 2009,
and email correspondence with the composer, July 1, 2011.

9. Email correspondence with the
composer, July 1, 2011.

10. Personal interview, June 10, 2009,
and email correspondence with the composer, July 1, 2011.

11. Personal interview with the composer, June 10, 2009.

12. Ibid. It is a lovely coincidence that
Reeds is the name of one of Doolittle's

most recent pieces and the final work
discussed in this study.

13. Personal interview, June 10, 2009,
and email correspondence with the composer July 1, 2011.

14. Doolittle is "attached" to her capitalization choices when it comes to titles
of her pieces. The capitalization used in
this chapter reflects Doolittle's preferences. Email correspondence with the
composer, July 1, 2011.

15. See R. Murray Schafer, *The
Soundscape: Our Sonic Environment and
the Tuning of the World* (Rochester, Vt.:
Destiny Books, 1994). This seminal ex-
plication of Schafer's thinking was originally published in 1977 by Knopf, as *The
tuning of the world*.

16. Doolittle skipped the summer
of 2003 when she went to the Bread and
Puppet Theater, and then returned to the
Wolf Project for a final time in 2004. She
confesses to "missing it a lot." Personal interview with the composer, June 10, 2009.

17. A love of nontraditional music
sources and performing environments
connects Doolittle to Oliveros.

18. Doolittle is clear to point out that
field music was "inspired by the idea of a
pastorale – but not directly by nature!"
"*Hatchlings* is also really based on poetry
about turtles – not on turtles themselves!"
Email correspondence with the composer, July 1, 2011.

19. The length of the piece *Reeds* is
calculated to be three minutes per each
month of the year.

20. As with the other composers
interviewed for this study, Doolittle is
quick to clarify that nature inspires different works in many different ways and
to many different degrees.

21. *Other Species' Counterpoint*, 1.

22. Personal interview with the composer, June 10, 2009.

23. *Other Species' Counterpoint*, 1.

24. Ibid., 1–2.

25. Ibid., 2.

26. Ibid.

27. Ibid., 3.

28. Personal interview with the composer, June 11, 2009.

29. Telephone interview with the composer, September 2, 2008.

30. Email correspondence with the composer, June 30, 2010.

31. Ibid.

32. Doolittle shares with many other composers in this study a preference for extremely precise notation.

33. See Emily Doolittle, *night black bird song*, 1999, 1, note at bottom of page.

34. Ibid., 2. See measures 12 and 22.

35. Measures 88–91 are such a moment of return.

36. Doolittle recalled a moment when her grandfather, who listened to the work without knowing its title or provenance, remarked that he sure hoped the piece was about rain and birdcalls, because that's what it sounded like to him. According to the composer, she was relieved.

37. Obviously, the relative chattiness of humans and birds varies. Seemingly endless birdcalls and songs can overwhelm the quiet of dawn in many parts of the country, analogous to the ways cicadas can create a deafening sound mass at the right time on a hot summer's evening. My own experiences in Tallahassee, Florida, attest to both of these phenomena. Perhaps the number of birds I hear at any one time distorts my sense of the ratio of sound to silence characteristic of any single bird.

38. See measures 239, and then 241 and 242, of the 243-measure work. The piece ends with a dotted-quarter-note rest in all voices.

39. See measures 186 and 187.

40. Email correspondence with the composer, August 23, 2010.

41. Personal interview with the composer, June 11, 2009.

42. For the fullest explanation of cumulative form, see J. Peter Burkholder, *All Made of Tunes: Charles Ives and the Use of Musical Borrowing* (New Haven, Conn.: Yale University Press, 1995), 137–215. An essential difference between Ives's and Doolittle's handling may be in Burkholder's characterization of the move in Ives's works from complexity to clarification, which in the case of Doolittle's handling of the technique I hear as operating oppositely. For discussions of how the process works in particular pieces by Charles Ives, see Denise Von Glahn, *The Sounds of Place: Music and the American Cultural Landscape* (Boston: Northeastern University Press, 2003), 90–109, which considers his work "From Hanover Square North, at the End of a Tragic Day, the Voice of the People Again Arose," and the article "Charles Ives at Christo's Gate" in *twentieth-century music*, 5, no. 2 (September 2008): 157–178, which among other things lays out the ways Ives introduces the tune "Hello! Ma Baby" in his piece "Central Park in the Dark."

43. Email correspondence with the composer, August 23, 2010.

44. See *Other Species' Counterpoint*, 7, for Doolittle's quote of François-Bernard Mâche's *Music, Myth, and Nature or The Dolphins of Arion*, translated from the French by Susan Delaney (Philadelphia: Harwood Academic, 1992).

45. See measure 228.

46. Email correspondence with the composer, August 23, 2010.

47. Ibid.

48. Telephone interview with the composer, January 27, 2009.

49. *Other Species' Counterpoint*, 4

50. Email correspondence with the composer, August 23, 2010.

51. See also *Green Notes* (2000), *Falling Still* (2000–2001), and *Virelais* (2001).

52. Email correspondence with the composer, June 29, 2010.

53. Readers can listen to this set of pieces at Doolittle's website: http://www.emilydoolittle.com.

54. Email correspondence with the composer, June 29, 2010.

55. Telephone interview, January 27, 2009, and email correspondence with the composer, July 1, 2011.

56. Doolittle explained her notation: "# with one slash for quarter tone sharp; three slashes for three quarter tones sharp. Backwards flat for quarter tone flat; flat with downwards arrow for three quarter tones flat." Email correspondence, June 29, 2010.

57. Email correspondence with the composer August 23, 2010.

58. Email correspondence with the composer, June 29, 2010.

59. See "hoopoe lark," written variously in $\frac{6}{4}$, $\frac{7}{8}$, $\frac{4}{4}$, $\frac{2}{4}$, and $\frac{9}{4}$, and "pileated pocket grouse," written in $\frac{4}{4}$, $\frac{5}{4}$, $\frac{7}{8}$, $\frac{5}{4}$, and $\frac{3}{4}$. The variety of meters recalls Talma's similarly flexible but exactingly notated *Summer Sounds*.

60. Email correspondence with the composer, June 29, 2010.

61. Telephone interview with the composer, January 27, 2009. *all spring* became part of Doolittle's dissertation project, although it was not originally intended as such, as the composer explained: "I needed a large piece for my dissertation, so I chose to use it. It was nice that it corresponded with the topic of my written dissertation, though that wasn't actually a requirement." She originally wrote it out of a desire to collaborate with Rae Crossman. Email correspondence with the composer, July 1, 2011.

62. As discussed in the introduction, it is difficult to find the right word to describe what Doolittle is doing when she evokes birdlike sounds in music. Although Doolittle has used the word "translate" in reference to *music for*

magpies, the same word is clearly problematic in *all spring*, as are the words "imitate," "reproduce," "simulate," and "transcribe." Libby Larsen talks about "musicalizing" nonmusical events or entities, and this word has possibilities, although it also suggests a qualitative difference between birds' sounds and human music that Doolittle would likely reject.

63. The poem "all spring" is reprinted with the kind permission of the poet, Rae Crossman.

64. Emerson's famous image of a "transparent eyeball" from his essay "Nature" comes to mind: "Standing on the bare ground, my head bathed by the blithe air, and uplifted into infinite space, all mean egotism vanishes. I become a transparent eyeball – I am nothing; I see all; the currents of the Universal Being *circulate through me* – I am part or particle of God." See Ralph Waldo Emerson, "Nature" (New York: Literary Classics of the United States, the Library of America, 1983), 10. Italics my own.

65. Email correspondence with the composer, August 23, 2010.

66. In her dissertation, Doolittle refers to Clément Janequin among a list of early composers who "wove" animal sounds into their music. See *Other Species' Counterpoint*, 5.

67. "How Whales Hear" by Zhe-Xi Luo. At the time of this article, Zhe-Xi Luo was assistant curator of vertebrate paleontology at Carnegie Museum of Natural History. See http://www.carnegiemuseums.org/cmag/bk_issue/1997/julaug/feat4.htm (accessed October 30, 2011).

68. Ibid.

69. Dr. Roger Payne (b. 1935) is a biologist and environmentalist educated at Harvard and Cornell. In 1967, he and Scott McVay discovered and recorded humpback whales' songs. Their recordings quickly became source material for

composers and activists. The original "Songs of the Humpback Whale" was recently remastered and reissued. See http://www.livingmusic.com/catalogue/albums/songshump.html (accessed October 30, 2011).

70. George Crumb, *Vox Balaenae* (*Voice of the Whale*). Program notes by composer in CD booklet, Jecklin Edition JD 705.

71. David Rotherberg and Marta Ulvaeus, eds., *The Book of Music and Nature: An Anthology of Sounds, Words, Thoughts* (Middletown, Conn.: Terra Nova/Wesleyan University Press, 2001). Readers are encouraged to listen to the CD that accompanies the book. It contains a sampling of musics by humans and nonhuman others. Among the works included is Pauline Oliveros's "Poem for Change."

72. Telephone interview with the composer, January 27, 2009.

73. Marsha Green founded Ocean Mammal Institute in 1994. She has a PhD from Temple University in animal behavior and physiological psychology and advises the national government on policies affecting whale health, especially as regards the impact of sonar testing. She is an adviser to the Whalesong Project, which was founded in 2000 by Dan Sythe. See http://www.whalesong.net/index/php/humpback-faq/songs for an extended discussion of humpback whale songs and singing.

74. At the top of the score, Doolittle acknowledges Patrick Miller for the recording of the humpback whale song, Thomas Götz for the recording of the gray seal, Luke Rendell for the sperm whale song, and Henrik Brumm for the musician wren sounds. In an improvisatory section beginning at 5'33", the soprano is invited to play the percussion instruments "and even add percussion instruments that are not used elsewhere in this piece" (see score, page 6).

75. Doolittle's complex attitudes toward technology echo a comment Oliveros made in her interview with Jann Pasler. In the context of a conversation that focused on Oliveros "using electronics to replicate sound in certain kinds of ways" the composer explained: "I would like not to be aware of the technology: I'd like to be aware of the music." See Jann Pasler, "An Interview with Pauline Oliveros," AWC *News/Forum* (Spring/Summer 1991): 13.

76. See Walter Zimmermann interview with John Cage, referenced in the Pauline Oliveros chapter.

77. Telephone interview, January 27, 2009, and email correspondence with the composer August 23, 2010.

78. Ibid.

79. Email correspondence with the composer, August 23, 2010.

80. A similar situation occurred in Louise Talma's *Summer Sounds*, where that composer employed quarter tones and glissandi to evoke the sounds of sunrise in "Dawn."

81. See Emily Doolittle, *Social sounds from whales at night*, 2007, instructions to the singer, page 1 of the score.

82. Email correspondence with the composer, August 23, 2010.

83. Ibid.

84. Email correspondence with the composer, August 9, 2010, and July 1, 2011. Doolittle explained the importance of the Newfoundland Sound Symposium to her creation: "The history of experimental and interdisciplinary music there is part of how we started conceiving of ideas for the piece." Emily Doolittle, program notes for *Reeds*.

85. Transcribed from the composer's comments recorded on the video version of *Reeds*. I am grateful to Emily Doolittle for making available to me a DVD of the premiere performance.

86. See Schafer, *The Soundscape*, 147 and 212–213, for descriptions of the terms

soundwalk and *listening walk*. Doolittle's long acquaintance with Schafer and participation in his summer Wolf Projects would have exposed the composer to these ideas.

87. This practice recalls Beach's footnote at the bottom of "A Hermit Thrush at Morn": "These bird-calls are exact notations of hermit thrush songs, in the original keys but an octave lower."

88. See program for *Reeds*.

89. Ibid.

90. Ibid. In a personal interview with the composer, June 11, 2009, Doolittle shared her fascination with spring peepers and her plans to get their sound into a piece.

91. The composer's remarks are taken from the DVD video recording she shared with me.

92. Program notes written by Catherine Lee, the oboist of the Umbrella Ensemble.

93. Doolittle names Section II "A Hermit: Hermit Thrush."

94. Ibid.

CONCLUSIONS

1. The AAUW was founded in 1881 by Ellen Swallow Richards and Marion Talbot. Over the years it has awarded millions of dollars to individual women to support their research and further their education. It was the AAUW that in 1919 awarded Marie Curie over $150,000 to purchase the one gram of radium that she needed to carry out her experiments. While not focused on supporting women in the arts, its general mission of advocating for women's education makes it a force for good throughout society.

2. This might have been the case regardless of Beach's personal circumstances. Few American women born in the 1860s had access to or were encouraged to pursue education beyond that necessary to prepare them for their assumed roles as wives and mothers.

3. See Fisher and Ury, *Getting to Yes* (New York: Penguin Books, 1991), back cover.

BIBLIOGRAPHY

Allen, Aaron. "'Fatto di Fiemme': Stradi-
vari and the Musical Trees of the Pan-
eveggio." Laura Auricchio, Elizabeth
Heckendorn Cook, and Giulia Pacini,
eds. *Arboreal Values: Trees and Forests
in Europe, North America, and the Ca-
ribbean, 1660–1830.* Forthcoming.
———. "Ecomusicology." *The Grove Dictionary of American Music.* New York:
Oxford University Press, 2013. See also
Oxford Music Online http://www
.oxfordmusiconline.com.
———. "Ecomusicology: Ecocriticism
and Musicology." *Journal of the American Musicological Society* 64, no. 2
(2011): 391–394.
———. "Prospects and Problems for
Ecomusicology in Confronting a Crisis
of Culture. *Journal of the American
Musicological Society* 64, no. 2 (2011):
414–419.
Allen, Una L. "The Composer's Corner:
Wherein Contemporary Writers of
Teaching Material Express Views Re-
garding Certain of Their Own Compo-
sitions. No. 10: Mrs. H. H. A. Beach."
Musician 35 (July 1930): 21.
The American Chestnut Foundation.
"Mission." http://www.acf.org/mission
_history.php (accessed January 2, 2010).
Ammer, Christine. *Unsung: A History of
Women in American Music.* 2nd rev.
and expanded ed., Portland, Oregon:

Amadeus Press, 2001. Originally pub-
lished by Greenwood Press, Westport,
Connecticut, 1980.
Anderson, Lorraine, ed. *Sisters of the
Earth: Women's Prose and Poetry about
Nature.* 2nd ed. New York: Vintage
Books, 2003.
Appleby, Joyce. "The Power of History."
The American Historical Review 103, no.
1 (Feb. 1998): 1–14.
Aspria, Marcello. "Perfume and Gender
Identity." *Scented Pages.* http://www
.scentedpages.com (accessed July 16,
2009).
Bailey, Candace. *Music and the Southern
Belle: From Accomplished Lady to Con-
federate Composer.* Carbondale: South-
ern Illinois University Press, 2010.
Bartók, Béla. *Bluebeard's Castle: Opera in
One Act.* English Version by Christo-
pher Hassall. New York: Boosey and
Hawkes, 1963.
Bauer, Marion. "Indian Pipes." New
York: G. Schirmer, 1923.
———. "Up the Ocklawaha." Bryn
Mawr, Pa.: Hildegard Publishing,
1998.
Bauer, Theodore H. "Women's Clubs a
Dominant Factor in Music." *Musical
Monitor* 8, no. 9 (June 1919): 431.
Beach, Amy. "A Hermit Thrush at Eve."
Bryn Mawr, Pa.: Hildegard Publish-
ing, 1997.

———."A Hermit Thrush at Morn." The Arthur P. Schmidt Co., 1922. The University of New Hampshire, Milne Special Collections, Mrs. H. H. A. Beach Papers, MC 51, box 8, folder 17.

———. "To the Girl Who Wants to Compose." *Etude* 35 (November 1918): 695.

———. "The Twenty-Fifth Anniversary of a Vision." *Proceedings of the Music Teachers National Association.* 1932, 27th Series. Oberlin, Ohio: Music Teachers National Association, 1933.

Beach, Mrs. H. H. A. "How Music Is Made." *Keyboard* (winter 1942): 11, 38.

———. "Bird Songs Noted in the Woods and Fields by Mrs. H. H. A. Beach for this Article." *The Designer* (May 1911): 7.

Beach, Mrs. H. H. A. Papers, Milne Special Collections. The University of New Hampshire.

Bernstein, Jane A., ed. *Women's Voices across Musical Worlds.* Boston: Northeastern University Press, 2004.

Block, Adrienne Fried. *Amy Beach, Passionate Victorian: The Life and Work of an American Composer, 1867–1944.* New York: Oxford University Press, 1998.

———, asst. by Nancy Stewart. "Women in American Music, 1800–1918." In Karin Pendle, ed., *Women and Music: A History.* Bloomington: Indiana University Press, 2001.

Bolls, Pamela Tanner. "Who Does She Think She Is?" Mystic Artists Film Productions Documentary, 2009. www.whodoeshethinksheis.net (accessed June 29, 2011).

Bond, Victoria. Personal interview with the author, July 6, 2006.

———. Personal interview with the author, January 16, 2009.

———. Personal interview with the author, June 20, 2009.

———. Program Notes, January 7, 2009.

———. *Peculiar Plants* (2006–2008). Lyrics by Victoria Bond and Kenneth Cooper. Revised July 1, 2008.

Bonner, John T. *The Evolution of Culture in Animals.* Princeton, N.J.: Princeton University Press, 1983.

Branch, Michael P. *Reading the Roots: American Nature Writing before Walden.* Athens: University of Georgia Press, 2004.

Breton, Mary Joy. *Women Pioneers for the Environment.* Boston: Northeastern University Press, 1998.

Brooks, Benjamin. "The How of Creative Composition: A Conference with Mrs. H. H. A. Beach." *The Etude* (March 1943): 151, 208.

Brower, David. "The Third-Planet Operators Manual." *New York Times Magazine* (March 16, 1975): 53–54.

Brower, Harriet. *Piano Mastery: Talks with Master Pianists and Teachers and an Account of a von Bulow class, Hints on Interpretation by Two American Teachers (Dr. William Mason and William H. Sherwood) and a Summary by the Author. With Sixteen Portraits.* New York: Frederick A. Stokes Company, 1915. http://www.gutenberg.org/files/15604/15604-h/15604-h.htm#XXVI_EUGENE_HEFFLEY.

Broyles, Michael. "Art Music from 1860 to 1920." In David Nicholls, ed., *The Cambridge History of American Music,* 227–232. Cambridge, UK: Cambridge University Press, 1998.

Bruhn, Siglind. *Musical Ekphrasis: Composers Responding to Poetry and Painting.* Hillsdale, N.Y.: Pendragon Press, 2000.

Buell, Lawrence. *The Environmental Imagination: Thoreau, Nature Writing, and the Formation of American Culture.* Cambridge, Mass.: Harvard University Press, 1995.

———. *Writing for an Endangered World: Literature, Culture, and Environment in the U.S. and Beyond.* Cambridge, Mass.: Harvard University Press, 2001.

Burke, Edmund. *On the Sublime and Beautiful.* Vol. 24, part 2, *The Harvard Classics.* New York: P. F. Collier, 1909–1914; Bartleby.com, 2001. www.bartleby .com/24/2 (accessed June 9, 2008).

Burkholder, J. Peter. *All Made of Tunes: Charles Ives and the Use of Musical Borrowing.* New Haven, Conn.: Yale University Press, 1995.

Carson, Rachel. *Silent Spring.* Boston: Houghton Mifflin, 1962.

Cather, Willa. "Willa Cather Mourns Old Opera House." In Judith Tick, ed., *Music in the USA: A Documentary Companion.* Oxford, UK: Oxford University Press, 2008.

Cheney, John Vance. "The Skilful Listener." In Edmund Clarence Stedman, ed., *An American Anthology, 1787–1900.* http://www.bartleby.com/248/1008 .html (accessed July 18, 2007).

Chittenden, Elaine M. "Endangered and Threatened Plants in Michigan." W. J. Beal Botanical Garden, Michigan State University, 1996.

Citron, Marcia J. *Gender and the Musical Canon.* Cambridge, UK: Cambridge University Press, 1993.

Clare, John. "The Thrush's Nest." www .poemhunter.com/poem/the-thrush -s-nest/ (accessed July 12, 2007).

Clark, Suzannah, and Alexander Rehding, eds. *Music Theory and Natural Order from the Renaissance to the Early Twentieth Century.* Cambridge, UK: Cambridge University Press, 2001.

Classen, Constance, David Howes, and Anthony Synnott. *Aroma: The Cultural History of Smell.* London: Routledge, 1994.

"Composer Louise Talma: A Conversation with Bruce Duffie." http://www .bruceduffie.com/talma/html (accessed June 3, 2011).

Cook, Susan C., and Judy S. Tsou. *Cecilia Reclaimed: Feminist Perspectives on Gender and Music.* Urbana: University of Illinois Press, 1994.

Cooper, Susan Fenimore. *Essays on Nature and Landscape.* Ed. by Rochelle Johnson and Daniel Patterson. Athens: University of Georgia Press, 2002.

———. *Rural Hours.* Ed. by Rochelle Johnson and Daniel Patterson. Athens: University of Georgia Press, 1998.

Coupland, Douglas. *Generation X: Tales for an Accelerated Culture.* New York: St. Martin's Griffin, 1991.

Cronon, William. "The Trouble with Wilderness." In William Cronon, ed., *Uncommon Ground: Rethinking the Human Place in Nature.* New York: W. W. Norton, 1996.

Curran, Alvin. *Maritime Rites.* New World Records, 80625–2 15, 2004. Compact disc.

Dell'Antonio, Andrew, ed. *Beyond Structural Listening? Postmodern Modes of Hearing.* Berkeley: University of California Press, 2004.

Dillard, Annie. *Pilgrim at Tinker Creek.* New York: Harper Collins, 1974.

Doolittle, Emily Lenore. "Other Species' Counterpoint: An Investigation of the Relationship between Human Music and Animal Songs." PhD dissertation, Princeton University, 2007.

———. Personal interview with the author, June 10, 2009.

———. *night black bird song,* 1999.

———. "Emily Doolittle." http://www .emilydoolittle.com.

———. *Social sounds from whales at night,* 2007.

Dorsey, Sarah. "Louise Talma (1906–1996) and the MacDowell Colony: A Saving Grace." Paper presented at the Feminist Theory and Musicology Conference (FTM10), Greensboro, North Carolina, May 28, 2009.

Dragone, Luanne. www.omnidisc
.com/Talma>Biography.html#
INTERVIEW (accessed May 20,
2011).

Duffie, Bruce. "Joan Tower: The Composer in Conversation with Bruce
Duffie." *New Music Connoisseur*
(Spring 2001), rev. in February 2006.
http://my.voyager.net/~duffie/tower
.html (accessed June 28, 2006).

Duncan, Robert. "An Interlude of Rare
Beauty." Reprinted in *Three Songs for
soprano and piano*, by Pauline Oliveros.
Baltimore, Md.: Smith Publications,
1976.

Ecocriticism Study Group of the American Musicological Society. http://
www.ams-esg.org.

Edwards, J. Michelle. "Bauer, Marion
Eugenie." *Grove Music Online*. www
.oxfordmusiconline.com (accessed
December 30, 2010).

Eisler, Rianne. "The Gaia Tradition and
the Partnership Future: An Ecofeminist Manifesto." In Irene Diamond
and Gloria Feman Orenstein, eds.,
*Reweaving the World: The Emergence
of Ecofeminism*. San Francisco: Sierra
Club Books, 1990.

Elder, John. *Pilgrimage to Vallombrosa:
From Vermont to Italy in the Footsteps of
George Perkins Marsh*. Charlottesville:
University of Virginia Press, 2006.

Emerson, Ralph Waldo. "Nature." In *Emerson: Essays and Lectures*. New York:
Literary Classics of the United States,
the Library of America, 1983.

Evenden, Neil. *The Social Creation of Nature*. Baltimore, Md.: Johns Hopkins
University Press, 1992.

Farnham, Eliza W. *Life in Prairie Land*.
New York: Harper and Brothers, 1846.

Fay, Amy. *Music-Study in Germany: The
Classic Memoir of the Romantic Era*.
New York: Dover Publications, 1965.

Feder, Susan. *Joan Tower: Silver Ladders,
Island Prelude, Music for Cello and*
Orchestra, and Sequoia. Electra/None-
such Records 79245-2. Compact disc
liner notes.

Feld, Steven, and Keith Basso. *Senses
of Place*. Santa Fe, N.M.: School of
American Research Press, 1996.

Fisher, Roger, and William Ury. *Getting
to Yes: Negotiating Agreement without
Giving In*. New York: Penguin Books,
1983.

"Fog." http://en.wikipedia.org/wiki/Fog#
cite_note-15 (accessed July 20, 2010).

Fuller, Margaret. *Summer on the Lakes, in
1843*. With an introduction by Susan
Belasco Smith. Urbana: University of
Illinois Press, 1991.

Gaard, Greta, and Patrick D. Murphy.
*Ecofeminist Literary Criticism: Theory,
Interpretation, Pedagogy*. Urbana: Uni-
versity of Illinois Press, 1998.

Gardiner, William. *The Music of Nature:
or, An Attempt to Prove That What is
Passionate and Pleasing in the Art of
Singing, Speaking, and Performing Upon
Musical Instruments, Is Derived from
the Sounds of the Animated world: with
curious and interesting illustrations*. Boston: Sanborn, Carter and Bozin, 1856.
First published in London, 1832.

Gatta, John. *Making Nature Sacred: Literature, Religion, and Environment in
America from the Puritans to the Present*. Oxford, UK: Oxford University
Press, 2004.

Gianquitto, Tina. *"Good Observers of
Nature": American Women and the
Scientific Study of the Natural World,
1820–1885*. Athens: University of Georgia Press, 2007.

Glotfelty, Cheryll, and Harold Fromm.
*The Ecocriticism Reader: Landmarks in
Literary Ecology*. Athens: University of
Georgia Press, 1996.

Goss, Madeleine. "Marion Bauer." In
*Modern Music-Makers: Contemporary
American Composers*. New York: E. P.
Dutton, 1952.

de Graaf, Melissa. "Contributions of Jewish Women to Music and Women to Jewish Music." http://www.jmwc.org/pdf/MarionBauer.pdf (accessed December 30, 2010).

Graham, Mark. "Queer Smells: Fragrances of Late Capitalism or Scents of Subversion?" In Jim Drobnick, ed., *The Smell-Culture Reader*. Oxford, UK: Berg Publishers, 2006.

Green, Cynthia. "Interview with Composer Libby Larsen." *International League of Women Composers Journal* (June 1992): 24–27.

Grimley, Daniel M. *Grieg: Music, Landscape and Norwegian Identity*. Woodbridge, UK: Boydell, 2006.

———. "Music, Landscape, Attunement: Listening to Sibelius's Tapiola." *Journal of the American Musicological Society* 64, no. 2 (2011): 394–398.

Grolman, Ellen K. *Joan Tower: The Comprehensive Bio-Bibliography*. Lanham, Md.: Scarecrow Press, 2007.

H. F. P. "Believes Women Composers Will Rise to Greater Heights in World Democracy." *Musical America* 25 (April 21, 1917): 3.

Hale, Philip. "Symphony Night." *Boston Journal*, n.d., S2, p. 51.

Harjo, Joy. "Eagle Poem." In *In Mad Love and War*. Middletown, Conn.: Wesleyan University Press, 1990.

Harvey, Eleanor Jones. *The Painted Sketch: American Impressions from Nature, 1830–1880*. Dallas, Tex.: Dallas Museum of Art in association with Harry N. Abrams, c. 1998.

Herrick, R. "To Daffodils." *The Golden Treasury*, ed. by Francis T. Palgrave, 1875. http://www.bartleby.com/106/110.html (accessed January 5, 2011).

Hill, Gladwin. "Ecologists Fear Peril to Nature." *New York Times*, June 8, 1975, 15.

Hisama, Ellie M. *Gendering Musical Modernism: The Music of Ruth Crawford, Marion Bauer, and Miriam Gideon*. Cambridge, UK: Cambridge University Press, 2001.

Høeg, Peter. *Smilla's Sense of Snow*. Trans. by Tiina Nunnally. New York: Dell, 1992.

Horrocks, Peggy A. "The Solo Vocal Repertoire of Marion Bauer with Selected Stylistic Analyses." PhD diss., University of Nebraska, 1994.

Hughes, Adella Prentiss. *Music Is My Life*. Cleveland, Ohio: World Publishing, 1947.

Hughes, Rupert. *Contemporary American Composers*. Boston: L. C. Page, 1900.

Kennan, Kent Wheller. *The Technique of Orchestration*. 2nd ed. Englewood Cliffs, N.J.: Prentice-Hall, 1979.

Kolodny, Annette. "Unearthing Herstory: An Introduction." In Cheryll Glotfelty and Harold Fromm, eds., *The Ecocriticism Reader*. Athens: University of Georgia Press, 1996.

Krehbiel, Henry Edward. *Music and Manners in the Classical Period*. 3rd ed. New York: Charles Scribner's, 1899.

Larsen, Libby. *downwind of roses in Maine*. Minnesota: Libby Larsen Publishing, 2009.

———. *Mass for the Earth: Missa Gaia*. Koch International Classics 3–7279–2 1995. Compact disc.

———. *Missa Gaia*. Boston, Mass.: ECS Publishing, 1992.

———. Personal interview with the author, March 28, 2009.

———. Personal interview with the author, March 29, 2009.

Leckie, Nancy E. "An Analysis of Joan Tower's *Wings* for Solo Clarinet." DMA dissertation, Arizona State University, 1992.

Leonard, Kendra Preston. *The Conservatoire Américain: A History*. Lanham, Md.: Scarecrow Press, 2007.

Leopold, Aldo. *A Sand County Almanac and Sketches Here and There*. New York: Oxford University Press, 1949.

LePage, Jane Weiner. *Women Composers, Conductors, and Musicians of the Twentieth Century: Selected Biographies.* Vol. 3. Metuchen, N.J.: Scarecrow Press, 1988.

Levin, David Michael, ed. *Modernity and the Hegemony of Vision.* Berkeley: University of California Press, 1993.

Levy, Beth E. *Frontier Figures: American Music and the Mythology of the American West.* Berkeley: University of California Press, 2012.

Lochhead, Judy. "Joan Tower's *Wings* and *Breakfast Rhythms I and II*: Some Thoughts on Form and Repetition." *Perspectives of New Music* 30, no. 1 (Winter 1992): 132–156.

Locke, Ralph P., and Cyrilla Barr. *Cultivating Music in America: Women Patrons and Activists since 1860.* Berkeley: University of California Press, 1997.

Mâche, François-Bernard. *Music, Myth, and Nature or The Dolphins of Arion.* Trans. by Susan Delaney. Philadelphia: Harwood Academic, 1992.

Marian MacDowell Papers. Manuscript Division, Library of Congress, Washington, D.C.

Martin, Laura C. *Gardens of the Heartland.* New York: Abbeville Press, 1996.

Martinelli, Dario. *Of Birds, Whales and Other Musicians.* Scranton, Pa.: University of Scranton Press, 2009.

Marx, Leo. *The Machine in the Garden: Technology and the Pastoral Ideal in America.* Oxford, UK: Oxford University Press, 1964.

McKibben, Bill, ed. *American Earth: Environmental Writing since Thoreau.* New York: Literary Classics of the United States, 2008.

Merchant, Carolyn. *The Death of Nature: Women, Ecology and the Scientific Revolution.* San Francisco: HarperSanFrancisco, 1983.

———. *Earthcare: Women and the Environment.* New York: Routledge, 1995.

———. *Ecology: Key Concepts in Critical Theory.* 2nd ed. New York: Humanity Books, 2008.

———. *Reinventing Eden: The Fate of Nature in Western Culture.* New York: Routledge, 2004.

Michigan State University "Beal Botanical Gardens." http://anthropology.msu.edu/saints_rest_gallery/explore/fp_bealbotanical.html (accessed December 31, 2009).

Mies, Maria, and Vandana Shiva. *Ecofeminism.* London: Zed Books, 1993.

Miller, Perry. *Nature's Nation.* Ed. by Kenneth B. Murdock. Cambridge, Mass.: The Belknap Press of Harvard University Press, 1967.

"Miss Smilla's Feeling for Snow." http://en.wikipedia.org/wiki/Miss_Smilla's_Feeling_for_Snow (accessed July 8, 2010).

Mockus, Martha. *Sounding Out: Pauline Oliveros and Lesbian Musicality.* New York: Routledge, 2008.

Mohr, Charles. "Tampering with Nature Perils Health, U.N. Environment Unit's Report Warns." *New York Times,* April 20, 1975, 3.

Moore, Mary Carr. "Is American Citizenship a Handicap to a Composer?" *Musician* 40 (September 1935): 5, 8.

Morris, Edmund. "Oases of Silence in a Desert of Din." *The New York Times,* May 25, 1975, 13–14.

Nash, Roderick Frazier. *Wilderness and the American Mind.* New Haven, Conn.: Yale University Press, 1982.

Network Science. http://netsci.org/Science/Special/feature11.html (accessed December 31, 2009).

Neuls-Bates, Carol. *Women in Music: An Anthology of Source Readings from the Middle Ages to the Present.* Boston: Northeastern University Press, 1996.

———, ed. *Women in Music.* Rev. ed. Boston: Northeastern University Press, 1966.

Norwood, Vera L. "Heroines of Nature: Four Women Respond to the American Landscape." In Cheryll Glotfelty and Harold Fromm, eds., *The Ecocriticism Reader: Landmarks in Literary Ecology*. Athens: University of Georgia Press, 1999.

———. *Made from this Earth: American Women and Nature*. Chapel Hill: University of North Carolina Press, 1993.

Novak, Barbara. *Nature and Culture: American Landscape and Painting, 1825–1875*. Rev. ed. New York: Oxford University Press, 1995.

Oliveros, Pauline. "Alien Bog." Pogus Productions P21012–2, New York, 1997. Compact disc liner notes.

———. *Deep Listening: A Composer's Sound Practice*. Lincoln, Neb.: iUniverse, 2005.

———. "Deep Listening." http://www.deeplistening.org/site/ (accessed May 17, 2010).

———. "An Interlude of Rare Beauty." Baltimore, Md.: Smith Publications, 1976.

———. "My 'American Music': Soundscape, Politics, Technology, Community." *American Music* (Winter 2007): 389–404.

———. Personal interview with the author, February 16, 2005.

———. *The Roots of the Moment*. New York: Drogue Press, 1998.

———. *Software for People: Collected Writing, 1963–1980*. Baltimore, Md.: Smith Publications, 1984.

———. *Sonic Meditations*. Baltimore, Md.: Smith Publications, 1974.

———. *Three Songs*. Baltimore, Md.: Smith Publications, 1976.

———, Stuart Dempster, and Panaiotis. "Statements on the Experience" *Deep Listening*. New Albion Records NA 022 CD, 1989.

Origlia, Clara. "Sensory Semiotics: Culture-Sensitive, Holistic Research Approaches to Explore Sensory Complexity." Paper presented at the ESOMAR Fragrance Research Conference, Lausanne (Switzerland), March 2003, and published online by the World Association of Research Professionals.

Otto, Rudolf. *The Idea of the Holy*. Trans. by John W. Harvey. Oxford: Oxford University Press, 1923; 2nd ed., 1950.

Outka, Paul. *Race and Nature: From Transcendentalism to the Harlem Renaissance*. New York: Palgrave Macmillan, 2008.

Pasler, Jann. "An Interview with Pauline Oliveros." AWC *news/forum* (Spring/Summer 1991): 8–14.

Pater, Walter. *The Renaissance*. New York: The Modern Library, 1919.

Phelps, Almira Hart Lincoln. *Familiar Lectures on Botany, Practical, Elementary, and Physiological with an Appendix, Containing Descriptions of the Plants of the United States and Exotics, etc. for the Use of Seminaries and Private Students*. New York: Huntington, 1839.

Phillips, Dana. *The Truth of Ecology: Nature, Culture, and Literature in America*. Oxford, UK: Oxford University Press, 2003.

Pickett, Susan. *Marion Bauer*. Unpublished manuscript.

Platon, Nicholas. *Crete*. Geneva: Nagel Publishers, 1966.

Plummeridge, Charles. *Music Education in Theory and Practice*. London: Falmer, 1991.

Potter, C. W. "A History of Influenza." *Journal of Applied Microbiology* 91, no. 4 (October 2006): 572–579. doi: 10.1046/j.1365–2672.2001.01492.x. PMID 11576290 (accessed June 19, 2011).

Powell, Maud. "Here Is a Poem by Maud Powell." *San Francisco Examiner*, December 22, 1912, 1.

Public Broadcasting Service. "Deep Time: Miocene." http://www.pbs.org/wgbh/

evolution/change/deeptime/miocene .html (accessed January 5, 2010).

Rausch, Robin. "The MacDowells and Their Legacy." In Carter Weisman, ed., *A Place for the Arts: The MacDowell Colony, 1907–2007*, pp. 50–132. Hanover, N.H.: The MacDowell Colony, 2007.

Redhing, Alexander. "Eco-musicology." *Journal of the Royal Musical Association* 127, no. 2 (2002): 305–320.

———. "Ecomusicology between Apocalypse and Nostalgia." *Journal of the American Musicological Society* 64, no. 2 (2011): 409–414.

Ross, Stephanie. *What Gardens Mean.* Chicago: University of Chicago Press, 1998.

Rothenberg, David, and Marta Ulvaeus, eds. *The Book of Nature and Music: An Anthology of Sounds, Words, Thoughts.* Middletown, Conn.: Wesleyan University Press, 2001.

Ruether, Rosemary Radford. *Ecofeminisms: Symbolic and Social Constructions between the Oppression of Women and the Domination of Nature.* Charlotte: University of North Carolina Press, 1991.

———. *New Woman, New Earth: Sexist Ideologies and Human Liberation.* Boston: Beacon Press, 1995.

Schafer, R. Murray. *The Soundscape: Our Sonic Environment and the Tuning of the World.* Rochester, Vt.: Destiny Books, 1994.

Schama, Simon. *Landscape and Memory.* New York: Knopf, 1995.

Scherer, Barrymore Laurence. "Ellen Taaffe Zwilich: A Composer Not Afraid to Feel." *The Wall Street Journal*, May 5, 2009 (accessed December 30, 2009).

Schrepfer, Susan R. *Nature's Altars: Mountains, Gender, and American Environmentalism.* Lawrence: University Press of Kansas, 2005.

Schwartz, Elliott, and Barney Childs, eds. *Contemporary Composers on Contemporary Music.* New York: Da Capo Press, 1978.

Showalter, Elaine, ed. *Speaking of Gender.* New York: Routledge, 1989.

Smith, Catherine Parsons, and Cynthia S. Richardson. *Mary Carr Moore, American Composer.* Ann Arbor: University of Michigan Press, 1987.

Smith, Mark, M. *Sensing the Past: Seeing, Hearing, Smelling, Tasting, and Touching in History.* Berkeley: University of California Press, 2007.

Solie, Ruth A., ed. *Musicology and Difference: Gender and Sexuality in Music Scholarship.* Berkeley: University of California Press, 1993.

Soper, Kate. *What Is Nature?: Culture, Politics and the Non-Human.* Oxford, UK: Blackwell, 1995.

Stap, Don. *Birdsong: A Natural History.* New York: Oxford University Press, 2005.

Stewart, Nancy Louise. "The Solo Piano Music of Marion Bauer." PhD dissertation, University of Cincinnati, 1990.

Straus, Joseph N. *Twelve-Tone Music in America.* Cambridge, UK: Cambridge University Press, 2009.

Stravinsky, Igor, *Symphony of Psalms for Mixed Chorus and Orchestra.* London: Boosey and Hawkes, 1948.

Sullivan, Walter. "Vanishing Shield?" *New York Times*, April 13, 1975, 212.

Talma, Louise. *Soundshots.* Bryn Mawr, Pa.: Hildegard Publishing, 2000.

———. Letter to Mr. James D. Ireland, Jr., Office of Music Programs, National Endowment for the Arts, Washington, D.C., 20506, August 11, 1974.

Talma, Louise, Collection, Music Division, Library of Congress.

Taubenberger, Jeffery, and David Morens. "1918 Influenza Pandemic." Centers for Disease Control and Prevention (accessed June 19, 2011).

Theisen, Alan. "A Multifaceted Approach to Analyzing Form in Elliott Carter's *Boston Concerto*." PhD dissertation, the Florida State University, 2010.

Thoreau, Henry D. *Faith in a Seed: The Dispersion of Seeds and Other Late Natural History Writings.* Washington, D.C.: Island Press, 1993.

———. *Selected Journals of Henry David Thoreau.* Ed. by Carl Bode. New York: Signet, 1967.

———. *Walden.* Ed. by J. Lyndon Shanley. Princeton, N.J.: Princeton University Press, 1989.

Tick, Judith. "Charles Ives and Gender Ideology." *Musicology and Difference: Gender and Sexuality in Music Scholarship.* Berkeley: University of California Press, 1993.

———. *Music in the USA: A Documentary Companion.* Oxford, UK: Oxford University Press, 2008.

———. *Twentieth Century Music: How It Developed, How to Listen to It.* Albany Records, Troy 297, 1998. Liner notes.

Toliver, Brooks. "Eco-ing in the Canyon: Ferde Grofé's Grand Canyon Suite and the Transformation of Wilderness." *Journal of the American Musicological Society* 57, no. 2 (2004): 325–367.

Tower, Joan. *Amazon.* New York: Associated Music Publishers, 1978.

———. *Big Sky.* New York: Associated Music Publishers (BMI), 2000, 2006.

———. *Black Topaz.* New York: Associated Music Publishers (BMI), 1976.

———. *Black Topaz – Joan Tower.* New World Records, 80470–2, 1995. Compact disc.

———. *Joan Tower.* New World Records-CRI, NWCR 582, 2007. Compact disc.

———. *Sequoia.* New York: Associated Music Publishers (BMI), 1981.

———. *Snow Dreams,* New York: Associated Music Publishers, 1986, 3.

———. Telephone interview with the author, August 15, 2006.

———. Telephone interview with the author, September 3, 2010.

———. *Rain Waves.* New York: Associated Music Publishers (BMI), 1997.

———. *Rain Waves.* The Verdehr Trio. Crystal Records, CD943 2002. Compact disc.

"Victoria Bond: Catalog of Works." http://www.victoriabond.com/catalog.html (accessed June 12, 2006).

Von Glahn, Denise. "American Women and the Nature of Identity." *Journal of the American Musicological Society* 64, no. 2 (2011): 399–403.

———"Charles Ives at 'Christo's Gates.'" *Twentieth-Century Music* 5, no. 2 (2008): 157–158.

———. *The Sounds of Place: Music and the American Cultural Landscape.* Boston: Northeastern University Press, 2003.

Von Gunden, Heidi. *The Music of Pauline Oliveros.* Metuchen, N.J.: Scarecrow Press, 1983.

Walker, Melissa. *Reading the Environment.* New York: W. W. Norton, 1994.

Warren, Karen J. *Ecofeminist Philosophy: A Western Perspective on What It Is and Why It Matters.* Lanham, Md.: Rowman and Littlefield, 2000.

Waterman, Helen, ed. *Sonic Geography: Imagined and Remembered.* Toronto, Canada: Penumbra Press and the Frost Centre for Canadian Studies and Native Studies, 2002.

Watkins, Holly. "Musical Ecologies of Place and Placelessness." *Journal of the American Musicological Society* 64, no. 2 (2011): 404–408.

———. "The Pastoral after Environmentalism: Nature and Culture in Stephen Albert's Symphony: RiverRun." *Current Musicology* 84 (2007): 7–24.

Whitesitt, Linda. "Women as 'Keepers of Culture': Music Clubs, Community Concert Series, and Symphony Orchestras." In Ralph P. Locke and

Cyrilla Barr, eds., *Cultivating Music in America: Women Patrons and Activists since 1860.* Berkeley: University of California Press, 1997.

William James Beal Botanical Garden visitors' brochure. East Lansing, Mich.: University Publications.

Williams, Raymond. *The Country and the City.* New York: Oxford University Press, 1973.

Wolfe, Linnie Marsh, ed. *John of the Mountains: The Unpublished Journals of John Muir.* Boston: Houghton Mifflin, 1938; republished Madison: University of Wisconsin Press, 1979. http://www.sierraclub.org/john_muir_exhibit/ (accessed May 27, 2011).

Worster, Donald. *The Wealth of Nature: Environmental History and the Ecological Imagination.* New York: Oxford University Press, 1993.

Wright, Susan. "Challenging Literacies: The Significance of the Arts." A paper reprinted on the Australian Association for Research in Education (AARE) website: http://www.aare.edu.au/oopap/wri00006.htm.

Zim, Herbert S., and Paul R. Shaffer. *Rocks, Gems and Minerals: A Guide to Familiar Minerals, Gems, Ores and Rocks.* New York: St. Martin's Press, 2001.

Zimmermann, Walter. *Desert Plants: Conversations with 23 American Musicians.* Vancouver, British Columbia, Canada: A.R.C. Publications, 1976.

Zwilich, Ellen Taaffe. CD 3–74877–2 HI KOCH International Classics, 2000. "Liner Notes."

———. "Notes." Merion Music, Inc., Bryn Mawr, Pa.: Theodore Presser, 1999.

———. Personal interviews with the author, October 15, 2001, and October 25, 2004.

———. *Symphony No. 4 ("The Gardens") for Orchestra, with Mixed Chorus and Children's Chorus.* Bryn Mawr, Pa.: Theodore Presser, 2000.

———. "The Gardens: Birth of a Symphony." Michigan Council for the Arts and Cultural Affairs.

INDEX

Page numbers in *italics* represent illustrations.

DENISE VON GLAHN is Professor of Musicology and Director of the Center for Music of the Americas, in the College of Music at the Florida State University. She is author of *The Sounds of Place: Music and the American Cultural Landscape* (Northeastern University Press, 2003), which won an ASCAP–Deems Taylor Award, and is co-author (with Michael Broyles) of *Leo Ornstein: Modernist Dilemmas, Personal Choices* (IUP, 2007), which won the Irving Lowens Award of the Society for American Music.